Word Choice

Mechanics and Other Conventions

Punctuation

Language

Perrin's

Index to English

Sixth Edition

Wilma R. Ebbitt
The Pennsylvania State University

David R. Ebbitt

Scott, Foresman and Company
Glenview, Ill.
Dallas, Tex.
Oakland, N.J.
Palo Alto, Cal.
Tucker, Ga.

Library of Congress Cataloging in Publication Data
Ebbitt, Wilma R
    Index to English.

    Revision of the second section of Writer's guide and
index to English by P. G. Perrin, first published in 1939
under title: An index to English.
    Bibliography: pp. 9-10.
    1. English language—Rhetoric. I. Ebbitt, David R.,
1919-   joint author. II. Perrin, Porter Gale,
1896-1962 An index to English. Section 2. III. Title.
PE1411.E2 1977   808'.042   76-25588
ISBN 0-673-15036-4

Acknowledgment is made to Curtis Brown Ltd. for permission to use
"The Blushing Bride" from I Know What I Like by Georgina Coleridge.
Copyright © 1959 by Chatto and Windus; 1963 by Georgina Coleridge.

2 3 4 5 6 7 8 -RRC- 82 81 80 79 78 77

Preface

This Sixth Edition of *Index to English* is intended to help today's college students develop confidence and gain competence in writing. Students are faced with the problems that bedevil every writer, experienced or inexperienced—problems relating to punctuation and mechanics, syntax and choice of words, structure and style. If they are to say what they want to say in a manner that earns the attention and wins the respect of an audience that matters to them, they must keep making decisions as they plan, write, and rewrite their papers. They are more likely to make wise decisions if they have on their desks a resource book they will turn to regularly for information and advice.

So that users of this handbook can find what they want quickly and easily, we have retained from previous editions the alphabetical arrangement of articles and the extensive system of cross references. So that the treatment of usage will be immediately helpful, we have retained the simple division of standard English into formal, informal, and general. The Introduction, addressed to the student, describes the book, explains its rationale, and tells how it can be used—for course work, for individual reference, for browsing.

To help students write so that what they have to say will be understood, respected, even enjoyed by their readers, we provide them with some rules, remind them of certain conventions, and suggest some of the uses that can be made of both highly formal and decidedly informal English. Recognizing, however, that the practical functions of formal and informal are sharply limited for undergraduates, we recommend that they set out to master general American English, the variety of English that all educated Americans read and that all need to be able to write. We also consider it the variety most suitable for classroom instruction. Because general English is the English that students read both for course work and for relaxation, they can accept its rules and conventions as belonging to the real world (rather than the ozone layer) of letters. The great majority of the illustrative passages in the *Index*—whether taken from books, learned journals, popular magazines, and newspapers or adapted from the writing of students—represent this most useful and versatile variety.

On the issue of standards, we endorse neither anarchy nor absolutism. We don't believe that college students, or college graduates, should be encouraged to think that just any rush, or gush, of words on paper necessarily has value. Nor do we believe that students should be misled into thinking that there is only one Good English—least of all the Good English that demands observance of the rules embalmed in prescriptive handbooks and guides to linguistic etiquette.

On certain specific matters, students need—and will find—unequivocal advice. In the articles keyed to the correction chart we have made the *Index* as prescriptive as honesty and realism permit. But we refuse to condemn as "wrong" failure to observe a rule that has never been observed consistently by gifted writers, and we think it a waste of time to keep deploring practices that (though anyone may choose *not* to adopt them) have long been accepted in widely esteemed periodicals. When a locution is considered wrong, or illiterate, or merely distasteful by a sizable number of educated readers, we say so. When the same locution appears regularly in publications edited by men and women of skill, taste, and intelligence, we point out that fact as well. The student can then decide whether or not to use it in a particular rhetorical situation.

The correction articles answer directly and explicitly such questions as "What mark of punctuation do I need here?" "Should this verb be singular or plural?" "What can I do to improve the continuity of this paragraph?" But they also take into account appropriateness to the writer's subject and purpose and audience, and to the writer's self. And in most of the articles relating to usage, style, and rhetorical strategies, appropriateness is the primary criterion students are urged to apply.

In usage articles, after identifying the current status of a locution—standard or nonstandard; if standard, formal, informal, or general—we often include the alternatives: the "*pretty* good time" of informal and the "*fairly* good time" of general; the formal *arising* and the general *getting up*. The student who has read the Introduction knows that the varieties overlap and that on occasion good writers deliberately shift from one variety to another. In a paper that is predominantly in general English, then, the informal *about* may be used instead of *almost* ("I was about done") as a tactic for moving a bit closer to the reader. Here and elsewhere, we neither deny students a choice nor simply list alternatives and invite them to take their pick. What we try to do is guide them toward making intelligent choices, choices that reflect their awareness of the rhetorical context in which they are writing.

Index to English does not limit application of the labels "general," "formal," "informal" to words and phrases. It applies them as well to punctuation, to sentence patterns, to transitions, and to the styles that are the end result of the countless choices that every writer makes, deliberately or intuitively. For writing—certainly good writing—is all of a piece, and even worse than the categorical separation of words into "right" words and "wrong" is the separation of usage from style and of style from rhetoric.

Nor does the *Index* limit discussion to small writing problems that can be safely detached from the context in which they occur. Many of the articles bear on the composing of whole essays—on prewriting and getting started, on the choice of details, on the means of achieving logical sequence, on the organization and development of special types of papers, on how to stop. And many articles, like those on grammar, linguistics, usage, the English language, and the origin of words, introduce readers to broad areas of scholarship. From these, as well as from many of the shorter articles, references open the door to further study.

A word about editorial procedure: In order to keep the topic of each article in sharp focus, irrelevant material has been deleted from illustrative quotations; and when what remains is grammatically a complete sentence, it is presented without opening or closing ellipsis.

In planning this edition, the publishers solicited advice from many teachers. Among those whose suggestions influenced the direction the revision took were Julia A. Alexander of the Colorado School of Mines, Ronald E. Buckalew and Martha Kolln of The Pennsylvania State University, Don Norton of Brigham Young University, and William H. Pixton of Troy State University. Again, as in the Fifth Edition, we warmly acknowledge the contributions of James Fitzpatrick of Continental Bank, Jay Robinson of the University of Michigan, James Sledd of the University of Texas, and Joseph M. Williams of the University of Chicago.

Our thanks to Richard Welna of the editorial staff of Scott, Foresman, who proposed this collaboration and cast the deciding vote when we disagreed. More often than not he did so to the satisfaction of at least one of us. Our thanks, too, to Robert C. Gruen for his care and patience in seeing the manuscript through the press.

We dedicate this edition, with admiration and affection, to the memory of Porter G. Perrin, originator of the *Index to English*. He was right from the start.

Wilma R. Ebbitt
David R. Ebbitt

Introduction

What do I want to say on this subject?

What am I trying to accomplish in writing about it?

Who are my readers? What sort of people are they? What are their tastes and interests, their values and prejudices?

How can I make them share what I think and feel about my subject? Should I tell them outright what my convictions are, or should I simply put before them the evidence that has impressed me and invite them to form their own opinions?

Shall I treat the subject seriously, or are my readers the kind who respond best to a humorous approach? Shall I write as if I'm addressing them from a lecture platform, or shall I try for the style and tone of an evening of good talk with old friends?

Questions like these are the big questions in writing, the ones you need to face up to first when you set about planning and drafting a paper, the ones you need to keep steadily in mind as you write and rewrite. Essentially they are questions of rhetoric—how to find, organize, and present your ideas so as to achieve a specific purpose as you address a specific audience on a specific topic.

But though settling on the major strategies that are the concern of rhetoric is certainly the most important job in writing, it's not always the one that gives the most trouble. Many writers find themselves puzzling longest and fretting hardest over questions of grammar, word choice, and mechanics:

Do these two ideas belong in one sentence, or should they be in two? If in one, how should they be connected? Is the relationship between them most accurately expressed by *and* or *because* or *therefore*?

If I begin my paper with *I*, will it sound egotistical? Can I use *you* without making the reader think I'm putting words in his mouth? And if I use *him* as the pronoun after *author*, will I be accused of male chauvinism? Would it be better to use *his or her* or *her/his*, or should I avoid the issue by changing everything into the plural or by rewriting the sentence in the passive voice?

Can I open a paragraph with *and*?

Should I say *among* or *between*, *different from* or *different than*, *if I was going* or *if I were going*, *the girl I knew* or *the girl whom I knew*?

Shall I say *flush* or *blush*, *request* or *ask*, *cannot* or *can't*?

What punctuation do I need here—a comma, a semicolon, or a colon?

It's or *its*? *There* or *their*? *Traveled* or *travelled*—one *l* or two?

Questions like these, especially if they are considered separately as isolated items, can cause frustration and irritation. True, some of them have clear-cut answers, to be found in almost any dictionary or handbook. *It's*, the contraction for *it is*, is wrong when used as the genitive (*its*, not *it's*, color). Similarly, *their* and *there* have separate meanings which should not be confused. *Traveled* and *travelled* are both correct; American dictionaries give *traveled* as first choice. The comma has certain functions that it does not share with other marks of punctuation; the semicolon has separate functions; so has the colon.

But in some sentences either the comma or the semicolon is satisfactory, and in other sentences either the semicolon or the colon would do. There are conventions to be learned, habits to be established, alternatives to be noted, so that the right punctuation comes automatically, or so that, when there is a choice, it will be made on sensible grounds – because it fits with other choices that have been made.

What is true of punctuation is often true of diction: there is no one "right" answer to the question of which word to use. *Request* and *ask* are both correct; which word is preferable depends on the style of the paper, which in turn depends upon purpose and audience. Both *can't* and *cannot* appear regularly in print; in a specific context, one would be better – because more appropriate – than the other.

In these cases and a great many more, rhetoric and style and usage intersect; for rhetoric includes style (*how* we say *what* we say), and style is the sum of many individual choices in syntax and usage and even punctuation. It is when all these choices come together to create one prevailing manner of expression that a paper can be said to have a particular style.

If good writing depends upon skill in handling rhetorical problems, why do we spend so much time fussing about small, individual points of usage? Perhaps the situation is less paradoxical than it sounds. Seen in proper perspective – not as a series of *do*s and *don't*s – many questions of usage turn out to be questions of rhetorical strategy.

Initially, questions about usage arise because there are different varieties of English and because these varieties don't fit equally well into every social and rhetorical situation. What is appropriate in casual talk is not always appropriate on paper. What sounds natural to an audience of teenagers baffles an audience of old people. What amuses readers in one context alienates them in another. Knowing what kinds of English there are and recognizing how and why the alternatives differ puts you in a position to suit your style to your subject and to your audience and to the occasion. When you write English that is appropriate to the rhetorical situation, you're making the right use of the language. Good English is not just arbitrarily "good." It's good because it's right for the job.

The varieties of English

There are many ways of classifying the English we use, both the spoken and the written. *Index to English* is concerned primarily with written varieties of the language in their edited form—that is, with writing that has been gone over with some care. Its purpose is to help you increase your skill and confidence in writing standard English.

Standard and nonstandard English. Standard English is the dialect used, and therefore approved, by the dominant middle class in our society. The other cultural variety of English is nonstandard English, which includes usages from numerous regional and social dialects. In speech the distinction between standard and nonstandard hinges on a fairly small number of pronunciations, words, word forms, and grammatical constructions habitually used by people of noticeably different educational backgrounds and social standings. In writing the distinction is chiefly based on a carryover of those speech habits, with spellings taking the place of pronunciations. Nonstandard English, which appears in published writing chiefly in dialog and in other prose that attempts to reproduce nonstandard speech patterns, is inappropriate in the writing that college students are normally expected to do. (For *Index* articles on nonstandard words and forms, see the cross references in the article Nonstandard English.)

In this *Index* we divide standard English into general, formal, and informal. The labels "general," "formal," and "informal" broadly correspond to the social and rhetorical situations in which the varieties commonly occur. Since they shade into each other, with large areas of overlap, the categories should not be rigidly interpreted nor the labels rigidly applied. While some words are clearly more formal than others—*disputatious*, for example—and some more informal—like *hassle*—many can be labeled only in context. A word that stands out as inappropriately formal in one paper might, in a different one, pass as general. To say that a passage is formal, then, doesn't mean that the vocabulary and sentence structure are exclusively formal. It means that there are enough traits usually associated with that variety of the written language to give the passage a formal feel or tone even though much of it—perhaps most of it—may be general in style.

The boundaries between the varieties continue to shift, as they have been doing for hundreds of years. Today's good formal English is close to what would have been considered general English in the essays of a half century ago, while what might be called the High Formal of the 1800s has almost disappeared. General English, meanwhile, has become increasingly relaxed, taking in more and more words, phrases, and constructions from informal. Even short periods of time bring changes in the status of individual usages. A word or phrase that's looked on as informal one year may appear often enough in well-edited publications to be considered general a year later, as the verb *bug* (to plant a secret listening device) did in the early 1970s. A formal word may catch on in general English (as *charisma* and *ambience* did), enjoy a vogue, and then either return to its source or become a permanent part of the general vocabulary. Given such short-term change, the best way to keep in touch with what's going on in the language is not by relying on dictionaries and guides to usage, which are inevitably out of date, but by reading current books and newspapers and magazines and by listening to all the voices that reach your ear, directly and by way of radio and television. You may not—and shouldn't—adopt all the new locutions; but you will be aware that the language is a living, changing thing, and your range of choices will be expanded.

Formal English. Old-fashioned formal English—what we have referred to as High Formal—survives today chiefly in oratory—in some political speeches, some sermons, some eulogies and other ceremonial addresses, as at graduation time. At its best, old-fashioned formal demonstrates that the English language is a magnificent instrument that can not only disseminate information with clarity and precision but also spark the imagination, stir the emotions, lift up the heart. At its worst, it is empty verbal posturing, or arid, sleep-inducing pedantry, or a stiff parade of big words and stilted phrasings.

Formal written English is found today in some textbooks—particularly those for advanced courses—and in some learned journals. Outside academic circles it appears in books and articles addressed to well-educated audiences willing to make a greater intellectual effort than is called for by a good read. Formal is appropriate for writing on philosophy, religion, aesthetics, literature, theoretical science, and so forth. But though its subject matter may be intellectual, its tone need not be solemn. Wit and formal English have a long history of collaboration.

The vocabulary of formal English smacks of the literary, the scholarly, the philosophical. It includes words seldom used in ordinary conversation (*desultory, ubiquitous, importunate*) and a high proportion of nouns like *distinction, concept, hiatus,* which generalize about experience rather than present it directly. For those familiar with them, the words are often rich in suggestion (*omen, luminous, transcend*) or have some special appeal of sound or rhythm (*immemorial, quintessence*), while the abstract nouns and technical terms permit the exact and concise statement of ideas.

Though formal English uses short, compact sentences for emphasis, its typical sentence is fairly long, and the elements in it are carefully ordered. Here is an example of current formal English:

The children, we hear, are badly taught and cannot read, spell, or write; employers despair of finding literate clerks and typists; the professions deplore the thickening of jargon which darkens counsel and impedes action; scientists cry out in their journals that their colleagues cannot report their facts intelligibly; and businessmen declare many bright people unemployable for lack of the ability to say what they mean in any medium.—Wilson Follett, *Modern American Usage*

Such deliberate, studied arrangement of elements in a series ("employers despair . . . ; the professions deplore . . . ; scientists cry out . . ."), as well as careful, often self-conscious word choice ("the thickening of jargon which darkens counsel and impedes action"), characterizes formal writing, making its impact quite different from that of the more casual styles of most general and all informal English.

Throughout this *Index* formal preferences are regularly identified, not because formal English is called for in most college writing but because, in college and out, what you write is likely to have readers who insist that some (seldom all) of the conventions of formal English be followed.

When you set out to write a paper in formal English, you risk numerous pitfalls. The bad imitations of formal called officialese are prize exhibits of unreadable pomposity, while more literary efforts are plagued by big words and fine writing. And there is the problem of sustaining a formal style – not writing just one or two neatly balanced sentences but continuing to show control of phrases and clauses, mastery of the rules of close punctuation, conservative taste in usage, and a vocabulary adequate to the demands of the subject and the style. In short, writing a successful essay in formal English is a challenging undertaking. Meeting the challenge when the occasion arises is one measure of your sophistication as a writer.

Informal English. Informal written English is the variety of standard English that most of us use naturally in letters to members of our families and to close friends, in diaries and journals, and in other kinds of personal, intimate expression. It is also used – sometimes appropriately, sometimes not – when writers who share no intimacy with the readers they are addressing try to reduce the distance between themselves and their audiences.

Although it actually differs a good deal from the English we use in casual, spontaneous conversation, informal written English suggests speech in several of its characteristics. It swings over a wide range, sometimes mixing vocabulary from formal English with verb forms from nonstandard. It makes free use of slang and draws on the shoptalk that develops in every occupation and the in-group vocabulary that attaches to every sport. The writer takes many syntactic shortcuts, sometimes omitting subjects, usually skipping optional relative pronouns ("I hear he's in town" instead of "I hear that he is in town"), regularly using contractions. Some of the sentences of informal are short and elliptical ("Bet I won more than you" instead of "I'll bet that I won more than you won"); others are unusually long, with asides and afterthoughts keeping the structure loose and rambling.

In published nonfiction the extended use of informal English is limited to some periodicals addressed to special audiences (rock fans, surfers, motorcyclists), to the columns of determinedly personal columnists in more general publications, and to letters from readers. Often, published informal represents the hyped-up "Hey, there, you guys and gals" school of artificial intimacy, but it may also echo the flatness of much ordinary speech, as in these excerpts from campus newspapers:

I can't see why girls should be given a free ride. They're just being used as the window dressing and guys are being played for suckers.

Joanne Woodward gets to use a southern accent and drink a lot for her role. She is quite good but it is not much of a part.

In small doses, however, informal English appears in a great variety of newspapers, magazines, and books, where writers of general English use informal words and phrases to move closer to their readers. The following sentences, from a range of sources, share the feel of informal and the personal note that is one of its chief characteristics:

You can bet your sweet patootie they haven't. – Richard Dougherty, *Newsweek*

Both parties have been stuck with old geezers in their sixties ever since. – James Reston, *New York Times*

Around 3:30 in the afternoon, he'd been fooling with his hair, spraying, setting, combing, until it was perfect. – Laurence Gonzales, *Playboy*

When I was 10, gangs of hoods would stone us Jewish kids. – Audrey Gellis, *Ms.*

A single outing with one dame when he was 60 later cost him a couple hundred grand in paternity suit fees. – Tony Hiss, *New York Times*

And, of course, there is his behind. He has a fabulous behind. – Sally Quinn, *Washington Post*

If you have a chance to write a paper in informal English, don't make the mistake of assuming that it won't be any more of a problem than writing to your kid sister or your best friend. Your readers probably won't include your sister or your friend, but they will include your instructor and your classmates. And while no one should be applying the standards of formal written English or even the more relaxed ones of general English, all of them have a right to insist on being able to understand what you say. In a letter to family or hometown friends, you can take a lot for granted: they know local places and people and happenings you refer to without needing to have everything spelled out in detail; they know the special connotations of some of the words you use; they know your regional and social dialects. But it's certain that not everyone in your class knows these things, nor will everyone be as willing as family and friends to puzzle over what you're getting at.

So your job will be to put informal English to work for you – to preserve its easy, casual tone while ridding it of its sloppiness and vagueness. That will take some doing.

General English. Occupying the great middle ground between formal and informal is general written English. It's the variety of standard English that educated people most often read and that they themselves most often write. The words in its vocabulary include *spacious* as well as *roomy, precipitation* as well as *rainfall, nutty* as well as *eccentric, rip off* as well as *steal;* but unless there's a special reason for using the formal or informal words, *roomy, rainfall, eccentric,* and *steal* will be its choices. Writers of general English are likely to use words that are concrete, close to experience, referring to things, people, actions, and events more than to abstractions. The turns of phrase reflect those of speech *(look into, give up, take over);* coordinating conjunctions like *and* and *so* are much more common than conjunctive adverbs like *furthermore* and *consequently.* Typical sentences are moderate in length, with few interrupting phrases or elaborate constructions.

General written English is much less conservative than formal, more controlled than informal. Though it's more likely than informal to follow strict conventions of subject-verb agreement, it doesn't do so as consistently as formal does. It often ignores formal distinctions, as between *can* and *may, raise* and *rear.* Yet it's slower than informal to accept slang. And while the writer of general English is less conservative than the writer of formal English, he may be quite as careful. Indeed, because his style is not so restricted by conventions, he has more choices to make than the formal writer does.

General English is the most versatile and the most serviceable of the three varieties of standard written English this *Index* deals with. Because it can reach so many, it's the variety you will use in most of your writing while you're in college and after you've graduated. But keep alert to the opportunities informal and formal English offer you. Mixing the varieties of English is common practice in current writing. In many magazine articles, you'll find an informal phrase dropped into a passage whose predominant tone is general or formal—possibly for shock effect, possibly because the writer wants to show a new side of himself, possibly because he wants to mock his own seriousness or a view held by his audience. Or an essay that has been light and casual may move to a thoughtful, measured, formal conclusion.

Sudden shifts in style that have no discernible motive are distracting and suggest that the writer has lost control. Sometimes he has. But a good writer knows what he's doing: by calling attention to *what* he's saying by the *way* he says it, he makes shifts in style perform double duty. Even though most of your writing may be general, then, the more you acquaint yourself with the alternatives that formal and informal English offer, the better you will be able to use them when you want to achieve rhetorical effects that rely on contrasts in style.

Using *Index to English*

Index to English applies the principles of usage described in this Introduction. Because it deals with English as it exists—in publications addressed to moderately educated and to well-educated audiences, as well as in student essays—many of its articles don't offer a simple Right and Wrong, Do and Don't. Often they give both the formal choice and the general choice, sometimes the informal choice as well. When you have a particular job of writing to do, with a particular audience in mind, the relevance of the choices will come clear.

The articles in the *Index* are alphabetically arranged. They fall roughly into six categories:

1. Articles on particular words and constructions, like *among, between; definitely; like, as; not about to; who, whom.* Information about the standing of a locution in current usage is often supported by examples quoted from newspapers, popular magazines, scholarly journals, and books. (The fact that something is printed doesn't mean that it's recommended; bad writing may appear in respectable publications.) Read the article to see where the locution is placed among the varieties of English, and then decide whether it fits your style in the particular rhetorical situation. The entry titles for articles on words and phrases are the only ones that are not capitalized.

2. Articles to be used in correcting and revising papers. Signaled by longhand abbreviations, these articles are listed in the correction charts on the inside front and back covers of this book. They offer straightforward advice – practical *do*s and *don't*s. Go to them when your corrected papers have been returned to you, but also get in the habit of consulting them *before* you submit your essays, while you're in the process of revising your first drafts. Checking what you've written against their instructions and illustrations will help you decide whether you've punctuated a sentence correctly, used the expected case of a pronoun, made clear what a modifier relates to.

3. Articles on composition, rhetoric, and style. Prewriting, Beginning an essay, Thesis statement, Organization, Outline form, Paragraphs, Coherence, Transition, Emphasis, Unity, and Concluding an essay – these and other articles carry you through the stages of writing a paper. Some articles deal with specific topics in rhetoric – Argument, Cause and effect, Classification and division, Comparison and contrast, Definition, Deduction, Fallacies, Induction, Logical thinking. Style is treated more directly in such articles as Abstract language, Diction, Doublespeak, Figurative language, Nominalization, Parallelism, and Periodic sentence.

4. Articles offering information and advice on a range of topics that are useful in special writing situations: Footnote form, Business letters, Research papers, Technical writing, and so on.

5. Articles on grammar, offering definitions and discussions of standard grammatical terms and concepts – Collective nouns, for example, and Parts of speech, Relative clauses, Subjunctive mood.

6. Articles about language and language study, such as British English, English language, Linguistics, Sexist language, and Usage.

Refer to the *Index* when you're faced with a writing assignment (see Prewriting), as you write, as you revise what you've

written, and when your corrected essay is returned to you for
further revision. Besides following up the cross references that
most articles contain, look up any term you come upon that is
new or unclear to you—*modal auxiliaries,* for example, or *deep
structure.* Most such terms are explained in articles of their
own.

Index to English is intended to be more than a reference work
for college writers. It is a book to browse in and to annotate. By
updating the slang and vogue words and by noting changes in
usage, fresh figures of speech, allusions, and turns of phrase,
you can keep the *Index* alive at the same time that you keep
yourself in touch with your language.

Many articles include references to books and journals where
you can find further discussion. In the references, the titles of
the journals *American Speech* and *College Composition and
Communication* have been abbreviated to *AS* and *CCC.*

Books to which frequent reference is made are cited by author's name only:

Atwood, E. Bagby. *A Survey of Verb Forms in the Eastern
United States.* Ann Arbor: Univ. of Michigan Press, 1953.

Bolinger, Dwight. *Aspects of Language.* 2nd ed. New York: Harcourt, 1975.

Bryant, Margaret M. *Current American Usage.* New York:
Funk, 1962.

Christensen, Francis. *Notes Toward a New Rhetoric.* New York:
Harper, 1967.

Copperud, Roy H. *American Usage: The Consensus.* New York:
Van Nostrand, 1970.

Evans, Bergen, and Cornelia Evans. *A Dictionary of Contemporary American Usage.* New York: Random, 1957.

Follett, Wilson. *Modern American Usage: A Guide.* Ed. and
compl. by Jacques Barzun. New York: Hill, 1966.

Fowler, H. W. *A Dictionary of Modern English Usage.* 2nd ed.
Rev. by Sir Ernest Gowers. New York: Oxford Univ. Press,
1965.

Francis, W. Nelson. *The Structure of American English.* New
York: Ronald, 1958.

Fries, Charles Carpenter. *American English Grammar.* New
York: Appleton, 1940.

Hungerford, Harold, Jay Robinson, and James Sledd, eds. *English Linguistics: An Introductory Reader.* Glenview, Ill.:
Scott, 1970.

Jacobs, Roderick A., and Peter S. Rosenbaum. *English Transformational Grammar.* Waltham, Mass.: Blaisdell, 1968.

Jespersen, Otto. *Essentials of English Grammar.* 1933; rpt.
University, Ala.: Univ. of Alabama Press, 1964.

Joos, Martin. *The English Verb.* Madison: Univ. of Wisconsin
Press, 1964.

Long, Ralph B. *The Sentence and Its Parts.* Chicago: Univ. of
Chicago Press, 1961.

Long, Ralph B., and Dorothy R. Long. *The System of English Grammar*. Glenview, Ill.: Scott, 1971.

Mencken, H. L. *The American Language*. Abridged 4th ed. Ed. Raven I. McDavid, Jr. New York: Knopf, 1963.

Pooley, Robert C. *The Teaching of English Usage*. Urbana, Ill.: National Council of Teachers of English, 1974.

Pyles, Thomas. *The Origins and Development of the English Language*. 2nd ed. New York: Harcourt, 1971.

Quirk, Randolph, et al. *A Grammar of Contemporary English*. New York: Seminar, 1972.

Roberts, Paul. *Understanding Grammar*. New York: Harper, 1954.

Sledd, James. *A Short Introduction to English Grammar*. Glenview, Ill.: Scott, 1959.

Summey, George, Jr. *American Punctuation*. New York: Ronald, 1959.

Whitehall, Harold. *Structural Essentials of English*. New York: Harcourt, 1956.

Williams, Joseph M. *The New English*. New York: Free Press, 1970.

Two stylebooks are frequently referred to: *A Manual of Style*, 12th ed. (Chicago: Univ. of Chicago Press, 1969), and *United States Government Printing Office Style Manual*, rev. ed. (Washington, D.C.: Government Printing Office, 1967), cited as *U.S. Style Manual*.

A

a, an

The choice between *a* and *an* depends on the initial sound, not on the initial letter, of the word that follows. *A* is used before all words beginning with a consonant sound: a business, a European trip, a D, a usage. *An* is used before all words beginning with a vowel sound, including words spelled with initial silent *h:* an apple, an F, an honor, an hour, an uncle.

In words beginning with *h* but not accented on the first syllable, like *histo'rian, hyster'ical, h* was formerly not pronounced, so *an* was used. Although the *h* is now often pronounced, some people continue to say and write *an histor'ical event* (but *a his'tory*). In contemporary usage *a* is more common in such locutions, but *an* also occurs: "an habitual set of choices" (Josephine Miles, *CCC*).

Repeating *a* or *an* before each noun of a series keeps the various words distinct: a pen, a sheet of paper, and an envelope.

See *awhile, a while; half; kind, sort* 2.

 ## Abbreviations

Write in full the word or words inappropriately abbreviated. Or use the correct form of the abbreviation marked.

1. Appropriateness. Abbreviations are appropriate in manuals, reference books, business and legal documents, scholarly footnotes, and other works in which they are conventionally used in order to save space. They are also suitable in informal writing — notes for your own use, letters to friends. Otherwise, use only those abbreviations that are fully established in standard usage (see 2) or those that regularly occur in discussions of a particular subject.

2. Standard abbreviations. *Dr., Mr., Mrs., Messrs.* are always abbreviated when used with names. (A comparable term of address, *Ms.*, is technically not an abbreviation but a combination of *Miss* and *Mrs.*) A number of abbreviations, such as *St.* (see *saint*), *B.C.* and *A.D., a.m.* and *p.m., Jr.* for *Junior,* and abbreviations for government agencies like *CIA* and *SEC,* are standard. In formal writing, titles like Reverend, Professor, President, and Senator and naval and military ranks are not abbreviated. In general writing they may be abbreviated when initials or given names are used: Professor Hylander *or* Prof. G. W. Hylander (*but not* Prof. Hylander).

Scholarly writing still uses some abbreviations of Latin words. The following are no longer customarily italicized:

cf. (*confer*)	compare (for which *see* may be used)
e.g. (*exempli gratia*)	for example
ibid. (*ibidem*)	the same (used in footnotes)
i.e. (*id est*)	that is

Abbreviations less commonly used are often italicized: *c.* or *ca.* (*circa,* "about," used with uncertain dates), *seq.* (*sequentes* or *sequentia,* "following").

Dictionaries give abbreviations either in the main alphabetical list of words or in a special list.

3. Period with abbreviations. Where standard practice requires the period, its omission (as in *eg*) is a careless slip. Only one period is used after an abbreviation at the end of a sentence.

Periods are increasingly omitted from the abbreviations of names of government agencies (*CIA, FBI, HEW*) and of other terms if the abbreviation is generally used instead of the name (*AFL-CIO, CBS, GNP, ID, IQ*), and from abbreviations like *mph, hp, kwh, rpm* in scientific contexts or when used with figures (780 rpm). They are not used with the two-letter abbreviations for states adopted by the United States Postal Service (*PA, TX*).

Abbreviations that are pronounced as words (*WASP, UNESCO*) are called acronyms. Dozens of acronyms entered the language during World War II (*Nazi, Gestapo, radar, sonar, Wac, Wave*), and thousands have been created since that time (*NATO, SALT, laser*). A recent example is *Candu,* from Canadian deuterium-uranium reactor.

For abbreviation of dates, see Months. Compare Contractions, Numbers, Origin of words 3d.

ability to

The accepted idiom is *ability* plus a *to*-infinitive (ability *to do,* not *of doing*): He has the ability to design beautiful buildings. The idea is often better expressed by an adjective or verb: He is able to [He can] design beautiful buildings; He designs beautiful buildings.

able to

Able to followed by a passive infinitive (like *to be done* or *to be ended*) sounds awkward: This was not able to be done because of lack of time. *Revised:* This could not be done because of lack of time. *Or* They were not able to do this because of lack of time. Though *can* or *could* can sometimes replace *be able to,* in standard English they do not combine with another modal auxiliary as *be able to* does: *will* be able to attend, *might* be able to come. See Modal auxiliaries.

about

About has a variety of uses. Check these for trouble spots.

1. *about–around.* In describing physical position these are nearly interchangeable, though *around* is the more common (about the barn – around the barn). In the sense of "nearly" or "approximately," *about* is more common (about 70°), but both are standard American usage. In telling time, *around* (around two o'clock) is considered more informal. Reference: Copperud, p. 21.

2. *about–almost.* In the sense of "almost" (about finished), *about* is standard but mainly informal.

3. *at about.* In formal English *at about* is avoided on the grounds that something must be either *at* or *about*. But *about* is being used here as an adverb, and the preposition-adverb pattern is well established: at approximately noon; in about ten minutes. Reference: Bryant, pp. 31–32.

4. *about* followed by an infinitive is a convenient general idiom for "on the point of": He was about to make a third try. The negative *not about to* (an emphatic "not going to") is more informal.

above
Above is primarily a preposition (above the clouds) and an adverb (dark above and light below). Its adverbial use in such phrases as "the evidence cited above" and its use as an adjective (the above prices) and as a noun (the above is confirmed) are fully established if not universally accepted. For example, *above* as an adjective is avoided by some careful writers but not by others: "for a comment on the above use of the word 'claims' . . ." (Theodore Bernstein, *Watch Your Language*). References: Bryant, pp. 3–4; Copperud, p. 2; Pooley, pp. 120–22.

Abridged clauses
In an abridged clause, the subject and a form of *be* are deleted: When [she was] first hired, she made little impression. See Clauses 2b.

Absolute phrases
An absolute phrase (sometimes called a nominative absolute or an absolute clause) is a sentence modifier—that is, it modifies the sentence as a whole, not just a part of it. The most common type of absolute phrase consists of a participle or an adjective modifying a noun that has no grammatical connection with the rest of the sentence:

The battle lost, the army surrendered.
She begins to scream, *her face white with terror.*

1. Structure. An absolute phrase is sometimes explained as the result of deleting a form of *be* (or of *have* or of both *be* and *have*) from an underlying sentence: The battle *was* [*had been*] lost; Her face *is* white with terror. Because the underlying sentence does not have the same subject as the main clause, its subject is not deleted in the absolute phrase. In this respect it differs from a participial phrase; the subject of the sentence underlying a participial phrase is deleted because that subject is identical with the subject of the main clause: *Losing the battle,* the army surrendered. (It is the army that loses the battle and the army that surrenders.)

2. Absolute phrases as formulas. Some absolute phrases have been used so frequently that they have become fixed formulas or idioms: all things considered, other things being equal, this being the case, God willing.

3. Absolute phrases and style. Absolute phrases are economical, offering a compact way of singling out details of a scene or relating parts of a whole:

He entered the room, *eyes bloodshot, tie askew.*

The curtain rises on a dark stage, *its horizon lit by a full moon.* — Arlene Croce, *New Yorker*

It was about four of a winter afternoon, *the sky about thirty feet up, the flats looking like a testing ground for biological warfare, the horizon smoking away.* — Theodore Solotaroff, *The Red Hot Vacuum*

Suddenly the President leans forward, and with a vigor far surpassing any I have previously seen him show, *his voice rising almost to a shout, his forefinger pounding on the edge of the desk,* he adjures the Secretary to get the Navy going on the Elk Hills petroleum reserve. — John Hersey, *New York Times Magazine*

But the somewhat formal quality of absolute phrases makes them out of place in casual writing: *Camp made,* the kids went to bed. And absolute phrases that contain auxiliaries *(being, having, having been)* may be heavy and clumsy-sounding: *The description of the scene having been completed,* the stage is set for the crucial action. A dependent clause is often smoother and, in situations where relationships of time or cause are important, more precise.

Absolute phrase: The dry falls were formed by the erosive glacial waters, *the ice cap having changed the course of the Columbia.*

Clause: . . . *after the ice cap had changed the course of the Columbia.*

See Dangling modifiers. References: Christensen, Ch. 2; Dorothy Petitt, *CCC*, Feb. 1969, pp. 29–34; Martha Solomon, *CCC*, Dec. 1975, pp. 356–61.

Absolutes, comparison of

Logically, absolutes like *perfect* and *final* can't be more or most, less or least. But see Comparison of adjectives and adverbs 4.

 **Abstract language**

Make this word or passage more concrete or more specific.

Abstract words refer to emotions, qualities, concepts, relationships: *love, courage, square root, symmetry.* They contrast with concrete words like *kiss, lion, computer,* and *hoop,* which refer to things we can see or touch or otherwise perceive with our senses.

Abstract terms are essential in communicating ideas, and abstract language can be just as precise as concrete language. But writing that relies heavily on an abstract vocabulary sometimes seems to lose contact with the world of human experience.

If your writing is criticized as too abstract, try these remedies:

1. Provide concrete examples. If you're writing about courage, describe a courageous action or contrast a brave act with a cowardly one. The shift from the concept to the example will make it natural to use concrete terms. Or supplement an abstract statement with a concrete expression of the same idea:

The survey's assumption that the bodily symptoms in question are indicators of psychological distress leads to the conclusion that the working class tends to somatize its emotional troubles, whereas the middle class experiences them more directly. In other words, clammy hands and upset stomach are apt to be the poor man's substitute for angst. – Charles J. Rolo, *Atlantic*

2. Replace general terms with specific ones. *General* and *abstract* are sometimes used interchangeably, and so are *specific* and *concrete;* but the pairs are not identical. Although we can easily classify a word as concrete or abstract, we can say that a term is specific or general only if we compare it with a related term. In the series *Volvo, car, vehicle,* all the words are concrete; but judged in relation to each other, *car* is more general than *Volvo* and more specific than *vehicle.* In the series *emotion, love, lust,* all the words are abstract; but *love* is more specific than *emotion* and more general than *lust.* Thus a concrete term is not always specific, nor is an abstract term always general.

Prose that strikes the reader as "abstract" often contains a high proportion of general terms, both concrete and abstract. Instead of using the general, abstract term *immorality,* specify the kind of immoral act you have in mind (*adultery, bribery, robbery*). Instead of the general, concrete term *lawbreakers,* use *muggers, vandals, burglars, rapists, speeders* – naming the kind of lawbreakers you're actually writing about. It's the specifics of a subject just as much as concrete language that make a style concrete.

3. Choose your abstract terms with care. What often causes trouble is not the use of abstract terms but the particular ones chosen. If you find that every sixth or seventh word you write is a noun ending in *-ence, -ity, -ment,* or *-tion (permanence, responsibility, management, utilization),* your style will be abstract and heavy. Many abstract nouns are related to verbs or adjectives: *intention (intend), goodness (good), refusal (refuse), stupidity (stupid), response (respond).* Given a choice between representing an action in an abstract noun or in a full verb, you will generally write a livelier, clearer sentence if you choose the verb:

The achievement of clarity of thought has a clear dependence on the correctness of the formulation of the problem.

To think clearly, you need to formulate your problem correctly.

Although neither sentence contains any concrete words, the second is decidedly more direct and easier to read than the first. Its style is more concrete.

See Description, Details, Nominalization.

Accent marks

Accent marks and other diacritical marks placed over, under, or through letters are used, most commonly in dictionaries, to indicate pronunciation. Now that the dieresis to mark the syllable break in words like *cooperate* and *reentry* has largely disappeared, virtually the only accent marks in English are those retained on words taken from foreign languages:

Acute (´): attaché, resumé, détente
Cedilla (¸): français, garçon
Grave (`): cortège, derrière
Circumflex (ˆ): crêpe, rôle
Dieresis (¨): naïve
Tilde (˜): cañon, piñon
Umlaut (¨): doppelgänger

In general writing, accent marks are usually dropped; newspapers rarely use them. An accent mark is sometimes used in English words to show that a syllable is pronounced, especially in verse: "blessèd artifacts" (John Hall Wheelock, "There Is a Place"). See Foreign words in English.

accept, except

Accept means "receive" or "say yes to"; *except,* as a verb, means "leave out" or "exclude." See *except, accept.*

Accusative case

In English six distinctive pronoun forms are often called accusative (or objective) forms and usually occur in the object function: *me, her, him, us, them, whom.* See Case 2; Gerunds 2; Infinitives 4b; *it's me;* Objects; *who, whom.*

Acronyms

Abbreviations pronounced as words are called acronyms (*WASP, WHO*). See Abbreviations 3.

Active voice

All verbs except those consisting of a form of the verb *be* and a past participle (*is cooked*) are in the active voice. See Voice. Compare Passive voice.

actually

Actually, like *basically* and *definitely,* is overused in speech. It is seldom necessary in writing even when meant literally: "My nomination for the 'most neglected book' is actually a trilogy" (Carlos Baker, *American Scholar*).

ad

Ad, the clipped form of *advertisement,* has no period. Like other clipped words it belongs to general and informal speech and writing.

A.D.

Since *A.D.* stands for *anno Domini* and means "in the year of our Lord," it precedes the date: 240 B.C. to A.D. 107. Logically, a century can't be labeled *A.D.;* and though some writers use the abbreviation as if it meant "after Christ" (the second century A.D.), the practice is not appropriate in scholarly or other formal writing.

ad hoc, ad hominem

Most Latin phrases beginning with the preposition *ad* are italicized in English, especially formal English. The most common exceptions are *ad hoc* and *ad hominem.* The first is most frequently used to describe committees established for a special purpose (ad hoc committees), as opposed to standing committees; the second describes arguments attacking a man's character instead of his reasoning (arguments ad hominem).

Adjectival clauses

Adjectival, or adjective, clauses modify nouns and pronouns: The man *who is speaking* is my uncle. See Adjectives 5, Relative clauses, Restrictive and nonrestrictive.

Adjectives

The function of an adjective is to modify—that is, to restrict or limit—a subject, object, or indirect object.

1. Position. We recognize adjectives in sentences chiefly by their position in relation to the nouns they modify, especially by the fact that they can stand between an article *(a/an, the)* and a noun or between a word like *our, this, some* and a noun: an *old* parka, their *youngest* son, this *characteristic* gesture, some *favorable* opportunity.

According to its position in a sentence, an adjective is either attributive or predicate. Attributive adjectives are placed next to their nouns, usually preceding (as in *tiny* brook, *horseless* carriages) but occasionally following (as in time *available*). Predicate adjectives come after a form of the verb *be* or some other linking verb, stated or implied *(taste, feel, turn)*: The day is *warm;* That pie smells *good.* They precede the verb only in inverted sentence order: *Silent* was the night.

2. Forms. We also recognize some adjectives by their form. While many adjectives do not have a form that sets them off from other parts of speech *(high, civil)*, others consist of a noun or verb plus a derivational ending or suffix. Some suffixes that are still being used to create adjectives are *-able* and *-ible* *(translatable, edible), -al (critical, hypothetical), -ed (sugared, four-footed), -ful (playful, soulful), -ish (darkish, childish), -less (harmless, fearless), -ous (callous, ferrous),* and *-y (cranky, dreamy, corny).*

Many adjectives are compared by adding *-er* or *-est* to the positive (or base) form or by preceding the positive form with *more* or *most: warm, warmer* or *more warm, warmest* or *most warm; talkative, more talkative, most talkative.* See Comparison of adjectives and adverbs.

3. Types. Traditionally, adjectives have been given three labels:
a. *Descriptive* adjectives are said to modify the noun by naming a quality or condition of the object named: a *gray* shutter, *vivid* colors, *difficult* words. They are ordinarily compared and may themselves be modified by qualifiers, words like *almost, very, quite.* Because new members are constantly being added, this class of words is said to be open.
b. *Limiting* adjectives point to, locate, or number: *her* book, *this* car, *third* period. See 5b.
c. *Proper* adjectives, derived from proper nouns, originally are limiting (French possessions) but also become descriptive (French culture). Sometimes they mingle both functions, as *Elizabethan* in "the Elizabethan drama" both limits drama to a period and brings to mind qualities of a group of plays. Proper adjectives are also an open class and may even be compared: He is *Frencher* than the French.

A proper adjective may be used so frequently in a merely descriptive sense that it becomes a simple adjective, written without a capital: *bacchanalian, pasteurized, diesel, india* ink.

4. Adjectives as subjects and objects. Preceded by an article, words that are ordinarily adjectives occur in the functions of nouns: the *just,* the *rich,* a new *low.* Though most such words don't have genitive or plural forms, some do (new *lows*).

5. Adjectival function. Since phrases, clauses, and words that are usually other parts of speech may, like adjectives, restrict or limit a subject, object, or indirect object, we can speak of an *adjectival* function.
a. Phrases and clauses used in adjectival function:

The man *with his hat on* is Harry.
I like the one *on the end* best.
Everyone *who approves* will raise his right hand.
That was the summer *we went to Bermuda.*
He asked the first man *he met.*

b. Other parts of speech in adjectival function. Participles are verbals that function as adjectivals: a *coming* attraction, a *deserved* tribute. They may combine with regular adjectives: a *long-billed* bird. They are not normally compared.

One of the most characteristic traits of English is the use of nouns in the adjectival function: a *glass* jar, the *Roosevelt* administration, *adjective* modifier, *high-school mathematics* test. In form, such words are nouns: they all may be inflected for plural and genitive. In context, because they occur in the same position adjectives occur in, we may call them adjectivals. Thus in isolation they are nouns; in context they may be either adjectivals (*home* cooking), adverbials (He went *home*), or nominals (My *home* is your *home*).

Traditionally, *this, that, his, other, former, two, second, both,* etc., have been called limiting adjectives. (*This, that, these,* and *those* have also been called demonstrative adjectives. See Demonstrative adjectives and pronouns.) Some grammarians find it clearer to classify all these words as determiners that usually perform adjectival functions. Unlike regular adjectives, they cannot be compared, they ordinarily do not occur as predicates, they are lexically empty, and they belong to a closed class — new ones are not added. See Determiners.

See Parts of speech. References: Francis, pp. 268–81; Quirk et al., pp. 231–67; Roberts, Chs. 4, 14; Sledd, pp. 79–80, 92–93.

adj Adjectives and style

Reconsider your choice of the adjective marked.

The adjectives you use should make your statements more precise or more forceful.

1. Adjectives that fail. Some adjectives are redundant. In *briny ocean, briny* adds nothing because all oceans are briny; *stark* adds nothing to *tragedy* or *madness* because most tragedies and madnesses are stark. All emergencies are sudden, so *sudden emergency* is redundant. Very general adjectives are often weak: *good, bad, beautiful, wonderful, terrific, fantastic, incredible, awful,* and so on communicate an attitude toward something, rarely any of its characteristics. The reader wants to know the particular sort of *good* — generous? virtuous? affable? delicious? efficient? Many adjectives that are exact enough have been used so frequently with certain nouns (*fond* farewell, *beady* black eyes) that they have become trite. Though most of us use inexact adjectives in conversation, in writing we should think twice before using any combination of adjective and noun that comes automatically to mind. See Triteness.

2. Adjectives that clutter.   If you try too hard to paint a picture, you may pile up too many adjectives. Deleting most of them from this passage would improve the style:

In a hotel dining room there is not the clamorous, raucous bedlam of its immediate surroundings, but a refined, subdued atmosphere, pervaded by distinct, faintly audible sounds. The orchestra, with a barely perceptible diminuendo, concludes the melodic, slow-tempo arrangement, climaxed by the beautiful strains of the "Merry Widow" waltz — rising, falling, fading with plaintive supplication.

The stylistic effect is even worse when the words in adjectival position are nouns. Piling nouns in front of nouns produces prose that is heavy and hard to understand: The chairman selection committee progress report date has been changed = The date for the progress report of the committee on selecting a chairman has been changed. If a string of prepositional phrases is not very graceful, a string of nouns is less so.

3. Adjectives that work. Used sensibly and sensitively, adjectives reinforce meaning and improve style. As Herbert Read puts it, "Appropriate epithets may be either exact or happy." In most factual writing the first requirement of adjectives is exactness; they must answer the needs of the material. And in writing that makes a definite attempt to capture the feelings and sensations of the reader, the adjectives must also deserve the epithet "happy"; that is, they must seem to fit, as in this account:

He had a quick impression of hard-faced men with gray eyes burning some transparent fuel for flame, and said, "I won't go back. If you don't arrest me, I'm going on to the Pentagon," and knew he meant it, some absolute certainty had come to him, and then two of them leaped at him at once in the cold clammy murderous fury of all cops at the existential moment of making their bust . . . and a surprising force came to his voice, and he roared to his own distant pleasure in new achievement and new authority – "Take your hands off me, can't you see? I'm not resisting arrest. . . ." – Norman Mailer, *Harper's*

According to E. B. White, "The adjective hasn't been built that can pull a weak or inaccurate noun out of a tight place." True enough. And Carl Sandburg is said to have warned a writer, "Think twice before you use an adjective." This is probably sound advice for anyone who automatically attaches an adjective to every noun and so produces what a critic of the works of H. P. Lovecraft called "adjective-benumbed prose." But adjectives can help a writer describe his subject as he has seen it, and if he chooses the right ones – adjectives that are happy as well as exact – they will help the reader see it too.

See Description. Compare Adverbs and style.

Adverbial clauses

Adverbial clauses, so named because they function like adverbs, are dependent clauses that may be introduced by a variety of subordinators, including *as, as if, because, since, when, where:* He walks *as if his shoes are too tight; When they finally arrived,* all the tickets were sold. See Adverbs 2, 3.

Adverbs

Traditionally, the adverb as a grammatical category has been a ragbag, including a variety of words that modify verbs, adjectives, other adverbs, and whole clauses and sentences. Some words in the category, like *almost, very, quite, yes, no,* obviously differ in certain respects from more typical adverbs – they cannot be compared – and could be set off as different parts of speech; but because some of their functions resemble those of adverbs, they can also be regarded as adverbial and assigned to appropriate subgroups. Grammarians continue to experiment with new classifications.

1. Forms. Most adverbs are formed by adding *-ly* to adjectives or participles: *badly, deservedly, laughingly, surely.* Some adverbs have developed from Old English forms without a special adverbial sign: *now, then, here, there.*

A number of adverbs have the same forms as adjectives, including these:

bad	doubtless	hard	much	slow
better	early	high	near	smooth
bright	even	late	new	straight
cheap	fair	loose	right	tight
close	fast	loud	rough	well
deep	first	low	sharp	wrong

Most of these unchanged adverbs are matched by forms in -*ly*, with which they may or may not be interchangeable. See Adverbs and style.

Most adverbs are compared, either by adding -*er* and -*est* or by preceding them with *more* and *most*. See Comparison of adjectives and adverbs.

2. Functions. Adverbs are typically used in two functions:
a. To modify single words, phrases, and clauses: He came early (*early* modifies *came*); They were practically in the street (*practically* modifies *in the street*); Fortunately, no one was home (*Fortunately* modifies all of *no one was home*). In direct and indirect questions, *when, where, why,* and *how* perform adverbial functions even though they are not in the adverbial position at the end of a statement:

When did he leave? (*Compare* He left yesterday.)
Do you know why he left? (*Compare* He left because he was tired.)

As in all information questions, the item being questioned — in this case a time, place, reason, or degree question-word — is shifted to the beginning of its clause.
b. To connect separate sentences or the independent clauses of a compound sentence (see Conjunctive adverbs):

We found the dormitories empty, the classrooms silent and deserted. *Consequently* we returned to the city.

They agreed to call the matter closed; *however,* they were by no means convinced.

Phrases and clauses may also have the function of adverbs (see Phrases) and thus be classed as adverbials: He came *in the morning; After the exam* he quit; *When it was time to go,* she didn't know what to do.

Is *home* in "He went home" or *days* in "He works days" an adverb or a noun? The simplest solution is to define such words formally as nouns but functionally as adverbials. In most contexts and by most tests, *home* and *day* would be nouns: they occur in all noun contexts and with all noun inflections. But since they may also occur in positions normally occupied by adverbs, we can say that in such sentences they are nouns in adverbial functions or adverbials. The -*al* of *adverbial* indicates that we are defining these words by their syntactic function in the context, not by their form.

3. Position. Different subclasses of adverbs occupy different positions in sentences, and often a single subclass can occupy more than one position. Among the one-word adverbs, for example, qualifiers (like *very* and *extremely*) precede the words they qualify, different negatives (like *never* and *not*) occupy different positions with respect to the verb, and adverbs of manner (like *worse, keenly, openly*) often may stand initially, medially, or finally:

The air was *extremely* clear.
Tom had *never* liked pizza. Tom *never* had liked pizza.
Patiently she replied. She replied *patiently*. She *patiently* replied.

Some adverbial phrases and clauses have comparable mobility. In "When the tide turned, all the boats headed for the channel," the opening clause could be shifted to the end or, enclosed by commas, could be inserted between *boats* and *headed*. Whether its position should be changed is a matter of style.

See Parts of speech. References: Stanley Greenbaum, *Studies in English Adverbial Usage* (Coral Gables: Univ. of Miami Press, 1970); Long and Long, Ch. 38; Quirk et al., pp. 267–84, 743–56.

adv Adverbs and style

Correct the form of the adverb marked, change its position, or reconsider your choice of adverb.

1. Use the standard form of the adverb. You can say "He sang loud" or "He sang loudly"; both are standard. The short form is often preferred in general and informal English, the *-ly* in formal English. The choice is a matter of style. Problems arise when you fail to recognize the situations in which standard English does *not* offer a choice.

a. Omitting the *-ly* ending: Some adverbs have the same form as adjectives (see Adverbs 1). But most adverbs are formed by adding *-ly* to the adjective (*considerably, regularly, suddenly*). In such instances, the form without *-ly* is nonstandard: It hurt *considerable*; He did it *regular*. Use the *-ly* ending unless your dictionary recognizes its omission as standard.

b. Adding an unnecessary *-ly*: Even when an adverb has two forms, they are not always interchangeable. Although you can say "Drive slow" or "Drive slowly," you can't replace *close* with *closely* in "That shot came too close."

After a linking verb, a predicate adjective is called for, not an adverb: The breeze smelled sweet (*not* sweetly). Compare *bad, badly*.

Adding *-ly* to a word that already ends in *-ly* (*kindlily* for *kindly*) is a blunder. To make an adverbial from an adjective ending in *-ly* (*leisurely, orderly, worldly*), put the adjective in a prepositional phrase headed by a noun like *manner* or *way:* He approached us in a friendly way; she handled the subject in a scholarly manner. Adjectives in *-ly* that indicate time may function as adverbs unchanged: The train departed hourly.

2. Placing adverbs for clarity and style. Many adverbs can occupy different positions in a sentence (see Adverbs 3). When you have a choice, first of all place the adverb so that it makes the meaning clear: not "She answered the questions that the students asked patiently" but "She patiently answered the questions that the students asked" — if it was the answers and not the questions that were patient. Other considerations are rhythm and emphasis. Some writers hesitate to insert an adverb into a phrasal verb: instead of *have easily seen*, they write *have seen easily*. But *have easily seen* is smoother and more idiomatic. Normally an adverb should not be placed between a verb and its object. "He expects employees to obey promptly all his orders" should be revised to "He expects employees to obey all his orders promptly." See *only*, Split infinitive.

3. Making adverbs count. The use of adverbs, like the use of adjectives, should be at least precise and if possible happy. Adverbs are used unhappily when they are used unnecessarily and redundantly (Shrill horns scream *threateningly;* automobiles careen *wildly;* giant buses lumber *heavily* along), when they qualify excessively (the *seemingly* difficult problem of race relations), and when they set up a flutter of unstressed syllables (as in the first part of this sentence). Sometimes writers use an adverb to shore up an imprecise adjective or verb when an exact adjective or verb would be neater and at least as expressive:

Scholarships should be kept *for those who are academically industrious* [for the studious].

When no one was looking, I took the goggles and *swiftly made my way* [hurried] out of the store.

Many of the adverbs regularly used in conversation are better omitted in writing: *continue [on], refer [back].*

References: Copperud, pp. 6 – 7; Follett, pp. 50 – 55.

adverse, averse
Adverse is an adjective meaning "unfavorable" or "hostile" (adverse conditions). *Averse,* also an adjective, means "opposed" (I would not be averse to a short vacation).

advise
Besides meaning "to give advice," *to advise* is used to mean "to inform, to give information." In this sense the verb is commonly used for information that is rather formally given: Reporters were advised by an administration spokesman that. . . . In other situations simple *tell* is more appropriate: Peter tells us he won't be back next year.

affect, effect
Affect is usually a transitive verb meaning "influence" (This will affect the lives of thousands) or "put on" (He affected a stern manner). The noun *affect* is a technical term in psychology. *Effect* is most common as a noun, meaning "result": The effects will be felt by thousands. But it is also a formal verb meaning "bring about": The change was effected peaceably.

aggravate

In general and informal usage *aggravate* ordinarily means "annoy" or "irritate": The higher he turned the volume, the more aggravated I got. Formal writing still limits *aggravate* to the sense "make worse," as to aggravate a wound or a situation: Friction between faculty and administration was aggravated by cuts in the budget. The same division occurs in the use of the noun *aggravation*. References: Copperud, p. 8; Pooley, pp. 122–24.

agr Agreement

Make the verb or pronoun marked agree in form with the word to which it is related—its subject if it is a verb, its antecedent if it is a pronoun.

When used together, certain parts of speech "agree," or correspond in form in such a way as to express relationships of number, person, or gender. Several instances of agreement are illustrated in this pair of sentences:

This habit, which in *itself is* harmless, *is* likely to lead to *others* that *are* decidedly harmful.

These habits, which in *themselves are* harmless, *are* likely to lead to *another* that *is* decidedly harmful.

In English, agreement is largely a matter of linguistic etiquette. There are not many situations in which a change in grammatical form buttresses a difference in meaning. But when these situations occur, they are important: making your meaning clear—especially in writing—may hinge on your choosing the right form of a pronoun or the correct number of a verb.

1. Subject and verb agree in number (Those birds *were* seen; that bird *was* seen). There are four main causes of problems in subject-verb agreement: (a) phrases and clauses between subject and verb; (b) collective nouns as subjects; (c) compound subjects; and (d) dialect differences in verb inflection.
a. Most mistakes in agreement occur when a writer makes the verb agree with a word that is not the subject and that differs from the subject in number. The word is often a noun ending a clause or phrase that intervenes between subject and verb: An *analysis* of the extent to which audio-visual aids are used in schools *make* me conclude that books are no longer the chief means of education. The singular subject *analysis* calls for the corresponding verb form *makes,* but the writer has been misled by the plural noun *schools* immediately preceding the verb and perhaps also by *aids.*
b. The problem with collective nouns is, first of all, whether to treat the subject as singular or plural. If you're thinking of the group as a unit, make the verb singular (The first *couple* on the floor *was* Tom and Jane). If you're thinking of the individuals that make up the group, use a plural verb (When we found ourselves near where the old *couple were* living . . .). Once this

problem has been solved, you simply need to make sure that the verb and any related pronoun are used consistently. If the team *was* very much on edge, the reason was that *its* (not *their*) big game was only a week away. Sometimes the pronoun will determine the verb form: When we found ourselves near where the old couple *were* living, we dropped in to see *them*. "We dropped in to see *it*" (even after *was living*) would be impossible; hence the *were-them* combination. See Collective nouns.

c. Problems with compound subjects usually arise either because a compound subject is felt to be singular or because the writer is uncertain about the conventions governing the use of correlative conjunctions. Some compound subjects designate a unit that calls for a singular verb: Bacon and eggs is my favorite breakfast. Other compound subjects may represent a unit to one writer, separate things to another:

Her loyalty and patriotism *was* unparalleled in the history of her people.

Her loyalty and [her] patriotism *were* unparalleled in the history of her people.

Before deciding to use a singular verb with a compound subject, be sure your audience will not only recognize your intention but accept the logic behind it. Only subjects that are closely allied (*loyalty* and *patriotism*) can reasonably be construed as a unit. This principle rules out "Her beauty and duplicity *was* apparent even to me," which would be taken as an error in agreement.

When both elements of a compound subject connected by the correlative conjunctions *either . . . or* or *neither . . . nor* are plural, the verb is naturally plural; and when both elements are singular, the verb is usually singular. When one of the subjects is singular and the other plural, the traditional rule is that the verb should agree with the nearer subject (Neither the ideas nor the style *is* satisfactory; Neither the style nor the ideas *are* satisfactory). Although actual usage varies, this is a sensible rule to follow. See Compound subject, Correlative conjunctions.

d. Some American dialects, notably Black English, lack an ending in the third-person singular, so that *do* and *see*, for example, are treated like standard English *can* (he can, he do, he see). Writers for whom this is the natural grammatical pattern feel the standard forms (he does, he sees) to be unreal and superfluous. When writing in a variety of standard English, they have the double problem of adding the ending to most present-tense, third-person-singular verbs (*starts, stops, sees*) and of not adding it elsewhere, as in plural verbs and past-tense forms. See Principal parts of verbs 2.

2. A third-person pronoun agrees with its antecedent in number and gender. If the antecedent (the noun to which it refers) is plural, the pronoun is *they, their(s)*, or *them*, depending on its use in the sentence. If the antecedent is singular, the choice of pronoun is more complicated because gender enters in. Generally, if the noun refers to a male, we use *he, his*, or *him*, and if to a female, *she, hers*, or *her*. Otherwise, including situations where the sex is unknown or irrelevant, we use *it(s)*: The baby dropped *its* rattle; The dog was looking for *its* master.

Problems sometimes arise when the antecedent is a noun referring to a member of a group containing both sexes or a group of uncertain composition (each member of the class), or when it is one of the so-called indefinite pronouns, such as *one, anyone, everyone, no one, anybody, everybody,* or *nobody,* which, like *person,* are best regarded as indefinite nouns. When one of these words has a sphere of reference which includes only one sex, that sex generally determines the pronoun used: No one in the Girl Scout troop looked forward to *her* test [though *their* might be used here if everyone was taking the same test]. More often the reference includes both sexes, either actually or potentially. The problem then is that the common-gender *they* — because it developed rather indeterminately out of the plural *they* — is frequently looked upon as plural. In spite of the parallel with *you,* which also has both singular and plural functions, with the singular having likewise developed out of specialized uses of an original plural, many fail to recognize or acknowledge that *they* in indefinite reference is usually a singular pronoun. A form of *they* to refer to words like *everyone* (Everyone in the class turned in their papers Tuesday) is now firmly established in informal English, is increasingly accepted in general, but is strongly resisted in formal. See Sexist language, *they.*

3. A demonstrative adjective, or determiner, (*this, that, these, those*) usually agrees in number with the noun it modifies (*That coat* is expensive; *These shoes* cost more than my old pair did). See *kind, sort.*

agree to, agree with

One agrees *to* a plan and agrees *with* a person. One thing agrees *with* another. Other idioms are: I agree *in* principle; we agreed *on* a plan of attack; he agreed *to* fly or *on* flying or *that he would* fly.

ain't

Though in speech millions of Americans regularly use *ain't* as a contraction for *am not, is not, are not, has not,* and *have not,* it is never used in formal writing or in ordinary expository prose. When *ain't* does appear in general writing, it is almost always a deliberate attempt to suggest informality or down-to-earth common sense:

It will never reach the audience Welles might have and should have reached, because there just ain't no way. — Pauline Kael, *New Republic*

Those tiresome people with their tiresome quotes from Socrates about the fact that youth is going to the dogs are just trying to reassure themselves that it's all just a little bit more of the same. It ain't. — John M. Culkin, *New York Times*

See Divided usage. References: Bryant, pp. 16–17; Copperud, p. 9; Evans and Evans, p. 23.

all
Note the spelling of these words and phrases:

1. *all ready* (adjective phrase): At last they were all ready to begin.

2. *already* (adverb of time): They had already begun.

3. *all together* (adjective phrase): We found them all together in an old trunk.

4. *altogether* (adverb, equivalent to *wholly*): That's another matter altogether.

5. *all right* (adjective phrase): The seats seemed all right to me.

Alright now appears frequently enough to be accepted as a variant spelling by some dictionaries. Others specifically label it a misspelling, and many authorities consider it nonstandard. Reference: Copperud, p. 11.

Alliteration
Alliteration is repetition of the same sound, usually at the beginnings of several words in a series or at the beginnings of stressed syllables within several words. Besides possibly appealing to the reader's or listener's ear, alliteration serves to bind the phrase, or sometimes a whole series of phrases, into a unit: "the crowded, cloistered colleges of Oxford" (Paul Elmer More); "carried by wind and water and soil and seed" (John F. Kennedy).

Alliteration is one of the figures of sound that contribute to the musical effect of poetry. It is appropriate in formal prose that has oratorical or poetic overtones, and it occurs in some passages of description that are deliberately evocative: "like strange sea shells, their silken-nacreous lining welcoming the wind" (*New York Times*). But conspicuous alliteration is out of place in ordinary expository prose unless it helps reinforce meaning, as in "those crunching, nut-cracking Soviet consonants" (Alfred Kazin, *Starting Out in the Thirties*); otherwise it tends to attract attention to the expression at the expense of the idea. In writing of any kind, unconscious alliteration is likely to be distracting and may be disastrous. Check your first draft to get rid of unintentional alliteration that results from one combination of sounds summoning up another.

Compare Assonance.

all of
In general and informal usage *all* is followed by *of* in many constructions: All of the milk was spilled; They passed all of the candidates; You can't fool all of the people all of the time. In formal usage the unnecessary *of* is often omitted: all the milk, all the candidates, all the time. With personal pronouns and the relatives *who* and *which, all* may follow the pronoun (we all), or *all of* may precede it (all of us). *All of which* and *all of whom,* as subjects of relative clauses (four attempts, all of which failed),

are especially common and are more formal than their alternatives, *who all* and *which all* (four attempts, which all failed).

all that

"It didn't seem all that important," "It wasn't all that bad," and similar uses of *all that* work well enough in conversation and in informal writing but are likely to be criticized for imprecision in more formal contexts.

all the farther

Although in some parts of the country *all the farther* is heard in informal and general speech (This is all the farther I'm going), standard written English uses an *as . . . as* construction: This is as far as I'm going. Reference: Bryant, pp. 19–20.

Allusion

Loosely, an allusion is a brief reference to an event, person, or place, real or fictional, that is not a part of the subject under discussion. Strictly, an allusion differs from a reference in that it does not name the event, person, or place but mentions it indirectly. "This latter-day Paul Revere calls on us to arm against our home-grown revolutionaries" is a reference to Revere. "His signal is always a single lantern in the church steeple" alludes to Revere, leaving it to the reader to make the connection through his knowledge of Longfellow's poem.

In more elaborately contrived prose, a writer may incorporate well-known phrases from a literary work, as in this sentence with its deliberate echoes of *Hamlet* and *Macbeth:*

There is nothing new in heaven or hell not dreamt of in our laboratories; and we should be amazed indeed if tomorrow and tomorrow and tomorrow failed to offer us something new to challenge our capacity for readjustment.—Carl L. Becker, *The Heavenly City of the Eighteenth Century Philosophers*

By stimulating memory of a context—a historical event, the career of a celebrity, a scene in a play—a pertinent allusion enriches the passage in which it appears and at the same time gives the reader the pleasure of recognition. But the writer needs to know his audience: an obscure or esoteric allusion will not only be wasted but may be resented as pretentious. Like other aspects of style, allusions should fit the rhetorical situation.

Reference: Follett, p. 58.

allusion, illusion

Allusion, discussed in the preceding article, should not be confused with *illusion*, a misapprehension or a misleading appearance (Smoking a pipe can create an illusion of wisdom).

almost

Most for *almost* is informal. See *most, almost*.

also

Also as an adverb ordinarily stands within a sentence, not at its beginning (They also serve who only stand and wait), but inversion may shift an *also* to initial position: Also defeated was the party's candidate for mayor. As a loose conjunction meaning "and," *also* is a weak sentence opener: He subscribed to eight magazines. Also he belonged to the Book-of-the-Month Club.

In many cases the information introduced with initial *also* should have been included in the preceding sentence: He subscribed to eight magazines and belonged to the Book-of-the-Month Club.

See Conjunctive adverbs. Reference: Copperud, p. 13.

alternative

Alternative comes from the Latin *alter,* "the second of two." Some formal writers, in deference to the word's origin, confine its meaning to "one of two possibilities," but it is regularly used to mean one of several possibilities and is so defined in dictionaries.

although, though

Although and *though* connect with the main clause an adverbial clause of concession — that is, a statement that qualifies the main statement but does not contradict it.

Although [Though] the rain kept up for almost three weeks, we managed to have a good time.

We managed to have a good time, though [although] the rain kept up for almost three weeks.

Here there is no distinction in meaning; the choice between the two may be based on sentence rhythm. *Although* is slightly more formal.

Often one of two clauses connected by *but* can be turned into an *although* clause for a slight change of emphasis:

We had rehearsed the act time and time again, but we all missed our cues the first night.

Although we had rehearsed the act time and time again, we all missed our cues the first night.

Although can't be substituted for *though* in a sentence like "He did it, though."

See *but.* References: Bryant, pp. 216–18; Follett, pp. 60–62.

alumnus, alumna

A male graduate is an *alumnus,* a female graduate an *alumna.* Two or more male graduates are *alumni,* two or more female graduates *alumnae.* The graduates of coeducational schools — males and females together — have traditionally been called *alumni;* but *graduates* itself is a sound, and sexless, alternative. Also sexless is *alums,* the plural of the clipped word, *alum.* See Sexist language.

a.m. and p.m.

These abbreviations (for *ante meridiem,* "before noon," and *post meridiem,* "after noon") are most useful in tables and lists of times but are also used in general writing for specific hours, usually with figures: from 2 to 4 p.m. (*not* I went there in the p.m.). Though *m.* is the abbreviation for noon (12 m.), *12 noon* is more common; midnight is *12 p.m.* See Hours.

Ambiguity

Make your meaning unmistakable.

A word or phrase or sentence that is ambiguous is one that can be interpreted in two or more ways. Though the context usually shows which of the possible meanings is intended, the reader is momentarily confused and occasionally remains so. The most common sources of confusion are:

1. Inexact reference of pronoun, especially in indirect discourse: He *told* his father he had been talking too much. Rewrite as: He admitted to his father that he had been talking too much; or as: He criticized his father for talking too much. Or recast as direct speech. See Indirect discourse, Reference of pronouns 1.

2. Modifiers that can be misinterpreted.
a. Squinting modifiers may refer to either of two words or constructions: The governor penalized those officeholders who had opposed him *for good reason.* Rewrite as: The governor had good reason for penalizing those who had opposed him; or as: The governor penalized those who had had good reason to oppose him. The sentence "Some people I *know* would go there anyway" could not be misinterpreted if it began, "Some people *whom I know,*" or if it read, "Some people would go there anyway, I *know.*"
b. Modifiers should be clearly identified as restrictive or nonrestrictive. "Out-of-state students who were delayed by the blizzard will not be penalized for late registration" seems to mean that only the out-of-state students who were held up by the storm will be excused; but if the meaning intended is that all out-of-state students are home free, then commas are needed after *students* and *blizzard.* See Restrictive and nonrestrictive.
c. Modifiers should not mislead even momentarily. In revising a first draft, be on the lookout for puzzlers like the headline "Police Repair Man Killed by Car." See Hyphen 5.

3. Incomplete idioms, especially in comparisons: "I like Alice as well as Will" might mean "I like Alice as well as Will does," "I like Alice as well as I do Will," or "I like both Alice and Will."

4. Changing meanings.   Many words are undergoing changes in meaning. Sometimes the shift can be completed without risk of ambiguous communication because the context makes the intention clear. Before *car* came to apply primarily to an automobile, such restricting labels as *motor, railroad,* or *street* prevented misunderstanding. But when such safeguards are not present, serious misunderstanding may occur. See *censor, censure; disinterested, uninterested; imply, infer; incredible, incredulous; rhetoric; transpire.*

5. Intentional ambiguity. The literary artist may deliberately suggest multiple meanings, inviting the reader to draw inferences, to understand more than is said. Sleepy readers will see only what's on the page.

See Comma 6.

American

Because there is no simple adjective that corresponds to the United States of America (as *Italian,* for example, corresponds to Italy), *American* is ordinarily used. It is obviously inexact, since Canadians and Mexicans and Brazilians and others are as American (in the continental sense) as we are; and many Latins refer to themselves as Americans. But it is no more inexact than many other words, and the usage is standard. Use *American* as the adjective and the name of an inhabitant. Reference: Copperud, p. 14.

Americanism

Americanism, as a usage term, means a word or construction originating in the United States *(hydrant, zipper, realtor)* or first borrowed here, as from an African language *(goober, juke, okra),* an Indian language *(hominy, caucus, mugwump),* or from Spanish *(canyon, rodeo, lariat).* It also refers to a sense of a word added in the United States *(campus, carpetbagger, creek). A Dictionary of Americanisms,* edited by Mitford M. Mathews (Chicago: Univ. of Chicago Press, 1951), lists such vocabulary.

Americanism may be extended to include words continued in the United States after becoming obsolete in England *(loan* as a verb, *gotten)* or any item of usage characteristic of the United States and not of other areas of the English-speaking world. The label *American* or *chiefly U.S.* in dictionaries records such facts of usage. Americanisms in this extended sense are included in *A Dictionary of American English,* edited by Sir William A. Craigie and James R. Hulbert (Chicago: Univ. of Chicago Press, 1938–1944).

among, between

Between is used with two, *among* with more than two. But see *between, among.*

amount, number

Number is used only of countable things: a number of mistakes, a number of apples. *Amount* is preferred with mass nouns (a small amount of money, a certain amount of humor). Distinguishing between the two words often improves clarity and is therefore recommended. See Mass nouns. Compare *fewer, less.*

Ampersand

Ampersand is the name for the & sign (originally a linking of the letters of Latin *et*), called also *short and.* Because its primary use is to save space, it belongs only where abbreviations are appropriate. Otherwise, write out *and.*

Analogy

Analogies may be either figurative or literal. A figurative analogy suggests a resemblance between things or situations that on the surface are totally unlike: a mathematical equation and a Mozart quintet, for example, or a football team and an epidemic. There are no actual resemblances between an undefeated team and the Black Death; what they have in common is the capacity to mow down everything in their paths. This shared characteristic can be expressed in terms of the proportion a:b::c:d—the team figuratively slaughters its opponents as the Black Death killed its victims in the fourteenth century.

Literal analogies uncover relationships between two members of the same class, often revealing unexpected correspondences between widely separated historical events or persons. The attitude of young people toward marijuana laws in the 1960s has been analogized to the attitude of their grandparents toward liquor laws in the 1920s.

Whether compressed into a metaphor (the Muhammad Ali of the political ring) or elaborated through an entire essay, an apt analogy throws new light on the subject. Presenting the unfamiliar in terms of the familiar (the earth's strata in terms of the layers of an onion) is a common method of exposition. Here a writer relies on analogy to introduce his interpretation of recent changes in international relations:

> There has been a radical transformation of power. In traditional conflicts, states were like boiled eggs: War—the minute of truth—would reveal whether they were hard or soft. Today interdependence breaks all national eggs into a vast omelet. Power is more difficult to measure than ever before.—Stanley Hoffman, *New York Times*

Analogy becomes the basis for argument when a writer tries to persuade his audience that because two situations are alike in some respects (current proposals for gun registration in the United States and gun registration in Nazi Germany), they are alike in still another (if enacted into law, the current proposals will result in government seizure of all civilian-owned guns). Although analogies are seldom sufficient to carry the full burden of proof, they can induce strong conviction; and if the likenesses cited have real bearing on the point at issue and the differences are not fundamental, analogies have logical force as well.

Whether used to explain or to persuade, an analogy can stir the imagination and stimulate thought. For both writer and reader, a good analogy opens the door to a fresh, inventive approach.

See Comparison and contrast, Figurative language.

Analogy in language

In linguistics *analogy* is the name for the natural tendency in users of a language to make their speech more regular by forming new words on the pattern of existing ones, bringing old words closer together in form, or bringing less common constructions into line with more familiar patterns. It results from the fact that, in general, the patterns of a language form a consistent though complex system (most English noun plurals end in -*s*, past tenses in -*ed*, and so on). It is easiest to observe analogy in the attempts of children to master their language. Before they learn the irregular conventional forms used by grownups, they regularize on the basis of the patterns they are familiar with, saying *mans*, perhaps, for *men* or *singed* for *sung*.

Analogy has removed many irregularities in the body of the language. Of various plural forms used in Old English, -*s* has won in all but a few words, and analogy is still bringing more words to that form, like *formula, formulas*. Occasionally the spelling of words is changed by analogy, as -*b* was rather recently added to *crumb* and *thumb* from analogy with *comb* and *dumb* — showing that analogy does not always result in a simpler form. Other words are in the process of changing: *cole slaw* is often replaced by *cold slaw*, and *alright* is slowly making its way from analogy with *already*. New words are formed on analogy with old ones, like *astronaut, telecast*.

The extension of *was* to the plural — a common form in nonstandard English, based on the analogy of most English verbs in the past tense (I did, we did; he went, they went) — illustrates not only the force of analogy but also the fact that the result, however logical and consistent, is not necessarily acceptable. To become standard English the analogical form must be frequently used by educated writers and speakers — and "we was" is not.

See *due to*. References: Raimo Anttila, *An Introduction to Historical and Comparative Linguistics* (New York: Macmillan, 1972), Ch. 5; Leonard Bloomfield, *Language* (1933; rpt. New York: Holt, 1961), Ch. 23; Bolinger, pp. 403–405; E. H. Sturtevant, *Linguistic Change* (Chicago: Univ. of Chicago Press, Phoenix Books, 1961), Chs. 2, 6.

Analysis

Analysis is the term applied to a wide range of intellectual undertakings — attempts to grasp the nature of a thing or concept, to separate a whole into its parts, to discover the similarities and differences between two or more things, to investigate origins, to attribute effects. The aim of analysis is to increase one's understanding of a subject. A writer may also use analysis as a guide to action; that is, he may analyze a rhetorical situation in order to decide how best to arrange his material or what details to include or what arguments to advance. See Cause and effect, Classification and division, Comparison and contrast, Definition, Logical thinking.

and

1. Appropriate uses. *And*, the most frequently used connective, joins two or more elements of equal grammatical rank:

Adjectives: a *pink* and *white* apron; a *blue, green,* and *white* flag
Adverbs: He drove *very fast* and *rather carelessly.*
Nouns: trees and *shrubs; trees, shrubs,* and *plants*
Verbs: I *found* the book and *opened* it at the exact place.
Phrases: in one ear and *out the other*
Dependent clauses: While the boys were swimming and *[while] the older folks were resting,* I was reading.
Independent clauses: The first generation makes the money and *the second spends it.*

2. Inappropriate uses. In careless writing, elements of unequal grammatical value are sometimes connected by an unnecessary *and:*

Main verbs and participles: Three or four men *sat* on the edge of the lake with their backs to the road, [and] apparently *watching* the ducks.

Independent and dependent clauses: A contract has been let to install new copper work on the Post Office [and] *which will give it the facelifting it needs.*

And sometimes appears where no connective is needed or where some other connective would show more clearly the logical relation: "Shah was a founding member of the Club of Rome and [but?] while he retains his membership, he did not attend last fall's gathering in Berlin" (Elizabeth Hall, *Psychology Today*). See Coordination 2.

3. To begin sentences. In current writing of all varieties, *and* may stand at the beginning of a sentence. Used with restraint, it can contribute to movement and emphasis. Overused, it can be damaging to both, as well as boring for the reader.

4. Omitted or repeated. *And* may be omitted in a series (Cousins, uncles, aunts – all the relatives were there), but if repeated again and again this omission contributes to a telegraphic style inappropriate in general writing. *And* may also be used between the items in a series as an effective way of giving emphasis to each: "I do not mean to imply that the South is simple and homogeneous and monolithic" (Robert Penn Warren, *Southern Review*).

and etc.

Etc. is the abbreviation for *et cetera,* in which *et* means "and." Therefore *and* before *etc.* is redundant. See *etc.*

and/or

Though *and/or* is used primarily in legal and business writing, it may be useful when three alternatives exist (*both* items mentioned or *either* one of the two): *fruit and/or vegetables* means "fruit" or "vegetables" or "fruit and vegetables." Its use in general writing is objected to by many readers both because *and/or* looks odd and because *and* or *or* alone is very often sufficient. Reference: Copperud, p. 16.

angle

Angle meaning "point of view" or "aspect" (from an economic angle) is general but carries a strong suggestion of jargon. In the sense of "scheme" or "plan" (What's his angle?), *angle* is slang.

Antecedent

An antecedent is the word, clause, or sentence that a pronoun or pronominal adjective refers to. It usually stands before the word that refers to it, but not always: We did not hear their call again, and when we found the Thompsons, they were almost exhausted. (*The Thompsons* is the antecedent of the pronominal adjective *their* and of the pronoun *they*.) For relations between antecedents and their pronouns, see Agreement 2, Reference of pronouns.

Anticipatory subject

In sentences like "It was Ann who found the food stamps" and "There are more important things than graduating," *it* and *there* are anticipatory subjects. See *it; there is, there are*.

Anticlimax

An anticlimax ends a series with an element much weaker than what precedes it. It may be intentional, as a form either of serious irony or of humor, or unintentional, a lapse of judgment on the writer's part: She had a warm and sympathetic personality, a quick and perceptive intelligence, beautiful features, and real skill at bowling.

Antithesis

The stylistic device of using neighboring statements that contrast sharply in meaning is called antithesis. Often the statements are presented in parallel form: He is shamed for being backward; he is scolded for being forward.

Antonyms

An antonym is a word that means approximately the opposite of another word: *hot, stingy, boring* are antonyms of *cold, generous, entertaining*. Most books of synonyms also give antonyms, as do the synonym entries in dictionaries. Reference: Bolinger, pp. 211–15.

any

1. Uses. *Any* is used primarily as an adjective (Any dog is a good dog) but also as a pronoun (Any will do).

In comparisons of things of the same class, idiom calls for *any other:* This book is better than any other on the subject. But *any* alone is used when different classes are compared: I like a movie better than any book.

2. Compounds with *any*. Anybody, anyhow, anything, and *anywhere* are always written as single words. *Any rate* is always two words: at any rate. *Anyone* is written as one word when the stress is on the *any* (Anyone would know that) and as two when the stress is on the *one* (I'd like any one of them). *Anyway* is one word when the *any* is stressed (I can't do it anyway) and two when the stress is about equal (Any way I try, it comes out wrong). If the word *whatever* can be substituted for the *any* (Whatever way I try, it comes out wrong), *any way* should be written as two words.

3. Pronouns referring to *anybody, anyone*. *Anybody* and *anyone* are singular in form and take singular verbs: anybody [*or* anyone] feels bad at times. They are referred to by *he, his, him* (Anybody knows what *he* deserves) or, since they often apply to a person of either sex, by a form of *they* with the meaning "he or she," "his or her," "him or her": "It is not usually possible to achieve intimacy with anybody in the back seat of a car; you have to live with them in every sense of the phrase" (Edgar Z. Friedenberg, *New York Review of Books*). Formal usage insists on a singular pronoun. See Agreement 2, *he or she, they*. Compare *every*. References: Evans and Evans, p. 36; Fries, p. 50.

4. Other forms. *Anyways* is regional for the generally used *anyway*, and *anywheres* is nonstandard for *anywhere*. Though objected to by many, *any more* now frequently appears in print as one word: "They want to protect all those traditional events whether or not they mean something anymore" (Herbert Warren Wind, *New Yorker*). *Any more* (or *anymore*) in a strictly affirmative context (Any more I do that) is a regional idiom.

Anyplace (now usually written as one word) has become a general synonym for "anywhere": "Life can be as good and rich there as anyplace else" (Granville Hicks, *Saturday Review*).

Reference: Copperud, p. 18.

Aphorisms

An aphorism gives good advice or expresses a general truth in concise form. See Epigrams and aphorisms.

apos Apostrophe

Insert an apostrophe where it belongs in the word marked; or take out an apostrophe that is incorrectly used.

Typical mistakes in the use of the apostrophe are *mans* for *man's, mens'* for *men's, it's* for *its*, and *their's* for *theirs*. Review these uses of the apostrophe:

1. In genitives. The most common use of the apostrophe is in spelling the genitive (possessive) case of nouns and of the words traditionally labeled indefinite pronouns (*anyone, nobody, someone . . . .*): Dorothy's first picture; the companies' original charters; everybody's business is nobody's business; the boys' dogs. It should be used in singular genitives of time and value even though they carry no idea of possession: a day's hike, this month's quota, a dollar's worth. In formal writing it is also preferred in plural genitives of this kind (two weeks' work), but usage is divided (teachers college). For special examples of possessive form, see Genitive case. Reference: Follett, pp. 434–35.

2. In contractions. The apostrophe shows the omission of one or more letters in contractions: *can't, I'm, I'll, it's (it is)*.

3. In plurals. An apostrophe has ordinarily been used in plurals of figures, letters of the alphabet, and words being discussed as words: the 1920's, three *e*'s, the first of the two *that*'s. But current usage is divided, and the plurals of figures in particular are often made with no apostrophe: "In the mid-1950s, Hoffa was scratching to take over the union" *(Newsweek)*.

4. In representing speech. An apostrophe may be used to show that certain sounds represented in the usual spelling were not spoken: "He turned to someone else on the landing outside and said, 'Paddy, 'ere, 'e doesn't want 'is duff,' and went to walk on" (Brendan Behan, *Borstal Boy*). This is a legitimate use, but too many apostrophes distract the reader. It is better to suggest occasional pronunciations of this sort than to try to represent all of them.

Apostrophes are not used in the genitive of the personal pronouns: *his, hers, its, ours, theirs, yours;* and they should not be introduced into words that do not have them. *Till* is not *'till* or *'til.*

Apposition, appositives

Beside a noun or noun-equivalent in a sentence, we may place another nominal expression called an appositive: My aunts, *Mary and Agnes,* moved to Boulder in 1969. The noun headword, or head, and its appositive refer to the same person or thing. Typically, the appositive is set off by commas, but sometimes no punctuation is needed (He caught so many fish that we called him Jim *the fisherman*).

An appositive agrees in case with its head; the case of the head is determined by its relation to the rest of the sentence: The winners [subject as head], Al and *I*, will lend bus fare to the losers [object as head], you and *him*. See Headword.

Don't insult your readers by using appositives unnecessarily. For example, in referring to the President of the United States, either the President's name or "the President" is sufficient identification.

References: Jespersen, pp. 93–95; Quirk et al., pp. 620–48.

Arabic numerals

Arabic numerals are the ones we normally use: 1, 2, 3, etc. See Numbers 3.

Archaic words

When words drop out of all spoken and written use, they are said to be obsolete. When they are old-fashioned but still used occasionally or in special circumstances, they are called archaic. Examples are *anon* for *at once* or *soon*, *betimes* for *quickly*, *parlous* for *dangerous*, *doth* for *does*, and the *thou* and *saith* of some church services. Archaic words should be used only for very good stylistic reasons. They seldom fit in general writing.

Argument

Aside from its everyday meaning of "disagreement" or "dispute," *argument* is used in three distinct ways. It refers to an entire speech or essay that is designed to produce conviction. Or it refers to the line of thinking, the string of key propositions that runs through a piece — "the argument" of a book or a poem. Or it designates a reason for believing what might otherwise seem doubtful; in this sense "an argument" can be a single sentence. Thus in presenting his argument (first sense) to Congress, a legislator may use as his argument (second sense) the thesis that wiretapping should be discontinued, and he may offer as one of his arguments (third sense) the proposition that wiretapping is an illegal invasion of privacy.

Argument in the first sense may make appeals that are primarily intellectual or primarily emotional. Either kind of appeal can be used well or badly, for good purposes or bad.

Sometimes argument is distinguished from persuasion on the basis of purpose: argument is designed to change the mind of an audience; persuasion is designed to make an audience act. Normally both purposes are included when argument is classed as one of the four forms of discourse.

See Analogy, Deduction, Fallacies, Forms of discourse, Induction, Logical thinking, Rhetoric, Syllogisms.

arise

Arise is the formal word for *get up*. See *rise, arise, get up*.

around

Around, like *about*, can be used to mean "approximately." See *round, around*.

Articles

Traditionally *a* and *an* are known as indefinite articles, *the* as the definite article. Traditional grammars call articles adjectives; structural grammars call them function words; transformational grammars group them under determiners. See *a, an;* Nouns 3c; Parts of speech.

as

Among the meanings of *as* are "while" (As we walked along, he told us stories) and "because" (His speed is amazing, particularly as he weighs 260 pounds). *While* is preferable to *as* if the emphasis is on the time of the action (While we were walking along, he told us stories). And though *as* is used to mean "because" (or "since") in all varieties of English, many readers dislike the usage, which can easily be ambiguous: As we have continued responding to erratic change in Asia, our position has inevitably become more complex. (Does *as* mean "because" or "while"?) Reference: Copperud, p. 22.

For the growing tendency to use *as* where *like* would be expected, see *like, as.*

as . . . as

1. *As I* or *as me*. In a sentence like "He dislikes her as much as I/me," meaning determines whether the nominative *I* or the accusative *me* is used. The nominative implies the sense "as much as I dislike her"; the accusative, "as much as he dislikes me."

In a sentence like "They sent for someone as big as I/me," the choice of *I* or *me* does not affect the meaning. Both the nominative and the accusative are good English.

For a third type of sentence – "He is as big as I/me" – in which there is no preceding noun or pronoun in the accusative position, usage has always been divided. The nominative *I* is preferred in formal contexts and is insisted upon by many stylists.

2. Omitted *as*. Writers frequently omit the second *as* in a comparison of equality (as big as) when it is joined by *or* or *if not* to a comparison of inequality (bigger than): It was as large or larger than last year's crowd. But many readers and writers regard the omission as inelegant and prefer the complete form: It was as large as, or larger than, last year's crowd. Sometimes the second comparison can be moved to the end of the sentence: It was as large as last year's crowd, if not larger. Reference: Bryant, p. 57.

3. *As . . . as* and *so . . . as*. As . . . as is much more common than *so . . . as* in simple comparisons of degree (as big as that, as late as you like). Unlike *so . . . as*, it is suitable for both affirmative and negative statements. Many handbooks have urged that *as . . . as* be used only in affirmative statements (She's as clever as any of them) and *so . . . as* in negative statements (She's not so clever as she thinks); but the distinction has never become established in practice. Reference: Bryant, pp. 26–27.

as if, as though

In formal English the subjunctive is commonly used after *as if* and *as though:* He acted as if [or as though] he *were* losing his temper. In general English the indicative is usual: He acted as if [or as though] he *was* losing his temper. See Subjunctive mood.

as, like

As is the conjunction (He voted as he was expected to); *like* is the preposition (He voted like the rest). See *like, as.*

Assonance

Assonance is the repetition of vowel sounds in words having different consonant sounds (*brave – vain, lone – show*). It is characteristic of verse and also occurs in prose, especially in heightened style: "that ideal country, of green, deep lanes and high green banks" (Osbert Sitwell). Like unintentional alliteration, unintentional assonance can be distracting.

as though

As though is commonly followed by the subjunctive in formal English but not in general English. See *as if, as though.*

as to

As to is often a clumsy substitute for a single preposition, usually *of* or *about:* Practice is the best teacher as to [in, for, of] the use of organ stops. In some locutions it is completely unnecessary: [As to] whether college is worthwhile is a question we must all try to answer. But in specifying a subject initially, it is preferable to more cumbersome expressions like *as regards, as concerns, with respect to:* As to the economic value of going to college, the effect on earning power is clearly established.

as well as

When an *as well as* phrase between subject and verb gives a strong impression of adding to the subject, some writers treat it as part of the subject and let it influence the number of the verb: The singer as well as four of the band members *were* arrested. In such cases the phrase is not set off by commas. According to traditional grammarians, however, the phrase is parenthetical, is usually set off by commas, and has no bearing on the verb: "This volume, as well as others, consists of a collection of basic articles" (Robert R. Wilson, *ISIS*). Reference: Pooley, p. 80.

at about

At about can be reduced to either *at* or *about.* But see *about* 3.

athletics

When the collective noun *athletics* refers to sports and games, it usually takes a plural verb and pronoun: Our athletics *include* football, basketball, and baseball. When *athletics* refers to a skill or activity, it usually takes a singular verb and pronoun: Athletics *is* recommended for every student.

author

An author writes a book. Does a writer author a book? *Author* as a verb is widely used (by publishers, among others) but also widely disapproved. It may be most defensible in referring to publication by a group (the report was authored by the President's Commission on Campus Unrest) and to autobiographies of celebrities "as told to" professional writers. Reference: Copperud, p. 27.

Auxiliaries

A verb used with another verb to form a phrasal tense or, in the case of *be*, to change the active voice to the passive is called an auxiliary verb or helping verb. The most common auxiliaries, *be* and *have*, are used in forming the progressive and perfect tenses and the passive voice: I am going; He has gone; They were lost. The modal auxiliaries — *can, may, shall, will, must, ought to, should, would,* and *might* — are used to refer to future time and to suggest possibility, necessity, or obligation: He will go; You should reply; He must leave.

As a group, the auxiliaries play a major role in the structure of sentences, not only in questions (Does he know?) but also in negatives (He has not left), in emphatic affirmatives (They *are* working), and in substitutes for verb phrases: Jo could not have enjoyed the evening, and neither could Mary [have enjoyed the evening]. When no *be*, auxiliary *have*, or modal auxiliary is available for a question, negation, or affirmation, the meaningless *do* fills the structural position.

He works late.
Question: Does he work late?
Negation: He does not work late.
Affirmation: He *does* work late.
Substitution: If anyone works late, he does.

A few other verbs, such as *get*, resemble these structurally defined auxiliaries in some respects (*was arrested, got arrested*) but do not participate in the basic syntactic patterns (instead of "Got he arrested?" we say, "Did he get arrested?"). See Modal auxiliaries, Parts of speech, Tenses of verbs, and entries on the individual verbs. References: Jacobs and Rosenbaum, Chs. 14–15; W. Freeman Twaddell, *The English Verb Auxiliaries,* 2nd ed. (Providence: Brown Univ. Press, 1965).

awful

In formal English *awful* means "inspiring with awe." In informal English it is a convenient utility word of disapproval — "ugly, shocking, ludicrous" (awful manners). General writing avoids the confusion by seldom using the word except to intensify meaning: " . . . delusions that are being chosen by an awful lot of people in preference to standard, orthodox explanations" (Elizabeth Janeway, *Atlantic*). This use of either *awful* or *awfully* (an awfully long wait) is deplored by some authorities. References: Copperud, p. 28; Pooley, p. 127.

awhile, a while

Awhile is an adverb (They talked awhile). Strictly, a prepositional phrase in which *while* is a noun should be in three words (for a while, in a while), but *awhile* is increasingly common: "It had been found that many nonimmigrants, after they had been here for awhile, decided that they would like to stay" (Marion I. Bennett, *Annals*).

 Awkward

---

Rewrite the passage to make the phrasing smoother and more effective.

Awkward is a general word of disapproval sometimes used in correcting essays. It may refer to unnecessary repetition of a sound or word, unsuccessful alteration of normal word order, overloading of a sentence, or any phrasing that attracts unfavorable attention or handicaps a reader. Several kinds of awkwardness occur in this passage:

Primarily an agricultural country, New Zealand's dairy products are of a quality unknown to pollution-threatened, chemical-saturated America. As high as anywhere in the world are New Zealand's sanitation standards, and rigid animal inspection procedures are, even in the sparsely populated areas, rigidly enforced. These facts, combined with cattle and sheep which graze all year round on natural grass pasture lands, produce products with a uniquely wonderful fresh-tasting flavor.

The way to correct a phrase or sentence marked *awkward* is to rewrite. *Index* articles that deal with and illustrate specific weaknesses that may be labeled *awkward* include Coordination, Nominalization, Passive voice, Reference of pronouns, Repetition, Shifted constructions, Subordination, Wordiness, Word order.

B

bad, badly

Bad is ordinarily used as the adjective (a bad apple) and *badly* as the adverb (He speaks badly). Because the position after a linking verb is usually filled by a predicate adjective, we would expect "I feel bad about it," as well as "He looks bad" and "It tastes bad." But after *feel, badly* is widely used to modify the subject, particularly in speech. In formal written usage, *bad* is preferred. In general writing, the choice often depends on which form fits the rhythm of the sentence.

Bad as an adverb (I played bad all day) is informal.

Badly meaning "very much" (He wanted it badly) is standard, and *badly off* is general as a group adjective: "But we are not Satan. Fallen though we are, we are not that badly off" (John Morris, *American Scholar*).

References: Bryant, pp. 35–36; Copperud, p. 102.

Bad grammar

Bad grammar is used as a term of reproach and is applied to all sorts of locutions, from "I ain't got none" to imaginary confusions in the use of *shall* and *will*. It is too vague and emotional a term to be useful. See *grammatical, ungrammatical.*

Balanced sentence

When parallelism in a sentence produces structures that are noticeably alike in length and movement, the sentence is said to be balanced: "But we must go on or we will go under" (Douglas MacArthur, *Centennial Review*). Though associated with ornate style, balance can make any statement emphatic, often by bringing out likenesses or differences: "Grammar maps out the possible; rhetoric narrows the possible down to the desirable and effective" (Francis Christensen, *Notes Toward a New Rhetoric*). See Parallelism.

be

1. Forms. The forms of *be* are more numerous and more varied than those of any other English verb:

Present: I am, you are, he is; we, you, they are
Past: I was, you were, he was; we, you, they were
Infinitive: be
Present participle: being
Past participle: been

Sometimes *be* (in all persons) is used as a present subjunctive and *were* (both singular and plural) as a past subjunctive.

Some old forms survive in stock phrases (the powers that be) and in the nonstandard "You ain't [sometimes "be'n't"] going, be you?" Nonstandard also uses *was* in the plural (Was the Adamses there?), leveling the past tense to one form *(was)*, like the past of other English verbs.

2. As a linking verb. *Be* is the most common linking verb, joining a subject and a predicate noun (Jerome was the secretary) or predicate adjective (She is sick). When it joins a subject and a pronoun, the pronoun is in the nominative case in formal written English (It was *he*), in the accusative in informal (It was *him*). "It's I" is formal for the general "It's me." See *it's me*.

When the infinitive *be* has a subject and complement, both are in the accusative form: I wanted *him* to be *me*. When the infinitive has no subject, formal usage has a nominative as the complement (I wanted to be *he*); general usage more often has an accusative (I wanted to be *him*).

3. As an auxiliary verb. Forms of *be* are used with the present participles of other verbs to make the progressive tense: I *am* asking; he *was* asking; you *will be* asking. Forms of *be* with past participles form the passive voice: I *am* asked; you *will be* asked; he *was* asked. In general English a form of *be* may be omitted in the second of two clauses with subjects of different number: One was killed and six wounded. Formal style would have "were wounded."

4. As a verb of independent meaning. *Be* is sometimes considered a verb of independent meaning when indicating states or positions: He was at home anywhere; The fire was just across the street. In its unmistakable use as an independent verb with the sense "exist," "live" (Hamlet's "To be, or not to be"; Can such things be?), *be* is now rare.

See *ain't*, Subjunctive mood.

because

Because introduces an adverbial clause giving the reason for the statement in the main clause: *Because* we were getting hungry, we began to look for a convenient restaurant. *Since* and *as* can be used in such clauses, but they are less definite, more casual.

Because also finds some use in informal contexts where a more formal style would insist on *for*—that is, where *because* introduces the premise for a conclusion, not the cause of an effect:

Informal: Komarov clearly had some control over his ship, because he was able to orient it well enough to accomplish re-entry.

More formal: Komarov clearly had some control over his ship, for he was able to orient it well enough to accomplish re-entry. — *Newsweek*

See *as, for, reason is because.* For *because of,* see *due to.*

Begging the question

Begging the question is the logical fallacy of assuming a conclusion that needs to be proved. The debater who bases his argument for reform on the assertion "This unfair method of voting must be changed" begs the question of the method's fairness. Though in a broad sense we all beg questions all the time—"Use enough evidence to prove your point" begs the question of how much is enough—as a deliberate tactic in argument, begging the question is notably unfair. See Fallacies.

Beginning an essay

Revise the opening of your essay to make it lead more directly and smoothly into your subject or to arouse your reader's interest.

The best advice for beginning a short paper is "Get on with it." An elaborate windup is silly when the pitch is to be no more than a straight throw in a backyard game of catch. And an opening that indulges in philosophizing ("Since the days of Plato's Academy, violence and learning have been alien entities") or announces a grand strategy ("In the paragraphs that follow, I shall attempt, first by analyzing and then by synthesizing, . . .") is equally silly in a two-page paper on a campus controversy.

Ordinarily, the first step is to let your reader know what you are writing about—not by telling him what you are going to discuss but by discussing it: "We think of the drug addict as unwilling or unable to work, but he works harder to get his dope than most of us do to get our daily bread" ("Addicts in the Wonderland of Work," *Psychology Today*). This does not rule out a personal approach; there may be good reason for you to tell why you have chosen your topic or how you are qualified to discuss it. It does rule out beginnings that fail to begin.

In addition to getting the essay under way, the opening paragraph or two should interest a reader enough to make him want to continue. But straining for humor or excitement or cuteness or sentiment is no way to go about it. Such attempts often distract or mislead. And as imitations of the techniques used by some professional journalists, they are likely to fail: the humor doesn't amuse; the excitement doesn't stir; and so on. Instead of trying out gimmicks, move into your topic and treat it with the interest *you* feel. If it doesn't interest you, your chances of making it interest your readers are slim. If it does interest you, and if you write about it as honestly and directly as you know how, your readers will keep reading.

For long papers – from five to ten pages, say – somewhat more elaborate beginnings are justified and perhaps necessary. But getting on with the discussion remains fundamental. If you sketch the historical background of a problem, make sure that this material contributes to solving the problem.

beside, besides
Beside is used chiefly as a preposition meaning "by the side of," as in "beside the road," "beside her"; it is used figuratively in a few rather formal idioms like "beside the point," "beside himself with rage." *Besides* is used as an adverb meaning "in addition" (We tried two other ways besides), as a preposition meaning "in addition to" (Besides ourselves, no one was interested), and as a conjunctive adverb (He didn't think he ought to get into the quarrel; besides, he had come to enjoy himself).

between, among
Among implies more than two objects: They distributed the provisions among the survivors. *Between* is most strictly used of only two: They divided the prize between Kincaid and Thomas. But attempts to limit *between* to use with only two items have failed. When the relationship is between individual items, *between* is the word to use no matter how many items there are:

There are often two or more possible arrangements between which a choice must be consciously made. – H. W. Fowler, *Modern English Usage*

This is so . . . of some part of the debate between Einstein, Bohr, Wolfgang Pauli, and Max Born. – George Steiner, *Atlantic*

When treating a group as a collective unit, use *among:* Divide the books among the poor. References: Bryant, pp. 38 – 40; Copperud, p. 32; Pooley, pp. 129 – 31.

between you and me
Although *you and I* as the object of a preposition or a verb is frequently heard and has a long history in written English, anyone who uses it now is apt to be thought only half-educated. *Between you and me* is always correct. See Hypercorrectness.

bi-

Although *bicentennial* offers no problem, there is much confusion about some time words beginning with *bi-*. *Bimonthly* and *biweekly*, for example, may mean either "every two . . ." or "twice a. . . ." And *biennial* means "every two years" whereas *biannual* means "twice a year." Where the context does not distinguish exactly the time meant, it is safest to use phrases like "every two months," "twice a day," "twice a year."

Bible, bible

When referring to the Christian Scriptures, the word is capitalized but not italicized: You will find all that in the Bible. In the sense of an authoritative book, the word is not capitalized: *Gray's Manual* is the botanist's bible.

These are the usual forms of particular references to parts of the Bible: the Old Testament, the New Testament, the Ten Commandments, Exodus 20 (or Exodus XX), Exodus 20:3-17, I Corinthians 4:6. The adjective *biblical* is seldom capitalized.

Bibliographical form

The details of bibliographical form in a research paper may differ from author to author, from publication to publication, and especially from discipline to discipline. In some sciences, for example, a list of the references cited replaces the full bibliography of the humanities, only the first word of a book title is capitalized, the title of a journal article is omitted entirely, and the name of a journal is abbreviated. Whatever the style your instructor recommends, remember that the first rule for bibliographical form, as for footnote form, is consistency. Follow one style of documentation throughout.

The entries in a bibliography are listed alphabetically, according to the last name of each author. When no author is given, the first important word of the title—whether of a book, of a chapter or selection in a book, or of an article in a magazine, newspaper, or encyclopedia—serves as the key word for alphabetizing (*Manual* for *A Manual of Style*). Each entry begins at the left margin. Subsequent lines are indented five spaces.

The entries that follow conform closely to recommendations in the *MLA Style Sheet,* second edition. (There, short forms of the names of publishers are approved. If your instructor wants you to use short forms, examples can be found in the list on pages 9–10.) Examine each entry carefully to see what elements are included, what order they appear in, and how they are punctuated.

A book by a single author and a second book by the same author

```
Katz, Jerrold J.  The Philosophy of Language.  New York:
     Harper & Row, 1966.
_____.  Semantic Theory.  New York: Harper & Row,
     1972.
```

Instead of repeating the author's name, use a twelve-space line.

A book by more than one author

Brady, James E., and Gerard E. Humiston. <u>General Chemistry</u>:
     <u>Principles and Structure</u>. New York: Wiley, 1975.

Do not reverse the names of co-authors following the first author's name:
Bryant, Barbara, William Jensen, and Ann Wagner. If there are more
than three authors, substitute *et al.* for all but the first: Gorenstein,
Shirley, et al.

A work in more than one volume

Sewall, Richard B. <u>The Life of Emily Dickinson</u>.   2 vols.
     New York: Farrar, Straus & Giroux, 1974.

If the books in a multivolume work are published over a period of years,
the full span is given: 1909–49.

An edition other than the first

McArthur, Lewis A. <u>Oregon Geographic Names</u>.   3rd ed.
     Portland: Binfords, 1952.

An edition revised by someone other than the author

Robertson, Stuart. <u>The Development of Modern English</u>.   2nd
     ed.   Rev. by Frederic G. Cassidy.   Englewood Cliffs,
     N.J.: Prentice-Hall, 1954.

An edited work

Agnon, S. Y. <u>Twenty-one Stories</u>.   Ed. Nahum N. Glatzer.
     New York: Schocken Books, 1970.

A compilation by an editor

Baratz, Joan C., and Roger W. Shuy, eds. <u>Teaching Black</u>
     <u>Children to Read</u>.   Washington, D.C.: Center for
     Applied Linguistics, 1969.

A selection, chapter, or other part of a compilation

McKeon, Richard.   "Rhetoric in the Middle Ages." <u>Critics</u>
     <u>and Criticism</u>.   Ed. R. S. Crane.   Chicago: Univ. of
     Chicago Press, 1952.

A translation

Merleau-Ponty, Maurice. <u>Phenomenology of Perception</u>.   Trans.
     Colin Smith.   London: Routledge, 1962.

A book that is part of a series

Degler, Carl N. <u>Affluence and Anxiety: America Since 1945</u>.
     2nd ed.   The Scott, Foresman American History Series.
     Glenview, Ill.: Scott, Foresman, 1975.

A reprinted book

Whitehead, Alfred North. <u>Modes of Thought</u>.   1938; rpt.
     New York: Putnam, Capricorn Books, 1958.

A signed article in a newspaper

Cady, Steve.   "Dreams Grow from Asphalt." <u>New York Times</u>,
     13 July 1975, Sec. 5, p. 3, cols. 6-7.

An unsigned article in a weekly newsmagazine

"Nixon's Fight for Life." <u>Newsweek</u>, 11 Nov. 1974, pp. 26-29.

An article in a monthly magazine

Litten, Walter.   "The Most Poisonous Mushrooms." <u>Scientific</u>
     <u>American</u>, March 1975, pp. 90-101.

A journal article

```
Ong, Walter J.  "The Writer's Audience Is Always a Fiction."
    PMLA, 90 (1975), 9-21.
```

PMLA is the title of the journal, and 90 is the volume number. Because the journal (unlike most newspapers and magazines) is paged continuously throughout the calendar year, only the year is given, in parentheses, after the volume number. But if the volume does not coincide with the calendar year, as in the following example, the month is included. Note that when the volume number is given—without "Vol."—page numbers are not preceded by "pp."

A journal article with corporate authorship

```
NCTE Commission on Composition, "Teaching Composition: A
    Position Statement," College English, 36 (October
    1974), 219-20.
```

A signed encyclopedia article

```
We[intraub], S[tanley].  "George Bernard Shaw."  Encyclopaedia
    Britannica.  Macropaedia 16, 1974.
```

A book review

```
Wood, Michael.  "Incomparable Empson."  Review of William
    Empson:  The Man and His Work, ed. Roma Gill.  New
    York Review of Books, 23 Jan. 1975, pp. 30-33.
```

An unpublished dissertation

```
Teague, Frances Nicol.  "Ben Jonson's Stagecraft in His Four
    Major Comedies."  Diss. Univ. of Texas, 1975.
```

See Footnote form, Research papers. References: James D. Lester, *Writing Research Papers*, 2nd ed. (Glenview, Ill.: Scott, 1976); *The MLA Style Sheet*, 2nd ed. (New York: Modern Language Association, 1970).

Big words
A word is "big" if it is too heavy or too formal for the subject. See Diction 2.

black
Since the 1960s the term *Negro* has been replaced in a great deal of writing by *black*, usually not capitalized. *Afro-American* is also used.

born, borne
In most senses the past participle of *bear* is spelled with a final *-e*: The tax burden was borne by the middle class; The conclusion was borne out by the evidence; The ewes had borne many more lambs. But the spelling *born* is used in the senses "brought into being," "determined by birth," in the passive voice: A child was born; Corruption is born of public apathy; He was born to be hanged. Thus "She has borne three children," but "Three children were born to her." Both *borne* and *born* are used as modifiers: an airborne soldier, a born soldier.

both

Both is a favorite way of emphasizing two-ness: The twins were both there; Both Harry and his brother went. Though neither is necessary, each of the *both*s gives a legitimate emphasis. In "They were both alike," on the other hand, *both* awkwardly duplicates the meaning of *alike*. "The both of them," a fairly common spoken idiom, should be avoided in writing.

both . . . and

When used as a pair (both the tire and the tube), the coordinating conjunctions *both* and *and* are called correlative conjunctions. See Correlative conjunctions.

Bound modifiers

A bound modifier is a restrictive modifier: The horse *that I picked* came in third. See Restrictive and nonrestrictive.

Brackets

Brackets have specific uses in academic writing. Their main function is to enclose editorial interpolations within quoted material. Here they are used to clarify references: "The story answers precisely . . . to that told in the third paragraph of Curll's *Key:* 'But when he [Thomas Swift] had not yet gone half way, his Companion [Jonathan Swift] borrowed the Manuscript to peruse' " (Robert Martin Adams, *Modern Philology*).

In quoted material, *sic* in brackets indicates that an error in the original is being reproduced exactly: New Haven, Connecicut [sic]. Brackets may also be used to insert a correction: Cramer writes, "In April 1943 [the month was July], Jones published his first novel." And brackets function as parentheses within parentheses, particularly in legal documents and scholarly footnotes.

If your typewriter keyboard does not have brackets, you can make them with diagonals and underscores (/‾ _/) or put them in by hand.

In this *Index* brackets are used in examples to enclose words or marks of punctuation that might better be left out (In [the course of] the next year I read such books as . . .), to suggest improvements (The contraption made a noise similar to [like] a concrete mixer), and to indicate alternatives (He has proved [*or* proven] his case).

bring, take

Bring implies motion toward the speaker (Bring it with you when you come); *take* implies motion away from him (Take it with you when you go). When the speaker (or writer) is doing the moving, he is glad he *brought* his camera along; when he has returned, he is glad he *took* the camera and *brought* it back. In situations in which the point of view is of no significance, either form is used: Potatoes were brought [*or* taken] from Ireland to France.

bring up

Bring up (like *raise*) is general usage (That's the way I was brought up) for the more formal *rear* or *nurture*. It also means "to introduce" a subject: Having brought it up, he couldn't stop talking about it. See *raise, rear.*

British English

In the written language there are noticeable differences between British and American English in spelling. The British still prefer *-re* to *-er* in ending words like *center* and *theater*, though they use both forms; they still keep *-our* in a number of words where Americans use *-or;* they use *x* in a few words like *inflexion* where Americans use *ct;* they double more consonants, as in *traveller, waggon;* and they spell some individual words differently, such as automobile *tyre* for U.S. *tire.* They use hyphens more freely than we do (*no-one* and *hand-book*) and single rather than double quotation marks. Differences such as these are just pervasive enough to show that a book is of British or American origin but certainly not enough to interfere with comprehension.

The grammar of the popular levels of British and American English differs somewhat — contrast the speech of ordinary people in novels and movies of the two countries — though less than vocabulary. Collective nouns are more likely to be plural in British usage (the government intend); British writers differ in small matters like the position of *only,* the proper preposition with *different,* the use of *shall,* and various idioms (see *different*). A fairly long catalog of such minor differences could be drawn up, but their importance should not be exaggerated nor their occurrence allowed to obscure the fact that the resemblances far outnumber the differences and that the speech of the two countries represents two strands of the same language.

References: W. H. Mittins et al., *Attitudes to English Usage* (London: Oxford Univ. Press, 1970); Randolph Quirk, *The English Language and Images of Matter* (London: Oxford Univ. Press, 1972), Chs. 1–4.

Broad reference

A pronoun referring to a preceding idea rather than to a particular antecedent is said to have a broad reference. See Reference of pronouns 2.

bug

Both as a noun for an electronic listening device and as a verb for the planting of such a device (They bugged his home phone), *bug* has become established in general English.

bunch

In formal English, *bunch* is limited to objects that grow together like grapes or can be fastened together like carrots or keys. Used of people, *bunch* is moving into the general vocabulary: ". . . another monumental American myth — that Washington is run by a bunch of cynical, untrustworthy fools" (Nona B. Brown, *New York Times Book Review*).

burglar, robber, thief

All three take what is not theirs; but the robber uses violence or threats, and the burglar breaks into a building. See *rob*.

burst, bust

Burst is the unchanged past tense and past participle of the verb *burst*. *Bust* (with *bust* or *busted* as past tense and participle) is a nonstandard variant of *burst* in its literal meanings: dams and balloons burst (*not* bust).

But in contexts where the meaning is figurative, *bust* (frequently with the adverbs *up* and *out*) is now common, though still somewhat informal (The game was busted wide open). And of broncos and trusts and noncommissioned officers, *bust* is general; *burst* cannot be substituted in these senses. Nor can *burst* be substituted when *arrested* is meant, as in "He was busted for possession of marijuana."

Business letters

Business letters include not only the correspondence sent out by companies and corporations but also the letters of individuals to business firms, colleges, government agencies, newspapers, civic organizations, and so forth. When you write a letter to apply for a job or a scholarship, to obtain information, to request assistance, or to register a complaint, the recipient is most likely to give it serious attention if you have done your best with the packaging as well as the content.

1. Materials and appearance. Use good-quality white paper measuring 8½ by 11 inches. If at all possible, type your final draft. Keep a carbon of every business letter you write.

Most business letters are now written in block style without indentions, as shown in the sample. Convention calls for one line of space between inside address and salutation, between salutation and body, and between body and close. Three lines of space are usually left for the written signature. Other spacing depends on the length of your letter. In your drafts—and you may need to write several—work for an attractive, balanced page, with generous margins and plenty of white space at top and bottom.

If you can sensibly do so, limit your letter to a single page. When you must write more than one page, number the additional pages.

2. Heading. Give your full address and the date. Unless you use the abbreviations adopted by the Postal Service (which are not followed by periods), write out the names of states. Note that there is no comma between state and ZIP code and no punctuation at the ends of lines. If you use stationery with a letterhead that provides the address, type the date beneath it.

3. Inside address. Give the name and full address of the recipient, just as it will appear on the envelope, beginning each line at the left margin. How far down the page you begin the inside address will depend on the length of your letter. For good balance, a short letter should naturally begin lower than a longer one.

Whenever possible, direct your letter to an individual or at least to an office (Personnel Director) or a department (Personnel Department).

4. Salutation. When you are writing to a person you can name, the best greeting is the simplest:

Dear Ms. Nash:
Dear Mr. Mahoney:

Note that a colon follows the name. When the circumstances call for special formality, "Dear Sir" or "Dear Madam" is the right choice. If you are addressing an organization or an anonymous individual, the traditional greeting is "Dear Sirs" (or "Gentlemen") or "Dear Sir."

5. Body. Your first paragraph should make the subject of your letter clear. Let your reader know immediately the circumstances of your writing. If you're replying to a letter, answering an advertisement, or writing at the suggestion of someone known to your reader, say so. By making clear from the outset why you're writing, you help your reader concentrate immediately on what you have to say.

Your paragraphs will usually be much shorter than in an essay—often no more than two or three sentences. Use a new paragraph for each item or each subdivision of your message, so that your reader can swiftly identify the specific requests you're making or the information you're providing and can refer to them in his response.

The style of a business letter should be clear, direct, and as brief as is consistent with clarity and completeness. The tone should be brisk without being brusque. You don't want to waste your reader's time, but neither do you want to insult him. And while being concise, be careful not to mystify him. Provide all relevant information, especially if you are complaining about defective merchandise, outlining a proposal, or seeking a job.

Finding a suitable voice for your letter may require some effort, since you will often have little notion what sort of person your reader is. Under such conditions, attempting to make your writing seem personal may instead make it sound artificial and insincere. On the other hand, if you make no attempt to approach the reader as an individual, your writing may sound cold and aloof. The best technique, then, is to address the reader as a stranger but as an intelligent, respected stranger, who is probably short of time.

Don't make the mistake of trying to write in what you may think of as business style. The good business writer of today uses general English, avoiding both the clichés of commerce *(contact, finalize, angle, and/or)* and the pretentiousness of big words (like *ameliorate* for *improve, terminate* for *end*).

6. Close and signature. Begin the close at the left margin, in the middle of the page, or aligned with the heading—depending on overall balance—and follow it with a comma. For most business letters, "Sincerely," or "Sincerely yours," is appropriate. If you're writing as an official—as purchasing agent of a campus co-op, for example—give your title under your typed name:

```
Leslie Archer
Purchasing Agent
```

In typing her name, a woman may or may not choose to indicate her marital status:

```
Dorothy Olson

(Miss) Dorothy Olson

(Mrs.) Dorothy Olson

Dorothy Olson
(Mrs. Henry Olson)
```

7. Mailing. An envelope measuring 4 by 10 inches is best for business letters, but a smaller envelope ($3\frac{1}{2}$ by $6\frac{1}{2}$ inches) may also be used. Repeat the inside address on the envelope, and give your own name and address in the upper left corner.

Heading

```
                                    431 University Place
                                    Madison, Wisconsin 53706
                                    November 12, 1976
```

Inside address

```
Mr. Dwight Morrison
Program Director
WSTR Television
546 Main Street
Madison, Wisconsin 53703
```

Salutation

```
Dear Mr. Morrison:
```

Body

```
Members of the Sociology Club at the University of Wisconsin
have been examining the influence of the University on the
surrounding community, and we believe that some of our find-
ings may be of interest to your viewers.

In order to assess the importance of the University to local
business, we have talked with many shop owners about the prod-
ucts they carry to attract student customers.  We have looked
into the way political opinions in some Madison neighborhoods
have changed since students began taking an active role in
local elections.  And we have found that a tutorial project
started by students has begun to change some people's atti-
tudes toward the University.

Members of the Sociology Club would like very much to discuss
with you the possibility of using our study as the basis of
a special program.  Two or three of us could arrange to meet
with you at your convenience.
```

Close

```
                                    Sincerely yours,
```

Signature

```
                                    Marilyn Thompson

                                    Marilyn Thompson
                                    President
                                    Sociology Club
                                    University of Wisconsin
```

but

But is the natural coordinating conjunction to connect two contrasted statements of equal grammatical rank. It is lighter than *however*, less formal than *yet*, and, unlike *although*, does not subordinate the clause that follows it.

1. Connecting equals. The locutions connected by *but* should be of equal grammatical rank:

Adjectives: not *blue* but *green*
Adverbs: He worked *quickly* but *accurately.*
Phrases: He finally arrived, not *at lunch time* but *in the early evening.*
Clauses: The first day we rested, but *the second we got down to work.*
Sentences: The Rio Grande defied the best engineering minds of two countries for a century; but *$10,000,000 in flood-control work harnessed the treacherous stream.*

See *which* 4 for comments on *but which.*

2. Connecting statements in opposition. The statements connected by *but* should be clearly opposed: "He knows vaguely that the nation is not much good any more; he has read that the crust of the earth is shrinking alarmingly and that the universe is growing steadily colder; but he does not believe that any of the three is in half as bad shape as he is" (James Thurber, *My Life and Hard Times*). In "Our view was limited to about twenty yards down Tuckerman Ravine, but beyond that everything was in clouds," the statements are not genuinely opposed because "was limited" includes the idea of "only." So *but* should be deleted. The two clauses can better stand side by side as partial statements of a complex fact, an effect and its cause.

3. Minor uses.
a. As a subordinating conjunction, after some negative constructions and in some questions:

Nothing would do but I must spend the night with them.

I never go by a hospital and smell anesthetic, but I know we die. — Harvey Breit, *Esquire*

Who knows but everything will come out right?

b. As a preposition, equivalent to *except* (no comma preceding):

They asked none of the family but her.

A New Englander talks about everyone's income but his own.

c. As a formal adverb, equivalent to *only:* In that village there was but one light on after midnight.
d. As a relative pronoun in formal constructions like "There was no one in town but knew [who did not know] the whole story."

4. At beginning of sentences. *But,* like *and,* often stands at the beginning of sentences, especially if the sentences are short. The separation emphasizes the contrast with the preceding clause. But when a clause beginning with *but* (or *nevertheless* or a similar word) is followed by another clause beginning with *but,* both the contrast and the logic break down.

5. Punctuation. Two clauses connected by *but* should ordinarily be separated by a comma. The contrast in ideas makes punctuation desirable even when the clauses are relatively short: I couldn't get the whole license number, but it began with AOK. One of the most common punctuation errors is the use of a comma after an initial *but:* But [,] it was too late for the aging man to regain his lost skill. No punctuation should separate *but* from the clause it introduces.

References: Copperud, p. 39; Fowler, pp. 68–69.

but that, but what

Although formal style avoids *but that* as a subordinating conjunction after a negative (I do not doubt [but] that he will come), it is common in general and informal. In the same construction *but what* sometimes appears. Here, too, *that* can be substituted. References: Bryant, pp. 46–47; Copperud, pp. 38–39.

but which

If you write a clause that begins "but which," be sure it's preceded in the sentence by a *which* clause. See *which* 4.

c.

Often italicized, both *c.* and *ca.* are abbreviations for the Latin *circa*, "about," and are used to indicate that a date is approximate or uncertain. "Geoffrey Chaucer (c. 1340–1400)" means that Chaucer was born about 1340. The same uncertainty may be signaled by a question mark: (1340? to 1400).

can, may (could, might)

1. To express possibility, both *can* and *may* are used. *Can* is reserved for simple ability ("I can swim" meaning "I am able to swim") and for feasibility ("I can swim today" meaning "There is nothing to prevent me from swimming today"). *May* is also used to express feasibility, particularly in formal writing: "The Introduction only hints at the many paths the reader may follow" (Anna Benjamin, *Classical Philology*). Stylistically, habitual use of *may* in this sense can create an excessively tentative tone.

2. In requesting permission, *may* has a cool politeness appropriate to formal occasions: May I add one further point? Informally, *can* requests permission.

In granting or denying permission, *may* is also formal: "The Board adhered to the view that an employer . . . may not lawfully refuse recognition" (Howard Lesnick, *Michigan Law Review*). But except in institutional contexts, where the notion of authority is central, the more democratic *can* is apt to be chosen: "After forbidding the Colonel to speak of love to her, she . . . tells him he can" (Henry Hewes, *Saturday Review*).

3. Might and could, originally the past of *may* and *can*, are now used chiefly to convey a shade of doubt, or a smaller degree of possibility than *can* and *may:* He could be here by Sunday; I might have left it in my room. *Might could* is regional for *might be able to:* I might could borrow a car.

See Divided usage. References: Bryant, pp. 48–49; Copperud, p. 41; Long, pp. 138–42.

cannot, can not

Usage is divided; *cannot* is more common.

can't hardly

Since *hardly* means "probably not," *can't* (or *cannot*) *hardly* should be changed to *can hardly*. See Double negative.

can't help but, can't seem to

Can't (or *cannot*) *help but* and *can't* (or *cannot*) *seem to* are established general idioms:

The reader cannot help but question whether they, indeed, were so universally excellent. — Peter Wall, *Annals*

What they can't seem to tolerate is unemployment, the feeling of being useless. — Alfred Kazin, *Saturday Review*

Even so, *cannot help but* is avoided by many conservative stylists (who may prefer *cannot but*, or *cannot help* followed by a gerund: cannot help saying); and formal usage would have *seems unable to* rather than *cannot seem to*. See *seem*. References: Bryant, pp. 49–50; Copperud, pp. 41, 42.

cap Capital letters

Capitalize the word marked.

Certain uses of capitals, as at the beginning of sentences, for proper names, and for *I*, are conventions that almost everyone observes. Other uses of capitals are matters of taste. Formal English uses more capitals than general English, and newspaper style cuts them to a minimum. The best policy is to follow convention that is well established and not to capitalize in other situations without good reason.

1. Sentence capitals. Capitalize the first word of a sentence.
a. Capitalize the first word in a complete sentence that you enclose in parentheses and place between two other sentences. But don't capitalize it if you insert it in parentheses within a sentence or set it off with a dash or dashes.
b. Capitalize the first word in a sentence following a colon if you want to emphasize it (He promised this: The moment agreement was reached, the trucks would roll).
c. In dialog capitalize the first word of any quoted utterance but

not the second part of an interrupted quoted sentence: "Well," he said, "it was nice to see you again." Except in dialog, don't capitalize parts of sentences that are quoted: "Stressing that legal restrictions on surveillance are few, he rallied the assembled with the intelligence that 'the challenge is wide open' " (David M. Rorvik, *Playboy*).

2. Proper names. Capitalize proper names and abbreviations of proper names: names of people and places, months, days of the week, historical events (the Civil War, the Council of Trent, the New Deal), documents (the Treaty of Paris), companies and organizations, trade names, religious denominations, holidays, races and ethnic groups (but see *black*), languages, ships, named trains and planes, and nicknames. See Course names.

a. Capitalize *north, south,* and so on when they denote particular regions (She was much more familiar with the Southwest than with the East) but not when they indicate direction (They started west in 1849).

b. Capitalize *army, navy,* and so on when they appear in full titles (the United States Army, the British Navy) and when they stand for the teams of the service academies. In other cases usage is divided: the American army (or Army), their navy (or Navy).

c. Capitalize *college* as part of a full title (He went to Beloit College) but not as a level of schooling (Neither of them went to college).

d. Don't capitalize proper nouns that have become common nouns (*tweed, sandwich, bohemian, diesel engine, plaster of paris*). Many proper adjectives in senses that no longer suggest their origins are not capitalized (*india ink*) but other such adjectives usually are (*French cuffs, Bessemer process, Bordeaux mixture*).

e. Don't capitalize the names of the seasons except in *Fall term, Spring semester,* and so on, or for stylistic reasons.

3. Titles of books, articles, etc. Capitalize the first word and last word (and the first word after a colon), all nouns, pronouns, verbs, adjectives, and adverbs, and all prepositions of more than five letters: *With Malice Toward Some; Socialist Humanism: An International Symposium; Now Don't Try to Reason with Me;* "Biological Clocks of the Tidal Zone"; "Computer Control of Electric-Power Systems."

4. Titles, positions, relatives.

a. Capitalize personal titles before proper names: President Taft, Ambassador Clark, Senator Lodge, Sergeant York. When the title alone is used to refer to an individual (the Colonel was there), usage is divided, though "the President" for the President of the United States is still customary.

b. Capitalize the names for family members used as proper nouns: We had to get Father's consent. Do not capitalize when they are used as common nouns: My sister and two brothers are older than I am.

5. Deity. Capitalize *God, Jesus,* and nouns such as *Savior.* With pronouns referring to them, practice is divided: *He, Him, His,* or *he, him, his.*

6. *Street, river, park,* and so on. Capitalize such words as *street, river, park, hotel,* and *church* when they follow a proper name (Fifth Avenue, Missouri River). Abbreviations too should be capitalized: 2319 E. 100th St.

7. Abstract nouns. Usage is divided. Abstract nouns are likely to be capitalized in formal writing (less often in general) when the concept they refer to is personified or when they refer to ideals or institutions: The State has nothing to do with the Church, nor the Church with the State.

8. Quoted lines of verse. Follow the poet's capitalization exactly.

9. Stylistic capitals. Some writers use capitals as a form of emphasis, to lead the reader to stress certain words or give them more attention: "And a woman is only a woman, but a good Cigar is a Smoke" (Rudyard Kipling, "The Betrothed"). The effect is sometimes amusing, but unless you're feeling confident, avoid this practice.

References: *A Manual of Style;* Copperud, p. 42; *U.S. Style Manual.*

 # Careless mistakes

Correct the obvious and apparently careless mistake marked.

Careless lapses are inevitable in hurried work. But an essay is not expected to be hurried work. Comma faults and fragments, mistakes in the forms of verbs and pronouns (*broke* for *broken, it's* for *its*), missing words, and scores of other slips are likely to occur if you give too little time or too little attention to the final stages of preparing a paper.

Train yourself to proofread carefully. Check your manuscript for such elementary mistakes as these:

letters omitted (the *n* of *an,* the *d* of *used to,* a final *y*)

end punctuation omitted, including the closing quotation marks after a quoted passage

words run together (*a/lot,* in *a/while*)

words confused that are closely related in sound or spelling (*affect, effect; principal, principle; quite, quiet; than, then; there, their; to, too; whether, weather; who's, whose*)

Check for the unnecessary repetition of a preposition or a conjunction: It is only natural *that* with the sudden change in the administration *that* people are worrying about what new policies might be instituted.

If you are uncertain about the spelling of a word, consult your dictionary. If you are unsure what word, word form, construction, or punctuation to use, consult this *Index.*

Caret

This inverted v points to the place in a line of manuscript where something written above the line or in the margin should be inserted:

```
                                                      because
There was no reason for them not to get good grades,∧all
they did was study.
```

This is an acceptable way to revise papers so long as the revisions are few in number and are completely clear.

A caret used by an instructor as a correction mark indicates an omission.

Case Case

Correct the mistake in case.

The case of a noun or pronoun is one indication of its relationship to other elements in the sentence. (The second indication is word order.) The subject of a verb and the complement of a linking verb are in the subjective or nominative case (*Who* is *she?*); the object of a verb or preposition is in the objective or accusative case (I introduced *him* to *her*); certain modifiers of a noun (*his* hat, the *dog's* bone) are in the possessive or genitive case.

Except for the spelling differences in the genitive singular (*cat's*), the genitive plural (*cats'*), and the common plural (*cats*), the case of nouns presents no problems: the same form is used in both subject and object positions (Your *cat* chased my *cat*). Pronouns have more forms — especially those pronouns we use most often. And because we may be in the habit of using a few nonstandard forms in speech, the case of these pronouns causes some problems in writing. Most of the problems relate to the six pronouns that change form to indicate all three cases: *I, he, she, we, they, who* (and its variant *whoever*). Thus: *She* sings (nominative); The song pleased *her* (accusative); It's *his* song, not *hers* (genitive). Note that four of these pronouns have a second form of the genitive, used when the pronoun does not stand before a noun: *mine, hers, ours, theirs*. The pronouns *it* and *you* change their form only in the genitive (*its; your, yours*). These pronouns, as well as the indefinites, have the same form whether they are subjects or objects.

Here are the basic conventions to observe in standard written English:

1. Use the forms *I, he, she, we, they, who(ever)*
a. In subject position: *She* and *I* played on the same team; *He* asked *who* wrote the play (*who* is the subject of *wrote*, not the object of *asked*); *Whoever* wrote it had a good ear for dialog.
b. In apposition to a noun or pronoun in subject position: The winning couple, Phil and *I*, got a trip to Disneyland; *We*, Phil and *I*, got a trip. . . .
c. After a linking verb: It is *he* who should pay the bill. (But see *it's me*.)

2. Use the forms *me, him, her, us, them*

a. In object position: The song reminded Jack and *me* (object of verb) of our high-school graduation; College is harder for *him* than for *me* (object of preposition — see also *between you and me*). The object of the infinitive is often in the accusative case (I wanted to be *him*) in general writing and always in informal; the nominative (I always wanted to be *he*) is the rule in formal writing.

b. In apposition to a noun or pronoun in object position: Prizes went to the top students, Mary and *me*; The prizes went to us, Mary and *me*.

3. The special problem of *whom(ever)*. The object form *whom(ever)* is regularly used after a preposition: To whom was the remark addressed? But speakers and writers sometimes deliberately use *who* for the object of a verb when it stands at the beginning of a sentence, especially in questions. Although "Whom do we turn to for advice?" is the choice of some formal stylists, others would use *who*, which has become widespread in general usage: Who do we turn to for advice? See *who, whom*.

4. Use the genitive case of nouns and pronouns to indicate possession and the other relationships discussed in Genitive case 2, except when the *of* phrase is customary (the end of the street, the roof of the house): It was the other *man's* hat, not *his*; the mixup resulted from *their* putting them on the same hook. "*Their* putting" illustrates the standard form for a pronoun that is the subject of the gerund. When a noun is the subject of the gerund, the accusative is common in informal and general English and is the choice of some formal writers: He complained of the *book* (more formal: *book's*) going out of print. See Gerunds 2.

Avoid the nonstandard forms *hisself* (for *himself*) and *theirself* or *theirselves* (for *themselves*).

See Pronouns 1, 4; Genitive case.

case

In case for *if* (In case you're driving east, I'd like a ride) is a general idiom that is avoided in formal writing. *In any case* appears in formal usage but is objected to by some as vague and ambiguous. And the group preposition *in the case of* is frequently deadwood: In [the case of] television commercials, stereotypes are as inescapable as they are deplorable. Reference: Copperud, p. 43.

catholic, Catholic

Written with a small letter, *catholic* is a rather formal synonym for "universal or broad in sympathies or interests." In general American usage, *Catholic* written with a capital is taken as equivalent to *Roman Catholic*, both as a noun (She is a Catholic) and as an adjective (Catholic labor unions).

Cause and effect

Why something occurred (cause) or *what* will result from it (effect) often interests us as much as *what* happened.

1. Signals of cause-effect relations. Causal connections are conveyed by explicit statements (*A* caused *B; B* is the effect of *A*), by many familiar transitional words and phrases (*because* or *since, so that* or *in order that, thus* or *as a result*), and sometimes by the simple device of juxtaposing statements (In March he was told he had cancer; three months later he shot himself).

2. Discovering causes. Essays that investigate cause range from discussions of historical events and scientific experiments to arguments that attribute responsibility or predict the consequences of a policy. Almost all causal analysis has an argumentative edge to it, for the writer is always attempting to win acceptance for a *probable* interpretation of facts. He therefore has to do more than simply state his conclusion; he must justify and support it by demonstrating, offering specific information, knitting probable cause to known effect or probable results to an existing situation.

Because we have a habit of leaping to the most obvious answer, anyone analyzing causes and effects must discipline himself to keep an open mind until he has collected enough evidence to make a convincing case. But he needs to keep in check another tendency, too—the tendency to keep searching out causes that are more and more remote. There is no need to go back to Genesis to explain the genesis of an event of current, local interest. Finally, he should resist the tendency to end up showing not that something happened *because of* something else—the whole purpose of causal analysis—but merely that something happened *after* something else. Confusing temporal sequence with cause results in the logical fallacy of *post hoc, ergo propter hoc,* "after this, therefore because of this." See Fallacies, Logical thinking.

2. Testing causes. John Stuart Mill formulated five methods or canons for testing causal relationships. Outside the laboratory they have practical limitations, for they assume that all circumstances can be known, that controlled experiments can be repeated, and that only a single cause is operating. Even so, they are valuable in stressing the need for rigor in any causal inquiry. Here, followed by very simple examples, are Mill's canons, with punctuation modernized:

a. *The method of agreement.* If two or more instances of the phenomenon under investigation have only one circumstance in common, the circumstance in which alone all the instances agree is the cause (or effect) of the given phenomenon. (If several people have an attack of food poisoning after eating lunch in the same cafeteria, and if it is learned that the one item their meals had in common is smoked fish, it is probable—but not certain—that the smoked fish caused the food poisoning.)

b. *The method of difference.* If an instance in which the phenomenon under investigation occurs, and an instance in which it does not occur, have every circumstance in common save one, that one occurring only in the former, the circumstance in which alone the two instances differ is the effect, or the cause, or an indispensable part of the cause of the phenomenon. (If two people had exactly the same menu except that one added smoked fish, and if he became sick while his companion did not, the fish was probably — but not certainly — the cause of his illness.)

c. *The joint method of agreement and difference.* If two or more instances in which the phenomenon occurs have only one circumstance in common, while two or more instances in which it does not occur have nothing in common save the absence of that circumstance, the circumstance in which alone the two sets of instances differ is the effect, or the cause, or an indispensable part of the cause of the phenomenon. (This method combines the first two; it suggests the process of testing over an extended period of time used by doctors to isolate, through elimination of various possibilities, the cause of an allergy.)

d. *The method of residues.* Subduct from any phenomenon such part as is known by previous inductions to be the effect of certain antecedents, and the residue of the phenomenon is the effect of the remaining antecedents. (If only four people could have committed a crime and three can be proved not to have done it, then the fourth is presumed guilty.)

e. *The method of concomitant variation.* Whatever phenomenon varies in any manner whenever another phenomenon varies in some particular manner is either a cause or an effect of that phenomenon, or is connected with it through some fact of causation. (If a field which is heavily fertilized yields a better crop than one which has received half as much fertilizer and a much better crop than one which has received none at all, the farmer concludes that there is probably a connection between the amount of fertilizer he uses and the yield of the crop.)

Reference: Irving M. Copi, *Introduction to Logic*, 4th ed. (New York: Macmillan, 1972), Ch. 12.

censor, censure

When we *censure*, we condemn or disapprove. When we *censor*, we delete or suppress. But *censorious* refers to censuring.

center around

Although some condemn it as illogical, *center around* (The story centers around the theft of a necklace) is standard idiom:

We could sometimes look out on shooting and fights that seemed to center around this saloon. — Edmund Wilson, *New Yorker*

. . . accompanied by a propaganda war centered around her rightness and fitness for the throne. — Kerby Neil, *Modern Philology*

In formal styles precisionists may substitute *on* or *upon* for *around* or use *revolve* instead of *center*.

Centuries

The first century A.D. ran from the beginning of the year 1 to the end of the year 100, the nineteenth century from January 1, 1801, through December 31, 1900. Thus, to name the century correctly, add one to the number of its hundred except in the last year, when the number of the hundred is the number of the century, too. We live in the twentieth century.

For clarity, the hundred can be named, even in formal writing: Dr. Johnson lived in the seventeen hundreds. Similar practice—with and without the century—is standard in naming decades: the nineteen twenties, the thirties.

cf.

Cf., an abbreviation of the Latin *confer*, means "compare." See Abbreviations 2.

Chronology

One of the ways a good narrative achieves coherence is through chronology—what happened next. Because what happens goes on in a temporal sequence, a narrative finds its chief organizing principle and its momentum in *then* and all the related indicators of time—*later, next, after that, meanwhile, the following day, finally,* and so on. See Narration, Transition.

Circumlocution

A circumlocution is a roundabout way of saying what could be expressed concisely. See Wordiness.

claim

Used in the sense of "say" or "declare," *claim* suggests to many readers that the assertion should be regarded skeptically or scornfully: He claims to be opposed to thought control. Using it as a mere variant of *say* (He claimed he was taking Chemistry 301) can therefore be misleading.

Classification and division

Classification and division are related methods of investigating and writing about a subject. Division is the process of separating a single object (a car) or institution (a college) or concept (communism) into its parts or constituent elements. Classification is the process of bringing together objects, institutions, or concepts that have something in common: cars, colleges, political philosophies can be sorted into groups on the basis of their resemblances. Division reveals internal structure; classification identifies family likenesses. In writing an essay on college life, you might draw on both methods, analyzing the curriculum or campus social life and classifying students on the basis of their attitudes toward their courses or the ways they use their leisure time or some other principle.

As the example suggests, one group can be classified in many different ways, and the same object can be divided into different collections of parts, depending on the writer's purpose or interest. That interest will determine whether the division or classification should meet strict requirements of completeness (all parts or items accounted for) and consistency (no overlapping of parts or of groups). Some groupings are deliberately alogical, making no attempt to be either complete or consistent ("Some Nuts on a Knotty Family Tree"); their purpose is simply to entertain. But a writer interested in trying to organize his experience – the real purpose of classifying or dividing – will work hard to make his analysis reasonably complete and consistent. And if he has selected an original basis for dividing or classifying, he may offer his readers a new way of looking at the world.

See Logical thinking.

Clauses

Each combination of a complete subject with a complete predicate is traditionally called a clause. "He came home" is an independent clause; grammatically it can stand alone. "When he came home" is a dependent clause. In ordinary prose it does not stand alone as a sentence; it is preceded or followed by an independent clause (When he came in, he looked for the cat).

1. The clause structure of sentences. The sentences in *a, b, c,* and *d* both define and illustrate. Simple subjects and simple predicates are italicized. *IC* in brackets introduces an independent clause, *DC* a dependent one.

a. [IC] A simple *sentence* (like this one) *consists* of a single independent subject-predicate combination.

b. [IC] A compound *sentence has* two or more clauses of grammatically equal value; [IC] these *clauses are joined* by a coordinating conjunction, a conjunctive adverb, or (as in this sentence) by a semicolon. [IC] A *writer may decide*, for reasons of emphasis or rhythm, to break his compound sentence into two separate simple sentences [IC], and in such cases the only *difference* between the compound sentence and the separate sentences *is* punctuation.

c. [IC begun] A complex *sentence*, like the one [DC] [that] *you are* now reading, [IC continued] *has* at least one independent clause and one or more dependent, or subordinate, clauses, [DC] *which function* as nominals, adjectivals, or adverbials.

d. [DC] As the hyphenated *term indicates*, [IC] a compound-complex *sentence* (again illustrated by the sentence [DC] *you are reading*) *combines* the features of both compound and complex sentences: [IC] *it contains* two or more independent clauses and one or more dependent clauses.

See Adjectives 5, Adverbial clauses, Noun clauses, Relative clauses.

2. Reduced clauses. Though the typical clause as traditionally defined has an expressed subject and a predicate with a full finite verb, many constructions lack one or the other of these elements and yet function in sentences much as typical clauses do. These are accounted for in transformational grammars by a transformation that deletes either a repeated verb or a form of *be* and a repeated subject. Reduced clauses are of two types:

a. Elliptical clauses, in which a full verb can be reconstructed because it occurs earlier in the sentence:

I don't *believe it* any more than you [*believe it*].
They can *speak Russian* and so can Bill [*speak Russian*].

b. Abridged clauses, in which a subject and form of *be* are deleted:

While [*I was*] waiting, *I* read the newspaper.
When [*he was*]sixteen, *he* went to work.
Though [*he was*] a rapid reader, *he* disliked books.
After [*I had been*] standing in line for an hour, *I* left.
Though [*she was*] tired, *she* continued to work.

When the deleted subject is not the same as the subject of the main clause, the result is often a dangling modifier.

See Complex sentence, Compound sentence, Dangling modifiers, Elliptical constructions, Restrictive and nonrestrictive. References: Jerrold J. Katz, *The Philosophy of Language* (New York: Harper, 1966), pp. 119–51; Long and Long, pp. 143–58; Quirk et al., pp. 720–65.

Cliché

A cliché is a worn-out word or phrase (white as snow). See Triteness.

Clipped words

Ad [*vertisement*] and [*tele*]*phone* are clipped words. See Origin of words 3d.

 ## Coherence

Make clear the relation between the parts of this sentence or between these sentences or paragraphs.

Coherence—the traditional name for relationship, connection, consecutiveness—is an essential virtue in expository writing. It is essential because the reader's mind differs from yours; you must provide guidance from one idea, from one sentence, to another. To make a coherent presentation you have to arrange your ideas so that others can understand them.

Though careful planning in the prewriting stage will help to make clear the relationship of consecutive ideas, for the most part coherence must be tested after writing. To see if what you've written hangs together not only for you but for those who will read it, go over it as if you were encountering its content for the first time. Ask yourself, "Is the relation between these statements clear? Can a reader move from this sentence or from this paragraph to the next without losing the thread?"

A natural arrangement of material is not enough; you often need to signal the relationship between sentences and paragraphs. These signs, with suggestions for establishing coherence, are discussed in Conjunctions and style, Prepositions, Reference of pronouns, Transition. Reference: E. K. Lybbert and D. W. Cummings, *CCC*, Feb. 1969, pp. 35–38.

Collective nouns

A collective noun is a noun whose singular form names a group of objects or persons or acts. Here are some familiar examples:

army	contents	gang	number
athletics	couple	group	offspring
audience	crowd	herd	politics
class	dozen	jury	public
committee	faculty	majority	remainder

Some collectives have regular plural forms (*army – armies*); some (*athletics, offspring*) do not. The plural of a collective noun signifies different groups: The *audiences* of New York and Chicago differed in their reception of the play.

Some collectives are typically used in the singular (*committee is*) and some typically in the plural (*police are*). Most, however, are singular in one context, plural in a different one, depending on the way the writer is thinking about the group. When the group as a whole is intended, the collective noun takes a singular verb and a singular pronoun:

During the performance a *series* of barges covered with scenery *chugs* silently into place. — Edwin Wilson, *Wall Street Journal*

When the individual units of the group are intended, the noun takes a plural verb and plural pronoun:

Psychologists asked a *group* of young men and women what sex *they* wanted *their* first child to be. —*Psychology Today*

With this example, compare "Now that John is back, the *group has its* old solidarity."

Trouble occurs when a collective noun is treated inconsistently. The usual cause is that the writer has come to no firm decision about the group it names. He begins by treating the word as a singular, and as long as the verb follows it closely, he makes the verb singular: The inner *circle has* great influence. But if a plural modifier comes between the collective noun and the verb, he thinks of the members of the group rather than of the group as a unit, and he shifts to a plural verb: This inner *circle* of ambitious men *pose* a serious threat.

Inconsistency is also likely to occur when the writer's initial way of thinking about the collective and the meaning of a subsequent sentence come into conflict. He may want to keep a collective noun singular, but if the meaning calls for a plural construction, he is likely to make the shift unconsciously, sometimes in mid-sentence:

The entire *congregation troops* into the church, *seats itself*, and *remains* for a good two hours, while an aged curé berates *them* [consistency demands *it*] for *their* [*its*] sins.

In making constructions consistent, you will often find that, as in the example just given, it is the collective subject rather than its pronouns that needs to be changed. Beginning with "All members of the congregation troop into the church, seat themselves. . ." would avoid the problem.

Casual shifts in number are common in speech, but they may attract unfavorable attention in general writing, and they are almost certain to in formal prose. When reading over what you've written, be sure you haven't treated the same collective noun as both singular and plural.

See Agreement 1b, *each, every.* References: Bryant, pp. 6–7; Copperud, p. 50; Fries, pp. 48–50, 54, 57–59; Jespersen, pp. 210–12; Pooley, pp. 80–81.

Colloquial English

Usage that is characteristic of speech is colloquial. One familiar class of examples is made up of words that strive for emphasis, like *actually, really* (or *real*), *awful, terrible, terrific, fabulous, incredible, unbelievable.* In current writing the division between what is spoken and what is written is not nearly so sharp as it once was, though some spoken usages may be inappropriate in all but the most informal writing, just as some features of written English are inappropriate in all but the most formal speech.

Dictionaries sometimes mark words *Colloq.* to suggest that in the editors' judgment they are more common in speech than in writing. Many people mistakenly take the label to mean that the dictionary frowns upon their use, when in fact colloquial words are often accurate, expressive words that are used freely in good general writing. Because this misinterpretation of *colloquial* is so common, the label is less used in recent dictionaries and is generally avoided in this book. If a usage is more common in speech than in writing, that fact is stated; if the word or expression is standard English but is rarely found in general or formal writing, it is labeled informal.

See Spoken and written English.

 ## Colon

Use a colon here. Or reconsider the use of this colon.

The colon is a mark of anticipation, indicating that what follows the mark will supplement what preceded it.

1. Introductory uses. Use a colon before a series of words, phrases, or clauses when they are not preceded by an introductory word or phrase or when they are formally introduced by a set phrase like *as follows* or *including the following.*

Two "parallel economies" have now emerged in India: the "white economy," involving taxes, salaries, receipts . . . and the "black economy," involving bribes, unrecorded cash transactions, hidden inventories. . . .
—Ved Mehta, *New Yorker*

Classifying the poetry written from 1500 to 1900 in accordance with this distinction, we discover a sequence which runs as follows: predicative, then balanced; predicative, then balanced. — Josephine Miles, *PMLA*

Don't use a colon after less formal introductory words (*like, such as*) that make what follows a part of the clause: The shop carried a lot of ethnic recordings, like [:] West African, Moorish, Egyptian, and Arabian. And don't use a colon between a verb and its object or complement: The reason I went broke freshman week was that I had to buy [:] books, furniture, and tickets to a lot of things I knew I'd never go to; My three immediate goals are [:] to survive midyear exams, to get to Colorado, and to ski until my legs wear out.

When appropriate, use a colon to introduce quotations in factual writing, especially if they run to more than one sentence. The colon is more common in formal than in general and informal writing, and its suitability depends in part on the way you introduce the quotation. If it's built closely into the sentence, a comma is usual; if it's more formally introduced, a colon:

For example, the report cannot say, "It was a wonderful car," but must say something like this: "It has been driven 50,000 miles and has never required any repairs." — S. I. Hayakawa, *Language in Thought and Action*

2. Between clauses. Particularly in a formal essay, you may sometimes want to use a colon between the clauses of a compound sentence when the second clause is an illustration, a restatement, or an amplification of the first:

The supposition that words are used principally to convey thoughts is one of the most elementary of possible errors: they are used mainly to proclaim emotional effects on the hearers or attitudes that will lead to practical results. — H. R. Huse, *The Illiteracy of the Literate*

In less formal writing a semicolon or a period is common in this position. It is the one use in which the colon and the semicolon are sometimes interchangeable. (A semicolon should never be used to introduce a series or a quotation.)

3. Conventional uses.
a. After the salutation of formal letters: Dear Sir:
b. Between hours and minutes expressed in figures: 11:30 a.m.
c. In formal bibliographies and formal citations of books:

Sometimes between volume and page: *The Mt. Adams Review,* 160: 129–40 (A comma, however, is now more common.)

Between title and subtitle: *The Great Tradition: An Interpretation of American Literature Since the Civil War*

Between place of publication and publisher: Austin: Univ. of Texas Press

Between Bible chapter and verse: Genesis 9:3–5

d. In ratios and proportions when the numbers are written as numerals: concrete mixed 5:3:1. Two colons are used instead of an equals sign in a full proportion: 1:2::3:6.

4. Stylistic use. You may sometimes choose a construction that requires a colon in order to spotlight what the colon introduces: "It is a common dream: To stand beneath sun and blue sky, harvesting your own . . . fruits and vegetables" *(New York Times)*. The more common order, "To stand . . . is a common dream," is much less emphatic.

Sometimes, for stylistic effect, an experienced writer will use colons where other writers would use commas, dashes, semicolons, or periods. James Agee's *Let Us Now Praise Famous Men* contains many examples.

5. Capitals following. After a colon either a capital (as in the last quoted sentence) or a small letter may be used; but a small letter is much more common, as in the example in 2. Use a capital after a colon only when what follows it is long or complicated, with internal punctuation, or when you want to give it special prominence: "Beneath the surface, however, is the less tangible question of values: Are the old truths true?" *(Newsweek)*.

For other uses of the colon, see *A Manual of Style* and the *U.S. Style Manual*.

 ## Comma

Insert or remove a comma at the place marked.

The most common question about punctuation is "Should there be a comma here?" The general advice of this book is to use commas wherever they are considered obligatory and to use them elsewhere if they contribute to understanding. When choice is possible, the decision depends on appropriateness: the complex syntax and deliberate pace of much formal writing call for more commas than the simpler, brisker sentences of general English.

1. To separate independent clauses.
a. Use a comma before the coordinating conjunction when the clauses are rather long and when you want to emphasize their distinctness, as when they have different subjects:

For all its impressiveness, Monks Mound is only a part of the even more impressive Cahokia group, and Cahokia in turn is only one, albeit the largest, of 10 large and small population centers and 50-odd farming villages.—Marvin L. Fowler, *Scientific American*

When the independent clauses are short and closely related in meaning, the comma is often omitted:

Two years ago, the Dallas Cowboys had become dangerously long of tooth and the team's decline and fall seemed imminent.—Anson Mount, *Playboy*

But there is no rule that forbids using a comma to separate the clauses in a compound sentence, no matter what their length or relationship. Many experienced writers automatically place a comma before the conjunction, and so guard against the momentary confusion that a sentence like this one invites: A crowd

Uses of the comma

The following list of uses of the comma outlines the treatment in this article. The numbers and letters refer to sections and subsections.

1. **To separate independent clauses**
   a. Between clauses connected by a coordinating conjunction
   b. Between clauses connected by *but*
   c. Between clauses connected by *for*
   d. Between clauses not connected by a coordinating conjunction

2. **With preceding and following elements**
   a. After a dependent clause or long phrase preceding the main clause
   b. Before a dependent clause or long phrase following the main clause and not essential to its meaning

3. **To set off nonrestrictive modifiers**

4. **To enclose interrupting and parenthetical elements**
   a. Around interrupting elements
   b. Around conjunctive adverbs within clauses

5. **In lists and series**
   a. Between units in lists and series
   b. Between coordinate adjectives

6. **For clarity**

7. **For emphasis and contrast**

8. **With main sentence elements**
   a. Subject and verb
   b. Verb and object
   c. Compound predicates

9. **In conventional uses**
   a. In dates
   b. In addresses
   c. After salutations in all but formal letters
   d. After names in direct address
   e. In figures
   f. With degrees and titles
   g. With weak exclamations
   h. To show omission

10. **With other marks of punctuation**
    a. With parentheses
    b. With dash
    c. With quotation marks (Quotation marks 4b, 4c)

of spectators lined the walkway to see him [ ] and the President, in standard fashion, passed along the crowd *(New York Times)*.
b. Use a comma between two independent clauses joined by *but,* regardless of their length, to emphasize the contrast: "His achievements in office have been difficult to assess, but they have been formidable" (John David Hamilton, *Atlantic*).
c. Use a comma between independent clauses connected by the conjunction *for* to avoid confusion with the preposition *for:* They were obviously mistaken, for intercollegiate sports are always competitive.
d. Use a comma in place of a coordinating conjunction when you have good reason for doing so and when you can do so without inconveniencing or outraging your readers. In the great majority of cases such punctuation represents a comma fault (see Comma fault); but under certain circumstances a comma can appropriately stand between independent clauses that are not joined by a coordinating conjunction:

The intellect gets busy, means and methods are studied, purposes are assessed. — Gerald Warner Brace, *The Stuff of Fiction*

This writer is not merely good, she is *wickedly* good. — John Updike, *New Yorker*

The clauses here are short, parallel in form, and closely bound together in meaning. Semicolons, the most likely alternative punctuation, would slow the pace and add formality. In the following example the comma reinforces a contrast:

Both colloquial styles — consultative and casual — routinely deal in a public sort of information, though differently: casual style takes it for granted and at most alludes to it, consultative style states it as fast as it is needed. — Martin Joos, *The Five Clocks*

Sentences punctuated like these are increasingly common in print. Not all are successful. If the clauses are neither short nor closely related in form, and if one or more of them contains internal punctuation, the reader may have a hard time grasping the meaning: "The strongest and luckiest private constituencies win, social needs get pushed aside, as in the 50s, to explode a decade later" (Bill Moyers, *Newsweek*). Here, a reader who assumes that the writer is building a series is brought up short and forced to reread the sentence.

The choice of a comma alone instead of a coordinating conjunction (with or without a comma), a subordinating conjunction, or a semicolon is a matter of style. But convention needs to be taken into account. Before using the comma alone, consider your audience. Some very conservative readers look on such punctuation as invariably incorrect. If you can assume that your audience will not automatically condemn the practice, then be sure you are using a comma for a purpose. And, most important, be sure that your use of a comma won't make your readers' task more difficult.

See Fused sentence, Semicolon 1.

2. With preceding and following elements.
a. Use a comma after an introductory dependent clause or a long introductory phrase:

Since encouraging women to spend money was the main point of magazines directed at us, they had distinctive characteristics. —*Ms.*

Far from being a neutral instrument, the law belongs to those who have the power to define and use it. —Michael Parenti, *Democracy for the Few*

Often when the preceding phrase is short or when the dependent clause has the same subject as the independent clause, the comma is omitted:

During my convalescence [ ] I will meditate on a few items. —Goodman Ace, *Saturday Review* (short phrase)

Although Grant ignores such details [ ] he is shrewd not only about his colleagues but about his former colleagues. —Gore Vidal, *New York Review of Books* (subjects the same)

But some professional writers make a practice of putting commas after all introductory clauses and after all introductory phrases that contain verb forms. By doing so they establish a consistent pattern and avoid risking the confusion that sometimes results from lack of punctuation.

b. Use a comma before a dependent clause or a long phrase that follows the main clause if the subordinate element is not essential to the meaning of the main clause:

In addition, most of these men have just spent years in the regimented, choiceless life of prison, which makes a life of freedom and responsibility a frightening prospect. —Sol Chaneles, *Psychology Today*

Again and again they tried to start the engine, with the breeze freshening and the tide beginning to turn.

3. To set off nonrestrictive modifiers. Use a comma to set off word groups that do not restrict the meaning of the noun or verb or clause they modify. The italicized word groups in the following sentences are nonrestrictive:

From where I was standing, *almost directly above the trunk*, I could see many of the articles that had been lost.

Pigeons breed in the spring and the hen lays two eggs, *one of which usually hatches into a hen and the other into a cock.*

A modifier that restricts the reference of the word it modifies (as "that had been lost" restricts "articles" in the first of the illustrative sentences above) is essential to correct understanding and is therefore not set off by commas. Out of context, many modifiers could be either restrictive or nonrestrictive. The word groups in italics in the following sentences might or might not be set off, depending on the writer's meaning:

A winding road *which seemed to lead nowhere in particular* passed through the village.

The man *who was carrying a gun* walked across the campus and into the administration building.

See Restrictive and nonrestrictive.

4. To enclose interrupting and parenthetical elements.
a. Use commas around a word, phrase, or clause that interrupts the main structure of the sentence:

Next summer, no matter what happens, I intend to go to Africa.

The prank, I suppose, seemed amusing at the time.

My uncle, as was his habit, stopped for a drink on his way home from work.

Forgetting to complete the enclosure with a second comma can result in a confused sentence: "If factory workers and farmers became more efficient, Soviet citizens were told this week [ ] they would get more domestic goods, food, housing, hospitals and schools" (*Newport Daily News*).

Usage is divided over setting off short parenthetical expressions like *of course*. Enclosing them in commas is more characteristic of formal than of general writing. There is often a difference in emphasis as well as tone according to whether or not commas are used:

And of course there are those who talk about the hair of the dog. — *Providence Sunday Journal*

The question, of course, is not whether the family will "survive." — *Time*

b. Use commas around a conjunctive adverb that stands after the first phrase of its clause: It was this ridiculous proposal, however, that won majority approval. At the beginning of a sentence such adverbs may or may not be set off: Therefore [,] I have decided to withdraw my application.

But and other coordinating conjunctions are a part of the clauses in which they appear and should not be set off: But a solution must be found. Nor should *however* be set off when it modifies an adverb or adjective: However strongly you feel. . . . However tired you are. . . .

5. In lists and series.
a. Use commas to separate the units in lists and series: "He has read everything he could lay his hands on, manuscript and printed, that was written during the period: plays, sermons, ballads, broadsides, letters, diaries, and, above all, court records" (Edmund S. Morgan, *New York Review of Books*). See Semicolon 2.

Usage is divided over the use of a comma before the conjunction in a series: "letters, diaries, and records" or "letters, diaries and records." The comma is a safeguard against ambiguity: "He had small shoulders, a thick chest holding a strong heart [ ] and heavy thighs" (Richard Mandell, *Sports Illustrated*). See Series.

b. Use a comma between adjectives modifying the same noun. In the sentence "Though it was a hot, sticky, miserable day, Mrs. Marston looked cool in her fresh gingham dress," there are commas between *hot* and *sticky* and between *sticky* and *miserable* because each stands in the same relation to the noun *day*. "Hot *and* sticky *and* miserable" would make sense. There is no comma between *fresh* and *gingham* because *fresh* modifies *gingham dress*, not just *dress.* "Fresh *and* gingham" would not make sense.

Frequently in current writing, when only two adjectives modify the noun, no comma is used: a hot sticky day; the tall dark woman. There is no loss of clarity, but if you follow this style consistently, you deprive yourself of a rhetorical resource. By separating, a comma provides emphasis. Compare these two versions:

His long, greasy hair hung down to the shoulders of his worn, faded jacket.

His long greasy hair hung down to the shoulders of his worn faded jacket.

In the first, *greasy* and *faded* stand out as separate modifiers of their nouns.

C_6 6. For clarity. Use a comma to guide a reader in interpreting a sentence and to make it unnecessary for him to go back over it for meaning. A comma between clauses joined by *for* makes it clear that the word is functioning as a conjunction rather than as a preposition. Similarly, a comma can prevent the subject of one verb from being mistaken even momentarily for the object of another:

When the boll weevil struck, the credit system collapsed and ruined both landowners and tenants. *Not* When the boll weevil struck the credit system. . . .

Soon after the inspector left, the room was crowded with curious onlookers. *Not* Soon after the inspector left the room. . . .

A comma can also make immediately clear whether a modifier goes with what precedes or with what follows: A great crowd of shoppers milled around inside, and outside hundreds more were storming the doors. *Not* . . . milled around inside and outside. . . .

And a comma helps when a word is used twice in a row: What he does, does not concern me.

C_7 7. For emphasis and contrast. When two words or phrases are connected by *and,* they are not usually punctuated; but because a comma tends to keep distinct the elements it separates and to emphasize slightly the element that follows it, writers may use commas for these purposes alone: My brother was delighted with the prestige of his new position, and with the increase in pay.

Here a comma is used for emphasis, and irony: "Midge Decter is disappointed, again" (Jane O'Reilly, *New York Times Book Review*).

C_8 8. With main sentence elements.
a. Subject and verb. Though it sometimes occurs in old-fashioned formal usage, don't use a comma between a subject and its verb.

b. Verb and object. Don't use a comma between a verb and its object. (Words or phrases that must be set off by pairs of commas may, of course, intervene between subject and verb and between verb and object. See 4.)

c. Compound predicates. Use a comma between the verbs of a compound predicate only when the sentence is so long and involved that reading it is difficult or when you feel the need for special emphasis or contrast. This is a sensible rule and one that is insisted upon by many writers, teachers, and editors, though in published prose the verbs in a compound predicate are frequently separated by a comma without obvious cause:

Works by other writers in the past few months have reflected this fascination with language, but have delved deeper into the mysterious origins of words. — *Time*

9. In conventional uses.

a. In dates, to separate the day of the month from the year: May 26, 1971. When the day of the month is not given, a comma may or may not be used: In September 1846 *or* In September, 1846. If a comma precedes the year, punctuation should also follow: In September, 1846, the government fell.

b. In addresses, to separate smaller from larger units: Washington, D.C.; Chicago, Illinois; Hamilton, Madison County, New York; Berne, Switzerland.

c. After salutations in all but formal letters: Dear John,

d. After names in direct address: Jim, try that one again.

e. In figures, to separate thousands, millions, etc.: 4,672,342. In some styles no comma is used in figures with four digits: 2750.

f. To separate degrees and following titles from names: George Emmett, M.A.; Charles Evans Hughes, Jr. (this comma is now sometimes omitted); Elihu Root, Esq.

g. After a weak exclamation like *well, why, oh:* Oh, what's the use?

h. Sometimes to show the omission of a word that is required to fill out a construction: He took the right-hand turn; I, the left.

10. With other marks of punctuation.

a. When a parenthesis comes within a phrase or clause that is followed by a comma, the comma belongs after the parenthesis.

b. Use a comma or a dash, not both.

c. For the use of commas with quotation marks, see Quotation marks 4b, 4c.

References: Summey, index entries; Whitehall, pp. 126–29.

Comma fault

Revise the sentence marked by changing the comma to a semi-colon or a period, or by inserting an appropriate conjunction, or by rephrasing to make a more satisfactory sentence.

A comma fault (comma blunder, comma splice) occurs when a comma alone is used to separate the independent clauses of a compound or a compound-complex sentence: He stared at his visitor, it was too dark to see who it was. Occasionally such sentences are deliberately constructed for an intended effect: "I was awed by this system, I believed in it, I respected its force" (Alfred Kazin, *A Walker in the City*). The term *comma fault* marks uses of the comma that are not justified either by the structural similarity of the clauses or by the close relationship of their content.

There are various remedies for a comma fault:

1. Replace the comma with a semicolon or a period.

He stared at his visitor, it was too dark to see who it was.
Revised: He stared at his visitor. It was too dark to see who it was.

This is the simplest remedy but not always the best one. Sometimes inserting a period simply produces two weak sentences in place of one.

I think Americans should read this book, they would get a more accurate picture of problems in the Middle East.
Revised: I think Americans should read this book; they would get a more accurate picture of problems in the Middle East. [A period would produce two weak sentences. For a better revision, see 3.]

2. Join statements that belong together with a conjunction that makes their relationship clear. When the choice is a coordinating conjunction, the comma is ordinarily retained (see Comma 1a); when the choice is a conjunctive adverb, the comma is replaced by a semicolon (see Semicolon 1b).

An increase in student fees would enable us to balance the budget, this is clearly not the time for it.
Revised: An increase in student fees would enable us to balance the budget, but this [*or* budget; however, this] is clearly not the time for it.

3. Rewrite the sentence, perhaps subordinating one of the clauses, perhaps making a single independent clause. Work to produce a satisfactory sentence, not just to eliminate the comma fault.

I think Americans should read this book, they would get a more accurate picture of problems in the Middle East.
Revised: I think Americans should read this book because it would give them a more accurate picture of problems in the Middle East.

One part receives the stimulus from outside and transmits the impulse to the cell, this is known as the dendrite.
Revised: One part, known as the dendrite, receives the stimulus from outside and transmits the impulse to the cell.

If you can make a sure distinction between an independent clause and a dependent clause, you should find it easy to spot any comma faults in your sentences. Look first to see how many independent subject-verb combinations you have in each group of words punctuated as a single sentence. If there are two independent clauses, see if you have a connective between them. If there is no connective but only a comma, you have probably produced a comma fault. For exceptions, see Comma 1d. Compare Fused sentence.

Commands and requests

Direct commands, also called imperatives, are expressed by the simple (infinitive) form of the verb:

Hurry up!
Shut the door, please.
Fill out the coupon and mail it today.

In speech, the force of the command or request is shown by the stress and tone of voice, which are hard to represent on paper. Emphatic commands are punctuated with an exclamation mark, less emphatic ones with a period. Negative commands are expressed with *not* and the *do* form of the verb: Don't go yet.

Commands and requests can be made less abrupt through phrasing and the use of auxiliaries or adverbs of courtesy. Often in the pattern of a question, they are punctuated with either a period or a question mark, depending on the intonation intended.

Try to get them in on time.
Please think no more of it.
Would you be willing to take part in this program?
Would [*or* Will] you please close the window.
Let's go around and see what we can do with him.
Suppose we say nothing more about it.

In indirect discourse a command becomes an infinitive with *to* or a clause with *should:* He told us to write a 5000-word paper. *Or* He said that we should write a 5000-word paper.

References: Long, pp. 76–79; Quirk et al., pp. 402–405.

committee

Committee is a collective noun, usually construed as singular. When the writer is thinking of the several individuals who compose it, *the members of the committee* is preferable.

compare, contrast

Compare with *to* points out likenesses: He compared my stories to Maupassant's [said they were like his]. *Compare* followed by *with* finds likenesses and differences: He compared my stories with Maupassant's [pointed out like and unlike traits]. *Contrast* always points out differences.

When the things compared are of different classes, *to* is used: He compared my stories to a sack of beans. In the common construction with the past participle, either *to* or *with* is used: Compared with [*or* to] Maupassant's, mine are feeble. *In comparison* is followed by *with:* In comparison with Maupassant's, mine are feeble. *Contrast* ordinarily takes *with:* He contrasted my work with [*sometimes* to] Maupassant's. *In contrast*, however, usually takes *to:* In contrast to Maupassant's, my stories are feeble.

Comparison and contrast

To compare and contrast is to establish the similarities and the differences between two or more objects, people, places, institutions, ideas, and the like. Comparing is a natural way of communicating information. You can acquaint a reader with a subject that is unfamiliar to him by telling him how it is like and how it is unlike something he knows well. And you use contrast automatically in arguments when you set out to prove that one thing is better than another.

To make a comparison, first select the points that are significant for the purpose you have in mind. (Is cost a significant factor in deciding what make of car you want to buy? Is safety? Speed? Color?) Then find out how your subjects are alike and how they differ in each of these respects. In organizing your discussion, you may treat one of the subjects *(A)* fully before taking up the corresponding points in the other *(B);* or you may compare *A* and *B* point by point; or you may set out all the likenesses between *A* and *B* and then all the differences (or the reverse). In any case, it is not enough to offer a mass of details about each of the subjects under discussion. You must work out the comparison, relating details about one to the corresponding details about the other, so that the reader understands the ways in which the subjects differ and the ways in which they are alike.

See Logical thinking.

Comp Comparison of adjectives and adverbs

Correct the fault in comparing the adjective or adverb marked. To express degrees of what is named, adjectives and adverbs are compared — that is, their forms are changed by adding *-er* or *-est* to the root, or base, form *(long, longer, longest)* or by preceding it with *more* or *most (beautiful, more beautiful, most beautiful).*

1. Choosing the form. We say "a longer walk," not "a more long walk"; we say "a more beautiful picture," not "a beautifuller picture."

a. Some adjectives and adverbs add *-er, -est* to the root form (the positive degree).

	Positive	Comparative	Superlative
Adjective	early	earlier	earliest
	hoarse	hoarser	hoarsest
	unhappy	unhappier	unhappiest
Adverb	fast	faster	fastest
	soon	sooner	soonest

b. Other adjectives and adverbs precede the root form with *more, most.*

	Positive	Comparative	Superlative
Adjective	exquisite	more exquisite	most exquisite
	afraid	more afraid	most afraid
	pleasing	more pleasing	most pleasing
Adverb	comfortable	more comfortable	most comfortable
	hotly	more hotly	most hotly

Three-syllable adjectives and adverbs are ordinarily compared with *more* and *most*, those of one syllable with *-er* and *-est*. Two-syllable modifiers are usually compared with *more* and *most*, but many can take either form: *able – abler, more able – ablest, most able; empty – emptier, more empty – emptiest, most empty.* When you're in doubt, *more* and *most* are the safer choices. It was once possible to use both methods of comparison in one locution, as in Shakespeare's "most unkindest cut of all," but double comparatives and double superlatives are no longer standard English.

Some points of usage that arise with irregular forms of comparison are discussed in *former, first – latter, last;* and *last, latest.* Reference: Fries, pp. 96–101.

2. Using the comparative. The comparative expresses a greater degree (It is *warmer* now) or makes specific comparison between two units (He was *kinder* [*more kind*] than his wife). The two terms of a comparison should be actually comparable:

Comparable: His salary was lower than a shoe clerk's. *Or* than that of a shoe clerk. *Not comparable:* than a shoe clerk.

Comparable: His face was round and healthy looking, like a recent college graduate's. *Not comparable:* like a recent college graduate.

Logic calls for *other* with *any* in comparisons between a thing and the group to which it belongs: She is a better dancer than *any* of the *other* girls. The comparative is, however, frequently used absolutely, with no actual comparison involved (*higher education, the lower depths, older people*). In much advertising copy the task of supplying a comparison is left to the reader (*cooler, fresher, stronger, faster, more economical*).

3. Using the superlative. In formal and most general writing, the superlative is used to indicate the greatest degree of a quality among three or more people or things (He was the *jolliest* of the whole group; This is the *brightest* tie in the showcase). Informally, the superlative of two objects is common, and it is not rare in general writing: Roy and Joe did pushups to see who was strongest; Russia and China compete to see which can be most critical of the other's policies. Use of the superlative as a form of emphasis is also informal (She has the loveliest flowers; We saw the best show). The form with *most* is now largely restricted to formal social correspondence (You are most kind; She is most clever) in which no specific comparison is intended.

Superlatives are not completed by *other:* The Egyptians had obtained the highest degree of cultivation in medicine that had up to that time been obtained by any [*not* any other] nation.

References: Bryant, pp. 201–202; Fries, pp. 99–101; Pooley, pp. 112–14.

4. Comparing absolutes. Purists raise objections to the comparison of *black, dead, excellent, fatal, final, impossible, perfect, unique* on the grounds that there can be no degrees of *deadness* or *blackness* or *impossibility.* But in fact these words are frequently compared: a more equal society, a more complete victory, a more impossible situation; and the Constitution has "to form a more perfect union." Many absolutes are used figuratively with meanings that naturally admit comparison: This is the *deadest* town I was ever in. See Divided usage. References: Bryant, pp. 58–59; Pooley, pp. 112–14.

Complement

Complement often refers to the noun or adjective completing the meaning of a linking verb and modifying the subject: He was *busy;* He became *the real head of the business.* In some grammars *complement* is used to include direct and indirect objects. See Linking verbs, Predicate adjectives.

complement, compliment

As a noun, *complement* means "that which completes or is called for" (a full complement); as a verb, it means "to make complete" or – of two things – "to fill out each other's lacks" (the scarf and blouse complemented each other perfectly). *Compliment* is the noun (He received many compliments for his work) and verb (He complimented her on her victory) having to do with praise and congratulations.

Complex sentence

A complex sentence has one independent, or main, clause and one or more dependent clauses, ordinarily introduced by relative pronouns or subordinating conjunctions: She married the man *who* picked her up *when* she fell. See Clauses.

Compound-complex sentence

When one or more of the independent clauses of a compound sentence are modified by dependent clauses, the sentence is called compound-complex. Here the opening dependent clause modifies the first independent clause: "When its facilities were offered to Kansas State Teachers College, they were refused, for enrollment at that institution had already declined 500 below capacity" (John R. Silber, *Atlantic*). See Clauses.

Compound predicate

Two or more verbs with the same subject, together with their modifiers, form a compound predicate: Ruth *wrote* and *mailed* three letters.

Compound predicates help make writing economical. Note how far removed this sentence is from the type that gives only one small idea to a sentence:

The case is made more interesting if the great daily has, among other things, distorted political news, reported its political opponents with miserable unfairness and glaring prejudice, tried to goad the government into declaring war on Cuba, lowered the mental level of life in the community, debased the language, filled its pages with vast ads for pork butts, storm windows, under-garments, dollar sales, antiperspirants, failed to inform the public on matters of great importance, fought medical care for the aged, and so forth. – Saul Bellow, *Atlantic*

See Comma 8c.

Compound sentence

A compound sentence coordinates two or more independent clauses.

1. With coordinating conjunction. Usually the clauses of a compound sentence are connected by one of the coordinating conjunctions: "Lavin's stories are centered almost entirely on the lives of women, and they are informative in the most humane way" (Rosellen Brown, *Ms.*).

2. Without connective. A compound sentence may have a semicolon instead of a connective between the clauses: "They are generous-minded; they hate shams and enjoy being indignant about them; they are valuable social reformers; they have no notion of confining books to a library shelf" (E. M. Forster, *Aspects of the Novel*). Since each of these clauses could also be written as a separate sentence, it is apparent that the traditional definition of sentence is somewhat arbitrary. For the use of a comma instead of a connective, see Comma 1d.

3. With conjunctive adverb. The clauses of a compound sentence may be connected by a conjunctive adverb (*however, moreover, whereas, consequently, therefore* . . .) preceded by a semicolon: The FBI had proved themselves expert in publicizing their solution of crimes; consequently, some local police gave them only grudging support.

See Clauses, Conjunctive adverbs.

Compound subject

Two or more elements standing as subjects of one verb make a compound subject: "Capitalists, militarists, and ecclesiastics cooperate in education" (Bertrand Russell, *What I Believe*). The verb following a compound subject is usually plural: Christianity and humanity have gone hand in hand through history. See Agreement 1c.

Compound words

Compound words in written English are combinations of two or more words that are usually written as one word or hyphenated: *doorknob, notwithstanding, quarter-hour, father-in-law, drugstore*. Some compounds—especially those that express more than the sum of their parts—continue to be written as separate words: *the White House, high school, post office*. In speech these are usually distinguished by the stronger stress on the first words: compare *a white house* and *the White House*. See Group words, Hyphen, Plurals of nouns 5. For the spelling of particular compound words, consult your dictionary.

comprise

Traditionally, *comprise* means "consist of" or "include": The whole comprises its parts. In current usage the nearly opposite senses of "constitute," "compose," and "make up" are very common: "The four states that at one time comprised French Equatorial Africa . . ." (Harold G. Marcus, *American Historical Review*). But many writers, editors, and teachers insist that *comprise* be used only in its traditional sense. Since it is a relatively formal word, the more general *make up* is a better choice in most contexts.

concept

Concept as a vogue word is often used where *idea* would be more appropriate: "Research tests . . . whether concepts for [TV] shows are promising" (Jeff Greenfield, *New York Times Magazine*). See Vogue words.

Concluding an essay

Revise the ending of your paper to round out the discussion.

When you reach the end of your discussion, wrap it up. Don't simply stop, so that your reader wonders if the last page is missing. And don't keep rambling on until your reader is missing.

If your paper is a long one, you may need to review the ground you have covered, preferably in fresh phrasing. If the material is complex, you may need to pull together the points you have made and show how they add up and what they add up to. Short papers, like long ones, must add up to something.

When the reader of an essay finishes the last sentence and thinks "So what?" the writer has produced an essay that has no point, or—more likely—he has failed to make clear what that point is. A conclusion can't save a pointless essay by simply announcing a point; but by clarifying a fundamental causal relationship, by restating the essential argument, by bringing out an implication, the final paragraph or two can greatly strengthen an essay.

If your essay has been a voyage of discovery in which you've tried to define your own attitudes, you may end up with something like, "What I feel now is that my parents gave too much to me without thinking enough about me." Whether or not such a conclusion works depends on what has gone before. If that point has been gradually emerging throughout the essay, fine. If it hasn't—if, for example, you have only told about the size of your allowance, your charge accounts, the gifts on birthdays and at Christmas—then your ending will leave the reader perplexed and dissatisfied.

Final sentences should avoid tag ends and anticlimax as well as irrelevance. They should build to a firm conclusion, not trail away to a dying fall. They should wrap up the essay in such a way that the reader not only recognizes its completeness but feels satisfied that the last words were the right ones.

Concrete words

Concrete words name things that can be seen and touched: *box, building*. See Abstract language.

Conditional clauses

A conditional clause states a condition or action necessary for the truth or occurrence of what is expressed in the independent clause that the conditional clause modifies. *If, if not, unless,* and *whether* are the most common conjunctions for conditional clauses. Somewhat more formal words and phrases introducing conditions are *in case, provided, provided that, in the event that.*

1. For real or open conditions — statements of actual or reasonable conditions under which the main statement will hold — use the indicative verb forms:

If the red light is on, you know a train is in that block of track.
He will be there *unless something happens to his car.*
Whether he comes or not, I shall go just the same.

An older type of condition survives in some proverbs: Spare the rod and spoil the child. (*If you spare the rod,* you will spoil the child.)

2. For hypothetical conditions — theoretical but still possible — use *should . . . would* or the past tense: *If he should offer another $100,* I would take it. Or *If he raised his offer,* I would take it.

3. For contrary-to-fact conditions — those that cannot be met or that are untrue — use in general English the past tense of the verb in a present or future sense (If he *was* here, we would have seen him by now). In formal English, the plural form of the past tense is not uncommon in the third-person singular, usually called a subjunctive (If he *were* here . . .) and is firmly established in the first person (If I were you). Formal literary English may use inversion (Were he here . . .).

See *if, whether;* Subjunctive mood. References: Fries, pp. 104–107; Long, pp. 130–36; Quirk et al., pp. 745–49.

Conjunctions

Conjunction is the traditional term for a limited group of words without distinctive formal traits, which join words, phrases, clauses, or sentences. In this *Index* conjunctions are further defined and discussed according to their conventional classification:

Coordinating conjunctions (*and, but, for,* etc.)
Correlative conjunctions (*either . . . or, not only . . . but,* etc.)
Conjunctive adverbs (*however, therefore, consequently,* etc.)
Subordinating conjunctions (*as, because, since, so that, when,* etc.)

Since most conjunctions are also used as other parts of speech, especially as prepositions and adverbs (*as, for, so . . .*), the exact application of the term is not always possible, nor is the distinction between coordinating and subordinating conjunctions always apparent. Though relative pronouns (*who, which, that . . .*) also have a connective function, they are not classed as conjunctions. See Parts of speech.

conj Conjunctions and style

Make the conjunction marked more accurate or more appropriate to the style of the passage.

1. Conjunctions and meaning. In everyday speech we get along with a relatively small number of conjunctions — *and, as, but, so, when,* and a few others — because we can emphasize shades of meaning and exact relationships by pauses, tones, gestures. In writing, we lack these means of relating ideas, and a more thoughtful choice of connectives is essential.

Choose your conjunctions carefully. Don't toss in *but* when there is no contrast between statements (see *but* 2). Decide whether your meaning can be better conveyed by a coordinating conjunction or by a construction that uses the corresponding subordinating conjunction (*but* versus *though,* for example). And note distinctions between subordinating conjunctions. *As* means "because," but it is a weak *because* (see *as*); *while* may mean "although" or "whereas," but the core of its meaning relates to time. Sometimes, if a writer's thinking has been truly consecutive, the most satisfactory linkage will be implicit; a *therefore* or an *accordingly* will be unnecessary and unwelcome. See Transition and the articles on the particular conjunctions.

2. Conjunctions and style. Conjunctions should be appropriate to other traits of style. Often simple *but* is a better choice than *however:* The trail is easy walking as far as the canyon; from there on, however, it's no route for Sunday strollers. *Better:* . . . canyon, but from there on. . . . See Conjunctive adverbs 1.

Repeating a conjunction at the beginning of each element of a series makes each element distinct, avoids possible confusion, and achieves the advantages of strong rhythm and clear-cut parallelism:

I took an old shutter and fixed a sort of porch roof on it, and nailed it to a locust tree nearby, and set the nest with the eggs carefully on it. — Wendell Berry, *The Long-Legged House*

The tribal chants echoing from the seats were always fitting accompaniments to Mick's grunts and wails and hoots. — Robert Mazzocco, *New York Review of Books*

In contrast, omitting *and* before the last member of a short series may build an emphatic climax: "The most important of these, the most characteristic, the most misleading, is called *Some Glances at Current Linguistics*" (William H. Gass, *New Republic*). Or it may suggest that the series is only a sample, not a complete enumeration: "Many were the Northerners who, during and after the Civil War, went South to train, to educate, to rehabilitate Negro refugees and freedmen" (William H. Pease, *Journal of Southern History*).

See Conjunctive adverbs, Coordinating conjunctions, Correlative conjunctions, Subordinating conjunctions. See also Coordination, Subordination.

Conjunctive adverbs

A number of words that are primarily adverbs are used also as connectives. They are called conjunctive adverbs (or transitional adverbs or adverbial connectors or sentence connectors or sentence adverbials). Because their adverbial meaning remains rather prominent, their connective force is relatively weak. They are used after a semicolon between independent clauses and also after a period to introduce a new sentence. The most common conjunctive adverbs are:

accordingly	furthermore	namely
also (see *too*)	hence	nevertheless
anyhow	however	otherwise
anyway (informal)	indeed	still
besides	likewise	then
consequently	moreover	therefore

Adverb: No campaign, *however* violent, could make him vote.
Conjunction: The results were poor; *however,* we were not surprised.

1. Style. Because conjunctive adverbs are relatively heavy connectives, they are most appropriate in formal writing and in sentences of some length and complexity. In general writing they are more likely to serve as transitional devices between sentences than to connect clauses within a sentence. Excessive use of conjunctive adverbs is a major barrier to simple, straightforward writing.

Note these appropriate and inappropriate uses:

The armored saurians, the dodo, and a few other extinct creatures are supposed to have become unviable through their exaggerated specialties; usually, however, such excesses are not reached. [Appropriate with the formal sentence structure.]—Susanne K. Langer, *Philosophical Sketches*

In the morning I still felt sick; *nevertheless,* when the bugle sounded, I got up. [Inappropriately heavy in this context. Could substitute *but.* Better to rewrite as a complex sentence: Though I still felt sick the next morning, I got up when the bugle sounded.]

2. Position. Placing conjunctive adverbs inside their clauses instead of at the beginning gives the initial stress to more important words. When they are so placed, they are usually set off by commas, as in the first example in 1.

3. Punctuation. When used to introduce the second independent clause in a compound sentence, a conjunctive adverb is preceded by a semicolon, as in the second example in 1.

Connotation

Connotation means the associations a word or phrase carries, as distinguished from its denotation—what it refers to. It is connotation that makes the difference between *house* and *home,* between a *dutiful* child and an *obedient* one. See Denotation.

A writer needs to be conscious of what words connote as well as of what they signify. Although *flush* (in the sense "turn red") and *blush* are so close in meaning that they can often be substituted for each other, the overlap of the two words is not complete. We say "He flushed with anger" but not "He blushed with anger."

Although dictionaries give some information about the shades of difference among words, context tells more. The situation in which a word has regularly occurred, the variety of usage to which it belongs, the prevailing social attitude toward what it refers to and toward the people who use it (politicians, salesmen, children) all contribute to the public connotations of a word. Beyond that are the private connotations that stem from an individual's personal experiences. For one student, *school* has connotations of confinement, for another intellectual excitement, for still another sociability.

Heavily connotative words are sometimes called slanted, loaded, or evaluative; and writers are sometimes urged to replace them with words that are more nearly neutral. The advice is not always sound. We use words not only to give information about things but to express our own feelings about them and to influence the attitudes of others. It is natural to describe an action we admire as *courageous*, one we deplore as *foolhardy*. Neutral terms are preferable only when we are in fact neutral or when we are striving to give that impression.

Construction

A construction is a group of words which stand in some grammatical relationship to each other, as that of modifier and headword (black cat), preposition and object (to the roof), or subject and predicate (They walked slowly). Any grammatical pattern may therefore be spoken of as a construction.

contact

The verb *contact*, meaning "get in touch with, communicate with" (Will you contact Mr. Hubble?), is more acceptable in nonbusiness contexts today than it was a generation ago, though it remains rare in formal usage. Its popularity in general English may be explained by its inclusiveness, embracing as it does the notions of "call," "write," "visit," and even communication through intermediaries: "He contacted a leading American corporation, but the corporation heads were skeptical" (Grace M. Spruch, *Saturday Review*). See Divided usage. References: Bryant, pp. 60–61; Copperud, pp. 59–60.

Context

The word *context* is used in different ways.

1. Verbal context. In writing, the context is the discourse that surrounds and limits a word or passage. The context is tremendously important in revealing the particular meanings of words. The word *check*, for example, has forty or so dictionary senses. Yet in actual use, in definite contexts, it gives no trouble:

They were able to *check* the fire at the highway.
The treasurer's books *check* with the vouchers.
He drew a *check* for the entire amount.
The tablecloth had a red and white *check*.
He moved his bishop and shouted *"Check!"*
With difficulty he held his temper in *check*.
He had the *check* list on the desk in front of him.

And so on. Though *check* has more senses than most, a great many English words have more than one sense, so a particular meaning must be gathered from the context — and ordinarily can be. Context gives clues not only to the particular denotative sense of a word, as illustrated with *check,* but also to its connotative value. This fact is recognized whenever someone says, "By itself that might seem insulting, but in the context it couldn't possibly give offense." See Parts of speech 2c.

2. The context of allusions and quotations. An honest writer takes care that allusions and quotations are true to the context in which they occur, that they really represent the ideas of their authors. The complaints of politicians and government officials that their words have been quoted "out of context" are often justified.

3. Rhetorical context. Every piece of writing occurs in a rhetorical situation or context, which includes the writer, the subject, the writer's purpose, and the audience. The choice of material, the organization, and the style of a good essay all reflect the writer's sense of the rhetorical context. See Rhetoric.

continual(ly), continuous(ly)

In the sense "uninterrupted," with reference to time, formal stylists prefer *continuous(ly)*, but *continual(ly)* is also used: For weeks we observed an almost continuous eruption of the volcano. In the sense "recurring rapidly and often," the situation is reversed — conservatives insist on *continual(ly)*, but *continuous(ly)* is also standard: The governor broke his promises, not just repeatedly but continually.

Contractions

In writing, contractions like *can't* are forms that show pronunciation, usually by substituting an apostrophe for one or more letters of the standard spelling. They occur regularly in informal usage but are notably rare in formal. In general usage a writer will favor or avoid them just as he makes other rhetorical choices, considering the rhythm of the particular sentence, how much distance he wants between himself and his readers, and whether the subject and the occasion call for a relaxed or a restrained style. Contractions are necessary, of course, in actual representations of speech, as in dialog. See *have* 3.

contrast, compare

Contrast points out differences; *compare to* points out likenesses; *compare with* does both. See *compare, contrast*.

controversial

Controversial (a controversial book, a controversial person) labels the subject a source of disagreement, of argument. Unfortunately the word has acquired a connotation of warning: Better watch out for this one—some people disapprove! If the subject you are writing about has caused significant controversy, tell what the controversy is and why it's significant.

Conversion

When a word that usually functions as one part of speech is used as another part of speech, it is said to have undergone conversion or functional shift: a *must* book; a good *read;* in the *know;* the experience of *parenting;* I wouldn't *fault* him. The principle of functional shift is well established, but a writer should be cautious in experimenting with new conversions. The student who wrote the following sentence was experimenting—unsuccessfully: She stooped as if to *negative* her height.

convince, persuade

For a long time some uses of *convince* and *persuade* have overlapped: He persuaded (convinced) me of the necessity for action; He convinced (persuaded) me that I should act. *Convince* is now common in still a third context, where *persuade* is traditional: "Advisers to President Ford have apparently convinced him to avoid a meeting with the exiled Russian author, Alexander I. Solzhenitsyn" *(New York Times).* The use of "convince . . . to " instead of "persuade . . . to" (persuaded him to avoid) is deplored by conservative stylists. Reference: Copperud, p. 61.

Coordinate

Two or more grammatically equivalent words, phrases, or clauses are said to be coordinate: *bread* and *butter; in the sink* or *on the stove; dancing, singing, laughing; When he lectured* and *when he prayed,* everyone listened; *He wrenched his back,* and *she broke her leg.*

Coordinating conjunctions

The coordinating conjunctions, *and, but, for, nor, or, so,* and *yet,* are used to connect two or more elements of equal grammatical rank:

Words: books *and* papers; books, pamphlets, *or* magazines

Phrases: in one ear *and* out the other

Dependent clauses: She . . . wrote to young Lewis Rutherford cheerfully enough that his sister looked lovely and that the new baby was delightful.—R. W. B. Lewis, *Edith Wharton*

Independent clauses: At present the common cause between eccentric and hippie is proper hatred of the way things are, and the common inclination is for personal justice.—Jerome Lettvin, *Natural History*

Sentences: Perhaps I should wish that I had liked him better. But I do not wish it.—Renata Adler, *New Yorker*

See Conjunctions and style, Coordination, Series.

coord Coordination

Correct the faulty coordination.

Faulty coordination is not a lapse in grammar or usage; it is a failure to make logical relationships clear. Faulty coordination means that in the particular context the material calls for a relationship or emphasis different from the one reflected in the writer's use or arrangement of independent clauses.

1. Some examples of faulty coordination result from joining two statements that don't belong together: The condition of the house is deplorable, and the dining nook seats six comfortably. Revision should take the two statements out of the coordinate relationship by putting them in separate – and separated – sentences.

2. Sometimes faulty coordination can be corrected by turning one of the independent clauses into a dependent clause. "He went to France for the summer, and his novel was published" suggests that there is an obvious causal relationship between his going to France and the publication of his novel. In some contexts, this might make sense. But if the only relationship that can be established is a temporal one – two events happening at about the same time but not otherwise related – the sentence needs to be revised: "When he was spending the summer in France, his novel was published," or "At the time his novel was published, he was spending the summer in France," or in some other way.

3. In the example above, coordination might be confusing or misleading. Sometimes it is simply ineffective:

When I reached the intersection, I found a group of people gathered around a wrecked car. The left front tire had had a blowout, and the car had gone out of control and rolled over, and the driver was obviously dead.

The independent clause "the driver was obviously dead" needs to be taken out of the coordinate relationship it is in; to gain its proper effect, it should be made a separate sentence. Left in the series, it implies that the death of the driver had no more importance than the blowout and the crash.

See Subordination. Reference: Sledd, pp. 275–81.

Correlative conjunctions

Some coordinating conjunctions are used in pairs: *both . . . and, either . . . or, neither . . . nor, not only . . . but [also], whether . . . or.* Of these correlatives, *neither . . . nor* and *not only . . . but [also]* are slightly formal, showing a more conscious planning than is common in informal or general English: "Neither the gold drain nor the beautification of America deters them from going abroad" (Thomas L. Hughes, *Foreign Affairs*).

Like coordinating conjunctions, correlatives normally join expressions of the same grammatical rank:

Nouns: He said that both *the novel* and *the play* were badly written.

Adjectives: He must have been either *drunk* or *crazy.*

Prepositional phrases: They can be had not only *in the usual sizes* but also *in the outsizes.*

Verb phrases: The wind scoop not only *caught the cool breezes* but also *picked up the captain's conversation.*

Clauses: Whether *Mitch thumbed a ride through the mountains* or *Jenny made the long bus trip*, they were determined to be together during the vacation.

Like similar rules, the rule that constructions built on correlative conjunctions must be strictly parallel should be broken when it gets in the way of natural, rhythmic expression.

See Shifted constructions. Reference: Pooley, pp. 91–92.

could(n't) care less

Formerly (and too frequently) a lack of concern was expressed by "I couldn't care less." Recently the negative has been dropped; now "I could care less" is used to mean the same thing: "kids who never heard of Little Richard and could care less" (Ellen Willis, *New Yorker*). Neither form is suited to college writing, except perhaps to point up triteness in dialog.

Count nouns

Count nouns name things that can be counted as separate units. See Mass nouns, Noun 3c.

Counter words

Counter words are usually words of general approval or disapproval or else rather abstract words that are overused. Like slang, they are popular and current; unlike slang, they are ordinary words, used with no spark of originality. In Elizabethan times, *fair* as in "fair maid" was a counter word. In modern speech *fine, great, lovely, nice, pretty, poor* are samples. Some counter words do no harm in informal writing, but they are no substitute for more precise terms. See Vogue words.

couple

The primary meaning of the collective noun *couple* is "two persons or things associated in some way," as in "a married couple." In general and informal usage it is equivalent to the numeral *two* (a couple of pencils) or to *a few* (a couple of minutes). The *of* is frequently omitted in speech and informal writing and sometimes in general: "Yet some of his classmates do not sleep through the night, and live happily on a couple hours sleep" (Gay Gaer Luce and Julius Segal, *Insomnia*); but this use offends many readers. See Collective nouns.

Course names

In general discussions, only the names of college subjects that are proper adjectives (the languages) are capitalized. In writing a list of courses including one or more of these proper adjectives, it is possible to capitalize them all for consistency (and courtesy), though the distinction is usually kept: I am taking biology, chemistry, European history, English composition, and French. Names of departments are capitalized (the Department of History), and so are names of subjects when accompanied by a course number (History 347).

credibility

In journalese, *credibility* was joined to the vogue word *gap* to refer to public loss of faith in President Johnson's statements about the Vietnam War. In the Nixon administration the gap became a gulf, and *gap* went out of vogue. But *credibility* moved into officialese and flourished. Readers should remember that *honesty* and *credibility* (what will be believed) are by no means synonymous. Writers should shun *credibility* as a vogue word that has some of the connotations of *image.*

Cumulative sentence

A cumulative sentence makes its main statement at or near the beginning, usually in a short independent clause, and then goes on to add details in modifiers that are free or detachable. The modifiers may be parallel to each other:

Ragtime is a unique and beautiful work of art about American destiny, built of fact and logical fantasy, governed by music heard and sensed, responsive to cinema both as method and historical datum, shaken by a continental pulse. — Stanley Kauffmann, *Saturday Review*

Recognized and greeted by restaurant personnel, Zero becomes manic, draping hat and coat onto the headwaiter, wrapping his arms and one leg around the manager, then bellowing his way into the main room. — Robert Alan Arthur, *Esquire*

Or they may be built onto each other:

The cars have been piling into the infield by the hundreds, parking in there on the clay and the grass, every whichway, angled down and angled up, this way and that, where the ground is uneven, these beautiful blazing brand-new cars with the sun exploding off the windshields and the baked enamel and the glassy lacquer, hundreds, thousands of cars stacked this way and that in the infield with the sun bolting down and no shade, none at all, just a couple of Coca-Cola stands out there. — Tom Wolfe, *Esquire*

As the last example shows, the cumulative sentence offers a way of clustering or massing details; Wolfe's one sentence does the work of a dozen on the subject-verb-object pattern. Because it observes the natural order of speech — main statement first, then qualifications and particulars — a cumulative sentence can and often does give the impression of ease and naturalness. But unless the modifiers add strength or richness or support the initial assertion, the sentence may wander off into insignificant or irrelevant detail. In itself, a cumulative sentence is neither good nor bad. What counts is the skill with which it is constructed and the effect that it produces.

Compare Periodic sentence. Reference: Christensen, Ch. 1.

cupfuls, cupsful

Cupfuls is usual. See *-ful, full.*

curriculum

Curriculum has the Latin plural *curricula* and the English *curriculums.* The adjective is *curricular;* the compound adjective with *extra* is usually written as one word: *extracurricular.*

D

 **Dangling modifiers**

Revise the sentence so that the expression marked is clearly related to the word it is intended to modify.

A phrase is said to dangle (or to be misrelated) if its position makes it seem to relate to a word that can only make nonsense of the meaning or if, in a context that demands an explicit relationship, it has no clear relation to any word in the sentence.

In the sentence "Looking farther to the left, we saw the spire of a church," *looking* obviously modifies *we;* if the subject of the verb *look* were reconstructed, it would be *we:* [We were] looking farther to the left, *we* saw the spire of a church. In the sentence "Defined in psychological terms, a fanatic is a man who consciously overcompensates a secret doubt" (Aldous Huxley, *Proper Studies*), it is clear that *defined* modifies *fanatic,* for the same reason. The subject of *defined* must be *fanatic:* [A *fanatic* is] defined in psychological terms, *a fanatic* is a man who consciously overcompensates a secret doubt.

When the phrase does not refer to the subject—that is, when it has a different subject from the subject of the main clause—then the modifier dangles. In the sentence "To get the most out of a sport, the equipment must be in perfect condition," the reconstructed subject of the introductory phrase would be something like "[For *someone*] to get the most out of a sport, *the equipment* must be in perfect condition." But since *someone* is different from *equipment, someone* should not be dropped. If the sentence "At eleven, my family moved to Denver" is reconstructed, it reads "[When *I* was] eleven, *my family* moved to Denver." *I* does not equal *family,* so *I* should not be deleted. In the following examples, try to reconstruct the subject of the introductory phrase:

Upon telling my story to my adviser, he stopped and thought.

Born in England in 1853, John MacDowell's seafaring activities began after he had migrated to this country. [This type of dangling modifier, in which the phrase refers to a noun—*MacDowell*—represented only by its genitive form modifying the subject, sometimes appears in edited prose.]

Modifiers that dangle may also follow the independent clause:

Many signs read "Visit Our Snake Farm," driving toward the city.

Dangling modifiers are to be avoided chiefly because educated readers do not expect to find them. As a rule there is no real question of the intended meaning of the sentence, and in context the dangling phrases are not apt to be conspicuously awkward or as nonsensical as they seem in isolation. But they are distracting in any writing that is meant to be read attentively. By forcing the reader to search for (or guess at) the related noun, they can make a piece of writing needlessly difficult.

Such dangling constructions should not be confused with absolute phrases, in which the phrase has its own subject. Compare an absolute phrase, a correct modifier, and a dangling modifier:

Absolute phrase: The car paid for with my last dollar, I was at last out of debt.

Correct modifier: Paid for with my last dollar, the car became my first piece of personal property.

Dangling modifier: Paid for with my last dollar, I drove the car away elated.

In revising what you write, examine carefully every introductory verbal phrase, for the phrases most likely to dangle are those that begin with participles or infinitives or that contain gerunds. If you continue to have trouble relating them to the words they should modify, you might try giving them up and using clauses instead.

See Absolute phrases, Gerunds, Infinitives, Participles. References: Byrant, pp. 64–65; Copperud, pp. 64–66; William H. Pixton, *CCC*, May 1973, pp. 193–99; Roberts, pp. 351–52, 358–59, 366–67.

Dash

The dash—typed as two hyphens not spaced away from the words they separate—can be used singly to link a following word or word group to the main structure of a sentence or in pairs to enclose a word or word group that interrupts the main structure. Enclosing dashes indicate greater separation from the core context than enclosing commas, less separation—or less formality—than parentheses.

If used sparingly, the dash suggests a definite tone, often a note of surprise or an emotional emphasis equivalent to a mild exclamation. If used regularly in place of commas, colons, and semicolons, it loses all its distinctiveness and becomes merely a sloppy substitute for conventional punctuation. At its best the dash is an abrupt, emphatic mark.

1. Before a kicker. The single dash is often used to throw emphasis on what follows, which may be dramatic, ironic, humorous:

The old nations still live in the hearts of men, and love of the European nation is not yet born—if it ever will be.—Raymond Aron, *Daedalus*

We do not question the right of an author to spell, capitalize, and punctuate as he wishes—provided he follows consistently a recognizable system.—John Benbow, *Manuscript and Proof*

2. Before a summary or illustration. The dash is used singly or in pairs with word groups that summarize what has just been said or provide details or examples:

It takes a cataclysm—an invasion, a plague, or some other communal disaster—to open their eyes to the transitoriness of the "eternal order."—Eric Hoffer, *The True Believer*

He was strongly in favor of peace—that is to say, he liked his wars to be fought at a distance and, if possible, in the name of God.—George Dangerfield, *The Death of Liberal England*

3. Between independent clauses. A dash is sometimes used to link independent clauses when the second expands, develops, completes, or makes a surprising addition to the first. In this function, it is less formal than a colon:

And yet they had a thing in common, this oddest of odd couples—they both cared about the social graces.—George Frazier, *Esquire*

In one respect, Welles was unique among the Cabinet members—he did not think himself a better man than the President.—Margaret Leech, *Reveille in Washington*

4. Enclosing interrupting elements. Dashes are used to set off words and word groups, including complete sentences, that break with the main structure of a sentence:

Fitzgerald's people believed in their world—it really mattered who won the Princeton-Harvard game, it really meant something to appear at the theatre or the opera—and because they believed in their world they owned it.—Frank Conroy, *Esquire*

References: Summey, pp. 101-104; Whitehall, pp. 123, 129.

data

Formal usage follows the Latin, treating *datum* as singular and *data* as plural. In general usage *datum* is rare, and *data* is treated as a collective noun, taking a singular verb to emphasize the whole—"Data so far available makes it seem doubtful" (John Mecklin, *Fortune*)—and a plural verb to emphasize the parts—"There were still a good many data in the 33-page report" (William H. Honan, *New York Times Magazine*). References: Bryant, pp. 66–67; Copperud, pp. 66–67; Pooley, pp. 59–60.

Dates

The typical American form for writing dates is "August 19, 1976." The form "19 August 1976" prevails in British usage and in American military usage and is gaining popularity in the United States. If the full date is given within a sentence, the year is usually set off by commas; and if the day of the week is also given, full comma treatment is used: The legislature met on Wednesday, December 13, 1905. When only month and year are given (in August 1976 he died), no commas are necessary, though they are often used in formal styles.

The year is not written out in words except in formal social announcements, invitations, wills, and some other ceremonial situations and at the beginning of a sentence—and most writers manage to avoid beginning sentences with the year. Expressions like "January in the year 1885" are wasteful: "January 1885" is enough. In business writing and references, months having more than four (or five) letters are often abbreviated: Jan. 3, 1970.

In writing dates in figures only, American practice is month-day-year: 9/17/76; European practice is day-month-year, sometimes with the month in roman numerals: 17-IX-76.

Deadwood

Words or phrases that add nothing at all to the meaning or effectiveness of a statement are deadwood. See Wordiness.

Declension

Declension means the list or listing of the forms of nouns and pronouns (and in many languages the forms of adjectives and participles also) to show number (singular, dual, plural), gender (masculine, feminine, neuter), and case (nominative, genitive, accusative, and others in different languages). The English noun has two regular forms: the form ending in *s,* which serves as genitive and plural, though these are written differently (*sister's, sisters', sisters*), and the form without an ending, which is used for all other relationships. Personal pronouns in English have from two forms (*it, its*) to four (*I, my, mine, me*). Adjectives and adverbs are compared but not declined.

Deduction

Deduction is the process of drawing a conclusion from propositions known to be true, or accepted as true, or assumed to be true. You are reasoning deductively when you notice a ring around the moon and say, "We're in for some bad weather." Your unspoken premise, based on your own experience or perhaps on what you've read somewhere or heard from someone, is that the appearance of a ring around the moon means that bad weather is bound to follow. The essence of the deductive process is the *must* – drawing an inevitable conclusion (the weather will be bad) from two related propositions: (1) a ring around the moon forecasts bad weather and (2) there's a ring around the moon.

For the conclusion of a deductive train of reasoning to be valid and true, correct inferences must be made from true premises. See Fallacies, Logical thinking, Syllogisms. Compare Induction.

Deep structure

Generative-transformational grammarians distinguish between the surface form of a sentence and the more abstract relationships in its deep structure. In the five sentences "Bill bought Jane a stereo," "Bill bought a stereo for Jane," "Jane was bought a stereo by Bill," "A stereo was bought for Jane by Bill," and "It was a stereo that Bill bought for Jane," the surface subjects are *Bill, Bill, Jane, a stereo,* and *it;* but at a deeper level all the sentences have the same subject or agent – Bill – since he did the buying regardless of the form the expression of the fact is given. Yet this deep-structure subject *(Bill)* is the object of the preposition in the third and fourth sentences, and the deep-structure or underlying object *(a stereo)* is the subject on the surface of the fourth sentence.

Such a concept of sentences may enlarge your view of the sentences you write. You can experiment with ways of expressing the same deep grammatical relationships through different surface structures, noting the varying rhetorical effects of each. Our sentences about Bill and Jane and the stereo are an example. And each of these could also be embedded in a larger structure in various ways:

When Bill bought Jane a stereo, he surprised her.
Bill's buying Jane a stereo surprised her.
Jane was surprised by Bill's buying her a stereo.
That Bill bought Jane a stereo surprised her.
For Bill to have bought Jane a stereo surprised her.
The buying of a stereo for her by Bill surprised Jane.

These are only a few of the possibilities. Usually such considerations as focus, tone, transition from one sentence to another, and the rhythm of the sentence in its context will help you choose, often intuitively, between one surface structure and another.

This view of sentences can also sharpen your awareness of ambiguity and its sources. Although some sentences are ambiguous because a particular word can be interpreted in more than one way, others are ambiguous because the same surface structure may derive from two different deep structures. "Visting relatives can be boring" is ambiguous because *visiting relatives* may be derived from a deep structure with *relatives* as object (someone visits relatives) or from one with *relatives* as subject (relatives visit someone). Such ambiguity can be resolved by providing a surface structure to which only one deep structure can be related: To visit relatives can be boring.

See Clauses 2, Grammar 3c, Transformation. References: Noam Chomsky in Hungerford, Robinson, and Sledd, pp. 108–50; Paul Postal in *Language and Learning,* ed. Janet Emig, James T. Fleming, and Helen M. Popp (New York: Harcourt, 1965), pp. 153–75.

definitely

Definitely has been overused as a counter word to give emphasis or in the sense of "certainly" (I will not do it, definitely; He was definitely worse than usual; She definitely uses those methods; But definitely!) instead of in its more limited sense of "clear-cut, in a definite manner."

Definition

1. Types of definition. Definitions are of two main kinds:
a. A lexical or dictionary definition tells how a word is used in different contexts. Lexical definitions that appear in everyday

prose often use the verb *means* or *expresses* or, when connotations are foremost, *suggests: expectorate* means "spit"; *hooked,* applied to drug use, suggests hopeless addiction.

b. A real or logical definition (sometimes called a philosophical definition) identifies the essential characteristics of the thing that is the referent of the word. It joins subject and predicate with a form of the verb *be* on the model of the equation

term-to-be-defined	=	genus	+	differentia(e)
A ballad	is	a song		that tells a story

Thus, in "Logic is a specialized language dealing with the relationship of truth and falsity within a language" (Dwight Bolinger), *language* is the genus, and the two differentiae are *specialized* and *dealing with the relationship of truth and falsity within a language.*

Logicians have formulated rules for real definitions. One is that the definition must include all things designated by the term but exclude anything to which the term does not properly apply. Thus "A bachelor is a person who is unmarried" is unsatisfactory because the genus is too broad. In "A shoe is a leather covering for the foot," one of the differentiae—*leather*—is too restrictive.

Other traditional rules are these: A definition should not be circular (Hostility is the state of being hostile). Except when loss or lack is a distinguishing characteristic (as in *baldhead* and *bastard*), a term should not be defined negatively (Liberty is the absence of restraint). A term should not be defined metaphorically (Television is the opiate of the people), nor should a term be defined by a synonym (A pail is a bucket).

These rules have all been laid down in the interest of precision, and they should be observed when rigor is required (in answering examination questions on the special terms of a subject matter, for instance). But for some purposes the pattern of the logical definition is too confining or smacks too much of textbook style. Not all our definitions require the rigor of formal logic, and normally we want to say more about a term than can be compressed into the genus + differentiae formula.

2. Definition in exposition and argument. As a writer, you will have occasion to use both lexical and real definitions. When you do, you should make clear which kind you are using.

a. In the stipulative definition, a variety of lexical definition, the writer gives a word a special, limited sense that is necessary for his specific purpose:

I do not use the word "myth" to imply something entirely false. Rather, I use it to connote a complex of profoundly held attitudes and values which condition the way men view the world and understand their experience. — Richard Weiss, *The American Myth of Success*

A stipulative definition shouldn't be so remote from ordinary usage that it won't be taken seriously. Most readers will go along with the writer who says, "In this paper I will use the word *teen-*

ager to include twenty-year-olds," but will probably stop reading if they find, "In this paper *teenager* means everybody who knows what's really going on."

b. An extended definition gives information about the essential nature of a thing, like the one-sentence logical definition, but it is not restricted to the processes of classification and division that yield the genus and differentiae. It may use *description*, telling what the thing looks like; *chronology*, giving its genesis and development; *example*, giving instances of it; *comparison*, saying what it is like; *contrast*, saying what it is not; *causal analysis*, indicating what circumstances produced it and what consequences it has; and *testimony*, telling what authorities have said about it. Etymologies and synonyms may also be used to develop a definition. What the central elements in a definition are depends on what is being defined and also on where the writer's interest lies. A psychologist and a biologist define *man* in different ways.

An extended definition may be simply explanatory, with the aim of giving information about the subject in a readable, interesting essay. Or it may pave the way for further analysis: once he has established his definition of *tragedy*, a writer can go on to show that a new play is, or is not, a tragedy. Defining is also one way of conducting an argument. When opponents of legalized abortion argue that abortion is murder and its proponents argue that it is not, the issue is one of definition. Defining is often geared not to the purpose of explaining but to proving that a belief is sound or a policy wise.

3. Phrasing a definition. When a definition is given the prominence of a separate sentence, subject and complement — whether joined by *is* or by *means* — should normally be the same part of speech: noun matched by noun, adjective by adjective, and so on. Consider the sentence "Defining is to locate a thing in its class and then separate it from other members of the class." The meaning is clear, but the sentence would be easier to read if the two parts matched: "To define is to locate . . ." or "Defining is locating . . . and then separating. . . ."

Definitions that begin with *where* or *when* (Erosion is when rain washes away the topsoil) are common but are objected to in formal contexts. They occasionally occur — in this example metaphorically — in literary works of established reputation: "Morning is when I am awake and there is a dawn in me" (Henry David Thoreau, *Walden*). See *when, where*.

Degree of comparison

Smaller, smallest, more handsome, most handsome are expressions of degree. See Comparison of adjectives and adverbs.

Degrees

Ordinarily, academic degrees are not given with a person's name except in college publications, reference works, and articles and letters where the degrees indicate competence in a particular field, as in a doctor's comment on a medical matter. When used, the names of the degrees are abbreviated, and the abbreviations are separated from the person's name by a comma; in alumni publications they are often followed by the year in which the degrees were granted:

Harvey J. Preble, A.B. [*or* B.A.]   Harvey J. Preble, A.B. '08
Jane Thomson, Ph.D.   Jane Thomson, Ph.D. '61
Royce Walton, B. Arch., was master of ceremonies.

As a rule, except in reference lists, only the highest degree in an academic professional field is mentioned.

If the institution granting the degree is named, the following form is usual:

George H. Cook, A.B. (Grinnell), A.M. (Indiana), Ph.D. (Chicago)

Demonstrative adjectives and pronouns
The determiners *this, that, these, those* have traditionally been called demonstrative adjectives or demonstrative pronouns, according to their use in a sentence:

Adjectives: This car is fast. *Those* people never think of anyone else.
Pronouns: These cost more than *those. That*'s a good idea.

See Determiners; *kind, sort;* Pronouns 6; *that; this.*

Denotation
The denotation of a word is what the word refers to, as described in a dictionary definition: fuel = a substance that is burned to produce heat or power. When heating oil is in short supply or gasoline doubles in price, *fuel* takes on additional overtones, or shades of meaning, that go far beyond this literal definition. See Connotation.

Dependent clauses
A dependent, or subordinate, clause has a subject and verb but can't stand as a sentence: If he comes today. See Clauses.

Description
Description normally deals with the visible and tangible, telling how a thing looks or feels or tastes or smells. Abstractions can be described, too, but a writer who undertakes to produce a word picture of grief or pride or chaos is likely to find that he can best present them in terms of physical sensations. Description feeds on the concrete.

Although most common in narration, description is used in all types of writing. Discussions of all subjects, except perhaps the most theoretical, include patches of description, for only description can help the reader visualize a subject or know the truth about it through sensory experience.

1. Kinds of description. In describing an object or a scene, the writer may try to present what any impartial observer would

see — to come as close as he can to putting into words the image
a camera would record. Or he may try to present a scene as it
appears to an observer whose perception is highly colored by
emotion — for example, a fire in which he was temporarily
trapped or a fire as he imagines it appeared to someone who was
trapped in it. Thus descriptions range from the precise, informative reports of technical writing to impressionistic sketches.

2. The function of details. Most descriptive passages fall somewhere between factual reporting and poetic evocation; the writer tries to provide a picture of reality so clear that the actual
scene or object would be immediately recognizable and, in addition, to make the reader aware of how the writer (or the writer's
imagined observer) feels about it and understand why he feels
as he does.

Such description, if successful, will make the subject particular and individual. Second Beach in Middletown, Rhode Island,
will not be described in details that apply equally well to every
beach on the Atlantic coast. Instead, the writer will search out
the details that give the beach its special character and convey
them in words that communicate what he feels as well as what
he perceives. It is always best to make the details evoke the feeling. Outright statements of emotions (I was excited by the big
surf) or judgments (The beach is best in late September) are
singularly unconvincing in the absence of the stimulus that
gave rise to them. If the details are authentic, such assertions
become unnecessary, for the appropriate generalization will
have formed in the reader's mind. Good description shows; it
doesn't need to tell.

3. The selection and organization of details. When an observer
who has looked long and hard at his subject (even in memory)
begins to write about it, he has far more details than he can use.
Selection is vital. A profusion of unrelated details will only be-
wilder the reader. The beachcomber will not name all the shore
birds any more than he will number the grains of sand. Which
birds? What details about the sand? Leo Rockas gives a clue:
"The night club in Mozambique need only be plainly presented;
the corner supermarket had better be invested with novelty." As
in every writing situation, then, the audience must be taken into
account. What is commonplace to one group of readers will be
exotic to another.

Organization of the details in a description should be determined by the subject and the writer's purpose. Does the reader
need to understand the spatial relations in order to picture the
scene? The directions must be clear, with the writer making use
of indicators such as *here, there, on top, in the middle, below, to
the left, on the right, beyond, in the distance, on the horizon.*

4. The language of description. Again, selection counts. A rush
of adjectives may call attention away from the scene to the writing. Descriptive prose should be neither flat nor overexcited; it

should suit the subject and the feeling the subject is intended to evoke. Details can be conveyed most directly and compellingly in language that is concrete and specific. Concrete diction gives things color, shape, and texture; specific terms give them particularity and individuality.

See Abstract language, Adjectives and style, Details, Point of view. Reference: Leo Rockas, *Modes of Rhetoric* (New York: St. Martin's Press, 1964), pp. 29–54.

 ## Details

Develop the passage or the topic more fully by giving pertinent details.

The symbol *Det* is shorthand for "Give an example" or "What's your evidence?" or "Make this specific" or "Don't just *say* the house is in bad condition; make me *see* that it is." In revising a paper so marked, you need to supply particulars that will make your ideas or your impressions clearer, your argument more convincing, or your essay more readable.

The details of a physical object are its parts (the *webbed feet* of a duck) or its attributes or qualities (*scorching* wind, *smooth* leather). The details of an abstraction like pride are the words and attitudes and actions that justify our saying that someone is proud. The details of a novel are specifics of plot, character, style, and so on. Thus the details of any subject are its particulars. In a good paper they fit together, making a pattern, leading to a generalization, or inviting the reader to draw an inference. Besides giving substance to an essay, details enliven writing, capturing and holding the reader's interest. See Description, Induction. Reference: Christensen, Ch. 2.

Determiners

Determiner is a general term for several types of words, other than adjectives, that precede nouns in English. Chosen usually to fit the semantic context, determiners may be subclassified as articles (*a/an, the*), prearticles (*none, all, half, most, much,* etc.), and postarticles (*two, three; first, second; first, last; former, latter;* etc.). The three subclasses are illustrated in "*half* of *the last* installment."

The prearticles can serve as transitional devices between sentences when the noun has been deleted:

Several boys walked in. A *few* were wearing black leather jackets.

Demonstrative articles and the postarticles can serve the same function:

These were the last ones. The *first* were more interesting.

Genitive, or possessive, forms can also function as determiners "George's book was very interesting" becomes in some contexts "*George's* was very interesting"; and "My father is a teacher" becomes in some contexts "*Mine* is a teacher." In "George's book" and "My father" the genitive form occurs where the definite article *the* would occur. Since they occur in identical positions in the noun phrase, the definite article and the genitives belong to the same class of words.

See Parts of speech. References: Copperud, pp. 70–71; Arthur Norman in *Readings in Applied English Linguistics,* ed. Harold B. Allen, 2nd ed. (New York: Appleton, 1964), pp. 156–63.

Dialects

A dialect is the speech (sounds, forms, meanings) characteristic of a fairly definite region or group. It is speech that does not attract attention to itself among the inhabitants of a region (regional dialect) or among members of a group (group or class dialect) but that would be recognizably different to an outsider. Because the educated middle class is the dominant group in the United States, its dialect is called standard English.

The term *dialect* is also applied to written expression: there are writing dialects as well as speech dialects. Standard written English is the appropriate form for college work. But this does not mean that a college student should set out to purge his writing of all the words and word forms and phrases from a regional dialect or another group dialect. The guiding principle should be appropriateness: What are you writing about? Who is your audience? If you are reminiscing about your childhood or describing your homesickness, don't resist the natural impulse to use dialectal expressions. If your instructor and your classmates are familiar with the dialect you grew up using, you may also use it effectively in other essays. The more formal and impersonal your topic and the broader your audience, the less appropriate dialectal usages will be. In any circumstances avoid those that are likely to mystify your readers or strike them as simply ungrammatical (see *grammatical, ungrammatical*).

See English language 3. References: Hungerford, Robinson, and Sledd, Part II; Raven I. McDavid, Jr., *PMLA,* May 1966, pp. 7–17.

d Diction

Replace the word marked with one that is more exact, more appropriate, or more effective.

Diction means choice of words. Good diction is exact, appropriate, and effective. Faulty diction either fails to convey the writer's meaning fully or accurately or in some other way disappoints the expectations of the reader.

1. Choose the exact word. The exact word is the one that conveys better than any other the meaning you intend. Some mistakes in word choice result from confusing two words that resemble each other in some way *(delusion* for *illusion, predominate* for *predominant).* Others result from confusing two words that, although similar in basic meaning, are not interchangeable in all contexts. We can speak of a *durable* friendship or a *lasting* friendship; but though we describe shoes as *durable*, we do not say shoes are *lasting*. Idiom allows "the oldest existing manuscript" but not "the oldest living manuscript." In some instances, finding the exact word means searching for a more specific one, as *complained* is more specific and may be a better choice than *remarked*. Often it means settling for simpler expression. If you reach for a fancy phrase, you may come up with one that has nothing to do with your meaning: Because of pressure to do well on examinations, a *disquieting aura pervades* me even when I am relaxing. See Connotation, Dictionaries, Idiom, Meaning, Wrong word.

2. Choose the appropriate word. The words should fit both the subject and the relation between writer and audience. If your subject is technical, complex, serious, and if you are addressing readers who know something about it and want to learn more, you will probably use a rather formal vocabulary. If your subject is light or humorous and if you know your readers well or want to establish a sense of intimacy with them, you'll express yourself more informally.

Though a style can err on the side of excessive informality, probably the more common fault in college papers is inappropriate formality — "big" words selected more to impress an audience than to express meaning. Big words need not be long — *deem* (for *think*) is as big as *domicile* (for *house*); they are "big" in the sense of "pretentious." *Ignominious, cantankerous, lachrymose, florid, inscrutable, mortified, chronicled* — these words may be big in one context but not in another. You can catch the big words in what you write by reading your essays aloud. If you have used words that you would be unlikely to speak in or out of the classroom, reconsider them. See if you can't substitute words that are just as precise but more natural to you.

Although formal, general, and informal English overlap and are frequently mixed in current prose, you can seriously weaken what you write if you mix the varieties of usage carelessly. When informal name-calling interrupts a thoughtful paper on welfare, when high-flown poetic clichés break the mood of an honest piece of nature description, when *know-how* is applied to a painter's technique or *finalize* to a composer's efforts, readers will be distracted and disturbed. If you mix usage deliberately, have a good reason for doing so — to amuse or startle your readers, perhaps, or to emphasize the point you're making. Keep your audience in mind, and avoid overkill. If you find yourself being criticized for mixing usage, read and reread your essays before turning them in, and maybe ask a friend to read them as well, with an eye open for sore thumbs and an ear cocked for sour notes.

See Dialects, Fine writing, Formal English, Informal English.

3. Choose the effective word. If your words convey your meaning accurately and if they are appropriate to the rhetorical context, your diction will be competent, and it may be effective too.

But you will probably move beyond competence only if you pay very close attention to your style. Effectiveness nearly always means choosing words that convey your meaning directly and economically. It may mean deliberately repeating a word, or turning a familiar word to a new use, or choosing a word for its sound as well as its sense. In short, effective diction often requires the imaginative use of words; it calls for finding a middle course between diction that is commonplace and trite and diction that turns the reader's attention from what is being said to the way it is being said. See Abstract language, Adjectives and style, Adverbs and style, Conjunctions and style, Counter words, Euphemisms, Figurative language, Imagery, Nominalization, Repetition, Style, Triteness, Vogue words, Wordiness. See also articles on individual words: *claim, contact, drunk, finalize, hopefully, however, massive, relate, viable,* and so on.

Dictionaries

Next to a well-stocked mind and a good ear, your dictionary is your chief resource in writing papers. Refer to it to check spelling and word division; consult it when you are trying to choose the word that conveys your meaning most precisely; browse in it to increase your own word hoard.

A good dictionary tells what a word denotes in various contexts (see the several meanings of *office, cast, culture, critical* in your dictionary). It gives linguistic information about the word (its part or parts of speech, its inflections), something of its history, its synonyms and its antonyms, and the idioms in which it occurs. It may also suggest some of the connotations of a word. Watch for the labels that indicate limitations on the use of a word or of some sense of it—subject labels like *chemistry,* temporal labels like *archaic,* geographic labels like *British,* and usage labels like *nonstandard.* And be sure you know what the labels mean. Some dictionaries use *colloquial* to mark words that are characteristically used in conversation and in informal writing; some use *informal* for the same words.

Because dictionaries differ in the labels they apply and in the amount of labeling they do, determining the status of a word is not always easy. You may be told that *plenty,* as in "plenty hot," is *informal* or *colloquial* and therefore inappropriate for a formal essay, but you will not be warned that *adumbrate* is too formal and literary for general writing. Although a dictionary can give you a great deal of information, it can't substitute for a good ear and good judgment.

These dictionaries, listed alphabetically, are recommended for college work: *American College Dictionary,* revised edition (Random); *American Heritage Dictionary of the English Language,* new college edition (American Heritage and Houghton); *Standard College Dictionary* (Funk, text edition Harcourt); *Random House College Dictionary,* revised edition (Random); *Webster's New World Dictionary of the American Language,* second college edition (World); *Webster's New Collegiate Dic-*

tionary, eighth edition (Merriam). Each of these dictionaries has its own policies, procedures, abbreviations, restrictive labels, and order of definitions. To use your dictionary well, become familiar with the explanatory notes in the opening pages.

Your college library will have unabridged dictionaries—the three most recent are *Webster's Third New International Dictionary of the English Language* (Merriam, 1961), the *New Standard Dictionary of the English Language* (Funk, 1966), and the *Random House Dictionary of the English Language* (Random, 1966)—and dictionaries in special subjects like law, business, psychology, and economics.

See Connotation, Definition 1a, Denotation, Diction. References: Bolinger, pp. 582–89; James Sledd and Wilma R. Ebbitt, *Dictionaries and That Dictionary* (Chicago: Scott, 1962).

different

Formal usage prefers *different from:* The rich are different from you and me. General usage is divided between *different from* and *different than:* "The young TV generation has a completely different sensory life than the adult generation which grew up on hot radio and hot print" *(Newsweek). Different than* is particularly common when the object is a clause: "The story would be different for an investigator who accepts the verdict of the court than for one who doesn't" (Meyer Shapiro, *New York Review of Books*). The formal alternative would be the longer, wordy expression: . . . verdict of the court from what it would be for one who doesn't.

Different to is a British idiom, rare in American usage.

References: Bryant, pp. 69–70; Copperud, p. 72; Evans and Evans, pp. 135–36; Pooley, pp. 163–67.

Direct address

In direct address the audience being spoken to is named:

My friends, I wish you would forget this night.
What do you think, *Doctor,* about his going home now?

Words in direct address are usually set off by commas. See Indirect discourse.

Direct objects

In "Dogs chase cats," *cats* is the direct object of the transitive verb *chase.* See Objects 1, Transitive and intransitive verbs.

disinterested, uninterested

From its first recorded uses in the seventeenth century, *disinterested* has had two senses: "indifferent, uninterested" and "impartial, not influenced by personal interest." But the first meaning gradually disappeared from educated writing, and its revival in this century has met strong opposition—in part, at least, because assigning the two different meanings to two different words set up a distinction that prevented ambiguity. Even though *disinterested* in the sense "uninterested" is established in general usage, a writer who uses it should know that he risks being thought semiliterate: "I began to hate someone once who habitually said 'disinterested' when he should have said 'uninterested'" (Alexander Cockburn, *New Statesman*). Reference: Copperud, pp. 73–74.

Divided usage

Usage is said to be *divided* when two or more forms exist in the language, both of them in reputable use in the same dialect or variety. *Divided usage* doesn't apply to localisms, like *poke* for *sack* or *bag*, or to differences like *ain't* and *isn't*, which belong to separate varieties of the language. It applies to spellings, pronunciations, or grammatical forms in which those of similar education follow different practices.

Most of us have no idea how many of these divided usages exist within standard English. In addition to hundreds of instances of divided usage in pronunciation, most dictionaries record forms like these:

In spelling: *buses, busses; millionaire, millionnaire; catalog, catalogue*

In verb forms: past tense of *sing: sang* or *sung;* past tense of *ring: rang* or *rung;* past participle of *show: shown* or *showed;* past participle of *prove: proved* or *proven*

The point about divided usage is that both alternatives are acceptable. A person who has learned to say "It's I" does not need to change to "It's me," and one who says "It's me" need not change to "It's I." When there is a choice between variants of equal standing, choose the one that you use naturally, that is appropriate to your style, or, if you are taking pains to be tactful, the one that is customary among the audience you want to reach. Before criticizing another person's usage, make sure that it's not a variant that is as reputable as the one you prefer.

The entries in this *Index* include divided usages. When one or the other of two acceptable usages is likely to disturb many readers or listeners and arouse emotional attitudes, evidence is usually presented: there's security in knowing what is dangerous ground. For examples, see *can, may; different; disinterested, uninterested; dove, dived; due to; enthuse; farther, further; like, as;* Principal parts of verbs; *reason is because;* Sexist language; *slow, slowly.*

div Division of words

Break the word at the end of this line between syllables.

To keep the right-hand margin of a manuscript fairly even, you must divide some words at the end of a line with a hyphen. The following words are divided to show typical syllables: *mar gin, ca ter, hy phen, chil dren, long ing, hi lar i ous, cat ty, ac com plished, ad min is trate.* When you are not sure how to divide a word, consult a dictionary. Here are the basic rules:

1. Both the divided parts should be pronounceable: the break should come between conventionally recognized syllables. Words of one syllable, like *matched, said, thought,* should not be divided at all.

2. Double consonant letters are usually separable (*ef fi cient, com mit tee, daz zling, bat ted);* but they are kept together if there is no syllable break (*im pelled)* or if both belong to a root to which a suffix has been added (*stiff ly,* not *stif fly; yell ing,* not *yel ling).*

3. A single letter is never allowed to stand by itself: do not divide words like *enough* or *many.*

4. Words spelled with a hyphen (*half-brother, well-disposed)* should be divided only at the point of the hyphen to avoid the awkwardness of two hyphens in the same word.

Fuller directions will be found in the stylebooks of publishing houses, like *A Manual of Style.*

do

Do may be considered two verbs, one of which is a meaningless but structurally important auxiliary verb. The other *do* is synonymous in some of its uses with *perform.* In "Do they do the job well?" the first *do* is the auxiliary verb, the second a main verb. The forms of both are the same and quite irregular: *do, does, did, done.*

Do has many idiomatic meanings and is part of many idiomatic phrases: *do for, do away with, do in, do over, do up.*

See Auxiliaries, Tenses of verbs 2. References: Evans and Evans, p. 140; Quirk et al., pp. 684–98.

doctoral, doctor's, doctorate

Doctoral is an adjective, *doctorate* a noun: a man who has earned his doctorate has earned his doctor's degree (his Ph.D.) in a doctoral program.

don't

Don't is the contraction of *do not,* universally used in conversation and often in writing when *do not* would seem too emphatic or when the rhythm seems more comfortable with the shorter form. Until about 1900 *don't* was the usual third-person singular (*he don't, it don't, that don't)* in informal speech, but the usage is now regarded as nonstandard. References: Atwood, p. 28; Bryant, pp. 73–74; Fries, pp. 52–53.

Double negative

1. In standard English. Two negative words in the same construction are not used in standard English to express a single negation: not "He couldn*'t* find it *no*where," but "He couldn*'t* find it *any*where" or "He *could* find it *no*where." But two negatives may be used in general English to make an emphatic affirmative: "Its re-emergences into view, out of covering buildings, never are not dramatic" (Elizabeth Bowen, *A Time in Rome*). And in a few constructions one negative statement modifies another negative statement to give a qualified meaning or a meaning with some special emphasis: I wouldn't be surprised if he never spoke to us again; He isn't sure he won't be able to afford it; Don't think he isn't clever. The negated negative, or *litotes*, is used in some formal styles (a not unattractive young woman). See Negatives and style.

2. *Hardly, scarcely.* A concealed double negative sometimes occurs with *hardly* or *scarcely*. Since *hardly* means "almost not" or "probably not" and *scarcely* means the same a little more emphatically, a sentence like "The campus paper contains hardly nothing" should read "contains hardly anything," and "For a while we couldn't scarcely see a thing" should read "could scarcely." Reference: Bryant, pp. 106–107.

3. In nonstandard English. Two or more negatives are very often used in nonstandard English to express a simple negation: Ain't nobody there; Couldn't nobody find the body; I don't have nothing to lose. Such double negatives are not a backsliding from the current idiom of standard English; the form survives from an older period. In early English two negatives were used in all varieties of language. The objection to a double negative is not that "two negatives always make an affirmative," for they do not. The objection is simply that the double negative is not now in fashion among educated people. References: Bryant, pp. 75–76; Copperud, p. 75; Fries, p. 35.

Double prepositions
The *of* in double prepositions like *off of* and *outside of* is unnecessary. See Prepositions and style 2.

Doublespeak
Doublespeak is the use of language not to express but to obscure, disguise, or deny the truth. Dwight Bolinger has suggested that the label be applied to "jargon that is a sophisticated form of lying." Doublespeak is common in the pronouncements of governments and government agencies, corporations, and special interest groups of all kinds. In some cases doublespeak in the form of euphemisms is used to protect the feelings of the old, the poor, the mentally retarded, the crippled, or the criminal; but the inaction encouraged by bland doublespeak does more harm than hurt feelings. Deliberate manipulation of the language by the government during the Vietnam War and Watergate led to the formation of the Committee on Public Doublespeak by members of the National Council of Teachers of English. See Euphemisms, Gobbledygook. Reference: *Language and Public Policy*, ed. Hugh Rank (Urbana, Ill.: NCTE, 1974).

doubt

The word used to introduce a clause after a statement with the verb *doubt* (or *it is doubtful*) depends on whether the statement is negative or positive.

1. Negative (when there is no real doubt), *doubt that:* I do not doubt that he meant well. (For *doubt but,* see *but that, but what.*)

2. Positive (when doubt exists), *that, whether,* less often *if:*

But there is reason to doubt that this is so. — Wayne F. LaFave, *Supreme Court Review.*

A couple of days ago, Walter Heller . . . said that he doubted whether that level could be reached. — Richard H. Rovere, *New Yorker*

I doubt if this was ever a really important reason for his leaving London. — George Woodcock, *Esquire*

dove, dived

Dove as well as *dived* is acceptable as the past tense of *dive.* References: Copperud, pp. 75–76; Pooley, pp. 134–35.

drunk

It seems to take courage to use this general word. We either go formal—*intoxicated;* or grasp at respectability through euphemisms—*under the influence of liquor, indulged to excess;* or make a weak attempt at humor with one of the dozens of slang expressions like *looped, bombed, stoned.* But *drunk* is the word.

due to

No one complains when *due* (followed by *to*) is used as an adjective firmly modifying a noun: "The failure was due to a conceptual oversight" (William Jaffé, *Journal of Political Economy*). But there has been strong objection to the use of *due to* in the sense "because of" to introduce prepositional phrases functioning as adverbs: "Cooperative self-regulatory efforts among newspapers in a locality have become rare, partly due to the tradition of independence in the field" (*Harvard Law Review*). The objection—on the grounds that *due to* is adjectival only—ignores the fact that the change of a word from one part of speech to another is commonplace in English. And though the distinguished lexicographer John S. Kenyon presented evidence in 1930 that this use of *due to* had become standard, the prejudice (which he shared) remains widespread. As a result, some writers are afraid to use *due to* in any context. References: John S. Kenyon, *AS*, Oct. 1930, pp. 61–70; Bryant, p. 81; Copperud, p. 77; Pooley, pp. 135–38.

E

each

1. Though the pronoun *each* is singular (To each his own), we use it to individualize members of a group. As a result, it inevitably attracts plural forms. In informal and increasingly in general usage, *each* is treated as a collective when the plural idea is uppermost (compare *every*):

Each of the stages in child development produce typical conflicts. – Selma Fraiberg, *New York Review of Books*

Each of these peoples undoubtedly modified Latin in accordance with their own speech habits. – Albert C. Baugh, *A History of the English Language*

But in formal usage *each* is ordinarily singular: "Each of them was asserting its own individuality" (John Higham, *American Historical Review*).

Sometimes when *each* refers to both men and women, a writer will use *they* rather than *his* as one way of avoiding sexist language: Each of the weekend guests brought their own climbing gear. See Agreement 2, Sexist language.

2. As an adjective, *each* does not affect the number of the verb or related pronoun. When the subject modified by *each* is plural, the verb and related pronoun are also plural: "The editions that have appeared since World War I each have their weak and strong points" (James McManaway, *PMLA*).

References: Bryant, pp. 8–9; Copperud, p. 78.

each other, one another

Although some textbooks have insisted that *each other* refers to two only and *one another* to more than two, writers ignore the distinction. See Pronouns 3. References: Bryant, pp. 82–83; Copperud, pp. 78–79; Pooley, pp. 138–39.

Echo phrases

An echo phrase calls to mind a passage in literature or a popular saying. See Allusion.

Editorial we

Traditionally the anonymous writers of editorials use *we* and *our* (We believe that . . . ; It is our recommendation that . . .) rather than *I* and *my*. The practice makes sense because editorials supposedly speak for the group that publishes the periodical. See *I, we*.

effect, affect

The common noun is *effect,* meaning "result." As verbs, *effect* means "bring about"; *affect* means "influence" or "put on" (She affected a Southern accent). See *affect, effect*.

e.g.

E.g. stands for the Latin words meaning "for example." The best way to avoid possible confusion with *i.e.* is to use *for example.* See Abbreviations 2, *i.e.*

either

The pronoun *either* normally takes a singular verb: "Welsh and Irish are closer to each other than either is to English" (William W. Heist, *Speculum*). Reference: Copperud, p. 81.

either . . . or, neither . . . nor

When one element of a compound subject connected by *either* . . . *or* or *neither* . . . *nor* is singular and the other is plural, make the verb agree with the nearer subject. See Agreement 1c.

elder, eldest

These forms of *old* survive in references to the order of birth of members of a family—"the elder brother," "our eldest daughter"—and in some honorific senses like "elder statesmen."

Ellipsis

A punctuation mark of three spaced periods in a quotation, indicating the omission of one or more words, is called an ellipsis: "Four score and seven years ago our fathers brought forth . . . a new nation . . . dedicated to the proposition that all men are created equal." When the last words in a sentence are omitted, the end punctuation precedes the ellipsis, just as it does when the omission follows the sentence: "Four score and seven years ago our fathers brought forth on this continent a new nation. . . ."

The omission of a line or more of poetry is generally indicated by a full line of spaced periods. The omission of a paragraph or more of prose is traditionally indicated in the same way; but current practice often uses only an ellipsis at the end of the paragraph preceding the omission.

No ellipsis should be used when a quotation is just a phrase: It is worth asking whether we continue to be "dedicated to the proposition." (Not ". . . dedicated to the proposition. . . .")

In dialog, an ellipsis indicates hesitation in speech. It is also used as an end stop for a statement that is left unfinished or allowed to die away: "The town was poor then. And like so many who grew up in the Depression, we never expected we would have real jobs. There was no place for us in the world. It was depressing . . ." (John Thompson, *Harper's*).

References: *A Manual of Style; The MLA Style Sheet*, 2nd ed. (New York: Modern Language Association, 1970); *U.S. Style Manual.*

Elliptical constructions

An elliptical construction omits a word or two that can somehow be supplied, usually from a neighboring construction: I work much harder than you [work]. Grammarians differ in the extent to which they use ellipsis as a means of explanation. In the sentence "We had the same experience you did," some grammarians would say that the relative pronoun *that* has been omitted after *experience*, some that it is present in zero position, still others that no relative occurs, even implicitly. Constructions like "The more, the merrier" and "First come, first served" are commonly accepted as established idioms, not elliptical.

The choice between longer and shorter forms is a matter of style. Formal English tends to be explicit and uses relatively few ellipses. General and informal English use the shorter constructions freely. Compare Clauses 2a. References: Long and Long, pp. 143–53; Quirk et al., pp. 536–50.

else

In phrases with pronouns like *anyone*, *nobody*, and *someone*, *else* (not the preceding pronoun) takes the sign of the possessive: The package was left at somebody else's house.

emp Emphasis

Strengthen the emphasis of this passage.

Rightly used, emphasis indicates the relative importance of the points you are making, so that your reader recognizes the most important as most important, the less important as less important, the incidental as incidental. A lack of emphasis means a failure in guidance; misplaced emphasis means serious confusion.

1. Proportion. Give the point you want to emphasize the space and development its importance calls for. Ordinarily, mass is evidence of significance; we allot space on the basis of importance. When you finish a paper in a hurry, you may leave the major point undeveloped and therefore unemphatic. Sometimes you must lay a good deal of groundwork before you can present the central issue in an essay, but one of your jobs in revising is to see that you have not given preliminaries so much space as to mislead the reader.

2. Position. Generally speaking, the most emphatic position in a sentence, a paragraph, or a full essay is the end (hence the danger of leaving the final point undeveloped). The second most important is the beginning. Don't waste these natural positions of emphasis. In an essay you will often want to use both – stating your thesis in the opening paragraph and, after presenting the arguments that support it, restating it in your conclusion. In any case, don't let your major point get lost somewhere in between, and don't announce it at the beginning and then fail to get back to it. See Beginning an essay, Concluding an essay.

3. Separation. Use a comma, a colon, or a dash to set off part of a sentence and thereby emphasize it, lightly or heavily. Or begin a separate sentence or a new paragraph to achieve the same purpose. See Colon 4, Comma 7, Dash 1.

4. Repetition. As long as you don't overdo it, you can gain emphasis by repeating significant words and by repeating ideas in different words, perhaps in figurative expressions. Repeating a structural pattern, especially in a series that builds to a climax, is an excellent device for emphasizing. See Parallelism, Repetition, Series.

5. Economy. In the condensing that is a regular part of revision, pay special attention to the expression of the ideas that deserve major emphasis. Strip the sentences of any verbiage that blurs their clarity and blunts their impact. Emphatic statement need not be brusque, but it must be direct and uncluttered. See Wordiness.

6. Mechanical devices. Using underlinings, capitals, and exclamation marks for emphasis is likely to bore, annoy, or amuse the reader. Telling him that he should be interested ("It is interesting to note") or impressed ("Here is the really important point that we should all recognize") is likely to irritate him. Pretentious or portentous word choice has the same effect, and the intensifiers used in speech—*very, terribly, extremely, incredibly*—are almost uniformly ineffective in writing. On paper, "a very shocking incident" turns out to be less, not more, emphatic than "a shocking incident." So avoid mechanical devices as a means for achieving emphasis. They demand the reader's attention instead of earning it.

End stop

An end stop is a mark of punctuation—usually a period, exclamation mark, or question mark—used at the end of a sentence. In writing dialog, a double dash may be used as an end stop when a speech is interrupted. An ellipsis may be used as an end stop for a sentence that is intentionally left unfinished.

When two end stops would fall together at the close of a sentence, only one mark, the more emphatic or more necessary for meaning, is used. Here a question comes at the end of a sentence that would normally close with a period; only the question mark is used: "When we say, for example, that Miss A plays well, only an irredeemable outsider would reply, 'Plays what?'" (C. Alphonso Smith, *Studies in English Syntax*).

English language

To the linguistic historian there is no real beginning for any language. The earliest records of English date from the seventh century A.D., two centuries after invading Germanic tribesmen from northwestern Europe—Angles, Saxons, Jutes, and Frisians—had made their homes in the British Isles, bringing with them the differing but mutually intelligible dialects which are the direct ancestors of the English language. But through those dialects, English is connected to a prehistoric past—to an unrecorded language called Germanic, parent of the Low and High German languages, the Scandinavian languages, and English.

Through Germanic, English is connected to a still more ancient and unrecorded language called Indo-European, the parent of several language groups besides Germanic: Indo-Iranian, Armenian, Celtic, Albanian, Balto-Slavic, Italic, Hellenic, and the ancient tongues Hittite and Tocharian.

The history of English is often divided, somewhat arbitrarily, into three main periods: Old English (OE), c. 450–1100; Middle English (ME), c. 1100–1450; Modern English or New English (MnE or NE), c. 1450–, with this latter period sometimes subdivided into Early Modern English (EMnE), c. 1450–1700, and Modern English, c. 1700–. Some knowledge of the history of English can help a writer understand the richness and complexity of the medium he uses.

1. Vocabulary. Of all aspects of language, vocabulary is the surest index to cultural change. English is no exception to this rule, since its lexicon reflects ever-widening contacts with foreign speakers and foreign cultures as well as the inevitable expansion of word stock which goes hand in hand with an increase in cultural complexity. Throughout history, English speakers have borrowed words from foreign tongues; but they have also met their needs for new words by relying on native processes of word formation.

Latin, Scandinavian, and French have contributed most to the common vocabulary of English. Latin makes its mark early – first before the English-to-be had left their continental homes, next when Roman missionaries converted the English to Christianity in the OE period. Scandinavian influences strike still more deeply into the core of English vocabulary. Danish and Norwegian armies invaded England in the ninth century; in the tenth, colonists followed to establish permanent settlements in north and east; by the eleventh, Danish kings ruled England. Because Englishmen and Norsemen lived side by side, and because the languages were similar, many Scandinavian words entered English. French influence, resulting from the Norman conquest and occupation, is still more pervasive. For almost three hundred years, French replaced English as the tongue of law, learning, politics, and influence. One scholar has calculated that during the ME period alone over ten thousand French words were borrowed and that, of these, 75 percent survive.

Loan words from the modern period reflect the ever-widening circle of contacts. Terms from Low German (particularly Dutch and Flemish) result from late medieval trade across the channel; Italian and Spanish terms show English movements into the Mediterranean. Excursions to more distant lands provided English with loans from Turkish, Arabic, Persian, Indo-Aryan, Chinese, Japanese, Malayo-Polynesian, Australian, African, and Amerindian languages. Some words from exotic sources have entered the general English vocabulary (*apricot, caravan, coffee, taboo, tulip*); others belong to the common vocabulary of only one national variety of English (e.g., Amerindian loans in

American English); still others retain their exotic flavor and are used only in reference to foreign locales (*gaucho, amboyna, parang, punkah*).

Many words have made their way into English through books. Latin and Greek have contributed most to the learned vocabulary. The Christian missionaries to the earliest English brought terms related to learning and to church activities: *school, gloss, grammatic(al), master, verse* alongside *abbot, alms, cleric, hymn, priest*. OE borrowings of animal terms show that the world of books is opening: *dragon* (OE *draca*), *elephant* (OE *elpend*), *basilisk, camel, phoenix*. The language of English learning is predominantly Latin through the EMnE period, joined then by Greek as a complementary source. The scholarly, scientific, and technical vocabulary of the twentieth century reflects the persistent influence of the classical tongues: *aerospace, allobar, antibiotic, astrophysics, astronaut, biochemistry, chronograph, ecology, isotope, positron, spectroscope, telemetry*.

Of the native processes for forming new words, two have been most productive: compounding and word composition (see Origin of words). English vocabulary is rich in its collection of noun, adjective, verb, and adverb compound terms. OE *scops* (bards, poets) relied heavily on compounds to meet the demands of alliterative verse; OE prose writers used compounds almost as frequently, often preferring native formations to borrowed terms: e.g., *ānhorn, allmihtig, gōdspell* (literally, "good tidings"), instead of *unicorn* (L. *unicornus*), *omnipotent* (L. *omnipotens*), *evangel* (L. *ēvangelium*). Compounding has continued as a productive process throughout the history of English; examples abound in modern colloquial English: *highbrow, egghead, hotbed, deadbeat, lowbrow;* in the vocabularies of occupations, sports, and hobbies; and in technical vocabularies—*countdown, earthshine*.

History has worked changes in English word composition, but has never restricted its productivity. Over the centuries, some native affixes have disappeared altogether; some survive only as fossils (e.g., *for-* in *forbear*); still others have become restricted in use (e.g., *-dom, -hood, -th* as in *width*). But to its dwindling stock of natives affixes, English has added others, principally from Latin, Greek, and French. How completely English has assimilated foreign elements may be seen in the freedom with which it combines foreign and native word elements: to native bases are added foreign affixes— *goddess, endearment, mileage, hindrance, murderous, heathenism, womanize;* to foreign bases, native affixes— *graceful, faintness, courtship, unconscious, forbearance, martyrdom;* foreign elements from two sources are mixed—*postal, socialist, jurist, communism*. With its borrowings and its still flourishing native supply, English possesses a rich and precise system of formatives.

In spite of its cosmopolitan quality, the English lexicon remains fixed to its origins. Perhaps a quarter of the present English vocabulary goes back to the words of Old English, and many of these are the most frequently used of all. The modern descendants of OE words are changed almost always in pronunciation and nearly as often in meaning, as are borrowed words which have long been in common use. As objects change in shape or in the uses to which they are put, the meanings of the terms naming them change: *ship, car, weapon* are obvious examples; *atom* has a long history in English, but scientists change its definition each time they discover more about its structure. Words naming specific things can be generalized in application (*thing* was once a legal term); general terms can become specific (*deer* once meant "wild animal"); words can slide up and down an evaluational scale with the fortunes of the referents (*lust* once meant "pleasure," harmless as well as otherwise; a *marshall* was once a horse-servant, a *steward,* a pig-keeper). Writers must be on their guard for fluctuations in denotation and nuance but quick to seize potentialities in their rich lexical heritage. English offers an everyday vocabulary rich in its synonyms, an exotic vocabulary redolent of distant countries, a learned vocabulary precise in denotation and partially preserved by its literary character from rapid semantic change. The effective writer learns to exploit the nuances of synonymous terms, to respond to the demands of occasion on vocabulary level, and to recognize that the English lexicon is not a closed book.

2. Grammar. Although a modern student needs assistance in learning to read Old English, he will recognize more similarities than differences in the grammatical systems of Old and Modern English. The inflectional system of OE has been extensively simplified by historical changes, but in syntax the two stages show fundamental likenesses.

Space permits only hints of the inflectional complexity of OE. The OE noun, for example, had distinctive forms for singular and plural and for four cases (nominative, genitive, dative, accusative) and exhibited grammatical gender (nouns fell into one of several declensions, mainly according to gender). Articles, demonstratives, and adjectives agreed with nouns in gender, number, and case. Thus, where MnE has only the form *the,* OE had separate inflections for masculine, neuter, and feminine forms, for singular and plural, and for the various cases. Where MnE has an invariant form of the adjective, OE possessed a full array of endings for number, gender, and case.

From the complex of forms in OE comes the sparse inflectional machinery of MnE: *the* and *that* are remnants from an OE demonstrative article; *this, these,* and *those* come from a second demonstrative; *a, an* come from the OE word *ān* (one), separately inflected in OE. Adjective inflections disappeared entirely by the end of the ME period. The noun endings that remain in MnE trace back to OE origins: the *-s* of plural to *-as* in the masculine declension (*cyningas* "kings"); the *-s* of genitive to the OE genitive of the same declension (*cyning-es*). From other noun declensions, MnE retains only fossils: the *-en* of *oxen;* the *-ren* of *children* (a double plural); the vowel gradation of *man, men; goose, geese.* Verb inflections underwent similar processes of decay, particularly of personal endings, and in the conversion of strong (irregular) verbs to the weak pattern. This last change is reflected in the variations of past and past participle forms in British and American dialects: *dived* vs. *dove, climbed* vs. *clomb, blowed* vs. *blew, heaved* vs. *hove.*

Some syntactic changes have occurred. The MnE use of *do* in interrogatives (Do you dance?) and emphatics (You *do* dance) is an EMnE addition to the auxiliary system of English (cf. Chaucer's question form, "Lady myn, Criseyde, lyve ye yet?"). The auxiliary *be* in progressive forms first appeared in OE, and only slowly made its way into the English auxiliary system. Forms like "He is laughing" were not common until the sixteenth century; passive progressive (The house is being painted) does not develop until the end of the eighteenth. The full participation of progressive forms in the auxiliary system will be reached when a sentence like "The runner could have been being trained during that time" no longer strikes us with its rarity. But significant innovations are rare in the history of the English grammatical system. To look at deep rather than superficial features of English grammar is to convince oneself of how slowly they alter, no matter what happens to vocabulary and pronunciation, or to surface inflections. Purists sometimes maintain that changes in usage will render the language chaotic and unintelligible. As a consequence, writers are urged to cling to the *whom* in "Whom did you see?" Historical perspective helps us to see that English preserves its basic form, its semantically significant categories and relations, through many superficial changes.

3. Standardization and the spread of English. In modern times, English has undergone two developments which may at first glance seem contradictory. On the one hand, large groups of English speakers have migrated from England in apparent imitation of their continental Germanic ancestors, whose migrations resulted in the split of Germanic into separate languages. In North America, Australia, New Zealand, India, and Africa, new national varieties of English have arisen, but none has diverged far enough from its parent or its siblings to be considered a separate tongue. The failure of history to repeat itself may be attributed to the second major development in Modern English—standardization. In England after the ME period, a relatively uniform and powerfully dominant form of English spread to all parts of the island kingdom; in other English-speaking nations, similar tendencies toward standardization have kept the separate national varieties basically alike.

Dialect differences have always existed in English. The major varieties of OE—Kentish, West Saxon, Anglian (sometimes divided into Mercian and Northumbrian)—derive from differences among the dialects brought by Germanic invaders and lead in turn to the major varieties of ME. In the ME period conditions favored localism in the use of English—particularly the replacement of English with French in official documents, in Parliament, in law courts and schools, and in the literature intended for the upper classes. Although English emerged from its subservience in the thirteeth century and became common in official use in the fourteenth, the three major English poets of the fourteenth century—Chaucer, Langland, and the Pearl Poet—all wrote their separate native dialects.

Sixteenth-century poets, however, used a uniform written standard based on a late ME form of London English. Thus what is later known as standard English began as a regional dialect—the dialect of England's capital, naturally prestigious because it was the dialect of powerful and influential men. Early in the fifteenth century the standard spread into official documents written outside London, later in the century into private documents such as letters and journals. Printers felt a particular need for uniformity, especially in spelling and choice of word forms, and helped spread written standard by putting it before the eyes of a growing number of readers. Renaissance scholars and schoolmasters pushed standardization almost as actively, seeking to demonstrate that English was as proper a medium of learning as the classical tongues, pressing their claims by working for spelling reform and by providing English with grammars and dictionaries. What the Renaissance left untidy, eighteenth-century schoolmen sought to regularize and fix. Prescriptive grammarians labored to settle cases of disputed usage: to unravel the uses of *between* and *among*, to decide what case properly follows *than* and *as*, to explicate the differences between *shall* and *will*. Uniformity and correctness were cardinal linguistic virtues.

The benefits of standardization are many: learning to read is made easier as the number of variant spellings and forms is reduced; communication is facilitated; the growth of a national literature is undoubtedly encouraged when writers and audience share a common tongue. But there are disadvantages and dangers when standards are asserted so stringently that no room is left for variations introduced by the natural processes of linguistic change; greater dangers when, as has happened in the history of English, the standard dialect becomes a class dialect invested with the status of its speakers. The process began early in England with the feeling that one kind of pronunciation must be correct. Sir Thomas Elyot urged sixteenth-century nurses, if they could not teach a nobleman's son pure and elegant Latin, at least to teach "none englisshe but that which is cleane, polite, perfectly and articulately pronounced, omittinge no lettre or sillable." Such pronunciation was soon equated with the speech of "the better sort": educated and influential people who hovered about the seats of power. After the eighteenth century—a great age of snobbism, when aristocrats looked down their noses at the lower classes and lower classes did all they could to imitate their betters—spoken standard English became firmly established as a class standard, carefully maintained as an outward sign of status. Those who could not adapt betrayed their origins merely by opening their mouths.

Although most traces of provincial dialects disappeared from English writing after the fifteenth century, the dialects themselves continued to be spoken. Earlier dialect differences are, of course, the bases of modern British dialects, and also of differences between British English, American English, Australian English, etc. But American English has never diverged far from the parent language, partly because of cultural contacts, partly because standardizing processes in American English have retarded linguistic change. British and American usage remained close during the colonial period – the differences consisting mainly of vocabulary items. Growing nationalism after the Revolution led Americans to predict, and eagerly expect, a new American language, "as different from the future language of England, as the modern Dutch, Danish and Swedish are from the German, or from one another" (Noah Webster, 1789). But concern for preserving national unity suggested that American dialects must not be allowed to develop unchecked lest they become so different from one another as to make communication difficult: "a national language is a band of national union," wrote Webster, and as textbook writer for the new nation he pushed a standard of general (that is, national) custom:

. . . general custom must be the rule of speaking, and every derivation from this must be wrong. The dialect of one state is as ridiculous as that of another; each is authorized by local custom; and neither is supported by any superior excellence.

But American prescriptivism has tended to concentrate on the written word. Webster's "general custom" is easily translated into marks on a printed page, and general custom in pronunciation must inevitably be abstract as long as differences in speech exist. America has never had an official standard of pronunciation, based on the speech of a single locale or class. And American prescriptivism has paid more attention to grammar than to pronunciation. Southern, Northern, and Western speakers may sound different but still speak standard American English; the same is not true of Southerner, Northerner, or Westerner who utters "He don't never do that."

Class dialects do exist in the United States. When we use the terms *standard* and *nonstandard* English, we refer to the social status of the speakers of each, not to good or bad qualities inherent in the dialects themselves. And while it is true that standard English in the United States has been flexible and tolerant of regional variation and of importations from nonstandard, dialect conflict has emerged in our century. Massive migration to Northern cities, particularly from the South and South-Midlands, has brought Northern and Southern speakers into close contact. Because many of the migrants have been poor and ill-educated, their speech – regional in its origins – has been taken as indicative of their class. Thus in many Northern cities, Southern speech is equated with nonstandard speech. The new migrant—particularly if he is black—does not find the city welcoming him. Hostility toward him, toward his class or race, attaches easily to his language; in return, the migrant may see in Webster's "general custom" only the values of an oppressive class.

Dialects are not merely collections of sounds, forms, words. They are powerful social and psychological symbols—expressive of who one is, what groups he belongs to, what values he shares with others. Standardized languages have vital functions to perform in breaking down intense regionalism and in facilitating international communication: Englishmen, Americans, Canadians, Australians, New Zealanders can talk to one another; they can also talk to English speakers in India, Pakistan, Ceylon, Malaysia, Nepal, the Philippines, Nigeria, Rhodesia, Sierra Leone, Ghana, Kenya, the British West Indies, to name only a few of the nations where English holds some official status. Standardization has helped make English available as a communicative medium for educated people in Africa, Asia, and the Western world, as a potential link between peoples of diverse cultures. The link, however, can be easily broken by an over-zealous commitment to inflexible standards that take no account of the personal, social, and cultural validity of dialect difference. West Indian poets and novelists insist that their own English is the proper medium for their works; African writers do the same; some black authors in the United States insist that they write in Black English—a dialect symbolizing the values and attitudes of black people in coexistence with or rebellion against white society. If standard American English is defined too narrowly and without reference to the usage of social minorities—if it is identified too closely with the usage of the white middle class—we invite the division of America into fixed castes.

References: Histories: Albert C. Baugh, *A History of the English Language*, 2nd ed. (New York: Appleton, 1957); Thomas Pyles, *The Origins and Development of the English Language*, 2nd ed. (New York: Harcourt, 1971); Joseph M. Williams, *Origins of the English Language* (New York: Free Press, 1975). American English: G. P. Krapp, *The English Language in America*, 2 vols. (New York: Ungar, 1960); A. L. Marckwardt, *American English* (New York: Oxford Univ. Press, 1958); H. L. Mencken, *The American Language*, abridged 4th ed., ed. Raven I. McDavid, Jr. (New York: Knopf, 1963); Thomas Pyles, *Words and Ways of American English* (New York: Random, 1952). English words: George H. McKnight, *English Words and Their Background* (New York: Appleton, 1923); Mary S. Serjeantson, *A History of Foreign Words in English* (London: Routledge, 1935); J. A. Sheard, *The Words We Use* (New York: Praeger, 1954). Dialects: G. L. Brook, *English Dialects* (New York: Oxford Univ. Press, 1963); Raven I. McDavid, Jr., in Francis; Carroll E. Reed, *Dialects of American English* (Cleveland: World, 1967); Harold B. Allen and Gary N. Underwood, eds., *Readings in American Dialectology* (New York: Appleton,

1971). A survey of British dialects is in process of publication by Leeds University under the editorship of Harold Orton and Wilfred J. Halliday. Many publications have resulted from the survey of American dialects called *The Linguistic Atlas of the United States and Canada.* Bibliographical references may be found in the books by Reed and by Allen and Underwood.

Jay Robinson

enormity, enormousness

Because *enormity* looks like a more compact way of expressing the idea of "enormousness," it is often used in that sense, as most dictionaries indicate. But this use is deplored by those who restrict *enormity* to the meaning "enormously evil" or "great wickedness," as in "the enormity of the crime."

enthuse

Enthuse is a back formation (see Origin of words 3e) from *enthusiasm.* Although widely used in general and informal writing, it is still not established in formal usage, and many readers object to it. The only other locutions we have for the idea are the longer *be enthusiastic over* or *be enthusiastic about.* Reference: Copperud, p. 87.

Epigrams and aphorisms

An epigram is a short, pithy statement, in verse or prose, usually with a touch of wit. In prose this means a detached or detachable and quotable sentence. In consecutive prose, epigrams sometimes become too prominent, attract too much attention to themselves, or give the impression of straining for effect. But they can focus attention and phrase an idea so that it will be remembered: "Conscience is the inner voice that warns us that someone may be looking" (H. L. Mencken).

Closely related to epigrams are aphorisms—pithy statements that are more likely to be abstract and are not necessarily witty. The essays of Francis Bacon are packed with aphorisms:

To spend too much time in studies is sloth; to use them too much for ornament is affectation; to make judgment wholly by their rules is the humor of a scholar. . . . Read not to contradict and confute; nor to believe and take for granted; nor to find talk and discourse; but to weigh and consider. . . . Reading maketh a full man; conference a ready man; and writing an exact man.—Francis Bacon, "Of Studies"

A special type of epigram is the paradox, which makes a statement that as it stands contradicts fact or common sense or itself and yet suggests a truth or at least a half-truth: All generalizations are false, including this one.

equally as

Although *equally as* is an established idiom (Color is equally as important as design), one of the words is always redundant. With that in mind, use *equally* or *as*, not both: *Either* Color is as important as design *or* Color and design are equally important. References: Bryant, p. 85; Copperud, p. 88.

-ese
The suffix *-ese* is used to make new nouns, such as *Brooklynese, journalese, educationese, Pentagonese,* which have the disparaging sense of "lingo, jargon, or dialect": His mastery of sociologese left us impressed if uninformed.

Establishment
In the 1960s *Establishment* (sometimes not capitalized) became a vogue word for the powers-that-be: "In the intellectuals' lexicon 'the Establishment' now seems to include federal, state, and local government, business corporations, foundations and other philanthropic organizations, Big Labor, Big Science, and the administrators of universities" (Max Ways, *Fortune*). While sometimes simply descriptive, it is more often a term of abuse, expressing discontent with the ins and sympathy with the outs.

In *The New Yorker,* October 19, 1968, Henry Fairlie tells of launching the term in its present sense in the British *Spectator* of September 23, 1955. At that time Fairlie wrote: "By the 'Establishment,' I do not mean only the centres of official power — though they are certainly part of it — but rather the whole matrix of official and social relations within which power is exercised." *Establishment* has remained anything but precise but continues to refer to often sinister inner circles: "John O'Hara was underrated by the critical-academic axis sometimes called The Literary Establishment" (Matthew J. Bruccoli, *The O'Hara Concern*).

et al.
Et al. is the abbreviation for the Latin words meaning "and others." A footnote style may call for reducing a list of four or more authors to the first author named and *et al.* (See Footnote form.) In ordinary writing, and in some footnote styles, use "and others."

etc.
Though sometimes a convenient way to end an incomplete list, *etc.,* the abbreviation for the Latin phrase *et cetera* ("and the rest"), belongs primarily to business and reference usage: This case is suitable for large photographs, maps, blueprints, etc. In most writing *and so forth* or *and so on* is preferable when the reference is to things, and *and others* is preferable with lists of people. The incompleteness of a list can also be marked by an introductory phrase like *such as* after the category the list exemplifies: This case is suitable for large papers such as photographs, maps, and blueprints.

Ethnic labels
American English has more than its share of slang terms for members of racial and ethnic groups. While these may at times be used with no hostile intent — may even be used by members of the groups they name — our vocabularies would be healthier

without them. Besides the labels for peoples of European, African, and Latin American origins, these terms should be avoided: *Asiatic* (for *Asian*), *Jap* (*Japanese*), *Chinamen* or *Chink* (*Chinese*), as well as words like *gook*.

Etymology
Etymology is the study of word origins. See Origin of words.

Euphemisms
A euphemism is a word used in place of one that names more explicitly something unpleasant or something regarded as not quite nice: *perspire* for *sweat, passed on* for *died, senior citizens* for *old people, lavatory* or *powder room* or even *comfort facility* for *toilet.* Political, military, and promotional vocabularies offer countless examples. Occasionally euphemisms are warranted, to avoid causing pain or embarrassment, but ordinarily honesty is better — and makes for better writing — than evasion. The persistent substitution of *attacked* and *assaulted* for *raped* in news stories succeeded chiefly in making the substitutes ambiguous.

every

1. *Every, everybody, everyone* were originally singular and are still so to the extent that they nearly always take a singular verb: Every man on the team did well; Everybody loathes the mayor; Everyone takes the freeway. Usage is divided, however, for related pronouns that come later in the sentence. The singular is perhaps more common in formal writing, but the plural appears in all varieties: "Everybody who has praised the inaugural address cannot possibly be as enthusiastic as they sound, unless they are merely reacting to its music" (James Reston, *New York Times*). The plural is reasonable, since the reference is to a number of people. Instead of substituting a *he* for each *they,* formal written usage might replace *Everybody* with an explicit plural: All those who have praised. . . .

A plural pronoun is also used for clarity when the *every* phrase is the object of a verb with a singular subject: "The traditional leader then comes forward and thanks everyone for their attendance and invites them to lunch" (John A. Woodward, *Ethnology*). Treating the *every* words as collectives can sometimes prevent confusion and also avoid the awkward he-or-she problem. But some conservatives continue to insist that, in writing, related pronouns be singular. See *he or she.* References: Bryant, pp. 8–10; Fries, p. 50.

2. *Everybody* is always written as one word; *everyone* is usually written as one word, but when the *one* is stressed, it is written as two:

Everyone knew what the end would be.
Every one of us knew what the end would be.

3. *Every so often,* meaning "occasionally," should not be con-fused with *ever so often,* meaning "very frequently":

Every so often we have to get away from the city.
We go to the country ever so often in the summer.

One way to avoid confusing the two is to avoid using the exclam-atory *ever so often.*

4. *Everyplace,* meaning "everywhere," is avoided in formal usage. *Everywheres* is nonstandard.

Examples
Examples are instances that illustrate general statements. They clarify explanations, confirm assertions, and provide support for arguments. See Details, Induction.

except, accept
Except as a verb means "leave out, exclude": He excepted those who had made an honest effort. It is decidedly formal. *Excused* would be more appropriate for the same meaning in general writing.

Accept means "receive" or "respond to affirmatively" and is slightly formal: I accept with pleasure; He accepted the position (as contrasted with "He took the job").

Exclamation mark
An exclamation mark (or point) is used after an emphatic in-terjection, after a phrase, clause, or sentence that is genuinely exclamatory, and after forceful commands. Clear-cut exclama-tions are no problem:

Oh! Ouch! No, no, no!
Damn those mosquitoes!
It was the chance of a lifetime!

But many interjections are mild and deserve no more than a comma or a period: "Well, well, so you're in college now." Often sentences cast in exclamatory patterns are simply statements (What a memorable experience that was), and the type of punc-tuation is optional.

In deciding whether or not to use an exclamation mark, you should first ask yourself whether you intend an exclamation. Are you in fact expressing strong feeling or saying something that you want to give special emphasis to? Walt Kelly said, "Using the exclamation point is like wearing padded shoulders." But when used sparingly, to signal genuine emotion, the mark can serve the writer as the raised voice or dramatic gesture serves the speaker:

The Sun Also Rises is a major work, brilliantly constructed and colored —though last year I was taken aback to hear some students complain that Jake Barnes indulges himself in too much self-pity. How imperious the young can be when judging the victims of disasters they don't even trou-ble to learn about! — Irving Howe, *Harper's*

Exclamations

What distinguishes an exclamation from other kinds of utterance is its purpose: emphatic expression. In form, an exclamation may be a declarative sentence (She's late again!), a question (Can she be late again!), a command or request (Be ready when I call! Please be on time!), a verbless sentence (How terrible for you!), or an interjection (Ouch!). See Exclamation mark.

expect

In general and formal writing, *expect* is ordinarily limited to the senses "anticipate" (He expects to be a great success) and "require as reasonable" (Winsock, Inc., expects its employees to arrive on time). In American usage the sense "to suppose, presume, believe" in reference to past and present events (I expect there were times when Lincoln was heartily fed up) is likely to be limited to informal contexts. Reference: Copperud, p. 95.

Exposition

Most of the writing required in college courses is explanatory — writing that is intended primarily to inform and enlighten the reader. *Exposition* (or *expository writing*) is the traditional term for writing of this kind. When it is extended to include argument, *exposition* refers to all factual prose, in contrast to fiction. See Argument, Forms of discourse, Rhetoric.

F

fact

The fact is often deadwood that can simply be omitted: The study demonstrates [the fact] that workers can become affluent. Sometimes phrases with *fact* can be replaced by single words: In spite of the fact = *although;* due to the fact that = *because.* In the redundant *true fact, fact* alone should be retained.

factor

Windy phrases with *factor* should be deleted: Determination and imagination [were the factors that] brought the program its popularity. *Factor* itself, which means "something that helps produce a result," can often be replaced by a more precise, expressive word: A major factor [stimulus? influence? resource?] in creating the system was the artisan class.

Fallacies

As the term is used in logic, a fallacy is an error in reasoning. If a college announces that it awards scholarships only to students who are needy, then we are reasoning correctly when we assume that a particular student who receives a scholarship at that institution is needy. But it would be fallacious to say, on the basis of the same announcement, that every needy student in the college is receiving scholarship aid. Similarly, a person who acts on the premise that no X-rated movie is fit to see can't confidently assume that any movie not so rated *is* fit to see. *Non sequitur* ("it does not follow") is a comprehensive category covering all those errors in reasoning in which the stated conclusion does not follow from the premises or starting points.

Popularly, *fallacy* is extended to include all misleading statements and errors in interpretation, intentional or unintentional. In this sense, a speaker or writer who deliberately withholds facts, slants evidence, draws an unjustified inference, or argues beside the point commits a fallacy. So does the speaker or writer whose attempt to reach a sound conclusion is thwarted because he doesn't know enough about a situation or because he makes a mistake in interpreting his information.

The common fallacies go by names that are almost self-explanatory. *Hasty generalizing* means jumping to a conclusion before sufficient evidence has been gathered: The fact that two of every three students in my physics class are interested in a career in engineering indicates that engineering is the first choice of science majors these days. *Faulty generalizing,* which is based on weak or unrepresentative instances, may take the form of *card-stacking* (deliberately suppressing data that contradicts the conclusion) or *stereotyping* (applying labels to an entire group — calling all Scots stingy, for example).

Ignoring the question is the fallacy of shifting the grounds of the argument from the real issue to one that is not under debate. An *argumentum ad hominem* attacks not the issue itself but the character of those who support it. Setting up a *straw man* is arguing not against the opposing point of view but against a caricature of it. And using a *red herring* is introducing an issue that shifts the argument from its proper course. *Name-calling* is the irresponsible use of epithets and labels chosen for their connotations for particular audiences (for some audiences, *liberal* is inflammatory; for others, *conservative* is). *Hypostatization* is the appeal to an abstraction as an authority: "Science tells us" instead of "Heisenberg tells us in *Physics and Beyond. . . .*"

For other fallacies, see Begging the question, Cause and effect 2. See also Logical thinking.

farther, further

Some careful writers make a distinction between *farther*, referring to physical distance (Farther north there was heavy snow), and *further*, referring to more abstract relations of degree or extent (Nothing could be further removed from experience). But the distinction is not consistently maintained, even in formal English. References: Bryant, p. 87; Pooley, pp. 141–43.

feel

Although one of the accepted meanings of *feel* is "think" or "believe" (I feel that Barnum was right), *feel* should not be allowed to replace those verbs. Readers need to be reminded now and then that a writer thinks and has convictions.

fellow

Fellow is general and informal when used to mean "person, man, or boy" but formal in the sense "associate." It is most commonly used in writing in the function of an adjective: his fellow sufferers, a fellow feeling ("a similar feeling" or "sympathy").

female

In current usage the noun *female* seems most appropriate in somewhat formal or technical contexts in which the designation of sex is significant: "Each female is assigned a number of social security quarters at the beginning of the simulation" (James H. Schulz, *Yale Economic Essays*). As an adjective *female* has more general usefulness but does not entirely escape its pejorative or technical connotations. See Sexist language.

fewer, less

The rule is that *fewer* refers to number among things that are counted (fewer particles) and *less* to amount or quantity among things that are measured (less energy). Formal usage ordinarily observes the distinction; and though *less* is applied to countables fairly often in general writing—"I suggest they sell two less tickets to the public" (Dwight Macdonald, *Esquire*)—it grates on some readers' ears. References: Bryant, pp. 129–30; Copperud, p. 103.

field

The phrase "the field of" can almost always be omitted: He has long been interested in [the field of] psychiatry.

Figurative language

We use figurative language when we transfer a word from a context in which it is normally used (a smelly cheese) to one in which it is not (a smelly scandal). The moment we begin to look for figures of speech, we find them everywhere: we *play ball* when we cooperate, *chime in* when we join in a conversation, *tax* someone's patience when we talk too much. Many of these word transfers have been around so long that they have lost all their figurative, or image-making, power. (Who pictures an animal when he hears that someone has *weaseled* out of a situation?) Although *foot* continues to serve as the name for a part of the body, its reference has been extended to include the bottom or lowest part of a tree, a bed, a path, and a mountain, among many other things. In these uses, *foot* is a petrified, or dead, figure. (*Dead* is used here figuratively.)

A live figure is created when a word is extended to a new referent. We speak routinely of peeling an apple or a potato; Paul Auster, writing of the poet Laura Riding, speaks of her "trying somehow to peel back the skin of the world" (*New York Review of*

Books). The yoking of things not ordinarily thought of as alike or the phrasing of a perception in a fresh way may serve the double function of seizing the attention and of informing or persuading. Both functions are served by these figurative descriptions of musical performances, the first by a rock group, the second by a jazz pianist:

Aston Barrett's pounding bass line kicks you in the guts and Al Anderson's . . . guitar lead cuts through the air like a knife.—Michael Goodwin, *Rolling Stone*

He uses his considerable technique beautifully: His arpeggios, which whip and coil, have logic and continuity; his double-time dashes are parenthetical and light up what they interrupt; his single-note passages continually pause and breathe; no tempo rattles the clarity of his articulation, which has a private, singing quality.—Whitney Balliett, *New Yorker*

Traditionally, distinctions among figures of speech are made on the basis of the way the meaning of the word or phrase is transferred. In a metaphor it is often made directly: the bass line *kicks* you. In a simile it is made through *like* or *as:* the guitar lead cuts through the air *like a knife.* In other common figures the part stands for the whole (*wheel* for bicycle) or the whole for the part (*Navy* for a team at the Naval Academy) or the author for the works (*Shakespeare* for his plays). Hyperbole uses extravagant language for emphasis (a *thousand* apologies); understatement seeks the same effect by the opposite means (Enthusiasm for the draft was *not overwhelming*).

Personification gives life to abstractions and inanimate objects. In this elaborate figure General Motors, Chrysler, and Ford, losing sales to foreign automakers, are pictured as pompous aristocrats being hard pressed by snapping dogs:

The Auto Lords of Michigan continue to stride about the interior, making gruff and manly sounds, but their legs are beset with Saabs and Volvos, their ankles nibbled at by Datsuns and Volkswagens.—Michael J. Arlen, *New Yorker*

For other figures of speech, see Analogy, Imagery, Irony, Metaphor, Oxymoron. For figures of sound, see Alliteration, Assonance, Onomatopoeia, Puns. See also Figures of speech. Reference: Lawrence Perrine, *College English,* Nov. 1971, pp. 125–38.

Figures

Figures are the symbols for numbers. See Numbers.

Figures of speech

This figure of speech is trite, inconsistent, or inappropriate. Revise the passage.

A good figure of speech can add color, humor, interest, and information and may convey meaning more economically than its literal equivalent. But literal expression is always preferable to figures that are overused or carelessly chosen.

1. Replace trite figures. Use fresh ones that represent your own perceptions. Many figures that once were fresh and vivid are now clichés: *cool as a cucumber, a ribbon of concrete, Old Man Winter.* The writer who thinks about what he is setting down on paper either avoids them or at least tries to give them a new look. "A cucumber-cool manner" might get by where "cool as a cucumber" would bore the reader. But there are dangers in trying to disguise clichés. Although "A lot of water has flowed under the bridge" takes on some new life in "all the water, and war, that had flowed under the bridge" (Karl Miller, *New York Review of Books*), some readers may feel that water and war don't mix. Whenever possible, offer the reader an original figure, like James Thurber's road "which seemed to be paved with old typewriters." If you can neither freshen an old figure successfully nor invent a new one that works, stick to a literal statement of your meaning.

2. Untangle mixed figures. Sometimes, instead of coming up with no images at all, you may find yourself with too many:

The noise, like an enthusiastic roar from a distant sports stadium, yet as insistent as the surge of distant surf, grew till it was galloping up the quadrangle in massive waves.

Here sports fans, the ocean, and horses create a catastrophe. To catch such incongruous mixtures before the final draft, read what you've written as objectively as you possibly can. More difficult to spot are the mixed figures that involve dead metaphors. Keep in mind that a figure that is dead in most contexts may revive in some relationships, with ridiculous results. In the first of the following sentences, the student invents a figure that is apt. In the second, the word *faces,* which is regularly used to stand for "people," simply won't work with *sitting* or with suiting up:

As we dressed, comments were tossed about the room as casually as the rolls of tape we were using to tape our ankles. The familiar faces, sitting in their usual corners, were all getting into their uniforms.

Don't just read what you've written before you turn a paper in. Think about what it *says.* When your figures call up pictures of physical impossibilities or other absurdities because you have mixed images, they are bound to distract your readers from the point you're trying to make. If in speaking figuratively you seem to be speaking foolishly, your figurative language needs to be overhauled.

3. Replace inappropriate figures. A figure of speech may be inappropriate to the audience, to the subject, or to you as the writer. Whether used to explain or to amuse, similes, metaphors, and analogies drawn from biology or trout fishing or from the folklore of your home town won't work with an audience that knows nothing about those things. Describing bluegrass music with figures appropriate to a discussion of Beethoven's symphonies, or vice versa, makes sense only if you are trying, rather desperately, to be funny. And using figures that don't match your own attitudes or temperament — poetic figures, for example, when your natural style is down-to-earth, or hard-boiled ones when your approach is gentle and thoughtful — gives them an off-key prominence that will disturb readers.

A figure of speech can be judged good or not good only in a context, a rhetorical situation. When you write your final draft, judge each of your figures by its appropriateness to the audience, the subject, and your prevailing tone. If you decide that a figure doesn't fit, replace it with a suitable figure or with the literal equivalent. But don't discard a figure simply because it startles you when you read over what you've written. In the context of your essay "the moon crashed through the clouds" may be just right. See Figurative language.

finalize

Finalize has been in widespread use for more than a generation. Its near-synonyms, *finish, conclude,* and *complete,* lack the connotation "to make official" that give *finalize* its usefulness in some contexts: "Before they finalize new guidelines they will consult listeners in East Europe to make sure the proposed changes are having the right effect" (Mary Hornaday, *Christian Science Monitor*). But no writer can afford to be ignorant of the great prejudice against *finalize.* It was included in Maury Maverick's original list of gobbledygook in 1942, and some consider it gobbledygook today. Reference: Copperud, p. 104.

Fine writing

Fine writing is generally a term of dispraise, applied to writing that is too pretentious for the material or purpose. Fine writing betrays itself chiefly in the use of big words and in strained, artificial figures of speech. If you write more to impress an audience than to express an idea, you are likely to produce fine writing. See Diction, Figures of speech.

Finite verbs

A finite verb is one that is limited in number (singular or plural) and in person (first, second, or third), as contrasted with the nonfinite forms — the infinitives (*to drive, drive*), the participles (*driving, driven*), and the verbal nouns or gerunds (*driving*). Only finite forms can be the verbs of sentences and unreduced clauses.

fix

In formal usage *fix* means "fasten in place"; in general usage it means "repair" or "put in shape": The TV had to be fixed. As a noun meaning "predicament," *fix* has passed from informal to general: "In some respects economic theory is in the same fix as biology was years ago" (Henry M. Boettinger, *Harvard Business Review*).

flaunt, flout

Flaunt, to "wave, display boastfully," is frequently used with the sense "treat with contempt, scorn," the meaning traditionally assigned to *flout.* Readers aware of the traditional distinction deplore the confusion.

flounder, founder

Flounder means "stumble about, wallow." *Founder* is applied literally to horses ("go lame") and to ships ("sink"); in an extended sense it means "fail." *Flounder* is frequently used in this sense, but for the flounderer there's still hope.

Folk etymology

When people are puzzled by an unfamiliar word or phrase, they sometimes try to make it more regular or more meaningful by reshaping it from familiar elements: from *aeroplane* they made *airplane;* from Spanish *cucuracha,* English *cockroach;* from *saler,* "a salt-holder," first the redundant *salt-saler* and then *saltcellar,* which has no more to do with a cellar than the *sir-* in *sirloin* has to do with a knight (the *sir-* in the steak is *sur,* "above").

folk, folks

In formal writing, *folks* is uncommon. *Folk* is used in the senses "the common people" (usually of a certain region) and "people" (of a specified type). In general writing, *folks* for "people," often with the connotation "ordinary, everyday," and for "relatives, parents" is carried over from informal.

Footnote form

In any paper based on the words of others, the writer has an obligation to acknowledge the sources. This is primarily a matter of honesty and courtesy. In addition, documentation in the form of footnotes and bibliography invites the reader to judge for himself the evidence an assertion is based on and, if he wishes, to turn to the sources for further information.

You must acknowledge your sources not only when you reproduce a paragraph, a sentence, or even a significant phrase exactly but also when you reword or summarize. Whether you use direct quotations or not, you need to give the source of all facts, interpretations, and conclusions that are not common knowledge and that you have not arrived at through independent thought, experiment, or investigation. If you name in the text the original source of a quotation that you obtained from a secondary source, you should cite that secondary source in a footnote. To neglect to credit the authors and the works that the information and the ideas came from is plagiarism. See Plagiarism.

1. Placing footnotes. Each footnote is keyed to a number in the text that is placed slightly above the line after the statement or quotation. The footnotes, numbered consecutively throughout the paper, appear at the foot of the page (single-spaced with a triple space between the text and the first note and with a double space between notes) or, if the instructor so recommends, on separate sheets at the end. In either case the footnote form is identical. The footnote number is slightly raised and is separated from the note by one space; the first line of the note is indented five spaces.

2. Form for the first reference. The first time a source is identified in a footnote, the documentation is complete. In general, the form given here is that recommended in the *MLA Style Sheet*, second edition. (One exception is in the listing of publishers. The *Style Sheet* approves shortened forms of publishers' names, like those in the bibliography on pages 9–10 of this text.) Other footnote styles used in the humanities differ in details, and those used in most of the sciences are fundamentally different from the form described in this article.

In the examples given below, examine each footnote carefully to see what elements are included, in what order they appear, and how they are punctuated.

A book by a single author

^{1} Jerrold J. Katz, The Philosophy of Language (New York: Harper & Row, 1966), p. 42.

A book by more than one author

^{2} James E. Brady and Gerard E. Humiston, General Chemistry: Principles and Structure (New York: Wiley, 1975), p. 42.

If there are more than three authors, substitute "et al." for all but the first: Shirley Gorenstein et al.

A work in more than one volume

^{3} Richard B. Sewall, The Life of Emily Dickinson (New York: Farrar, Straus & Giroux, 1974), II, 251-58.

The roman numeral is the volume number. When the volume number is given, page numbers are not preceded by "pp."

An edition other than the first

^{4} Lewis A. McArthur, Oregon Geographic Names, 3rd ed. (Portland: Binfords, 1952), p. 468.

An edition revised by someone other than the author

^{5} Stuart Robertson, The Development of Modern English, 2nd ed., rev. Frederic G. Cassidy (Englewood Cliffs, N.J.: Prentice-Hall, 1954), pp. 36-52.

An edited work

^{6} S. Y. Agnon, Twenty-one Stories, ed. Nahum N. Glatzer (New York: Schocken Books, 1970), p. 27.

A compilation by an author

7 Joan C. Baratz and Roger W. Shuy, eds., <u>Teaching</u>
<u>Black Children to Read</u> (Washington, D.C.: Center for
Applied Linguistics, 1969), pp. 3-7.

A selection, chapter, or other part of a compilation

8 Richard McKeon, "Rhetoric in the Middle Ages," in
<u>Critics and Criticism</u>, ed. R. S. Crane (Chicago: Univ. of
Chicago Press, 1952), p. 271.

A translation

9 Maurice Merleau-Ponty, <u>Phenomenology of Perception</u>,
trans. Colin Smith (London: Routledge, 1962), pp. 88-90.

A book that is part of a series

10 Carl N. Degler, <u>Affluence and Anxiety</u>, 2nd ed., The
Scott, Foresman American History Series (Glenview, Ill.:
Scott, Foresman, 1975), p. 125.

A reprinted book

11 Alfred North Whitehead, <u>Modes of Thought</u> (1938; rpt.
New York: Putnam, Capricorn Books, 1958), pp. 26-27.

A signed article in a newspaper

12 Steve Cady, "Dreams Grow from Asphalt," <u>New York</u>
<u>Times</u>, 13 July 1975, Sec. 5, p. 3, cols. 6-7.

An unsigned article in a weekly newsmagazine

13 "Nixon's Fight for Life," <u>Newsweek</u>, 11 Nov. 1974,
p. 27.

An article in a monthly magazine

14 Walter Litten, "The Most Poisonous Mushrooms,"
<u>Scientific American</u>, March 1975, pp. 90-91.

A journal article

15 Walter J. Ong, "The Writer's Audience is Always a
Fiction," <u>PMLA</u>, 90 (1975), 19.

Because the journal (unlike most newspapers and magazines) is paged
continuously throughout the calendar year, the volume number is given
and only the year of publication is provided.

A journal article with corporate authorship

16 NCTE Commission on Composition, "Teaching Composition: A Position Statement," <u>College English</u>, 36 (October
1974), 219.

In this case, because this volume does not coincide with the calendar
year, the month is included. See the previous example.

A signed encyclopedia article

17 S[tanley] We[intraub], "George Bernard Shaw,"
<u>Encyclopaedia Britannica</u>, Macropaedia 16, 1974.

A book review

[18] Michael Wood, "Incomparable Empson," rev. of
William Empson: The Man and His Work, ed. Roma Gill, New
York Review of Books, 23 Jan. 1975, p. 30.

An unpublished dissertation

[19] Frances Nicol Teague, "Ben Jonson's Stagecraft in
His Four Major Comedies," Diss. Univ. of Texas, 1975, p. 71.

3. Form for later reference.
a. Subsequent references to a source you have already cited in full should be no longer than is necessary to identify the work. For example, a second reference to Michael Wood's review of the book on Empson should be reduced to "Wood" and the page number: Wood, p. 31. If more than one work by the same author is footnoted, then a subsequent reference to one of them must include at least the key word in the title. If two or more authors with the same last name appear in footnotes, a second reference to any one of them must include enough additional detail—first name or initials—for identification.

For reference to the footnote immediately preceding, *ibid.,* meaning "in the same place," can be used; but it saves very little space and if used inaccurately can cause serious confusion. See *ibid.*

b. When a single work is quoted frequently—as, for example, in an analysis of an article or book—the first footnote to it can state that all subsequent page references will be made in parentheses immediately following the quotations. For example:

Of his "defensibles," Follett says that *aggravate* "is perhaps the one least entitled to mercy" (p. 125).

4. Split note. If the author's name is given in full in the text, it can be omitted from the footnote. This does not apply to the title of a work, however. If title and author both appear in the text, the title should still begin the note.

See Bibliographical form, Research papers. References: James D. Lester, *Writing Research Papers,* 2nd ed. (Glenview, Ill.: Scott, 1976); *The MLA Style Sheet,* 2nd ed. (New York: Modern Language Association, 1970).

for
Since *for* always comes between the clauses it joins, it is classified as a coordinating conjunction, but coordinating *for* may mean the same as subordinating *because:* He was exhausted, for he had gone two nights without sleep. A comma is usually needed between clauses joined by *for* to keep it from being read as a preposition: The tutors must love the work, for the pay, which is only $300 a year plus room and board, can't be very attractive. The comma prevents the misreading: The tutors must love the work for the pay. See *because.*

Foreign words in English

1. Anglicizing foreign words. English has always borrowed words and roots freely from other languages and is still borrowing, especially from Greek and French. Words usually cross the threshold of English with their foreign spelling, perhaps with un-English plurals or other forms, and with no established English pronunciation. The process of anglicizing brings them more or less in line with English usage, but they may keep some of their foreign quality, like the *i* of *machine*, the silent *s* in *debris*, the *t* where we are tempted to put a *d* in *kindergarten*.

The speed and degree of anglicizing depends on how frequently the word is used, the circumstances in which it is used, and the people who use it. Formal writers and conservative editors keep the foreign spelling longer than writers and editors of general English. If the words come in through the spoken language, like those of the automobile vocabulary, they are anglicized sooner than if they come in by way of literature: *chassis, chauffeur, garage, detour.* Words that come in through and remain in literary, scholarly, or socially elite circles change more slowly, in both spelling and pronunciation: *tête-à-tête, faux pas, nouveau riche, laissez-faire.*

2. Using borrowed words.

a. Italics. Words which have not been completely anglicized are usually printed in italics in magazines and books and should be underlined in copy. Words on the borderline will be found sometimes in italics, sometimes not. Formal writers use italics more than general writers.

b. Accents and other marks. In books and magazines, words recently taken in from other languages are usually written with accent marks if they were so written in the language of their origin. After a time the accents are dropped unless they are needed to indicate pronunciation. Publications for the general public are more likely to drop accent marks *(expose, detente)* than are those for limited, scholarly audiences *(exposé, détente).* See Accent marks.

c. Plurals. English usually brings borrowed words into its own system of conjugation and declension *(campuses)*, though some words change slowly, especially words used mainly in formal writing *(syllabi* or *syllabuses)*. See Plurals of nouns 4.

See English language, Origin of words. References: Albert C. Baugh, *A History of the English Language*, 2nd ed. (New York: Appleton, 1957); Mencken; Pyles; Thomas Pyles, *Words and Ways of American English* (New York: Random, 1952); Mary Serjeantson, *A History of Foreign Words in English* (London: Routledge, 1935).

form Formal English

The word or passage marked is too formal for the subject or for the style of the rest of the essay. Revise, making it more appropriate.

Formal written English is appropriate (though not mandatory) in discussions of ideas, in research papers and other scholarly works, in addresses to be delivered on ceremonial occasions, and in literary essays intended for well-educated readers. It is usually not appropriate in accounts of personal experience, in papers about campus issues, in comments on current books, movies, TV shows, or popular records, or in other writing intended for general readers.

The vocabulary of formal style includes many words not used in general written English. *Form* in the margin of your paper may refer to a word that is too formal for the context: For a while it looked as though the bad habits he had picked up were irremediable [*Better*: could never be corrected]. Or it may point to a sentence pattern that suggests the deliberate pace of formal English and therefore mixes poorly with sentences that suggest the spontaneity of speech:

In addition to being younger than my classmates, I had retained, along with the babyish habit of sucking my thumb, a tendency to cry when I was not allowed to have my own way, thereby turning them against me. *Possible revision*: Besides being younger than my classmates, I still sucked my thumb. This irritated them, and I made things worse by crying when I didn't get my own way.

For discussion, see the Introduction, pp. 2–7.

Form-class words

These are the nouns, verbs, adjectives, and adverbs that function words bind together in sentences. See Parts of speech.

former, first — latter, last

Traditionally, *former* and *latter* refer only to two units — "the former called the latter 'little prig'" (Ralph Waldo Emerson) — and though, in fact, the use of *latter* with more than two is common enough to be standard, conservative readers would prefer "the last named" in references like this one: "The list of products . . . could include potassium, bromine, chlorine, caustic, and magnesium. The latter might become a very important lightweight metal" (Glenn T. Seaborg, *Bulletin of the Atomic Scientists*). *Former* should be used only with two. Reference: Copperud, p. 109.

First and *last* refer to items in a series, usually more than two:

The first president had set up a very informal organization. His last act was to advise his family on their future.

Latest refers to a series that is still continuing (the latest fashions). *Last* refers either to the final item of a completed series (their last attempt was successful) or to the most recent item of a continuing series (the last election). See *last, latest*.

Forms of discourse

For the last century or so it has been conventional to divide writing into four forms of discourse — narration, description, exposition, and argument. The classification is useful because it emphasizes purpose as the controlling element in a piece of writing, and studying the forms one by one allows concentration on certain traits of content, organization, and style peculiar to each type. The categories are not, however, sharply distinct — description contributes to all, notably to narration; many essays which are primarily argumentative include stretches of exposition; and so on.

Formulas

Every language has some fixed phrases that have become customary in certain situations: Once upon a time, Ladies and gentlemen, Good morning, Best wishes, Dear Sir, Yours truly, How do you do? Occasionally fresh substitutes can be found, but more often the attempt merely calls attention to itself. Such phrases, though stereotyped, are too useful to be called trite, and they are not, as most trite expressions are, substitutes for some simpler locution. When called for, they should be used without apology and without embarrassment. See Idiom, Subjunctive mood 2a.

Fractions

Fractions are written in figures when they are attached to other figures ($72\frac{3}{4}$) or are in a series that is in figures ($\frac{1}{2}$, $\frac{2}{3}$, 1, 2, 4) or are in tables or reference matter. In most running text they are written in words: In the local newspaper three fourths of the space was given to advertising, one eighth to news, and one eighth to miscellaneous matters. Hyphens may be used between the numerator and denominator if neither part itself contains a hyphen (*seven-tenths*), and they should be used to avoid confusion: though *twenty seven eighths* probably means "twenty-seven eighths," it could mean "twenty seven-eighths." But hyphens are less used than formerly and are not used at all when the numerator has the value of an adjective, as in "He sold one half and kept the other."

Decimals are increasingly used in place of fractions in factual writing, since they are more flexible and may be more accurate: .7; .42; 3.14159.

See Numbers.

frag Fragment

The construction marked is not a satisfactory sentence. Revise by joining it to a neighboring sentence, by making it grammatically complete, or by rewriting the passage.

A sentence fragment is a part of a sentence — usually a phrase or dependent clause — that is carelessly or ineffectively punctuated as a whole sentence. You can usually correct a fragment by joining it to the preceding or following sentence or by otherwise making it grammatically complete. But sometimes you'll find that rewriting is the best solution.

Below, with suggested revisions, are three common types of fragments.

1. A prepositional phrase punctuated as a sentence

The northern part of the city is mainly residential. On the eastern outskirts are the oil refining plants. And to the south beaches and parks.
Revision: The northern part of the city is mainly residential. On the eastern outskirts are the oil refining plants and to the south beaches and parks.

2. A participial phrase punctuated as a sentence

For sixteen years I did pretty much what I wanted. Being distrustful and avoiding anyone in authority.
Revision: For sixteen years I did pretty much what I wanted to, distrusting and avoiding anyone in authority.

3. A dependent clause punctuated as a sentence

I still remember him as the best teacher I ever had. Because right then he sat down and helped me work all the problems.
Revision: I still remember him as the best teacher I ever had, because right then he sat down and helped me work all the problems.

In an unexpectedly heavy turnout, over 80 percent of the citizens voted. A fact that shows how strongly they felt about the issue.
Revision: . . . the citizens voted—a fact that shows. . . . *Or* . . . the citizens voted. This fact shows. . . .

The deliberate setting off of a phrase or dependent clause for rhetorical effect is common in print. Unfortunately, it has become a cliché of heavy-breathing advertising copy (The magic of a coral atoll; Discovering the real you). But it can do good service as an organizational road sign that briskly points the reader toward the next topic—"But first, the new troops" (Lucian K. Truscott IV, *Harper's*)—or provides informal notice of the progress of the discussion—"Which brings us back to the absurdity of the backlash accusations" (Letty Cottin Pogrebin, *Ms.*). And fragments of some length can sometimes be used effectively to pile up details in descriptive writing:

Prairie wool blue-green, spring wheat bright as new lawn, winter wheat gray-green at rest and slaty when the wind flaws it, roadside primroses as shy as prairie flowers are supposed to be, and as gentle to the eye as when in my boyhood we used to call them wild tulips, and by their coming date the beginning of summer.—Wallace Stegner, *Wolf Willow*

See Clauses, Phrases.

Free modifiers

A free modifier is a nonrestrictive modifier. See Restrictive and nonrestrictive.

freshman, freshmen

The modifier is *freshman*, not only before nouns with an obviously singular reference (a freshman dorm) but before plural and abstract nouns (freshman courses, freshman orientation).

-ful, full

When the adjective *full* is used as a suffix to nouns of measure (*basketful, spoonful*) or of feeling or quality (*peaceful, sorrowful, soulful*), it has only one *l*. In the separate word, both *l*'s are kept (a basket full of apples).

The plural of nouns ending in *-ful* is usually made with *-s*: *spoonfuls, basketfuls*. When *full* is written as a separate word, the preceding noun is made plural: *spoons full, baskets full*.

fulsome

The *ful-* in *fulsome* misleads some readers and writers into thinking the word means "generous" or "hearty," but *fulsome praise* (a rather formal cliché) actually means praise that is overdone and insincere and therefore offensive. Because of possible ambiguity, *fulsome* is a good word to avoid.

Function words

Function words are the auxiliaries, conjunctions, determiners, and so forth that bind together form-class words. See Parts of speech.

further, farther

Both *farther* and *further* are used in referring to distance. See *farther, further*.

Fused sentence

Fused or *run-on sentence* is the name sometimes given to two grammatically complete sentences written with no mark of punctuation between them: If you ask me why I did it, I can only say that at the time it seemed the right thing to do [ ] that is my only explanation. To correct the error, begin a new sentence or insert a semicolon. Compare Comma fault.

Future time

English verbs do not inflect, or change their form, to express future time. Some of the means we use to refer to the future are illustrated in these sentences: I am leaving next week; He sails tomorrow; She is to speak on Saturday; He is about to resign; When I am elected, I will make an investigation; They will try to be on time; She is going to refuse. See Tenses of verbs.

Gender

Modern English does not have regular and distinctive endings for masculine, feminine, and neuter nouns, for articles and adjectives modifying them, or for many pronouns referring to them—grammatical gender. Instead, we call nouns masculine, feminine, or neuter according to the sex or lack of sex of their referents, using *he, she,* or *it* as their pronouns. We use *who* mainly for human beings, *which* and *what* for inanimate objects. Usually, then, in speaking of gender in English, we are talking about the choice of pronouns and about the meaning of the words that govern that choice.

Some English nouns refer to living things of either sex *(parent),* some to one sex *(father),* some to the other *(mother).* Some names for animate beings imply no sex distinction *(friend),* though compounds allow the distinction to be made *(girl friend).* When we ignore the sex of an animal, we use *it* to refer to the noun that names the beast, just as we sometimes use *it* of a child. We have no pronoun meaning "either-he-or-she." Traditionally, *he* has been used, but that usage is rejected by opponents of sexist language, who prefer *he or she, he/she,* or *they.* Though a fair number of nouns have endings that distinguish gender *(actor, actress; alumnus, alumna; comedian, comedienne),* they remain an unsystematized minority. Here, too, feminists call for sex-free labels.

In rather old-fashioned formal styles, the sun may be *he,* the moon *she.* In informal English, *she* sometimes replaces *it,* especially where affection or intimate concern is involved, as when a driver speaks of his car. See *he or she,* Sexist language.

General English

General English is the core of standard English. Spoken general English is what we hear in most talks for general audiences, in news broadcasts, and in the ordinary conversation of educated people. Written, edited general English is what we read in newspapers, magazines, and most books. The main focus of this *Index* is on written general English. See Introduction, pp. 2–7.

Genitive case

1. Signs of the genitive. The genitive (or possessive) function in English is shown in four ways:

a. Apostrophe-*s* or apostrophe alone. Singular nouns that do not end in the sound of *s* as in *chess* or of *z* as in *breeze* and plural nouns that do not end in the letter *s* add apostrophe-*s*: *boy's, one's, England's, men's, children's, freshmen's.* After plural nouns ending in -*s*, only an apostrophe is used: *workers' incomes, dogs' teeth, coaches' rules.*

For singular nouns ending in the *s* or *z* sound, practice varies, as do the recommendations of the stylebooks that encourage systematic rules for the sake of consistency. The system proposed by the *Manual of Style* calls for an apostrophe-*s* after all singular nouns except *Jesus, Moses,* classical names ending in -*es* *(Socrates, Xerxes),* and words like *conscience* and *goodness* before *sake;* these exceptions take an apostrophe only.

To indicate joint possession, the apostrophe is added only to the second of two coordinate nouns: "Martha and George's son."

In "Mary's and Tom's bicycles," separate objects are possessed, and an apostrophe-*s* is needed for each noun. References: *A Manual of Style,* pp. 129–30; Margaret Nicholson, *A Practical Style Guide for Authors and Editors* (New York: Holt, 1967), pp. 93–97; *U.S. Style Manual,* pp. 70–71.

b. The *of* genitive. Any genitive formed with an apostrophe or apostrophe-*s* can also be formed with an *of* phrase (the dancer's performance, the performance of the dancer). The choice between the two will usually depend on considerations of rhythm, idiom, and the syntactical pressures of neighboring phrases and clauses. Idiom calls for "the roof of the house," not "the house's roof." The *of* genitive is easier to work with when the noun in the genitive is to be modified by clauses or by other genitives. For example, both "the car's tires" and "the tires of the car" are acceptable, but if *car* is to be modified by the clause "that John used to drive," the *of* genitive is clearer: the tires of the car that John used to drive (*not* the car that John used to drive's tires). If we want to indicate that the car is John's, the *of* genitive avoids a perplexing succession of apostrophes: the tires of John's car (*not* John's car's tires).

There is also a possible difference in meaning between the two forms. "Jane's picture" probably means a picture belonging to Jane, but it might mean a picture of Jane. "A picture of Jane" can only mean that Jane is represented in the picture.

c. Double genitive. Using the *of* genitive and apostrophe-*s* together is an English idiom of long and respectable standing. It is especially common in locutions beginning with *that* or *this* and usually has an informal flavor: that boy of Henry's; friends of my father's; hobbies of Anne's. It is useful in avoiding the ambiguity mentioned above: "Jane's picture" is resolved as either "that picture of Jane" or "that picture of Jane's."

d. Genitive of the personal pronouns. The personal and relative pronouns have genitive forms without an apostrophe: *my, your, his, her, its, our, their, whose.* It is as important not to put apostrophes in these pronouns (and in the forms used without nouns: *ours, yours, theirs, hers*) as it is to put one in a noun in the genitive. See *its, it's;* Pronouns 1; *which* 2.

2. Uses of the genitive. The most common function of the genitive is to indicate possession: the professor's house, Al's dog, my daughter. It also indicates a number of other relationships:

Description: a man's job, children's toys, suit of wool

Doer of an act (the "subjective genitive"): the wind's force, the force of the wind; John Knowles's second novel; with the dean's permission, with the permission of the dean; the doctor's arrival, the arrival of the doctor

Recipient of an act (the "objective genitive"): the policeman's murderer, the murderer of the policeman; the bill's defeat, the defeat of the bill

Adverb: He drops in of an evening.

See Case, Gerunds 2. References: Bryant, pp. 50–51, 74–75, 93–94; Copperud, pp. 215–16; Fries, pp. 72–88; Jespersen, pp. 138–46; Quirk et al., pp. 192–203.

Gerunds

1. Form and function. A gerund—also called a verbal noun—is the *-ing* form of a verb used as a noun. It can serve in any noun function: as subject or complement of a verb (*Seeing* is *believing*) or as object of a verb or preposition (He taught *dancing*; The odds are against your *winning*). Like a noun, a gerund can be modified by an adjective (Good *boxing* was rare) or used as a modifier (a *fishing* boat, a *living* wage). Yet, like a verb, it can take a subject and an object and can be modified by an adverb: One despairs of the author [subject] ever [adverb] *constructing* a really forceful play [object].

A gerund may be in the present or the perfect tense and in the active or passive voice: *seeing, having seen; being seen, having been seen.*

Though the gerund has the same form as the present participle, it is used differently:

Gerund: Running a hotel appealed to him. (*Running* is the subject.)
Participle: He was busy running a hotel. (*Running* modifies *he.*)

2. Subject of a gerund. The subject of a gerund is sometimes in the genitive and sometimes in the accusative or objective (in nouns, the "common") case. Formal writing uses the genitive more than general writing does: "Such a view leads to the metaphor's becoming a brief poem in itself" (Alex Page, *Modern Philology*). General is likely to use the common case: "The Vice President's humorous remarks about Hofstra not picking up this ball are somewhat offset . . . by the record" (Clifford Lord, *College Board Review*).

In both formal and general, the circumstances in which the subject of a gerund occurs make one choice more probable than the other:

a. When the subject is a personal pronoun or a proper noun, the genitive is more usual than the common case: They wanted to discuss *my going* AWOL; We overlooked *Joe's swearing.* When the subject is a personal pronoun and begins the sentence, the genitive is required: *Our* [not *Us*] *worrying* won't solve anything; *His* [not *Him*] *lying* deceived nobody.

b. If the subject is a plural noun, it is likely to be in the common case even if it refers to persons: I don't approve of *men drinking* or *women smoking.*

c. If the subject is abstract or the name of an inanimate object, it is most often in the common case: It was an instance of *imagination getting* out of hand; The city was seized without a *shell being fired.*

References: Copperud, pp. 113–14; Evans and Evans, pp. 245–48; Pooley, pp. 107–12.

3. Phrases with gerunds. Gerunds are often used in phrases that function somewhat like dependent clauses: *In coming to an agreement,* they had compromised on all points; *By refusing to sing,* he embarrassed his father. The relation of the gerund phrase to the word it modifies should be immediately apparent; the reader should not have to pause to make sure just what the writer intended:

Dangling: In coming to an agreement, campaign promises were ignored.
Revision: In coming to an agreement, both sides ignored their campaign promises.

Dangling: After sleeping sixteen hours, my headache was finally gone.
Revision: After sleeping sixteen hours, I was finally rid of my headache.

See Dangling modifiers.

4. Idioms with gerunds. Some words are characteristically followed by gerunds, others by infinitives. For example:

Gerunds	*Infinitives*
can't help *doing*	compelled *to do*
capable of *painting*	able *to paint*
the habit of *giving*	the tendency *to give*
an idea of *selling*	a wish *to sell*
enjoys *playing*	likes *to play*

With many common words, either is used: the way *of doing* something, the way *to do* something.

Compare Infinitives, Participles. References: Jespersen, Ch. 31; Long and Long, pp. 192–96.

get up

In general English you get up when you stand up or get out of bed. See *rise, arise, get up.*

go

Go in the sense "become" is used as a linking verb in a number of idioms. While some (*go broke, go native, go straight*) are informal to general, others (*go blind, go lame*) are fully established in all varieties. *Go and,* as an intensive with no actual motion implied, is common in speech and turns up in some general writing: "He has gone and made a genuine commercial film" (Joseph Morgenstern, *Newsweek*). *Going for* in the sense "working to the advantage of" is general: "when women in England didn't have much going for them" (Emily Hahn, *New York Times Book Review*). Neither *go and* nor *going for* in these senses is appropriate in formal writing.

Gobbledygook

Maury Maverick, a congressman from Texas, coined the term *gobbledygook* for wordy, pompous, overweight prose that confuses and irritates more than it informs. Although government bureaus have produced their full share of examples, business, the military, the social sciences, and the humanities have shown an equal weakness for inflated jargon. Frequently gobbledygook serves the purpose of disguising the truth. See Diction 2, Doublespeak, Jargon. Reference: Copperud, pp. 118–19.

good, well

Good is usually an adjective in standard English; *well* is either an adjective or an adverb. "I feel good" and "I feel well" (adjectives) are both usual but have different meanings, *good* implying actual bodily sensation, *well* referring merely to a state, "not ill." In nonstandard usage, *good* takes the place of *well:* He played good; She sings good. Adverbial *good* is also heard in informal speech and frequently appears in printed representations of speech: "She's running good now," the mechanic said. Reference: Copperud, p. 119.

got, gotten

Either *got* or *gotten* is acceptable as the past participle of *get* except in the following senses:

  Got (not *gotten*) is often added to *has* or *have* to emphasize the notion of "possess" (I haven't got a cent) or of "must" (You've got to lend me a dollar). Though seldom used in formal writing, the emphatic *got* is fairly common in general: "A lot of adults are bored by Bach because they haven't got the faintest idea of what music is about" (Marya Mannes, *TV Guide*). References: Bryant, pp. 95–98; Copperud, pp. 119–20; Pooley, pp. 144–47.

gourmet

A gourmet is a connoisseur of food and drink. As a vogue word, the adjective *gourmet* is regularly applied to food, restaurants, and cooking that a gourmet could not stomach. If you mean "foreign," "expensive," or "fancy," use those words. To express general approval, *good* is available.

graduate

The idiom *to be graduated from* an institution has generally gone out of use except in formal and somewhat archaic writing and has been replaced by *graduated from:* He graduated from Yale in 1850. Omitting the *from*—He graduated high school in 1976—is a common usage that many still consider nonstandard. References: Bryant, pp. 102–103; Copperud, p. 120.

Grammar

Grammar has several different senses. Just as *history* can mean a field of study, events in the past, or the book that describes those events, so *grammar* can refer to a field of study, a set of abilities in our brains, or the book that describes those abilities.

1. As a field of study, grammar is as old as intellectual inquiry itself. The pre-Socratic philosophers in Greece in the sixth century B.C. had begun speculating about language and words (*grammar* comes from *grammatikos*, "one who understands the use of letters") long before the Stoics in 300 B.C. singled grammar out as a field separate from rhetoric and poetics. Since then scholars have continued to study the structure of language, not only because language is the central defining characteristic of humankind but because it seems possible that the very foundations of our knowledge and thought—perhaps even perception itself—are shaped by the grammatical structures of our language. Grammar thus becomes an entry to the study of mind.

2. *Grammar* may also refer to this capacity of mind, the ability every normal human being possesses to speak and understand sentences. Thus we all have a grammar in our heads. Every human being understands an indefinite number of new sentences he has never heard before. He can recognize grammatical and ungrammatical sentences (see *grammatical, ungrammatical* 1). He can recognize sentences which are ambiguous in several different ways. He also understands that some sentences relate to others, as this one does to the next two.

That some sentences relate to others is also understood by him. It is also understood by him that some sentences relate to others.

The goal of a linguist, a scholar who studies grammatical structure, is to describe in a written grammar this tacit knowledge, this internalized grammar, that all of us share.

3. Though the formal aspects of language have been studied for over 2500 years, linguists are debating more strenuously than ever before both what questions they should concern themselves with and how their answers should be formulated in written grammars. At the risk of gross overgeneralization, it can be said that the history of linguistic study in the last hundred years falls into three schools.

a. Traditional. Although this label is applied to a great variety of approaches, most traditional grammars start with semantic definitions for parts of speech and the inflections that are associated with them: nouns are names of persons, places, and things, and so on. Once the parts of speech have been described, the grammar describes functions: subjects, verbs, objects, modifiers, etc. The definitions are illustrated by examples. The reader of the grammar is expected to understand the labeling through the descriptions and examples and then to use his native knowledge of the language to apply the label in any new sentence that might contain the pattern. For example:

A sentence adverb modifies a whole sentence rather than any individual word or construction. It usually stands at the beginning of the sentence, though it may occur elsewhere: *Fortunately,* he left; He is *allegedly* still here; No one cares, *obviously.*

Confronted with the sentence "*Apparently,* she left," you could identify *apparently* as a sentence adverb on the basis of the explanation and examples. Such descriptions—semantically based as they are—require the ability of a native speaker to make them work. References: George Oliver Curme, *Parts of Speech and Accidence* (Boston: Heath, 1935), and *Syntax* (Boston: Heath, 1931); Otto Jespersen, *A Modern English Grammar on Historical Principles,* 7 vols. (1909–49; rpt. New York: Barnes, 1954); Long; Quirk et al.

b. Structural. When, in the early part of this century, anthropologists began to deal more and more with languages that had no written form and were totally unrelated to the Indo-European languages already well known, a new approach to grammatical description emerged in this country. Structural linguists tried to devise objective techniques for discovering the structure of a language without relying on semantics. They began by cataloging the sounds produced by native speakers, then identifying the smallest units that seemed to have meaning (morphemes), and then arranging these units into larger classes, not according to their lexical content but according to their customary relationships with other units. Once the parts of speech were classified, higher-order syntactic sequences were identified (noun–verb, verb–noun, preposition–noun, adjective–noun, etc.) and then further described functionally (subject–predicate, verb–object, modifier–head, etc.). A rough approximation of this technique can be found in Parts of speech. References: Francis; Fries; Sledd.

c. Generative-transformational. Through the 1940s and most of the 1950s, structural grammars were thought to be the new wave in English language education. Then in 1957 Noam Chomsky, a linguist at the Massachusetts Institute of Technology, published *Syntactic Structures* and revolutionized the study of language. Chomsky turned linguists away from formal discovery procedures, which he claimed were largely useless, and toward a model of language that tries to account in a formal set of rules for the ability of native speakers to produce and understand an infinite range of new sentences. Grammarians of the generative-transformational school assume the existence of a grammar in the mind of the native speaker. They seek to account for what all languages have in common, as well as for the peculiarities which distinguish English, say, from German; and they attempt to deal with the full range of language, from sounds to meaning, in an integrated theory.

Chomsky's initial formulations of generative theory have been considerably modified and revised in recent work, which has assigned more importance to semantics than to syntax (generative semantics and case grammar are the most important examples). And there are adherents of theories of language description other than generative—tagmemic grammars, stratificational grammars, dependency grammars, and others. But the dominant models for research into the structure of English and other languages have been generative-transformational. References: Adrian Akmajian and Frank Heny, *An Introduction to the Principles of Transformational Syntax* (Cambridge, Mass.: MIT Press, 1975); Noam Chomsky, *Language and Mind,* enl. ed. (New York: Harcourt, 1972); Charles J. Fillmore and D. Terence Langendoen, *Studies in Linguistic Semantics* (New York: Holt, 1971); Jacobs and Rosenbaum; Robert P. Stockwell, Paul Schachter, and Barbara Hall Partee, *The Major Syntactic Structures of English* (New York: Holt, 1973).

4. So far, we have ignored what may be the most common meaning of *grammar*. This is grammar in the sense of "good grammar" — making the "right" choice between *who* and *whom*, avoiding prepositions at the ends of sentences, not splitting infinitives, and so on. This is *grammar* in its normative sense. It concentrates only on those areas where usage varies from one social class to another or from the way English teachers think educated people speak to the way their students actually speak.

How we communicate depends on our social class, our geographical roots, the social situation we happen to be in, and our mode of communication — speaking or writing. What most schools teach as grammar are those features that allegedly distinguish written, fairly formal, supposedly upper-middle-class usage from all other varieties. It is a serious mistake to assume that this form of usage alone defines "correct" usage.

Thus when you use the word *grammar*, you have to distinguish a variety of senses:

Grammar is a field of scholarly inquiry dating back beyond Aristotle.

A grammar of a language is in the mind of every speaker of that language. Its "real" nature is entirely inaccessible to direct observation.

A grammar of a language is that set of rules which can be written down and which will generate the sentences of that language along with a description of each sentence. The object of this grammar is to "model" or explain grammar in sense 2.

Grammar in the sense of "He uses good grammar" is the ability we have acquired that allows us to demonstrate that we can observe certain usages that allegedly characterize the practice of upper-middle-class speakers and writers. A grammar of good usage consists of the prescriptions found in grammar books — usually fewer than twenty or thirty — that allow someone aspiring to membership in the "educated" community to speak and write as those already in that community allegedly speak and write.

This last sense of *grammar* is, unfortunately, the sense most familiar to American students. The associations that cluster about this sense make it very difficult for linguists to communicate the excitement of discovering something about grammar (sense 2) that he can write down in a grammar (sense 3) that reveals the elegantly complex organization of human linguistic knowledge.

Reference: Quirk et al., pp. 7–12.

grammatical, ungrammatical

Sentences can be grammatical in two senses:

1. Sentences are grammatical when they meet the structural requirements of the grammar used by an individual speaker. "Can't nobody tell me what to do" is ungrammatical for some speakers, but it is grammatical for others, if the grammar they have incorporated into their nervous systems allows them to construct that sentence for ordinary conversation (see Grammar 2). "Nobody can tell me what to do" might, conversely, be ungrammatical for those speakers who habitually put the modal auxiliary and negative first ("Can't nobody tell me what to do") but grammatical for those who do not. In this sense, *grammatical* simply describes the structure of a sentence that is normal for use by a particular speaker in his ordinary discourse. And in this sense nobody, except by mistake or by intention, utters an ungrammatical sentence. For example, the made-up sentence "I know the man who and the woman left" is ungrammatical for all speakers of English.

2. In common and school usage, sentences are said to be "grammatical" when they meet the requirements set by those who are in a position to enforce standards of usage. In this looser sense, "Can't nobody tell me what to do" is said to be "ungrammatical" for everyone, and a person to whom the construction is normal and systematic with reference to an internalized grammar (see Grammar 2) is said to be speaking "ungrammatical" English. In such cases the terms *grammatical* and *ungrammatical* are judgmental rather than descriptive: they name social behaviors acceptable or unacceptable to those whose judgments often carry the most weight in our stratified society. Such usages would be more accurately termed "socially acceptable" and "socially unacceptable." In many cases, advice based on this sense of *grammatical* can be quite accurate: most educated people in this country do not say "Can't nobody tell me what to do"; in writing, most make their subjects and verbs agree; most avoid *ain't* in all but relatively informal situations. On the other hand, rules for sociologically grammatical usage also involve a good deal of folklore, as many of the articles in this *Index* make clear.

See Usage. References: Harold B. Allen, ed., *Readings in Applied Linguistics*, 2nd ed. (New York: Appleton, 1964), Part IV; Noam Chomsky in *The Structure of Language,* ed. Jerry A. Fodor and Jerrold J. Katz (Englewood Cliffs, N.J.: Prentice-Hall, 1964), pp. 384–89; William Labov, *Language in the Inner City* (Philadelphia: Univ. of Pennsylvania Press, 1972), Ch. 5.

Group words

In English many groups of two or more words (that is, phrases) function like single words. Examples:

Nouns: hay fever, back door, holding company, home run, safety razor, baby blue, school year, sacrifice hit

Verbs: dig in, hold off, look into, flare up, follow through, follow up, close up, show up, blow up, back water

Prepositions: according to, in spite of, in consequence of, previous to, due to, in opposition to

In this book we ignore the superficial difference between a part of speech written as a single word and one that is written as a group of words. *Noun* (sometimes *noun phrase*) or *verb* or *preposition* refers both to single words and to group words functioning as noun or verb or preposition.

guess

Formal usage limits *guess* to its sense of "conjecture, estimate, surmise": "The employers can only guess whom the victims will choose to sue" (Henry L. Woodward, *Yale Law Journal*). But in general and informal usage *guess* is common in its looser senses of "think, suppose, believe": "They were foolish, I guess, in trying to hold history still for one more hour" (Larry L. King, *Atlantic*).

had better, had rather

Had better is the usual idiom in giving advice or an indirect command: You had better take care of that cold; You'd better go. The assimilation of the *d* in *you'd* to the *b* of *better* has given rise to the informal construction without either *had* or *'d*: "But I better get with it if I'm going to be a TV viewer" (Goodman Ace, *Saturday Review*). Reference: Copperud, p. 32.

Had rather and *would rather* are both used to express preference: He would rather ski than eat; He had rather ski than eat. Use whichever seems more natural. In speech both *had* and *would* contract to *'d:* He'd rather ski than eat. Reference: Bryant, pp. 104–105.

half

Though *a half* is traditionally considered the more elegant of the two idioms, little distinction can be found between *a half* and *half a* in current formal and general usage. For example, both "a half century earlier" and "nearly half a century removed" occur in a single issue of the *American Historical Review*. *A half a* (a half an hour) is an informal redundancy.

The number of the noun accompanying *half* or *half of* in a subject determines the number of the verb: Half of the book is . . . ; Half the men are. . . .

hanged, hung

In formal English people are hanged, pictures are hung. General and informal usage often ignores this distinction, using *hang, hung, hung* in all senses: "Of course, McCarthy hung himself at the hearing" (Isidore Silver, *New Republic*). Reference: Copperud, p. 133.

hardly

Hardly means "probably not," so don't add another *not*. See Double negative 2.

have

1. Independent meaning. As a verb of independent meaning *have* means "own, possess" in a literal sense (have a car) or a transferred sense (have the measles). Because *have* occurs so frequently as an "empty" auxiliary word, its meaning as an independent word is often reinforced by *got* (see *got, gotten*).

2. Auxiliary. *Have* plus a past participle makes the perfect tense (They have come); *shall have* or *will have* plus a past participle makes the future perfect tense (They will have gone by then); *had* plus a past participle makes the past perfect (They had gone to the beach before we arrived). In this use *have* is a function word—a signal of tense. See Tenses of verbs 2.

3. Contractions. *He, she, it has* contract to *he's, she's, it's* (He's not tried to in years; It's rained for a week). Contractions with *has* and *is* are indistinguishable: *He's gone* may be *He has gone* or *He is gone*. *I, you, we, they have* contract to *I've, you've, we've, they've*. Both *had* and *would* contract to *'d* (They'd already spoken; She'd already be waiting).

Would have, wouldn't have are sometimes written *would of, wouldn't of*, a nonstandard transcription of what is spoken as *would've, wouldn't've*.

4. *Had ought, hadn't ought.* *Had ought* (He had ought to take better care of himself) is a common nonstandard idiom, sometimes heard in informal speech. *Hadn't ought* (He hadn't ought to lie like that) is regional and informal. Reference: Atwood, pp. 38–41.

5. *Have to.* *Have to* and *must* are nearly synonymous in the affirmative (I *have to* [or *must*] go now), but in the negative there is a difference (I don't have to go; I mustn't go). *Have to* has the advantage that it can be conjugated in all tenses.

6. Other idioms. For *have got*, see *got, gotten*. See also *had better, had rather*.

Headword

A headword, or head, is a word modified by another word, especially a noun modified by one or more adjectives (his first long *sleep*), a verb modified by one or more adverbs (*walk* carefully), or an adjective or adverb modified by qualifiers (very *old*, more *intelligently*). The term is used differently by different linguists but always to mean the word around which the rest of the construction is built: *men*, old *men*, very old *men*, very old *men* in raincoats, very old *men* in raincoats who had been waiting outside. References: Paul Roberts, *Patterns of English* (New York: Harcourt, 1956), pp. 77–105; Long, p. 490; Sledd, pp. 226–27; Whitehall, pp. 9–18.

healthful, healthy

The distinction between *healthful* "conducive to health" (places and foods are healthful) and *healthy* "having good health" (persons and animals are healthy) is maintained in formal and some general writing, but by and large *healthy* is now used for both meanings.

help but

Conservative stylists avoid using *can't* (or *cannot*) *help but*. See *can't help but, can't seem to*.

hence

Hence is primarily an adverb but it is also used as a rather formal connective. See Conjunctive adverbs.

he or she

The pronoun *they* does not indicate sex, but *he, she,* and *it* are masculine, feminine, and neuter. Traditionally, *he* is used with indefinite pronouns like *anyone* and *everyone* and with noun antecedents that may refer to either men or women: Every student must accept responsibility for his acts. But feminists find this usage a prime example of sexist language and prefer *he or she* (or *he/she* or *s/he*) and *his or her*. Sometimes antecedents make a masculine pronoun inappropriate and the double pronoun convenient: "In enabling a young man or woman to prepare for life in a shorter period of time, we direct his or her attention to other values" (Edward H. Litchfield, *Saturday Review*).

For writers and readers to whom avoiding *he* and *his* after a sexually indefinite antecedent is not a matter of principle, *he or she* and its variants often seem unnecessarily awkward: "Any individual who is a candidate for promotion or tenure should her/himself make sure that records are complete" (Committee recommendation). When *he* or *his* is inappropriate, *they* is a frequent choice in general writing: In helping a young man or woman to prepare for life, we must direct their attention to other values. See Agreement 2, Sexist language. References: Evans and Evans, pp. 221, 239–40, 509; Thomas H. Middleton, *Saturday Review*, June 29, 1974, p. 40.

himself, herself

Himself and *herself* are used in two ways:

1. As reflexive pronouns, referring to the subject of the sentence: George has always taken himself too seriously; She looked at herself in the window.

2. As qualifiers, for emphasis: He told me so himself; I looked up, and there was the captain himself.

historic, historical

Unlike many pairs of adjectives ending in *-ic* and *-ical, historic* and *historical* ordinarily have quite different meanings. *Historic* usually has the sense "important in history, noteworthy, famous": "a historic act: the toast to the French fleet by which the archbishop . . . urged French Catholics to abandon royalist opposition" (James E. Ward, *American Historical Review*). *Historical* is much more neutral, meaning "based on the facts of history," "having occurred in the past," "suitable for study by historians or using their methods": "This autobiography . . . provides a wide range of historical persons and events" (Heinz E. Ellersieck, ibid.).

hopefully

From an adverb with the established meaning "in a hopeful way, full of hope" (The dog waited hopefully for a handout), *hopefully* became a vogue word meaning "it is hoped": "Hopefully, they will reveal the thickness of the planet's polar ice cap" (Jonathan Spivak, *Wall Street Journal*). Sometimes it means no more than "I hope": Hopefully she'll be down in a minute. So long as it is kept away from the verb and set off by commas, there is little chance of real ambiguity; but strong prejudice against the usage continues. Reference: Copperud, p. 131.

Hours

In consecutive formal writing, hours are often written in words: at four o'clock; around five-fifteen. In newspapers and in much general writing, figures are used, especially if several times are mentioned and always in designations of time with *a.m.* and *p.m.*: at 4 p.m., just after 9 a.m., around 4:30 p.m., from 10 to 12. The twenty-four hour system used in Europe and by the U.S. military makes *a.m.* and *p.m.* redundant: 9 a.m. = 0900; 9 p.m. = 2100.

however

Though particularly appropriate as a connective in the fully developed sentences of formal style, *however* is also the most common conjunctive adverb in general writing. There it typically serves to relate a sentence to what has gone before rather than to connect main clauses within the same sentence:

Murder is usually reported, and 86 per cent of all reported murders lead to arrests. Among those arrested, however, only 64 per cent are prosecuted. – Ramsey Clark, *Saturday Review*

However is more maneuverable than *but;* it can either introduce the clause it modifies ("However, among those arrested . . .) or, as in the example, follow the words the writer wants to emphasize ("Among those arrested"). To open a clause the simpler *but* is often the better choice.

See Conjunctive adverbs. Reference: Copperud, pp. 132–33.

hung, hanged

In formal English, pictures are hung, people are hanged. See *hanged, hung.*

Hyperbole

This very common figure of speech – obvious and extravagant overstatement – is a staple of humor; but we also use hyperbole regularly in ordinary conversation when we describe our troubles as *incredible,* our embarrassments as *horrible,* our vacations as *fabulous.* Such efforts to dramatize and intensify rapidly cease to have any effect, including the hyperbolic. They are particularly tiresome in writing. See Figurative language.

Hypercorrectness

Hypercorrect forms are used by speakers and writers who extend the patterns of supposed correctness beyond their established limits. Perhaps the most common example of hypercorrectness is the use of *I* for *me* in a compound object: It is a wonderful moment for my wife and I; They invited Jack and I; between you and I. Other common hypercorrect forms include *whom* for *who* (He is critical of the other members of the committee, whom he feels spend more time making accusations than solving problems), *as* for *like* (She, as any other normal person, wanted to be well thought of), the ending *-ly* where it doesn't belong (Slice thinly), some verb forms *(lie* for *lay, shall* for *will),* and many pronunciations. Hypercorrect forms are also called hyperurbanisms. References: Theodore M. Bernstein, *The Careful Writer* (New York: Atheneum, 1968), pp. 322–23; Margaret Schlauch, *The Gift of Language* (New York: Dover, 1955), pp. 264–68.

Hyphen

In *Manuscript and Proof,* stylebook of the Oxford University Press, John Benbow wrote, "If you take the hyphen seriously, you will surely go mad." To ward off madness, adopt a recent dictionary or stylebook as your guide and follow it consistently.

1. Word division. The hyphen is always used to mark the division of a word at the end of a line (see Division of words). Other uses are in part a matter of style.

2. Compound words. Some compound words are written as two words *(post office),* some as one *(notebook),* and some as a combination of words joined by hyphens *(mother-in-law).* The trend is away from hyphenation, toward one-word spelling. Even when a prefix ends and a root word begins with the same vowel, the current tendency is to write the word solid: *cooperate, reelect, preeminent.*

A number of compound adjective forms are conventionally hyphenated when they precede a noun: *clear-eyed, able-bodied, first-class.* Compounds consisting of an adverb plus a verbal are hyphenated when the adverb does not end in *-ly:* a well-marked trail *(but* a plainly marked trail).

3. Noun phrases. Usage is divided on hyphenating noun phrases used as modifiers, as in "seventeenth century philosophy." A hyphen is more likely in formal styles: seventeenth-century philosophy.

4. Miscellaneous uses. A numeral as part of a modifier (5-cent cigar, nine-inch boards) is hyphenated, and a hyphen is used between a prefix and a proper name: pre-Sputnik, pro-Doonesbury.

A "suspension" hyphen may be used to carry the force of a modifier to a later noun: the third-, fourth-, and fifth-grade rooms;
both thirteenth- and fourteenth-century texts.

5. To avoid ambiguity. Occasionally a pair of modifiers is ambiguous without a hyphen. "A light yellow scarf" may be either a
scarf that is light yellow or a light scarf that is yellow. *Light-
yellow* makes the first meaning clear; *light, yellow* the second.
Similarly, "new car-owner" and "new-car owner" prevent misunderstanding.

References: Copperud, pp. 133–36; Regina Hoover, *CCC*, May
1971, pp. 156–60; *A Manual of Style; U.S. Style Manual;* Summey, Ch. 10.

I

The pronoun *I* is still written as a capital simply because in the
old manuscripts a small *i* might have been lost or attached to a
neighboring word; the capital helped keep it distinct. The notion
that *I* should not be the first word in a sentence is groundless. *I*
should be used wherever it is needed. Circumlocutions to avoid
the natural use of *I* are usually awkward and are likely to attract
attention to themselves: "My present thinking is that relief projects are unsound" is a clumsy way of saying "I think now [or "I
think" or "I have come to think" or "At the moment I think"] that
relief projects are unsound." See *it's me, myself, we.*

ibid.

Ibid., an abbreviation of the Latin *ibidem* ("in the same place"),
is still used, though less often than formerly, in footnotes of
scholarly books, articles, and research papers. When it stands
alone (² Ibid.), it refers the reader to the preceding citation. When
it is followed by a page number (² Ibid., p. 37), it refers to a different page of the work just cited. With or without a page number, it always refers to the citation *immediately* preceding. If a
reference to a different work has intervened, the new footnote
gives the author's name followed by *op. cit.*, an abbreviation of
opere citato ("in the work already cited"), and the page number
or, more commonly now, simply by the author's name and the
page number.

In modern styles of documentation, *ibid.* has been widely replaced by the author's name or by his name followed by a shortened version of the title of his work. Even when *ibid.* appears, its
use is often restricted to a second reference on the *same page* of
the manuscript or publication.

See Footnote form 3.

id Idiom

The expression marked is not standard idiom. Revise it, referring to an article in this *Index* or to a dictionary if you are not sure of the correct form.

Idioms are certain phrases that are established in the language but are not easy to explain grammatically or logically. Some examples are "in good stead," "come in handy," "strike a bargain," "look up an old friend," "many's the time," "make good," "in respect to." We learn these phrases as individual units, and if we are native speakers, most of them cause us no trouble. No native speaker is likely to say "the time is many" or "hit a bargain" or "look down an old friend" (though "track down" — another idiom — might be a satisfactory substitute). Many idioms are completely frozen: you can use thousands of words as subjects and verbs of sentences, but you can't substitute any other adjective in the phrase "in good stead."

We have trouble with idioms we have not learned, and most commonly the error is in the choice of preposition. Because we know *conform to,* we may speak of a policy that is "in conformity to public opinion"; but the idiom is "in conformity with." In using the formal word *arise,* we might attach the preposition *off* instead of the *from* idiom demands. Because logic is no help, the prepositions must be learned in the phrases that determine their usage. Dictionaries generally show the preposition that is conventionally used with a particular word.

See *agree to, agree with; compare, contrast; different;* Gerunds 4; *it;* Prepositions and style 1; Subjunctive mood 2a; Verbadverb combinations. References: Copperud, p. 138; Fowler, p. 261.

i.e.

I.e. is the abbreviation for the Latin words meaning "that is." It is appropriate only in scholarly writing. See Abbreviations 2.

if, whether

Writers have a choice between *if* and *whether* before interrogative clauses (indirect questions) and clauses expressing doubt or uncertainty. *Whether* is almost always chosen in formal contexts: "It is appropriate to ask whether these decisions are to be considered a victory for those who champion individual rights" (Wayne F. LaFave, *Supreme Court Review*). Both words are used in general writing, but *if* is more common: "The survey first asked people if TV made them feel more opposed to the war or not" (*Newsweek*).

Whether is required when the clause begins a sentence (Whether it rains or shines . . .), is the object of a preposition (The question of whether . . .), modifies a noun (The question whether . . .), or follows *be* (The question is whether . . .).

Reference: Pooley, pp. 147–49.

illiterate

Illiterate and *literate* are used to refer both to the ability to read and write (There were few schools, and most of the peasants were completely illiterate) and to familiarity with what has been written (Any literate person should know the name Kafka). Usage called nonstandard in this book is often loosely referred to as illiterate in the second sense—that is, uneducated.

ill, sick

Ill is the less common, more formal word. See *sick, ill.*

illusion, allusion

An illusion misleads, an allusion refers. See *allusion, illusion.*

image

Image meaning a public conception or impression—"Ford . . . said he hopes to project the image of a president rather than a campaigner" (Associated Press story)—has moved from the jargon of the public relations man and the advertiser into general use. It can also be found in scholarly writing, applied at times to persons whose lives antedated the usage, if not the attitude behind it: "Even in France, where Franklin was widely admired and loved, he still remained self-consciously aware of his image" (Melvin Buxbaum, *Benjamin Franklin and the Zealous Presbyterians*). For some readers, the connotations of *image* in this sense are distasteful.

Imagery

An image is a word or group of words that makes an appeal to one of the senses: sight (*shiny, ghostly, mist, slime, green, thick brown hair*), hearing (*creaking, faraway shouts, the pounding of surf*), taste (*salty, dry, a pickled pear*), smell (*jasmine, fresh paint, a blown-out candle*), touch (*smooth, glassy, razor sharp, a stubbly beard*), and the muscular tension known as the kinesthetic sense (*squirm, jerky, jogging heavily along*). Though an image may appeal to more than one sense (*a rough, angry sea*), in a specific context one sense is usually dominant.

Imagery is especially characteristic of poetry, in which the content or activity of the mind is often rendered concretely— thought manifested in things. But most writers of expository prose also use imagery to keep in close touch with the visible and tangible world:

The first attempt of men to live collectively under the rule of reason ended in the bloodletting of the French Revolution. This was a sorry disappointment to liberals, but they accommodated it to their thesis by arguing that rational behavior could not be expected to sprout overnight from soil that had for centuries been eroded and poisoned by injustice and oppression.—Reinhold Niebuhr, *The Search for America*

Studying the images in a writer's work will usually show what has impressed him in his experience, what appeals to him— colors, lines, odors, sounds. Your own writing will be richer and stronger if it includes images drawn from your own experience. A borrowed image is likely to be a dead one. An image drawn from experience is a live image; and a live image is like a good photograph: it reveals something of the photographer as well as showing what he has photographed.

See Figurative language.

Imperative mood

The form of the verb that is used for direct commands and requests is said to be in the imperative mood: Bring the tapes when you come; Run! Imperatives have no overt ending and usually no expressed subject. See Commands and requests.

implement

The catchall bureaucratic verb *implement*, meaning to "give effect" to policies or ideas (It's a great scenario, but who's going to implement it?), might often be replaced by *fulfill, execute, put into practice,* and *carry out*, if only for variety. See Gobble-dygook.

imply, infer

Careful users of English make a distinction between *imply* and *infer*: a writer or speaker *implies* something in his words or manner, suggesting a conclusion without stating it; a reader or listener *infers* something from what he reads or hears, drawing a conclusion from the available information. Indeed, both implying and inferring can be wordless: The dean implied by his half smile that he doubted my story; They inferred from his silence that he disapproved of the new policy.

Having a word for each of these acts contributes to clear communication. But for centuries *infer* has also been used to mean "imply," and today many dictionaries recognize this meaning (as well as the traditional meaning) of *infer* as standard. Thus when clarity is essential, the safe course is not simply to distinguish between *imply* and *infer* but to provide a context that underlines your meaning: From the President's words, I infer that he. . . .

References: Copperud, p. 141; Follett, pp. 175–76; Fowler, p. 282.

Incoherence

Writing is incoherent when the relationship between parts (of a sentence, of a paragraph, of a whole paper) is not made clear. The cause may be that there actually is no relationship between the parts, or it may be that the writer has failed to indicate the relationship that he perceives. See Coherence, Transition.

Incomplete sentence

Punctuating a phrase or a dependent clause as if it were a complete sentence is often the result of carelessness. See Fragment.

incredible, incredulous

A story or situation is incredible ("unbelievable"); a person is incredulous ("unbelieving"). One way to avoid confusing the two is to refrain from using *incredible,* an example of trite hyperbole in current vogue.

Indention

To indent in manuscript or printed copy is to begin the first line of a paragraph some distance to the right of the left-hand margin – about an inch in longhand copy, about five spaces in typewritten copy. Hanging indention is indention of all lines below the first line, as in bibliographies and in many newspaper headlines, outlines, headings, and addresses of letters. If a line of verse is too long to stand on one line, the part brought over to the second line should be indented. For indenting quotations, see Quotation marks 1d.

Independent clauses

An independent clause (like this one) can stand alone as a simple sentence. See Clauses.

Indicative mood

Verb forms that make assertions or ask questions are said to be indicative or in the indicative mood. The indicative is the mood of most verbs in English sentences: They *sat* on the porch even though it *was* late October; *Will* you *come* if you *are* invited? Compare Imperative mood, Subjunctive mood.

Indirect discourse (indirect quotation)

When someone's words are reported in paraphrase or summary instead of being quoted exactly, they are in indirect discourse:

Direct: He said, "I won't take it if they give it to me."
Indirect: He said he wouldn't take it if they gave it to him.

An indirect question restates a question at second hand:

Direct: "Is everyone all right?" he asked.
Indirect: He asked if everyone was all right.

See Commands and requests, Questions, Quotation marks 2b, Tense 3b.

Indirect objects

An indirect object names the person or thing to which something is given, said, or shown: She gave *him* a prize. See Objects 2.

Induction

The process of reasoning known as induction originates in curiosity and ends in conviction. You are reasoning inductively when, after asking your friends how they feel about a proposed change in the pass-fail policy and after listening to what's being said on the subject around campus, you decide that the student body is strongly opposed to the change. Note that you haven't polled the student body; that would be nose-counting, not inductive reasoning. Instead, at some point in your gathering of information, you have made the "inductive leap," assuming that what is true of the people you have talked to and listened to is true of the whole group.

You can't be certain that it's true. But you can have confidence in your conclusion – you can assume that it is highly probable – if the evidence you have examined has been adequate, representative, and related to the issue.

In serious argument, induction usually takes the form of example after example offered in support of a generalization. As used in everyday life, inductive reasoning may seem to be little more than a hunch or an informed guess. But it is nonetheless important, for only by using induction can we spot trends, make predictions, and discover causal relations.

See Cause and effect, Deduction, Fallacies, Logical thinking.

infer, imply
The writer or speaker implies; the reader or listener infers. See *imply, infer*.

Infinitives
Infinitive is a Latin grammatical term for a verb form expressing the general sense of the verb without restriction as to person, number, or tense. In Old English the infinitive had a distinctive form, but in Modern English the root form of the verb is used, often with *to* before it.

1. The *to* infinitive and the bare infinitive. More often than not, an infinitive is used with the preposition *to:* He is the man *to see;* He was glad *to come;* He likes *to be visited*. But *to* is seldom or never used after the modal auxiliary verbs or after some full verbs: I can *see;* He must *carry* it; We let him *go*.

With or without *to*, the infinitive may be in the active voice (*to ask, to have asked*) or in the passive (*to be asked, to have been asked*). As the examples show, there are two tenses. The present infinitive indicates a time that is the same as, or subsequent to, the time of the main verb: He is here *to help;* They expected *to be asked*. The perfect infinitive indicates action previous to the time of the main verb: I am glad *to have been* one of his friends.

2. Functions of infinitives. Infinitives serve as subjects, as objects, as complements, and as modifiers. They in turn may have subjects, objects, complements, or modifiers.

Subject: To sit and read was his idea of a holiday. For you *to do* that again would be a serious mistake.

Object: He prefers *to wait* until Tuesday. The police attempted *to hold back* the crowd.

Complement: He seems *to be* happy.

Modifier: My friend is the man *to see*. Jane is the person *to do* that. He was happy *to stay* longer. The police are trying *to find out* what happened. *To avoid* colds, stay out of crowds.

3. Subject of the infinitive. When *for* + nominal precedes the infinitive, the subject of the infinitive is the nominal: For Tom to say that shocked us. When it does not, the subject is either the indefinite *someone* or *anyone* (To ignore the suffering in the world is criminal = For anyone to ignore the suffering in the world is criminal) or a referent expressed elsewhere in the sentence (To ignore the suffering in the world is criminal of them = For them to ignore the suffering in the world is criminal).

4. Infinitives and style.
a. Infinitives in a series. In a short, unemphatic series, *to* is not repeated: He decided to shower, shave, and dress. When the series is complex or when separate verbs deserve emphasis, *to* is repeated: These were his goals—to escape the city, to avoid routine, and to find contentment.
b. Case of pronoun. For the pronoun after the infinitive of a linking verb that has no expressed subject, general English usually has the accusative: I always wanted to be him. Formal favors the nominative: I always wanted to be he. But that locution makes the pronoun prominent, and another phrasing might be preferable: He was the one I always wanted to be.
c. Dangling infinitives. Infinitives that function as absolute phrases (to tell the truth, to be sure) are sentence modifiers and as such present no problems. But an infinitive, like a participle or a gerund, will dangle if it seems to relate to a word that it cannot sensibly modify or if, in a context that demands an explicit relationship, it has no clear relation to any word in the sentence.

Dangling: To swim well, fear of the water must be overcome.
Revised: To swim well, the learner must overcome fear of the water.

See Absolute phrases, Dangling modifiers.
d. Split infinitive. In a split infinitive, a word or phrase (usually an adverb) comes between *to* and the verb: to actively pursue. Some infinitives should not be split; some should be. In still other contexts, it is a matter of choice, with more splits occurring in general English than in formal. See Split infinitive.
    References: Jespersen, Ch. 32; Roberts, pp. 359–67.

Inflection

In grammar *inflection* refers to the change of form that some words undergo to indicate certain grammatical relationships, like singular and plural number for nouns or past and present tense for verbs. See Case, Comparison of adjectives and adverbs, Plurals of nouns, Pronouns, Verbs.

Informal English

The word or passage marked is too informal for the subject or for the style of the rest of the paper. Revise, making it more appropriate.

Informal written English is appropriate (though not mandatory) in letters to your close friends and to members of your family and may be the style you use in a diary or journal. Its casual, intimate tone makes it unsuitable for most college writing, though informal usages and locutions may be successfully introduced into papers written in general English if they are chosen with taste and judgment.

You'd be unlikely to use the informal *pretty* (pretty big, pretty soon, pretty old) in a chemistry report or a psychology examination, and you probably wouldn't describe Robert Frost as a "pretty good poet" in a paper for a literature course. But in writing about a local hero for an audience of classmates, you might call him a "pretty good quarterback." Whether or not *inf* should appear in the margin of your paper would depend on the context. If your style was generally relaxed and conversational, *pretty* would be appropriate. If your style placed some distance between you and your readers, *fairly* would be a better choice.

As applied to sections of essays or whole essays, *informal* usually implies sloppiness—rambling, loose-jointed sentences, vague references, trite slang, counter words, repetition, incoherence. If something you've written has been so marked, the best solution is to rethink what you wanted to say and rewrite the passage, aiming for clarity and precision.

For discussion, see the Introduction, pp. 2–7. See also Agreement, Counter words, Repetition, Slang, Spoken and written English, Triteness.

in, into, in to

In usually shows location, literal or figurative: He was in the house; He was in a stupor. *Into* usually shows direction: He came into the house; He fell into a stupor. But in general and informal usage, *in* is common when direction is meant: "Twice a week we get in the car, and drive down the Parkway" (Richard Rose, *St. Louis Post-Dispatch*). Reference: Copperud, p. 141.

The *in* of *in to* is an adverb and the *to* a preposition (They went in to dinner) or sign of the infinitive (They went in to eat).

Intensifiers

Qualifiers like *very, greatly, terribly, much* intensify the meaning of adjectives: He is much older than she. See Qualifiers.

Intensive pronouns

Reflexive pronouns—the personal pronouns plus *-self* or *-selves* —may be used as intensives: We ourselves are responsible. See *myself*, Pronouns 2.

Interjections

Interjections are expressions of emotion like *oh, ow, ouch, ah.* See Exclamations, Parts of speech.

Interrogative pronouns

Who, whom, whose, which, what are interrogative pronouns. See Pronouns 5.

Intransitive verbs

An intransitive verb takes no object: The money vanished. See Transitive and intransitive verbs.

Introductions

Don't "introduce" any paper you write unless such a beginning is absolutely necessary. See Beginning an essay.

Inversion

Inversion means placing the verb, or some part of the verb phrase, before its subject. This is the regular syntactical pattern in questions: Will she go? Did they enjoy it? Inversion is also used with expletive *there* and *it* (There was a man at the door) and in a few other situations: What a fool he is; Long may it wave; Here comes the thunder. Occasionally a declarative sentence may be inverted for emphasis: Down he went; This I know; That she was brilliant he had no doubt.

Irony

Irony implies something markedly different, sometimes even the opposite, from what is actually said. Light irony is humorous, as in the greeting "Lovely day!" in pouring rain. Heavy irony is usually a form of sarcasm or satire.

irregardless

Irregardless is redundant: both the prefix *ir-* and the suffix *-less* are negative. The standard word is *regardless*.

Irregular verbs

Verbs that do not form their past tense and past participle by adding *-ed* are irregular. See Principal parts of verbs.

it

It is the neuter third-person singular pronoun, used most commonly to refer to inanimates but sometimes to living things. Typically, it replaces preceding neuter noun phrases: Have you seen *the neighbors' new car?* — Yes, isn't *it* a mess? The antecedent may be a clause or a sentence: Some people say *that more money will solve the problem of our schools*, but I don't believe *it*. But sometimes *it* has no antecedent, as in impersonal statements about the weather, time, distance, or events in general, and in numerous idioms:

It's three hours since *it* began to rain, and *it's* still five miles to camp.
It isn't pleasant to live in Washington these days.
Damn *it*, we'll have to talk *it* out with the dean.

Though typically neuter, the antecedent of *it* may be an animal or a small child whose sex is unknown or irrelevant. *It* is also used with reference to collective nouns denoting persons (The faculty must decide for itself) and in sentences where individuals are identified (I'm not sure who the violinist was, but it could have been Oistrakh).

The more important uses of *it*, stylistically, are those where it fills the position of a subject or object fully expressed later in the sentence. In such sentences, "expletive" *it* is called the "formal" or "provisional" or "anticipatory" subject or object:

It is doubtful *that he should be given so much freedom.*
He found *it* painful *living in the same house with a person whose racial attitudes he detested.*
It was *Wordsworth* who called his gun a "thundering tube."

The advantages of such constructions are that they offer an alternative to lengthy separation of sentence parts that belong together (He found living in the same house with a person whose racial attitudes he detested painful) and a means of assigning emphasis: "It was Wordsworth who . . ." emphasizes *Wordsworth*; "Wordsworth called his gun a 'thundering tube'" emphasizes *thundering tube*.

See *its, it's; it's me; there is, there are.* References: Copperud, p. 154; Long, pp. 211–12, 342–45; Pooley, pp. 115–17.

Italics

In longhand and typewritten copy, underline words or passages to correspond to the conventions of using italic type.

Words or statements that would be printed in italics are underlined in manuscript. Although newspapers have generally abandoned italic type, most magazines and books use it, and in academic writing—course papers, articles in learned journals, dissertations, reference books—italics have standardized uses:

1. To indicate titles of books, plays, motion pictures, and other complete works, and to indicate titles of periodicals and newspapers. See Titles 2.

2. To mark words and expressions considered as words rather than for their meaning: There is a shade of difference between *because* and *for* used as conjunctions.

3. To mark unanglicized words from foreign languages: Good clothes were a *sine qua non.* See Foreign words in English 2a.

4. To indicate words that would be stressed if spoken. This easily abused device is more appropriate in dialog than in exposition.

5. To indicate key words, phrases, or sentences in an argument or explanation. Here also italics must be used sparingly if they are not to lose their force. See Emphasis 6.

References: *A Manual of Style; The MLA Style Sheet,* 2nd ed. (New York: Modern Language Association, 1970).

its, it's

Its is a possessive pronoun and, like the possessive pronouns *his, her, our, your,* and *their,* has no apostrophe: A car is judged by its performance. *It's* is the contraction for "it is" or "it has": It's a long road; It's been said before. Like other contractions, *it's* is more appropriate to informal and general than to formal styles.

it's me

The argument over "it's me" illustrates a conflict between theory and practice. The theory—that after a finite form of the verb *be* the nominative or subjective case should always be used—is consistently contradicted by the usage of good writers and speakers (see *be* 2). We tend to use the nominative form of a pronoun when it is the subject and stands alone directly before the verb, but we are likely to use the accusative in most other positions, especially when it comes after the verb—in "object territory," as it has been called. (Compare *who, whom.*) All the large grammars of English regard "it's me" as acceptable. References: Bryant, pp. 120–21; Copperud, p. 155.

-ize

The formation of verbs from non-Greek nouns or adjectives by adding the Greek ending *-ize* (often *-ise* in British usage) has been going on since the sixteenth century. Some readers object to recent extensions of the verbs in *-ize,* either because the new verbs duplicate in meaning verbs in common use (*fantasized, fantasied; formularize, formulate*) or because the proliferation adds to the stock of advertising jargon (*customize, personalize*), much of which is virtually meaningless. See *finalize.* Reference: Copperud, p. 155.

J

Jargon

1. Sir Arthur Quiller-Couch popularized *jargon* as the name for verbal fuzziness of various sorts—wordiness, a high proportion of abstract words, "big" words, and words that add nothing to the meaning. *Jargon* and *gobbledygook* are sometimes used interchangeably. Reference: Sir Arthur Quiller-Couch, *On the Art of Writing* (1916; rpt. New York: Putnam, Capricorn Books, 1961), pp. 100–26.

2. *Jargon* is also used for shoptalk or the specialized language of a group—doctors, printers, sociologists, photographers, chicken farmers, and so on. So defined, jargon is appropriate in certain circumstances, as when a physicist writes for fellow physicists, but not in others, as when he writes for a general audience.

In many groups and many situations there is a tendency to go beyond the necessary technical jargon and create a jargon in the first sense. Examples of the use of language to impress more than to inform include sociologese, psychologese, educationese, journalese, and bureaucratese.

See Doublespeak, Shoptalk.

job, position

Job is general for the formal *position:* He got a job at the oil re-
finery. The word *position* has more dignity, and what it refers to
is usually thought of as better paid; but because *position* can
sound pompous, many writers use *job* for all levels of employ-
ment.

Journalese

Journalese, once limited in meaning to a kind of writing found
in newspapers, can be applied as well to a kind of prose read by
radio and television news broadcasters. At its best it is slick and
smooth; but smooth or rough, it is loaded with jargon and lacking in character and conviction. The sensational personal reporting of earlier times has been replaced in large part by a bland
"communicating" of whatever the newsmakers – politicians,
bureaucrats, celebrities – have to say, no matter how meaningless or untrue. Whether based on handouts or on observation,
journalese is full of clichés, vogue words, gobbledygook, and
doublespeak. Yet for all their fondness for the in phrase from
Washington, New York, or Las Vegas, the writers cling to such
hoary headline words as *slay, flee, vow,* and *ailing* (ailing
Joanne Starr). And there are reminders of the old journalistic
love of violence, not only in the trite hyperbole of the sports
pages but in the "firestorms" of protest and in the "firefights"
and "shoot-outs" that journalese has transported from distant
wars and the Hollywood West to urban liquor stores and rural
gas stations.

As a result of the shortcomings of current journalese, the columnist or commentator who expresses himself with some originality is almost as welcome as one who has something original
to say. Journalese provides evidence that even professional,
grammatical writing can be awful.

Reference: Edwin Newman, *Atlantic,* October 1974, pp.
84–89.

just

The qualifier *just* is redundant in expressions like *just exactly*
and *just perfect*. The locution "just may [might]" or "may
[might] just" – "Mr. Kilpatrick may just be right" (*Centre Daily
Times*) – in which *just* means "just possibly," is a cliché.

K

kid

The noun *kid* for "child" and the verb *kid* for "tease" are now so
widely used in serious contexts that they should be regarded as
established in general, though not in formal, usage. A problem
with *kid* as a noun is that it now may mean not only someone

past puberty but someone past adolescence (the kids in graduate school). In many contexts a more specific term is needed.

kind, sort

The words *kind* and *sort* are involved in three different problems for writers.

1. Agreement. *Kind* and *sort* are singular pronouns with regular plurals. A problem arises only when singular *kind* or *sort* is followed by *of* and a plural noun. Then there is a strong tendency to treat the plural object of *of,* rather than *kind* or *sort,* as the head of the construction and to use plural demonstratives and verbs: These sort of books are harmless; "Those kind of overhead expenses" (Lewis H. Lapham, *Harper's*).

The construction is common in speech, and there are numerous examples of its use by esteemed writers—"these kind of marks have not been left by any other animal than man" (T. H. Huxley, "The Method of Scientific Investigation")—but strong objection to it continues. For one kind (or sort), then: *That kind* of book *is.* . . . For more than one: *Those kinds* of books *are.* . . . References: Bryant, pp. 124–25; Copperud, p. 160; Fries, p. 58; Jespersen, p. 202.

2. Kind (sort) of a(n). Although shunned in formal writing, *kind of a(n)* and *sort of a(n)* are general idioms: "People just didn't trust that kind of an approach" (Charles Mohr, *Esquire*). Formal style would have "kind of approach." Reference: Copperud, pp. 160–61.

3. Kind (sort) of. As adverbs equivalent to imprecise qualifiers like *rather* and *somewhat* in more formal usage, *kind of* and *sort of* are informal to general: "She was kind of plump" (Claude Brown, *Commentary*); "Everything just sort of limped along" (E. J. Kahn, Jr., *New Yorker*).

know-how

Although *know-how* occurs in every variety of writing, for many readers its connotations remain commercial and technical. To speak of the know-how of a great violinist, for example, would be inappropriate.

lab

The clipped form of *laboratory* is now common in all but the most formal usage.

last, latest

Both *last* and *latest* are used as superlatives of *late* (his last book; his latest book). But to avoid ambiguity, formal English uses *last* for the final item in a series and *latest* for the most recent of a series that may or may not be continued: "Mao Tsetung's latest battle is almost certainly his last" (Mark Gayn, *Foreign Affairs*).

latter

The use of *latter* in referring to the last of more than two items is standard, but conservative stylists prefer "the last named." See *former, first — latter, last*.

lay, lie

In standard English *lie (lay, lain)* is intransitive: He let it lie there; She lay down for a nap; The boards had lain there for months. *Lay (laid, laid)* is transitive: You can lay it on the table; They laid the keel; She had laid it away for future reference. In much spoken English *lay* does the work of both verbs, but in most writing they are kept distinct. The *-ing* forms sometimes give trouble, with *laying* appearing where *lying* is meant: I spent the summer laying around the house. Reference: Copperud, pp. 165–66.

learn, teach

Nonstandard English often uses *learn* in the sense of *teach*: He learned me how to tie knots. Standard usage makes the distinction: He taught me how to tie knots; I learned how to tie knots from him.

leave, let

Let, not *leave,* is standard English for "permit" or "allow." See *let, leave*.

lend, loan

In referring to material wealth, *lend* and *lends* are preferred to *loan* and *loans* in formal writing, but the past tense and past participle *loaned* is preferred to *lent* in all varieties: "About $4 billion have been loaned" (Adolf A. Berle, *The American Economic Republic*); "those who wished to lend" (George V. Taylor, *American Historical Review*). In general contexts, *loan* and *loans* are as common as *lend* and *lends* and are entirely reputable.

In the sense "grant, impart, furnish" or "adapt or accommodate (itself)," *lend* and *lent* are always preferred: "America always lent itself to personification" (Norman Mailer, *Harper's*).

Reference: Copperud, p. 170.

less, fewer

Use *fewer* for things that can be counted, *less* for things that can't. See *fewer, less*.

let, leave

A common nonstandard idiom is the use of *leave* for "permit" or "allow," meanings that standard English assigns to *let*. Both uses are shown in this sentence by a writer making a transition between the two varieties: "In high school I was cured of the practice of leaving [nonstandard] notebooks go, but I fell into the habit of letting [standard] homework slide."

Only with *alone* and the meaning "refrain from disturbing" are the two verbs interchangeable in standard English: Leave [*or* Let] me alone; Americans like to be let [*or* left] alone. References: Bryant, pp. 127–29; Copperud, p. 164.

Lexical meaning

In linguistics a distinction is often made between grammatical or structural meaning and lexical meaning. In "Birds were killed," the information that *bird* and *kill* give us is of the sort regularly provided by a dictionary or lexicon—hence, lexical meaning. The information given by the *-s* of *birds* (plural), *were* (past tense, passive voice), and the *-ed* of *killed* (past participle in this position) is of the sort provided by our awareness of the structure or grammar of the language—hence, grammatical or structural meaning. When we fully understand the sentence, we have grasped its total meaning.

liable

In formal and most general writing, *liable,* when followed by an infinitive, is restricted to predictions of undesirable results (The effects are liable to be disastrous). *Liable* plus infinitive to predict desirable results occurs most often in informal and casual general contexts: "Walleyes are year-round sport and . . . they're liable to hit any time of the day or night" (Roger Latham, *Field and Stream*). *Likely* and *apt* are not restricted in this way. Reference: Copperud, pp. 19–20.

lie

The transitive verb *lay* should not be substituted for the intransitive *lie:* you *lie,* not *lay,* down when you're tired; you *lay,* not *laid,* down yesterday. See *lay, lie.*

like, as

1. As prepositions. In all varieties of English, *like* is used as a preposition introducing a comparison: The description fits him like a plaster cast; Habit grips a person like an octopus; She took to selling like a bee to clover. *As* seems to be increasing as a hypercorrect form: "The University of Texas, as so many American campuses during the Kennedy years, has exploded with vitality" (Willie Morris, *North Toward Home*).

2. As conjunctions. In all varieties of English, *as, as if,* and *as though* are used as conjunctions introducing clauses of comparison: Habit grips a person as an octopus does; He walked as though he was hurt. *Like* as a conjunction is common in speech and appears frequently in informal and general writing: "It looks now like it will take us years of John Cage, Godard, Burroughs, *et al.*, to absorb it" (Theodore Solotaroff, *The Red Hot Vacuum*). But many people remain strongly opposed to *like* as a conjunction, and it is avoided in formal and much general writing. References: Bryant, pp. 133–35; Copperud, pp. 166–67; Fries, pp. 225, 239; Pooley, pp. 149–52.

3. The way. *The way* provides an escape from the *like–as* thicket for writers who shy from *like* and find *as* prissy: "Hemingway once told Callaghan, 'Dostoevski writes like Harry Greb fights.' Unfortunately, Callaghan writes the way Hemingway fights" (*Time*).

Linguistics

Linguistics is a broad discipline incorporating several perspectives from which language may be studied systematically. Linguists study the structures of languages and the universal structure of language; they study language history and the variations of language as correlated with geographical and social distance; they study how language is acquired and how it is used.

Linguistics differs from other disciplines devoted to the study of language by having at its center a theory of language derived from the study of formal, regular, and recurrent patterns in the structures of human languages. While theories of language differ and hence schools of linguistics exist, all linguists are empiricists, sharing a desire to be as objective and "scientific" as possible, rejecting conclusions not based in consistent theory and verified by significant data.

For some linguists, especially those termed structuralists or descriptivists (see Grammar 3b), significant data consist only of those features of language they can directly perceive either as marks on a page (writing) or as vibrations in the air (speech); consistent theory, for these same linguists, consists of a set of generalizations derived inductively from the data through means of formal discovery procedures. For other linguists, particularly those termed generative-transformational or generative (see Grammar 3c), significant data also include what the native speaker (including the linguist himself) senses or intuits about the structures of sentences, the relations of those structures to one another, and the correlation between structured sound and meaning. The structuralist's goal is to write grammars that will *describe* the surface regularities of sentences in particular languages. The generativist's goal is to *predict* the sentences that will occur in a particular language, given the set of rules for sentence construction that native speakers have internalized. The generativist is more interested in explanation than he is in description, and seeks deeper relations between surface structures and meanings in the organization of human cognitive capacities as these are revealed through a study of rules that all human languages have in common.

In addition to describing the grammatical, phonological, and semantic structures of modern languages, linguists are interested in other linguistic phenomena. *Dialectology* examines the characteristic linguistic patterns that distinguish groups of speakers of the same language. Geographical dialects have been most thoroughly studied; but in recent years social dialects have drawn increasing attention as higher education has encompassed all classes of speakers, forcing teachers to reconsider their own attitudes toward the variety of English spoken by those not part of the white, Anglo-Saxon, upper-middle-class community. *Historical linguistics* attempts to reconstruct the grammars of earlier forms of a current or dead language and to account for change in language. *Comparative linguistics* studies the relationship between languages that are genetically related to a parent language or between languages that differ or resemble each other structurally, without regard to their historical sources. Specialists in child language investigate the development of linguistic competence among infants and young children.

Other areas of linguistics are often termed *applied,* to emphasize that they touch on practical concerns as well as theory. In *lexicography* the findings of semanticists and dialectologists are being used in compiling dictionaries. In *foreign-language teaching,* the findings of comparative and contrastive linguistics have helped pinpoint those differences between a native language and a target language that would make learning the new language particularly difficult. In *machine translation* the findings of syntactic studies and semantics have been used in attempts, so far largely fruitless, to program machines to translate from one language to another. In *literary studies* transformational grammars have been used to analyze the syntactic, metaphorical, and prosodic structure of poems and the styles of various prose writers. In *composition courses* transformational grammars have been used to analyze the characteristics of mature sentence structure to help students write better. In *reading,* phonological studies have shown how the apparently chaotic system of English spelling is in reality a regular system that, far from preventing a child from learning to read, may actually help him. The findings of phonology have also been used to construct better communications systems. And the scientific attitudes of linguists have forced those concerned with usage to look at language as it really is used rather than as they would like it to be used.

As linguistics has developed theoretically and in its practical applications, a number of related fields have developed. *Psycholinguistics* studies the correlation between linguistic structures and experimentally describable behavior. *Stylistics* studies the linguistic characteristics of literary language. One kind of *linguistic philosophy* studies the nature of meaning in sentences from the point of view of deep and surface structures. *Linguistic anthropology* uses the semantic structures of individual languages and the verbal interaction of their speakers to discover distinctive patterns of culture. Related to this field is *sociolinguistics,* the specific study of the verbal interaction between and among social classes and linguistic variation as it correlates with the behaviors of definable social groups.

References: Bolinger; Francis P. Dinneen, *An Introduction to General Linguistics* (New York: Holt, 1967); Ronald W. Langacker, *Fundamentals of Linguistic Analysis* (New York: Harcourt, 1972); Archibald A. Hill, *Linguistics Today* (New York: Basic Books, 1969); Hungerford, Robinson, and Sledd; R. H. Robins, *A Short History of Linguistics* (Bloomington: Indiana Univ. Press, 1968).

Linking verbs

When a verb like *be* functions chiefly as a structural bridge between a subject and another noun or a modifier, it is called a copulative or linking verb. It is followed by elements that function as adjectives or nouns (single words, phrases, or clauses) and are traditionally known as predicate adjectives (This bottle was *full*) and predicate nouns or predicate nominatives (The man was a *carpenter*). Some grammarians prefer to call them complements, or subjective complements.

Many verbs besides *be* are used as linking verbs; one grammarian has counted about sixty. For example, instead of having a verb of full meaning like *colden,* English uses the verb *turn* or *get* and the adjective *cold* (which carries the chief part of the meaning) in such a sentence as "The weather turned cold." Many verbs are used both with full meaning of their own (The tree *fell* into the water) and as linking verbs (She *fell* silent; He *fell* ill). Other linking verbs are italicized in the following sentences:

He *became* a doctor. The butter *tastes* rancid. She *felt* sad. He *acts* old. The ground *sounds* hollow. He *grew* moody. He *appeared* to be recovering. This *looks* first-rate. His story *seemed* incredible.

Because many speakers have been taught that verbs are modified by adverbs, and because they are unaware that the same verb can function either as a linking verb or as a transitive verb, they correct correctness by substituting an adverb for the correct adjective: "He felt sadly" for "He felt sad." Such hypercorrectness sometimes appears in writing.

For the most common source of difficulty in using the linking-verb pattern, see Predicate adjectives. See also *bad, badly; be* 2; *it's me; look.* References: A. S. Hornby, *A Guide to Patterns and Usages in English* (London: Oxford Univ. Press, 1954), pp. 62–72; Gustave Scheurweghs, *Present-Day English Syntax* (London: Longmans, 1959), pp. 19–32.

literally

Literally means "actually, without deviating from the facts," but it is so often used to support metaphors that its literal meaning may be reversed. In statements like the following, *literally* means "figuratively" and *literal* means "figurative":

The Village in the twenties [was] a literal hotbed of political, artistic, and sexual radicalism. — Louise Bernikow, *New York Times Book Review*

In this struggle, women's bodies became a literal battleground. — Martin Duberman, ibid.

[New York City is] literally hanging by its fingernails. — Walter Cronkite, *CBS News*

Literal-minded readers find such locutions absurd.

literate

Literate is used to mean both "capable of reading and writing" and "acquainted with what has been written — educated." See *illiterate*.

loan

In referring to possessions, *lend* is more formal in the present tense. For the past tense, *loaned* is preferred in all varieties of English. See *lend, loan*.

Loan words

Loan words in English are words borrowed from other languages. See Foreign words in English, Origin of words 2b.

Localisms

A localism is a word or other expression in regular use only in a certain region, like the "baby cab" used in western Pennsylvania for "baby carriage." Though appropriate in conversation and informal writing, localisms are out of place in general and formal writing except to give a regional flavor. See Dialects.

locate

Locate is in general use for "find" (I can't locate the letter now). Although avoided by many stylists in the sense "settle" (The family located near Nashua), it may be useful when it refers to considered placement: "Thus the small department store is probably wise to locate close to its competition" (Richard H. Holton, in *Competition, Cartels and Their Regulation*, ed. J. P. Miller).

Locution

Locution is a handy term for referring to a word or a group of related words; that is, it may be applied to a single word or to a phrase or clause considered as a unit. In the preceding sentence, "a handy term," "that is," and "phrase" are locutions.

logic Logical thinking

Reconsider the logical relationship that is expressed or implied.

At some time or other everyone has protested, "That doesn't make sense," or "That doesn't follow from what you just said." Everyone, that is, has some notion of the difference between logical and illogical thinking, and when something doesn't make sense or fails to show a logical progression, everyone's impulse is to dismiss it.

In an essay illogical thinking is revealed in irrelevant material, faulty organization, incoherent sentences, words that blur or skew the meaning of what's being said. More narrowly, it shows up in faulty relationships between ideas. Often the seeming breakdown in logic is simply the result of careless writing. In taking issue with the statement, "The true university is a collection of books," a student wrote, "If I were to agree that a true university is no more than a collection of books, I would graduate well-read but not socially mature." This makes no sense, because simply agreeing or not agreeing with the statement about a true university could not determine the kind of education a particular student would receive at a particular school.

Presumably the student meant, "If a true university is no more than a collection of books, and if this is a true university, then I can expect to be well-read when I graduate but not necessarily socially mature." If the student intended to base an *if . . . then* relationship on his agreement with the statement, the logical conclusion would be something like, "then I would spend all my time in the library."

You can avoid such apparent lapses in logic by carefully reading what you write – seeing what you have said rather than what you meant to say – and revising your sentences before making a final draft. Much more serious are the kinds of illogical thinking that undercut a whole essay. When you write a paper to express an opinion, defend a point of view, argue for or against something, persuade or convince your readers, keep these recommendations in mind:

Limit your generalizations to what you can support with evidence.

Make sure that what you offer as evidence is authoritative and that it bears on the issue.

Make sure that you have attacked the actual issue instead of skirmishing around the edges or wandering off into another battle.

Make sure that no links are missing in the chain of reasoning that leads to your conclusion.

In reading over what you've written, take a hard look at your generalizations. Are they sound enough to support your argument? Are they based on fact and justifiable inferences, or are they little more than unexamined assumptions or expressions of prejudice?

When you find yourself saying that *A* caused *B* or that *B* is the result of *A*, think over your reasons for saying so. Are they convincing? Are there reasons for *not* saying so that you have deliberately omitted? Are your comparisons justifiable and your analogies plausible?

After enjoying the violent language you've used in condemning those who hold an opposing point of view, or admiring the moving words you've used in supporting those whose side you're upholding, ask yourself whether the faults of the former group or the virtues of the latter have anything to do with the issue itself. If they haven't, don't confuse your comments on them with logical thinking.

See Cause and effect, Classification and division, Deduction, Fallacies, Induction, Syllogisms.

Logic and language

Sometimes items of usage are objected to as being "illogical" — for example, "he don't," "the reason is because." But the real trouble with "he don't" is simply that it has become nonstandard. And when the objection to "the reason is because" is elaborated, it is usually that an adverbial clause (*because . . .*) is equated with a noun (*reason*) — a criticism that has to do with grammar rather than with logic. Logic proper is not involved in either objection.

Idiom illustrates particularly well the lack of correspondence between logic and usage. The meanings of many idioms are not the sum of the meaning of their separate words: hard to come by, a little water, many's the time, out of order. These show, more clearly than the general patterns and rules of English, that language is a human development, the result of millions of speech situations, not a preplanned system; it is not illogical but simply alogical.

Probably arguments from logic had an influence in establishing the double negative as nonstandard English; in Old and Middle English, the more negatives there were, the more forceful the negation. But arguments from logic have had few such successes, and the term *logical* can be applied to language only in its most general popular sense of "more or less systematic."

See Double negative, Idiom, *reason is because*.

Long variants

Some writers are tempted to add an extra prefix or suffix to a word that already carries the meaning they intend. They write *irregardless*, though *regardless* already means "without regard to," or they write *doubtlessly* for *doubtless*. Some like to use sonorous suffixes that add nothing to the meaning, like the *-ation* in *analyzation*, which means no more than *analysis*. Some other long variants that it is wise to avoid are *certificated* for *certified*, *confliction* for *conflict*, *emotionality* when only *emotion* is meant, *hotness* for *heat*, *intermingle* for *mingle*, *orientate* for *orient*, *ruination* for *ruin*, *subsidization* for *subsidizing*, and *utilize* when *use* is entirely adequate.

Occasionally a long form acquires a special sense: a *certificated* teacher is one who has a certificate from the state, licensing him to teach. But in general the more compact form is the right choice. See Diction 2, Gobbledygook, Jargon. Reference: Fowler, pp. 342–43.

look

When used as an intransitive verb meaning "use the eyes, gaze," *look* is modified by an adverb: look longingly, look searchingly. As a linking verb, equivalent to *appear, look* is followed by an adjective which modifies the subject: He looks well [*or* healthy *or* tired *or* bad]. See Linking verbs.

lot, lots

In the senses "much," "many," "a great deal," the various expressions *a lot, a lot of, lots,* and *lots of* have an informal flavor but are established in general (though not in formal) usage:

He tells Celine to make herself attractive and buys her a lot of new clothes. — Edmund Wilson, *New Yorker*

There is lots of talk. — *Fortune*

Reference: Copperud, p. 171.

 ## Lowercase

Use a lowercase (small) letter instead of a capital.

As an alternative or supplement to *lc,* the correction may be indicated by a slant line through the capitals:

It was a ̸great ̸experience.

Such unconventional use of capitals may work occasionally to indicate emphasis, but an exclamation mark is the safer choice. For the conventional uses of capitals, see Capital letters.

m.

Lowercase *m.* is the abbreviation for noon: 12 m. But see *a.m. and p.m.*

Main clauses

Main clauses (like this one and the next) are independent clauses. They can stand alone as sentences. See Clauses.

majority, plurality

Technically, a majority in an election is more than half the total number of votes cast, while a plurality is the largest number of votes cast for any one candidate but not more than half the total. Though the distinction is sometimes neglected, it is worth preserving for clarity.

In formal usage, *majority* is applied only to groups of at least three things that can be counted. In informal and general usage it is sometimes used also of the larger part of a single thing or mass: "A majority of the LP is taken up with bouncy dance tunes" (Robert Palmer, *New York Times*). *Most* is preferable.

Malapropisms

A malapropism is a ludicrous confusion of two words that sound somewhat alike but differ in meaning: *prodigy, progeny; contiguous, contagious.* The humor of malapropisms has faded since the eighteenth-century playwright Richard Brinsley Sheridan used them in the speeches of Mrs. Malaprop, a character in *The Rivals.*

Manuscript form

Your manuscript is not in the proper form. Revise or rewrite as directed.

Instructors usually establish their own specifications for manuscript form at the beginning of the course. Whatever the details, the goal is a clean, legible copy that can be read easily. Use regulation paper, leave adequate margins, number the pages, make corrections neatly, and observe your instructor's directions for endorsing the paper. See Division of words, Typewritten copy.

massive

Used with abstract nouns, *massive* has been a vogue word since the 1960s: massive retaliation, massive resistance, massive inequality, massive unemployment. Applying it only to icebergs would be a step in the right direction.

Mass nouns

Mass nouns denote masses that can be divided but not numbered as aggregates of separate units: *dirt, oxygen, wealth.* They are used with *the* (not *a* or *an*) or without an article in the singular, and ordinarily they have no plural. Mass nouns are opposed to count nouns, which can be counted as separate units, are used with both *a(n)* and *the* but not without an article in the singular, and have plurals: *a boy, the stick, horses.* See Nouns 3c. References: Jespersen, pp. 206–209; Sledd, p. 225; Williams, pp. 71–73.

may, can

In requesting or granting permission or expressing feasibility, *may* is the formal choice. *Can* expresses ability and is commonly used in place of *may* in general English. See *can, may.*

Meaning

The word, phrase, or sentence marked does not make sense in this context. Replace it with one that communicates the meaning you intend.

For a reader to question the meaning of what you have written indicates a serious failure in communication. Ordinarily the problem is not simply the use of one word for another that is reasonably close to it in sound or meaning—*comprehension* for *comprehensibility,* for instance. This would be marked *ww* (wrong word): the reader knows the word is wrong because he knows what the right one is. But *mng*, often followed by a question mark, means that the reader can't, or won't, make a guess at what you were trying to say. Rethinking and rewriting are in order. Compare Ambiguity, Coherence, Wrong word.

media, medium(s)

Medium and *media*, the Latin singular and plural forms, were taken directly into English, and formal usage consistently maintains the distinction in number, while recognizing the alternate plural *mediums:* "the moral possibilities of the mediums themselves" (Robert J. Reilly, *American Literature*). But *media*, like many other Latin plurals, has tended to become singular in American usage and is frequently so used in general writing, with *medias* sometimes as its plural. Word watchers find these usages highly objectionable: "Nomination for the most common error among men who should know better: 'The media is . . .' " (*Columbia Journalism Review*). Reference: Copperud, p. 176.

Metaphor

Metaphor, now widely applied to any nonliteral use of language, traditionally refers to the figure of speech that implies an identity or resemblance between two unlike things. When we are talking literally, we say that it is people or machines that *polish*, flags that *unfurl*, liquids that *stream*, and flowers that *bloom*. Yet a writer can, through metaphor, put these words to new uses and so make a description of even the simplest things both fresh and pleasing:

The wind continued to polish the grasses. And a purple finch unfurled his song. Twice, and now three times, its last sure note streamed into the sun-bloom. — Sally Carrighar, *One Day on Beetle Rock*

The power of metaphor goes beyond its capacity to please: it can provide a new view of things and so shape attitudes and change minds. It may create a sharp image with a single verb (White House action *defused* the demands of Congress), or it may call up a sequence of analogous situations:

Before prose rhythm can be sensibly considered, one must redefine reading. It cannot be a jet flight coast-to-coast. It must be a slow walk in the country, taken, as all walks should be, partly for the walking itself. — Richard A. Lanham, *Style: An Anti-Textbook*

And metaphor may amuse with what, put literally, would be insulting:

In "Execution Eve: And Other Contemporary Ballads," William F. Buckley Jr. slithers venomously across the usual broad terrain of sacred and secular topics. — Steven R. Weisman, *New York Times Book Review*

See Figurative language, Figures of speech, Mixed metaphors.

Metonymy

Metonymy is a figure of speech in which the thing named suggests the thing meant, as in "guns [war] or butter [peace]." See Figurative language.

might, could
These two words express a slighter degree of possibility than *may* or *can:* I might go; They could turn up. See *can, may.*

Misrelated modifiers
A misrelated modifier is so placed that it relates to the wrong word in the sentence. See Dangling modifiers.

Mixed metaphors
Speakers frequently run two inconsistent metaphors together: The new measure has taken a firm foothold in the eye of the public; If they are to win in November, they need a fresh face on the ticket—one that has not been straddling the economic issue. Writers, who can reconsider their words, have less excuse for such blunders and—since what they allow to stand can be read again and again—more reason for avoiding them. See Figures of speech 2.

Mixed usage
Indiscriminate, thoughtless mixing of vocabularies—formal with informal, poetic with technical—weakens writing. See Diction 2.

Modal auxiliaries
Can, could; may, might; must; ought; shall, should; will, would are called modal auxiliaries. They differ from other verbs in having no *-s* in the third-person singular, no infinitive, no participle, and therefore no compound or phrasal forms; instead, they themselves always occur as part of verb phrases, complete or elliptical. The generally similar *dare* and *need* are also sometimes treated as modal auxiliaries. See Elliptical constructions.

Modifiers
Typically, a modifier limits the meaning of its headword and makes it more exact (a *green* apple). Modification has never been satisfactorily defined, however, and for the present, students of English grammar must be satisfied with examples. In the following illustrations the words in italics modify the words in small capitals: A *cold windy* DAY; He FAILED *miserably;* She was *truly* SUPERB; *Undoubtedly* IT WAS THE CAT WHO STOLE THE BUTTERMILK; *Coming around the corner,* WE met him head on. See Absolute phrases, Adjectives, Adverbs, Dangling modifiers, Gerunds 1, Infinitives 4, Participles 2, Phrases, Restrictive and nonrestrictive.

Money
1. Exact sums of money are usually written in figures: 72¢, $4.98, $168.75, $42,810. Though round sums are likely to be written in words (two hundred dollars, a million dollars), figures may be used for them, too, when several sums are mentioned.

2. In consecutive writing, amounts are usually written out when they are used as modifiers: a million-dollar project. Informally, figures are often used: a $2 seat.

3. For amounts in millions and billions, the dollar sign followed by the number followed by the word is most common: $50 billion. Instead of "three and a half million dollars" or "$3,500,000," "$3.5 million" is increasingly used.

4. A sum of money is usually thought of as a single unit: More than $9 million *was* invested in paintings.

Months

In reference matter and informal writing, the names of months with more than four or more than five letters are often abbreviated in dates: Jan. 21, 1972; Dec. 2, 1904; *but* May (June, July) 12, 1904. In formal writing the names of months are not abbreviated. When only the month is given, or the month and year, abbreviation is rare in any style: He was born in January 1959; Every September he tries again. See Dates.

Mood

The mood of a verb, indicated by its form, tells whether the writer or speaker regards what he is saying as a statement of fact or a question concerning fact (indicative mood), as a wish or an expression of possibility or doubt (subjunctive mood), or as a command (imperative mood). See Commands and requests, Imperative mood, Indicative mood, Subjunctive mood.

more, most

Preceding the base forms of adjectives and adverbs with *more* and *most* is one way of expressing their comparative and superlative degrees. See Comparison of adjectives and adverbs 1.

most, almost

In speech, *almost* is often reduced to *most:* A drop in prices would appeal to most anybody. *Most,* used thus, is occasionally seen in factual prose ("Most everybody is gaining on us" — Paul A. Samuelson, *Newsweek*); but in all formal and most general writing, if you can substitute *almost* for *most* in a sentence (almost always, almost everywhere), *almost* is the word to use.

Ms.

Ms. is a substitute for both *Miss* and *Mrs.* Its use is favored by those who believe that a woman should not be labeled unmarried or married any more than a man is. If a first name is used after *Ms.* for a married woman, the name is hers, of course, not her husband's: Mrs. John Doe becomes Ms. Jane Doe.

In writing for college courses a choice between *Ms.* and *Miss* or *Mrs.* is most often necessary when the topic is a biographical or critical essay about a woman or her work—for example, a review of the poetry of Sylvia Plath. Sylvia Plath can be called Ms.

Plath or Miss Plath as the writer chooses. (As a poet, she remained Sylvia Plath during her marriage.) She can also be called Sylvia Plath or simply Plath. The latter usage is becoming increasingly common in published writing about women.

MS

MS, usually in caps, is the conventional abbreviation for *manuscript*. The plural is *MSS*. Though usage is divided, the *Manual of Style* and the *MLA Style Sheet* recommend that in most contexts the abbreviation be used without a following period.

must

In general English (but not in formal) *must* has become a noun meaning "necessity" ("It has never been a must"—Henry Brandon, *Saturday Review*) and an adjective modifier meaning "essential": ("This book is a must assignment for reporters"—Robert O. Blanchard, *Columbia Journalism Review*).

myself

Myself is a reflexive or an intensive pronoun referring back to *I*: I shave myself (reflexive); I saw the whole thing myself (intensive). In addition, *myself* and the other *-self* pronouns are now used, in some grammatical environments, in the same way as the corresponding personal pronouns:

The writing was then done by myself, taking perhaps fifteen days.—Hollis Alpert, *Saturday Review*

Then the two of us, President Johnson and myself, walked out.—Malcolm Kilduff, *Columbia Journalism Review*

For the *-self* forms, most conservative stylists would substitute the regular nominative or accusative (*me* in the first example above, *I* in the second). See *himself, herself;* Pronouns 2; *self*. References: Bryant, pp. 141–43; Copperud, pp. 184–85; Pooley, pp. 153–56.

N

namely and other introductory words

The beginning of wisdom with introductory words like *namely, that is, for example* is to use them as seldom as possible. Very often they can be omitted altogether in compact general writing: His topic was a particularly unpleasant one—[namely] rising prices.

Narration

Stories (factual as well as fictional), autobiographies, biographies, and histories are all narratives. Like accounts of natural or mechanical processes and reports of laboratory experiments, they relate a sequence of events. In college papers you will frequently be called on to narrate such sequences.

1. Chronological order. As a writer of narrative, you may have reasons for altering actual chronological order. To arouse interest, you may decide to begin in the middle, making the reader ask how a character got into a certain situation. Or you may give the ending first, so that the reader will see how each step contributes to the final outcome. Or you may use a flashback ("Six years ago we had had a similar experience") to explain antecedent causes or to draw a parallel.

Although the events in a narrative can be told in any order, the reader must finally be able to understand the actual order in which they occurred. To make that order clear, you must use appropriate indicators of time (*then, later, after that,* and so on) and the right verb tenses (*had said* instead of *said* in a flashback, perhaps). And you need to use indicators of causal relationships (*in order to, because, as a result*) if the reader is to understand why an event took place or what effects it had.

2. Pace. In narration you can compress the events of a decade into a single sentence or extend the happenings of an hour through ten pages. You may slow your narrative with patches of description so that the reader can visualize the scene or gain a vivid sense of what's taking place. Or you may vary the pace by using dialog to dramatize a crucial action. You can make similar changes of pace in objective, factual reporting – of an industrial process, for example, or of a traffic accident – speeding up simpler stages and slowing down complex ones for clarity. Varying the pace is one of the ways you can direct the attention of your audience and control its responses.

3. Distance and point of view. How the reader sees and interprets the events depends on the distance you establish between yourself and your subject and between yourself and your reader. You may be close to your subject, taking part in the action, even motivating it; or you may be a remote observer, reporting and analyzing. You can present yourself as a learner and invite the reader to share that perspective, or you can assume the role of a professional – someone who knows much more than the reader does. The prevailing point of view will help define the tone of what you write. See Point of view.

4. The point of the narrative. A good narrative relates a sequence of events in such a way that a point emerges: the reader grasps not only what took place but the significance of what took place. In an expository narrative the significance may be clearly stated. In other narratives – personal reminiscences, for example – a brief comment on the significance of the action may be justified; but the better the storytelling, the less need there will be for spelling out the so-what.

nauseous, nauseated

Nauseated usually means "sickened, disgusted" (I felt nauseated at the sight); *nauseous* usually means "causing sickness or disgust" (The food looked nauseous). But speakers, and some writers, frequently use "feeling nauseous" and "getting nauseous." The ambiguity involved (sickened/sickening) suggests the wisdom of retaining the distinction between the two words. Reference: Copperud, p. 186.

Negation

In mathematics, -3 is as much less than 0 as $+3$ is more than 0 and $-(-3) = +3$ because the only mathematical alternative to minus is plus. In language a contrary is likely to be stated by another positive (good–evil, short–tall); the negative usually means "less than" or "different from": *not good* is "less than good" but not necessarily "evil," and *not short* is "taller than short" but not necessarily "tall." In *not uncommon,* we get a reduced reduction: *uncommon* is "less than common"; *not uncommon* is "less than less than common" or "not quite common" – an unemphatic or understated affirmative.

On the other hand, when *not* negates the verb, and one or two additional negatives modify either the verb or some other sentence element (as in "He can't never do no work"), the multiple negatives may actually reinforce the negation. But this cumulative effect is no longer used in standard English. See Double negative.

Sometimes the negative form shows unexpected variation from the affirmative: "must go" and "have to go" are nearly synonymous; "mustn't go" and "don't have to go" are not.

See Negatives and style.

Negatives and style

When you use both negative and positive words in the same sentence, be sure the combination says clearly what you intend: "The vocational counseling office will try to increase their clients' inability to support themselves" should be rephrased either as "to increase their ability" or as "to remedy their inability."

Poor sentences often result from stating negatively what might better be put positively:

This mob violence does not reflect the sentiment of an overwhelming majority of the students.
Better: This mob violence reflects the sentiments of only a small minority of the students.

Some writers are fond of tricky negative constructions, including litotes, a variety of understatement in which an affirmative is expressed by the negative of its contrary: "Marquand is not unfond of poor Apley" (Alfred Kazin, *Saturday Review*). Litotes can be effective, but when overused it makes the writer sound coy, evasive, or simply tiresome. See Double negative.

Negro

Negro has been replaced by *black* in much general usage since the 1960s. See *black*.

neither

As a pronoun, *neither* is ordinarily construed as singular and followed by a singular verb. When the verb is separated from *neither* by a prepositional phrase with a plural object, a plural verb frequently appears in informal writing and sometimes in general: "Marx and Trotsky, neither of whom were notably gentle or vegetarian" (Dwight Macdonald, *Esquire*); but in these cases, too, grammatical convention calls for a singular verb.

As an adjective, *neither* modifies a singular noun (neither man), and by grammatical convention a pronoun referring to the noun should be singular (Neither man lost *his* temper).

References: Bryant, pp. 8–10; Copperud, p. 188; Fries, p. 50.

Newspaper English

Today, newspaper English is only one form of journalese. See Journalese.

nice

Nice, a counter word indicating mild approval, is useful in speech but so imprecise that it is out of place in most writing. In formal prose *nice* is usually restricted to meanings like "subtle" or "discriminating": Kirk raises a nice point in his article on Camus.

nobody, no one

The pronouns *nobody* and *no one* take singular verbs, and, strictly speaking, a pronoun referring to either of them should be singular: No one lowered his voice. But sometimes meaning demands a plural pronoun: "No one sings; they simply listen reverently" (Ray Jenkins, *New York Times Magazine*). In formal writing the sentence might be recast: No one sings; everyone simply listens reverently.

 ## Nominalization

Change the abstract nominalization into a concrete verb.

For most purposes the best writing is direct writing—writing that avoids three words where two will do, writing that represents an action in a verb and the agent of that action as its subject. The difference between indirect and direct writing is the difference between these two sentences:

It seems to be the case that certain individuals in attendance at this institution of higher education are in a state of anger over recent announcements on the part of the dean in regard to a necessity for greater restrictions where demonstrations are concerned.

Some students here are angry because the dean announced that he would not let them demonstrate as freely as they had.

Probably the most common source of indirect writing is the abstract nominalization, a noun that, according to transformational theory, has been derived from a full subject + verb in the deep structure of a sentence:

Tom *paid* the money   → Tom's *payment* of the money
The monks *reject* wealth   → The monks' *rejection* of wealth
The students *are responsible* → The students' *responsibility*

The direct subject-verb-object or subject-*be*-adjective construction is here made indirect and accordingly less vivid and forceful. If this kind of construction occurs often in your writing (about once every seven or eight words), readers are likely to find your style heavy, abstract, even pretentious, and possibly dishonest.

To improve such a style, first look for nouns made out of verbs: An investigation is being made of the causes for the decline in wheat production. When you find them (*investigation, causes, decline, production*), ask whether the crucial action is in the main verb or in one of these abstract nouns. If it is in the noun (*investigation*), change the noun to a verb (*are investigating*), find a subject for it (*they,* referring to a specific antecedent? *scientists? agricultural chemists?*), and rewrite the sentence around the new subject-verb:

An investigation is being made of the causes for the decline in wheat production.
Agricultural chemists are investigating what has caused wheat production to decline.
Agricultural chemists are investigating why farmers are producing less wheat.

See Deep structure, Passive voice 1, Subjects, Verbs 3. References: Roderick A. Jacobs, *CCC*, Oct. 1969, pp. 187–90; Sledd, pp. 300–301; Rulon Wells in *Style in Language,* ed. Thomas A. Sebeok (Cambridge, Mass.: MIT Press, 1960), pp. 213–20; Williams, pp. 311–21.

Nominative case

A noun or pronoun that is the subject of a finite verb, the complement of a linking verb, or an appositive to either is said to be in the nominative (or subjective) case. The form of the nominative singular is the common form of the noun, the form to which, typically, the endings for the genitive and for the plural are added. The pronouns with distinctive nominative forms are the personals — *I, you, he, she, it, we, you, they* — and the relative *who.* Though these are the usual forms for the nominative functions, see *it's me; who, whom.* See also Case 1, Subjects.

none

The use of *none* with a plural verb has often been condemned, usually on the grounds that *none* means "no one" or "not one" and so must be singular. Actual usage is divided. Plural *none* would be ungrammatical as a substitute for an uncountable (He talks nonsense, but none of it matters), but when the reference is to countables, *none* has long been used as a plural in the most reputable writing:

Almost none [of the letters] are either thoughtful in their approach or deliberative in their style. — Louis J. Halle, *New Republic*

None have been older than this sacramental alliance. — Sidney Hook, *New York Times Book Review*

None of these documents afford any solid support for those historians who have viewed Pike as a tool or accomplice in the Wilkinson-Burr schemes. — Harvey L. Carter, *American Historical Review*

References: Bryant, p. 8; Copperud, p. 190; Follett, pp. 227–28.

Nonrestrictive

A nonrestrictive modifier does not provide essential identification of the word modified and should therefore be set off by commas. See Restrictive and nonrestrictive.

ns Nonstandard English

Change the nonstandard word, form, or idiom to one in standard use.

He do, they is, theirself, nobody ain't got nothing: these are nonstandard. Among the articles that treat nonstandard words or forms are Adverbs and style; Double negative; *lay, lie; learn, teach;* Principal parts of verbs. See also the Introduction, p. 3; English language 3.

no place

Although *anyplace, everyplace,* and *someplace* for "anywhere," "everywhere," and "somewhere" have become common in general writing, *no place* for "nowhere" is still mainly informal. It is sometimes spelled as one word.

nor

By itself, *nor* is an emphatic negative conjunction, most commonly used at the beginning of a sentence in the sense "and . . . not": Nor was Paris the only place he visited. Before the last member of a negative series, *nor* gives an added distinctness and emphasis: "I did not see him or hear him" is less emphatic than "I did not see him nor hear him."

As a correlative conjunction, *nor* is paired with *neither.* See Correlative conjunctions.

not about to

Not about to is not the simple negative of *about to* but an idiom that stresses the remoteness of the suggested possibility: I'm not about to go along with their weird schemes. It occurs mainly in speech but also in writing, where it quickly becomes tiresome.

not hardly, not scarcely

Since *hardly* and *scarcely* both mean "probably not," an additional *not* is redundant. See Double negative 2.

Noun clauses

A noun clause is a dependent clause that fills a nominal position:
What I can do in society [subject] depends on *what my neighbors will tolerate* [object of a preposition]. Many noun clauses
are introduced by *that* or *whether*, some by *what, which, who,
whoever, whatever, why, when*, and other interrogatives.

Subject: That anyone could raise his grades by studying has never
occurred to him. *Whether or not he should go* had bothered him for days.
Why sociology has been growing so rapidly is a complicated question. (A
noun clause as subject suggests a formal style.)

Object: He knew [*that*] *it would never happen again.* (When the noun
clause is object of the verb, introductory *that* is often omitted in general
English.)

Complement: His favorites were *whoever flattered him.*

Appositive: The doctrine *that we must avoid entangling alliances* was
first stated by Washington.

Compare *that* in a noun clause (I know *that he loves me*) with
that in a relative clause (The man *that I love* left town). In the
noun clause *that* has no syntactic function. In the relative
clause *that* is the direct object.
See Relative clauses.

Nouns

Nouns are best identified by their forms and by the positions they
fill in sentences.

1. Forms. English nouns may be inflected for number and case.
Many have a plural ending in *-s* or *-es*: *hats, kindnesses, lec-
turers.* These and other forms of the plural are discussed in
Plurals of nouns.

The ending of the genitive singular is written with an apostrophe and an *s: boy's, manufacturer's.* The genitive plural adds
an apostrophe to the regular plural spelling *(boys', manufactur-
ers')* and apostrophe-*s* to plurals not ending in *-s (men's, sheep's).*
See Genitive case.

A few distinctive endings make nouns from other parts of
speech. They include *-er* or *-or, -ness, -th, -tion: buyer, advisor,
darkness, warmth, inflation.*

Some nouns in English have different forms for masculine
and feminine: *actor–actress, confidant–confidante, execu-
tor–executrix.* See Gender, Sexist language.

Nouns may be single words or compound words written solid,
as two words, or hyphenated: *bathroom, bookcase, stickup, hub
cap, go-getter.* See Group words, Hyphen.

2. Position and function. *Dog* and *day* are nouns by their forms:
they occur with plural and genitive inflections (a dog's leash, two
days' work). But since they can occur in positions normally filled
by adjectives (*dog* days) and adverbs (He works *days*), they can
be called, in context only, adjectiv*als* or adverbi*als*. Thus if we
call them *nouns*, we define them by formal characteristics; if

adjectivals or *adverbials,* by syntactic function. If they also function as nouns syntactically, as in "The *dog* is man's best friend" or in "*Day* will come eventually," then they are nouns in *nominal* function.

Within noun phrases, nouns may be preceded by determiners and adjectives and followed by appositives, prepositional phrases, and relative clauses. Here are examples of the chief syntactic uses of noun phrases and hence of nouns:

Subject of a verb: A high wind from the east blew for three days.
Object of a verb: The wind damaged *the trees, which were loaded with ice.*
Object of a preposition: In *the night,* on *a frozen pond,* fishing is no sport for *a feeble spirit.*
Complement: He has become *president of the firm.*
Attributive: The young woman's partner had the grace of a *baby* hippo.
Apposition: The first settler, *Thomas Sanborn,* came in 1780.
Modifier of a verb: He came *two months ago.*

3. Classes of nouns. In the traditional grouping of nouns that follows, many nouns clearly fall into more than one group:
a. Proper nouns, names of particular people and places, written with capitals and usually without *the* or *a:* Anne, Dale A. Robb, London, Georgia, France, the Bay of Naples. All other nouns are called common.
b. Concrete nouns, names of things that can be perceived by the senses: *leaf, leaves, road, trousers, intellectuals.* Concrete nouns are opposed to abstract nouns, names of qualities, actions, types, ideas, and so on: *goodness, theft, beauty, heroism.*
c. Mass nouns, names of material aggregates, masses, or other units not defined by their discrete parts and their shape: *food, money, health, water, chaos, intelligence.* Mass nouns are syntactically distinguished by the fact that they cannot be preceded by indefinite articles: *Intelligence* depends on *environment* and *heredity.* (When *environment* can be preceded by *an,* it is not being used as a mass noun.) Mass nouns are opposed to count nouns, which refer to things that are conceived of as discrete units: *car, book, street, machine, horse.* Count nouns require *a/an* to mark their indefiniteness: a car, a book, a street, a machine, a horse. Some words can be either mass or count nouns: Wood is used in building—Mahogany is a valuable wood; Steak is expensive—I ate a steak.
d. Collective nouns, names of groups of things regarded as units: *fleet, army, committee, trio.* See Collective nouns.

See Parts of speech. References: Francis, pp. 237–52, 298–312; Quirk et al., pp. 127–203; Sledd, pp. 68–73; Williams, pp. 70–79.

nowhere near

Though in general use, *nowhere near* has an informal tone: It was a good score but nowhere near as large as we'd hoped for. Formal usage would substitute "not nearly so large as." Reference: Bryant, pp. 148–49.

Number

Number in English grammar is the singular and plural aspect of nouns and pronouns and verbs. Number in nouns is most important, since it controls the number of verbs and pronouns. In verbs, overt indication of number is limited to the present tense except in the pair *was–were*. See Plurals of nouns, Reference of pronouns, Subjects.

number

Number is a collective noun, taking a singular verb when the group as a group is meant and a plural verb when the individual units are the concern. Ordinarily "a number of" takes the plural (A number of tickets have been sold) and "the number of" takes the singular (The number of tickets left to sell is discouraging).

Numbers

1. Figures. Figures are conventionally used for the following:
a. Dates (June 29, 1918; 6/29/18), except in formal social correspondence and some ceremonial contexts.
b. Hours with *a.m.* or *p.m.:* 5 p.m. (*but* five o'clock).
c. Street addresses and highway numbers: 2841 Washington Avenue, Route 99.
d. Pages and other references: p. 761; Act III, scene iv, line 28 (III.iv.28) *or* act 3, scene 4, line 28 (3.4.28).
e. Exact sums of money: $4.98, 75¢.
f. Measures expressed in the conventional abbreviations: 15 cc., 3 km, 6″, 10 lbs., 32° F.

The plural of a figure is formed by adding either *-s* or, somewhat more formally, apostrophe-*s* (six 5s or six 5's; the 1970s or the 1970's). For the genitive, the apostrophe is not usual with figures: They imported $12,000 worth of equipment.

Except in dates, street numbers, zip codes, telephone numbers, and a few other regular series, a comma is used to separate thousands, millions, etc., though it may be omitted in four-digit numbers: 2,736 (*or* 2736) bushels; $4,682,981.

2. Figures or words. Words are conventionally used for round numbers and indefinite numbers: ten million, hundreds, a dozen, a score. Words are also customary for numbers that begin sentences—"Nineteen-eighteen did not usher in the millennium" (Henry Steele Commager, *Saturday Review*)—and for ordinal numbers (*first, second, third*).

As a rule, newspapers use figures for numbers over ten, words for smaller numbers; magazine and book styles (most general writing) ordinarily use figures for numbers over one hundred except when the numbers can be written in two words: *four, ten, ninety-two, two thousand.*

This passage illustrates a typical book style in handling numbers:

Stage coaches reached new top speeds as their horses galloped over the improved roads. It had taken four and a half days to travel the 160 miles from London to Manchester in 1754; thirty-four years later the journey had been shortened to twenty-eight hours. — T. Walter Wallbank et al., *Civilization Past and Present*

Words and figures should not be mixed in a series of numbers applying to the same units. If one of the numbers is conventionally written in figures, use figures for all: from 9 (*not* nine) to 125 days. But large numbers are increasingly written in a combination of figures and words: "$3 billion" is quicker to grasp than "$3,000,000,000."

Numbers in two words between twenty-one and ninety-nine are usually hyphenated, though the practice is declining: *forty-two* or *forty two*. A hyphen is used between figures to indicate a range: The prediction was based on 40–50 personal interviews and 200–300 telephone calls. It should not be used if the numbers are preceded by *from* or *between:* from 40 to 50 (*not* from 40–50).

3. Arabic and Roman numerals. Arabic numerals (1, 2, 146) are used in almost all places where numbers are not expressed in words. Roman numerals, either lowercase (i, ii, cxlvi) or capitals (I, II, CXLVI), are occasionally used to number units in a rather short series, as in outlines, chapters of a book, acts of a play, though now less often than formerly. The preliminary pages of books are almost always given Roman numerals; the body of a book begins a new pagination with Arabic numerals. Sometimes Roman numerals are used for the date on title pages and in formal inscriptions.

See Fractions, Hyphen 4, Money. References: Copperud, pp. 193–94; *A Manual of Style; U.S. Style Manual.*

Objective case

The object forms of pronouns are said to be in the objective, or accusative, case. See Accusative case.

Objects

1. Direct objects. In the simplest kind of sentence, the direct object is a noun phrase that follows a transitive verb to which the object is related as one of the primary elements of the predicate: Grammar puzzles *normal people; * Alice saw *the white rabbit;* The man was building *a fence*. In more complicated sentences a variety of elements, which do not always follow their verbs, can stand as direct objects; and, of course, pronouns can replace noun phrases in the object relation: Everybody enjoys *eating steak;* Somebody said *that porpoises are smart; What he meant* I never knew; John met *them* earlier.

Often the direct object of an active verb can be made the subject of a synonymous sentence in the passive: *Normal people* are puzzled by grammar; *The white rabbit* was seen by Alice. See Passive voice.

Traditionally, direct objects are said to name what is affected or effected by the actions of their verbs, but this description appears incorrect for "He received a wound in the war" or "They experienced many humiliations." On a deeper level, however, what appear to be subjects (*he* and *they*) may be objects (Someone wounded him; Someone humiliated them). See Deep structure.

2. Indirect objects. What is called the indirect object names the person or thing to which something is given, said, or shown – the person or thing affected, not directly but indirectly, by the verbal action: He gave *the church* a memorial window; She showed *him* the snapshot. Like direct objects, indirect objects are noun phrases or their equivalents. They follow a special set of transitive verbs, precede direct objects, and are synonymous, in corresponding sentences, with prepositional phrases introduced by *to* or *for*: He gave a memorial window *to the church*.

3. Objects of prepositions. The object of a preposition is the noun phrase, or equivalent, that follows the preposition and bears to some other element in the sentence a relation which the preposition indicates: here, "some other element in the sentence" is the object of *to*. A relative or interrogative pronoun as object may precede the preposition: *What* are you talking *about?*

4. Other objects. Different grammarians use *object* in different ways. Noun phrases or adjectives that follow direct objects after a special set of transitive verbs and that are related to the direct objects as if they were joined to them by the verb *to be* are sometimes called object complements: They considered his behavior *a threat to the school's welfare*.

When a direct or indirect object is made the subject of a passive sentence and the other object or object complement remains after the verb, that remaining object is called a retained object: His behavior was considered *a threat*.

Many linguists reject as direct objects words in a sentence that can't be made the subject of a passive version of the same sentence: He resembles his father – His father is resembled by him; I have a cold – A cold is had by me; It cost a nickel – A nickel was cost by it.

References: Sledd, pp. 126–36; Jacobs and Rosenbaum, Ch. 18.

Obscenity

Although the vulgar terms for the sexual and the excretory body parts and functions – the so-called four-letter words – are used much more freely in print, as well as in speech, than they were a decade ago, they ordinarily serve either as counter words or as expressions of generalized emotion—for example, disgust. In either case, they don't belong in college writing. See Profanity.

of course

Of course should be used sparingly and fairly. It should not be used as a substitute for evidence: Of course, we all know the administration is corrupt. Nor should it be used to suggest that, for the writer, the esoteric is the everyday: Old English had, of course, no inflected passive. Reference: Copperud, p. 196.

off of

The double prepositions *inside of, outside of, off of* are heard regularly and are in general use in writing. Many formal stylists reject the *of*, particularly with *off*.

OK, O.K., okay

OK or *O.K.* or *okay* is informal and commercial English for "approval" (The foreman put his OK on the shipment), for "all right, correct" (It's OK with me), and for "endorse, approve" (If you'll OK my time sheet, I can get paid). As a verb the forms are *OK, OK'ed* or *OK'd, OK'ing* and *okay, okayed, okaying*. Reference: For the most extensive treatment of the history of *OK*, see the series of studies by Allen Walker Read, *AS*, 1963–1964. Mencken, pp. 169–71, summarizes some of Read's findings.

Old English

Old English is the form of English in use from about 450 to 1100. See English language.

one

1. The use of the impersonal *one*, referring to people in general or to an average or typical person, is formal in tone, especially if it is repeated: "the victories and defeats of one's children, the passing of elders, one's own and one's mate's" (Benjamin De-Mott, *Atlantic*); One can't be too careful, can one? Many writers consider a series of *one*'s pretentious and refer back to *one* with forms of *he*—"One can determine his own life" (J. A. Ward, *Journal of English*)—but some readers would regard *his* in this context as offensively sexist.

A shift from *one* to impersonal *they* is avoided in writing, and while a shift from *one* to impersonal *you* is not rare, it would be inappropriate in formal contexts and disapproved by many readers. The *you . . . you* pattern is most common in general English. See *they, you*.

2. The use of *one* for *I*—"One hopes he will enter a primary campaign" (William F. Buckley, Jr., syndicated columnist)—is a stylistic eccentricity.

3. *One* may be used to avoid repeating a noun in the second of two compound elements: Fred took the new copy, and I took the old one. The plural *ones* is often so used, and logically enough, since *one* is not only a number but an indefinite pronoun: She had a yellow poncho and two red ones. But *one* as a noun substitute is often deadwood, taking emphasis away from the adjective that carries the real meaning: The plan was certainly [an] original [one].

Reference: Jespersen, pp. 83–85.

one another

The reciprocal pronoun *one another* is used to refer to two as well as to more than two. See *each other, one another;* Pronouns 3.

one of those who

In formal English the clause following *one of those who* and similar locutions is usually plural because the relative pronoun refers to a plural antecedent:

He is one of those people who believe in the perfectibility of man. (*Who* refers to *people*.)

This is one of the books that make you change your ideas. (*That* refers to *books*.)

But because there is a strong tendency to regard *one* as the antecedent, a singular verb is common:

Leslie Fiedler is one of those literary personalities who has the effect of polarizing his readers. — Peter Michelson, *New Republic*

. . . one of those crucial questions that comes up again and again. — David Garnett, *American Scholar*

The more formal your context, the more necessary a plural verb. Reference: Copperud, p. 199.

only

According to the conventions of formal English, a single-word modifier should stand immediately before the element modified: I need only six more to have a full hundred. But usage often favors placing *only* before the verb: I only need six more to have a full hundred. The meaning is equally clear, and placing *only* with the verb is an established English idiom.

Even so, precise placement of *only* may be more satisfying to both writer and reader: "In this bicentennial year, let us only praise [*better:* let us praise only] famous men" (Gore Vidal, *New York Review of Books*). And so long as it isn't insisted on where it sounds stilted and unnatural, it can at least prevent silly statements like "He only had a face that [*better:* He had a face that only] a mother could love."

In this respect, *even, ever, nearly, just, exactly,* and other such limiting adverbs are similar to *only*. They can be placed so that they spoil the emphasis: I'm tolerant about such things, but his conduct even surprises me [*for* surprises even me].

References: Bryant, pp. 155–56; Pooley, pp. 87–90.

Onomatopoeia

By their pronunciations some words suggest particular sounds: *buzz, bang, clank, swish, splash, whir, pop, clatter*. Such imitative words are well established in the English vocabulary. Using sounds that match the sense of a passage in order to intensify its meaning is a stylistic device known as onomatopoeia. Ordinarily the writer works with existing words, sometimes adapting them in the process: "The wire is cut into bullet sizes, the slippery bullets slide from the chopping block on a gangway of grease, they are slithering, skiddering, and slippering into one another" (John Sack, *Esquire*). Onomatopoeia may also inspire outright imitation of sound, as in Tom Wolfe's description of stunting motorcycles: "thraaagggh." Conscious striving for words like *thraaagggh* can produce embarrassing results unless the writer's tongue is visibly in his cheek. See Alliteration, Assonance, Figurative language.

on, onto, on to

When *on* is an adverb and *to* a preposition in a separate phrase, they should be written as two words: The rest of us drove on to the city. The test is that *city* cannot be the object of *on*. Used as a preposition, they are written solid: The team trotted onto the floor; They looked out onto the park. Both *floor* and *park* are objects of the compound *onto*.

In the sense "to a place on"—The evangelist leaped up on(to) the platform—*onto* and *on* are sometimes used interchangeably.

Reference: Bryant, p. 152.

on the part of

On the part of is often wordy for "by," "among," "for," and the like: The new law resulted in less wild driving on the part of [by] young people; There has been a growing awareness of political change on the part of [among] scholars.

or

Or is a coordinating conjunction and, like *and, but,* and *for,* should connect words, phrases, or clauses of equal value. According to conventional rules, two subjects joined by *or* take a singular verb if each is singular, a plural verb if both are plural or if the one nearer the verb is plural:

Cod-liver oil or halibut oil is often prescribed.
Cod-liver oil or cod-liver oil capsules are often prescribed.
Cod-liver oil capsules or cod-liver oil is often prescribed.

Sometimes, writers use a plural verb after singular subjects joined by *or,* suggesting "either and perhaps both" rather than "not both but one or the other": "There is no evidence that Mao or Castro are taking advantage of their young fans" (Andrew Kopkind, *New Republic*). The lack of agreement would be condemned by most formal stylists. See Correlative conjunctions.

oral, verbal

Literally, *verbal* means "pertaining to words" and *oral* means "pertaining to the mouth." Insisting on the etymological distinction, some writers maintain that *oral* is the one true opposite of *written;* but *verbal* is used in the sense "unwritten" in all varieties of English: "Though written contracts were fairly often produced, a large proportion of the agreements seem to have been verbal" (Robert Sabatino Lopez, *Speculum*).

org Organization

Improve the organization of your essay by arranging the parts in an orderly sequence, or by making the movement clear through the use of appropriate signals and transitions, or both.

The main cause of poor organization is failure to get clear in your own mind the natural or logical divisions of your subject and the right relation of the parts of your discourse. Every essay should have a definable structure. In writing your paper, you should arrange the parts in an order that makes sense in terms of your purpose; and as you develop each part, you should take into account its place and importance in the whole scheme.

A poorly organized essay lacks direction—a logical movement from beginning to end. Or it lacks shape—proportions that do justice to the relative significance of the ideas. Or it lacks unity, with irrelevant material diverting attention from the main thread of the discussion. The best way to pinpoint such structural weaknesses is to outline your essay, reducing it to a skeleton of key statements. Then set about reorganizing and rewriting.

If rereading your essay and studying your outline leaves you convinced that the organization is basically sound, examine the ways you have introduced topics and linked up paragraph sequences. Even though you can justify the order of the parts of the essay, you may find that you've neglected to give the reader guidance in seeing the relationships you intend. If this is so, relatively simple repair work—improving connections and supplying transitions—should give the essay the direction, shape, and unity it *seems* to lack. The remedy is not drastic reworking of the entire structure but adding or rewriting sentences, particularly those at the structural joints that connect the main blocks of material. See Coherence, Outline form, Paragraph indention, Transition, Unity.

Originality

Original is applied to writing in two different senses. Content is original when it is gathered by the writer from his experience, from his observation of people, events, or places, or from documents like letters and newspapers. Most college papers should contain some original material. Merely rewriting a magazine article is certainly not a profitable exercise in composition. Putting together ideas taken from several such secondary sources has some value, since it requires selection and comparison. But the most useful work for growth in writing is composing papers in which a good deal of the content is original. The writing is more fun and the gain is much greater than in simply working over what others have done. (See Plagiarism.)

Originality in expression, in style, is a different matter. The English language has been used a long time, and absolutely new words and phrases are rare. You can, however, avoid the more threadbare figures and locutions—like "threadbare figures"— and an honest attempt to tell exactly what you see and believe will ordinarily result in straightforward, readable writing that has some freshness of expression. Trying too hard for originality will result in strained writing or "fine" writing, uncomfortable to writer and reader alike. When a style deserving the label *original* appears, it is usually the by-product of an active and independent mind, not the result of a deliberate search for novelty. See Figurative language, Figures of speech.

Origin of words

1. The study of the sources of words. Every word has a history. Some words, like *chauffeur, mores, television, parapsychology,* are relatively new in English; some, like *home, candle, go, kitchen,* have been in the language for centuries; others have recently acquired new meanings, like *satellite* (from a Latin word for "attendant," a term in astronomy which probably now means for most people either a dependent nation or a man-made object which orbits the earth, moon, or other celestial body). Etymology, the study of word origins, traces the changes of forms and combinations of word elements (as in *dis/service, wild/ness, bath/ room, room/mate*) and pursues the word or its component parts to Old English, or to the foreign language from which it came into English, and so on back to the earliest discoverable forms. Of some words, especially informal words like *dude, stooge, rumpus,* earlier forms are unknown; of others, like *OK* or *blizzard,* the sources are debated. But the efforts of generations of scholars have discovered fairly full histories for most words. These are given briefly in most dictionaries and more fully in the *Oxford English Dictionary* and in special works.

Many of our everyday words come down directly from Old English (*brother, go, house, tell*) or, if they are of foreign origin, were borrowed many centuries ago (*candle, debt, pay, travel*). Many French words, of both early and recent borrowing, entered the vocabulary by way of high society (*debutante, fiancée*). The vocabulary of philosophy and abstract thought has a large Latin element (*concept, fallacy, rational, idealism*), and the vocabulary of science has many Greek elements (*atom, hemoglobin, seismograph*).

The sources of words will often reveal something about our history, as the many Norman French and Latin words in law (*fine, tort, certiorari, subpoena*) remind us of the time, following 1066, when the government of England was in the hands of the Norman French. But it is more interesting to discover what meanings the words have had in their earlier career in English and in the foreign languages from which they have come. *Supercilium* in Latin meant "eyebrow"; *rehearse* is from a French word meaning to "harrow again"; *sarcophagus* is, according to its Greek originals, "a flesh eater," referring to the limestone coffins that hastened the disintegration of bodies; *profane* (Latin) meant "outside the temple" and gathered the meaning of "against religion, the opposite of sacred"; *alcohol* goes back to an Arabic word for a finely ground powder, used for painting eyelids, and came to be applied, in Spanish, to specially distilled spirits, and so to our alcohol. See English language.

Words have arrived and are still arriving in English through two general processes – the making of new words, by either creating or borrowing them, and the compounding or clipping of words and parts of words that are already in the language. Then the usefulness of this new stock of words is increased as the words undergo changes in form.

2. New words.

a. Creation of words. Coinage, or outright creation, is rare. Even *gas*, first used by Van Helmont (1578–1644), a Belgian scientist, probably had the Greek *chaos* as well as a Dutch or Flemish word behind it. *Kodak* is an actual creation, as are a good many other trade names, some familiar from advertising. Informal words like *dud* and *burble* were also creations, good-sounding words someone made up. F. Gelett Burgess invented *blurb*, defining it as "self-praise; to make a noise like a publisher." Imitative words like *buzz, honk, swish, whiz* are attempts to translate the sounds of nature into the sounds of language. Various exclamations of surprise, pain, scorn, may have started as emotional noises – *ow, ouch, fie, phooey* – and then became regular words. A word that is coined for a special occasion is a nonce word – *steakola*, for example, used in Illinois in 1961 to mean meat given by a butcher as a bribe to an inspector of weights and measures. As a rule, arbitrary coinages do not stick. Outright creation is a very minor source of new words.

b. Borrowed words. English has always borrowed words freely, from Latin, German, French and from other languages with which English-speaking people have come in contact. It has assimilated words of quite un-English form: *khaki* (Hindi), *tycoon* (Japanese), *ski* (Norwegian), *hors d'oeuvres* (French), *intelligentsia* (Russian). The various words for *porch*, itself Norman French but the oldest and the most English-seeming of the group, come from various languages: *piazza* (Italian), *stoop* (Dutch), *veranda* (Hindi).

Borrowing is still going on, though perhaps more slowly than at some periods. Some words come into formal English and remain formal words: *intelligentsia, bourgeois, chef d'oeuvre, objet d'art, Zeitgeist*, and many others of political, philosophical, scientific, or literary bearing. *Sphygmograph* and many other scientific words are recent compoundings of Latin and especially of Greek words which are not otherwise in English usage, so that they may be regarded as borrowings as well as compounds. Others come in as general words, especially when large numbers of people go abroad, as during a war (*blitzkrieg, camouflage*) or when a foreign invention becomes suddenly popular, as in *chauffeur, garage, chassis* of the automobile vocabulary. Some words brought by immigrants have stuck: *sauerkraut, kohlrabi, pronto, pizza, kosher, goulash, zombie.*

Many borrowed words are dropped before they gain any general currency. The useful words are more or less adapted to English spelling and pronunciation and become true English words. (See English language and, for suggestions about the use of recently borrowed words, Foreign words in English 2.)

3. Changes in form of words.

a. Word composition. Most new words are made by putting together two or more elements to create a different meaning or function, as *un-* added to *interesting* gives a word of the opposite meaning, *uninteresting,* or *-ize* added to the noun *canal* gives a verb, *canalize.* The fact that dictionaries separate words formed with prefixes into two groups, those that need to be defined and those that are self-explanatory, shows how deceptive affixes can be. The elements may be a prefix placed before the root word (*mis-related*), or a suffix added (*foolish-ness*), or a combining element like *mono-* (*mono-syllable, mono-rail*), or two independent words built together (*book-case, basket-ball, gentle-man*). Group words like *high school, out of town,* though not written as single words, could be included as a type of word composition.

A list of prefixes and suffixes that are still active in English would take several pages. Here are a few of the more common prefixes:

a- (not): asymmetrical, amoral, atypical
ante- (before): anteprohibition era
anti- (against): antiprohibition
bi- (two): bivalve, biplane, bicycle
dis- (not): disinterested, dispraise
in- (not): inelegant, independent
mis- (wrong): mistake, misnomer
pre- (before): preview, prenatal, preempt
re- (again): revise, redecorate

A few suffixes are:

-en (to form a verb): heighten, lighten, weaken
-ful (full): playful, spoonful
-fy (to make): electrify, horrify
-ish (to form an adjective): dryish, foolish, smallish
-ize (to form a verb): circularize

Combining elements include a number of words or roots, many of them Greek:

-graph- (writing): biography, photograph
micro- (small): microcosm, micrometer, microphone, microbiology

mono- (one): monotone, monorail
-phil- (loving): philanthropy, philately, Anglophile
tele- (distant): television, telemeter
-trop- (turning): geotropic, heliotropic

At first a compound has no more than the meaning to be expected from its elements: *unable = not able*. But often it will develop an independent sense which can hardly be guessed at from the meanings of its elements: *cupboard, loudspeaker*.

Several pairs of prefixes and suffixes have the same meaning, and often two words with the same meaning but somewhat different forms exist side by side, especially words with *in-* (not) and *un-* and nouns with *-ness, -ity*, or *-tion:*

aridness, aridity	indistinguishable, undistinguishable
completeness, completion	precocity, precociousness
corruption, corruptness	torridness, torridity
ferociousness, ferocity	unobliging, disobliging

b. Phonetic alterations. For a variety of reasons, one word may have two or more developments in its pronunciation, each form emphasizing a different shade of the older word's meaning. Here are four of the many Anglo-Saxon words that have had such double developments: from *ān* we get *one* and *a, an;* from *of* come *off* and *of;* from *thurh, through* and *thorough;* and from *ūtera, utter* and *outer*. In many such doublets the spellings do not differ, though the pronunciations, functions, and meanings do: *con'duct*, noun; *con duct'*, verb.

c. Blends. Informal English has a number of words that show the liberties that the users of language have always taken with their words and always will take. Some of their experiments have been added to the main English vocabulary.

One common type is blends, or portmanteau words, made by telescoping two words into one, often making a letter or syllable do double duty. *Squish* is probably a blend of *squirt* and *swish; electrocute*, of *electro-* and *execute; smog*, of *smoke* and *fog*. Blends are common in the names of many firms and products. Other examples include *motel, paratroops, cinemactress* (*Time* magazine was once obsessed with such blends), and a good many folksy efforts like *absogoshdarnlutely*.

d. Clipped words. One of the commonest types of word change is clipping, dropping one or more syllables to make a briefer form: *ad* from *advertisement, bus* from *omnibus, taxi* from *taxicab* (earlier, from *taximeter cabriolet*), *quote* from *quotation, hifi* from *high fidelity* (a blend of clips), *mob* (an eighteenth-century clip from *mobile vulgus*), *auto, movie, plane, phone*, and so on. Shoptalk has many clips—*mike* for *microphone* or *micrometer*. The speech of any closely related group is full of clips; campus vocabulary shows a full line: *econ, home ec, phys ed, grad, dorm, ad building, lab, exam, gym, prof, premed*, and scores more. Clipped words are written (when they are appropriate to the context) without apostrophe or period.

e. Back formations. *Back formation* refers to the derivation of a new word (for example, *orate*) from an older word assumed to be its derivative *(oration)*. The new word usually serves as a different part of speech, like *baby-sit* from *baby-sitter, opt* from *option, peddle* from *peddler, typewrite* from *typewriter*. Some back formations are long established *(beg, diagnose, browse, edit)*; some are still avoided by conservative writers *(emote, enthuse, sculpt)*; some are mostly for fun *(buttle, revolute)*.

f. Common nouns from proper names. Some words have come into general use because of an association with a person or place: *boycott,* from the name of an Irish land agent, Captain Boycott, who was so treated; *macadam,* from the inventor of the road surface, John L. MacAdam; *sandwich,* from the Earl of Sandwich; *jersey,* from the island of Jersey; *pasteurize,* from Louis Pasteur, who developed the process.

g. Playful formations. Blends and back formations are likely to have a playful note, and so do some other word shifts that can't be classified. Some become quite generally used: *dingus, doodad, beanery, jalopy.*

References: The authority on the history of English words is the *Oxford English Dictionary;* the *Dictionary of American English* and the *Dictionary of Americanisms* supplement it for words peculiar to the United States. Besides general books on English, the following pay special attention to origin of words: Valerie Adams, *An Introduction to Modern English Word Formation* (London: Longmans, 1973); W. Nelson Francis, *The English Language* (New York: Norton, 1963); Pyles; Margaret Schlauch, *The English Language in Modern Times,* 2nd ed. (London: Oxford Univ. Press, 1964); Joseph M. Williams, *Origins of the English Language* (New York: Free Press, 1975).

other

In comparing things of the same class, add *other* to *any:* That movie scared me more than any *other* I've seen. See *any* 1.

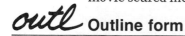 ## Outline form

Revise the form of your outline to observe the conventions given below.

1. The title. The title of the essay should stand three spaces above the outline. The heads should carry their full meaning and not refer back to the title by pronouns. See Titles 1.

2. Thesis statement. An optional practice—but a good one—is to put a sentence stating the subject and scope of the whole paper between the title and the first main head.

3. Numbering systems. The most widely used numbering alternates letters and figures, as shown in the examples in 7. Avoid intricate or confusing schemes of numbering.

4. Indention. Write the main heads flush with the left margin and indent subheads two or three spaces from the left—enough to place them clearly in a different column. Heads that run over a single line should be further indented.

5. Punctuation and capitalization. Don't use punctuation at the ends of lines in a topic outline. In a sentence outline the punctuation should follow regular sentence practice. Capitalize only the first word of a head and proper names; an outline head is not a title.

6. Heads.

a. Meaningful heads. Each head should be understandable by itself, especially if the outline is to be shown to someone for criticism or is to be submitted with the essay. The following would do as a scratch outline but would not be satisfactory for other purposes:

My Vocation

   I. The work I am interested in
  II. Why I prefer this type of work
III. What my responsibilities would be
IV. The chances for success

b. Heads of equal importance. The main heads of an outline, those usually marked by Roman numerals, should show the several main divisions of the material. Similarly, the immediate subdivisions of these heads, those usually marked by capital letters, should designate logical divisions of one phase of the subject. The same principle applies to further divisions under any subhead.

Unequal headings	*Equal headings*
Books I Have Enjoyed	Books I Have Enjoyed
I. Adventure stories	I. Adventure stories
II. Historical novels	II. Historical novels
III. *Walden*	III. Science fiction
IV. Autobiographies	IV. Autobiographies
V. What I like most	V. Books on mysticism

c. Headings in parallel form. Equivalent heads and subheads are expressed in parallel grammatical form. In a sentence outline, use complete sentences throughout; in a topic outline, use phrase heads only. Make all heads of the same rank parallel; that is, make the heads in one series all nouns or all adjectives or all phrases, or whatever is most appropriate.

Heads not parallel	*Parallel heads*
The Art of Putting	The Art of Putting
I. The stance is fundamental	I. The stance
II. The grip	II. The grip
III. Watch the backswing	III. The backswing
IV. Stroking the ball	IV. The stroke
V. Follow through with care	V. The follow-through

7. Division of main points. Since a topic is not "divided" unless there are at least two parts, a formal outline should have at least two subheads under any main head—or none at all. For every heading marked *I* there should be at least a *II*, for every *A* there should be a *B*, and so on.

Illogical single heads	*Logical subdivision*
The Tripartite System	The Tripartite System

I. The executive branch
  A. President and Cabinet
	I. The executive branch
	  A. President
	  B. Cabinet

II. The legislative branch
  A. The House
  B. The Senate
    1. Functions
	II. The legislative branch
	  A. The House of Representatives
	  B. The Senate
	    1. Special functions
	    2. Special privileges

III. The judicial branch
  A. The Supreme Court
	III. The judicial branch
	  A. The Supreme Court
	  B. Lower courts

When a main point cannot be divided, include any necessary detail in the head. For an organization in which the whole executive power lies in the president, this heading would be satisfactory:

I. The executive branch (the president)

8. Introduction and conclusion. Ordinarily an essay has a beginning, a middle, and an ending (or an introduction, a body, and a conclusion), but don't use such labels in the outline. They are too general to reflect specific content. Besides, the beginning and ending can rarely be represented by heads that are coordinate with the others. The first and last topics in the outline are from the main body of material, chosen with a special view to their fitness for starting and concluding the discussion.

Oxymoron

An oxymoron is a contradiction in terms used as a figure of speech — for example, "sweet bitterness," "loving hate," "mildly fatal," "making haste slowly," "literary illiterates" (Aleksandr Solzhenitsyn). *Oxymoron* is occasionally used with the extended meaning "a compound of incongruous elements": "He was that religious oxymoron, a gentle Calvinist" (George P. Elliott, *Commentary*).

pair

When not preceded by a number or other plural indicator, *pairs* is the preferred plural of *pair:* Pairs of figures were common in the design. Otherwise usage is divided:

These hypotheses are confounded in two pairs. — Roselle and Campbell, *Psychological Bulletin*

He found a car with one too many pair of skis. — *Time*

Paradox

A paradox is a statement that seems to contradict common sense. See Epigrams and aphorisms.

¶ Paragraph indention

Indent here for a new paragraph.

no ¶ No paragraph indention

Join this paragraph to the preceding one.

1. Indent for a new paragraph. A paragraph symbol in the margin of your paper means that you have failed to meet your readers' expectations. From their experience with books and magazines, they are in the habit of regarding a paragraph as a series of related statements, all bearing on the scene being described or the argument being advanced; and they expect to be forewarned by a paragraph break of any shift in focus or any turn in the course of reasoning. When they come to a stretch of prose that drifts or leaps from one topic to another, they are confused and distracted by the lack of unity and cohesion.

Your instructor may have other reasons for recommending indention. A single sentence or short sequence of sentences that makes a significant point may demand the emphasis it will gain by being set apart. Or a brief passage that marks a transition from one stage of the discussion to another may be more helpful to the reader if it is detached from the end of a long paragraph to stand on its own. And sometimes, even if there are close enough connections in the material to justify a very long paragraph, you may be advised to break it up simply to give the reader a mental breathing spell. Although it's not uncommon to find an 800-word paragraph in a scholarly journal where a closely reasoned argument is addressed to interested readers, most exposition and argument receives nothing like such close attention. Indention helps break a discussion into manageable units or (to use a familiar food metaphor) into digestible bites. In using indention this way, be sure to take advantage of natural subdivisions within the long paragraph. Don't divide the paragraph at a point that will separate two closely related sentences.

In general, the development of your topic should determine the length of your paragraphs. But take into account what your subject is: narrative and descriptive paragraphs are likely to be shorter than paragraphs of criticism or philosophy. And take into account the probable interest and attention span of your readers.

2. Join separate paragraphs. A succession of very short paragraphs, like a succession of very long ones, makes reading difficult. An unjustified paragraph break throws the reader off the track so that he loses the connection between one idea and another. In revising an essay, combine paragraphs in which the details or ideas are so closely related that they form a single stage in the development of the essay. In the process, make sure that you provide whatever transitional words or phrases may be needed to emphasize the unity.

While a transitional passage that sums up one substantial section of an essay and forecasts the next may be a very short paragraph—perhaps just one sentence—most paragraphs are from four to ten sentences long. If you have more than two paragraphs on a typed page of expository prose, look closely to be sure you can justify the breaks. A sequence of very short paragraphs may indicate that you are not developing your points adequately, not providing enough examples or details or comparisons. Or it may be that you have failed to recognize the close logical connections that pull your ideas together into larger units. In either case, a reader is likely to consider short, choppy paragraphs a collection of random observations rather than the unified development of a central idea. See Coherence, Transition.

par Paragraphs

Revise or rewrite this unsatisfactory paragraph.

A paragraph is a group of related statements that a writer presents as a unit in the development of his subject. It strikes the eye as a unit because it is physically set off by indention or spacing. It should also strike the mind as a unit because the statements in it are closely related, representing a stage in the flow of the writer's thought.

Here are the most common faults in paragraphs, with suggested remedies:

1. Lack of development. Rewrite the paragraph, including details and illustrations that will lead the reader to understand and accept its central point. See Details.

2. Lack of unity. Rewrite, deleting any material that fails to contribute to the central idea, or core of meaning, that is the focus of the paragraph and that justifies its inclusion in the paper. See Unity 2.

3. Lack of continuity. Revise or rewrite to make clear the relation between the statements that make up the paragraph. Occasionally you will find that you can improve the continuity by simply altering the order of the sentences. Sometimes you need to supply a transition between sentences. And sometimes you need to rethink and then rewrite. See Coherence, Logical thinking, Transition.

4. Lack of transition. Begin the paragraph with a word, phrase, or sentence that will integrate it firmly with the material that precedes it. See Transition.

5. Lack of a required topic sentence. Provide a topic sentence to strengthen the unity of the paragraph or to make clearer to the reader the direction your essay is taking. Not all paragraphs need topic sentences. But some do, either to announce the generalization that subsequent details will support, or to pull details together in a generalization, or to introduce or sum up a stage of the discussion. See Topic sentence.

Parallelism

When two words or groups of words are alike grammatically and structurally, they are said to be parallel. Parallel constructions range from matching pairs of adjectives (*cold and wet*) to series of phrases or clauses—"Some metaphors are harmless, some are useful, some are beautiful, and some are stumbling blocks to clear thinking" (Thomas H. Middleton, *Saturday Review*)—to sequences of elaborately balanced sentences. The extent to which a writer should deliberately employ parallelism depends on the context. The simple parallelism that contributes to clarity and efficiency is appropriate in all varieties of English. The exact, sustained, intricate parallelism of some balanced and periodic sentences is at home only in formal prose. See Balanced sentence, Cumulative sentence, Periodic sentence.

paral
//

Parallelism and style

Use parallel structures for elements that should logically be performing the same grammatical function.

Parallelism is one of the simplest, neatest, and most economical ways of achieving clarity. The sentence you have just read illustrates what it says. The three sentences that follow express the same idea without taking advantage of parallelism:

Parallelism is one of the simplest ways of achieving clarity. Neatness is a major contribution made by parallelism. A sentence that uses parallel structures is more economical than one that does not.

Parallelism is a mode of coordination. This means that as a general rule *and, but, nor,* and *yet* should match noun (or noun equivalent) to noun, adjective to adjective, infinitive to infinitive, dependent clause to dependent clause, and so on.

1. Put into the same grammatical forms and structures those words, phrases, and clauses that are alike in purpose and related in meaning (complementary or contrasting). "He was *brilliant* but *unstable*" (predicate adjectives modifying *he*) and "He was a *brilliant* but *unstable* person" (adjectives modifying *person*) both make use of parallelism. "He was *brilliant* but an *unstable* person" does not, though the purpose of *brilliant* and *unstable* remains the same: they are still describing the subject of the sentence.

Here are some sentences that use parallelism, followed in each case by a version that does not:

Parallel participles: Expanding the dimensions of the individual, or *contracting* them, continues to be the ultimate occupation of art in our time.—Harold Rosenberg, *New Yorker*
Not parallel (participle mismatched with infinitive): Expanding the dimensions of the individual, or *to contract* them, continues to be. . . .

Parallel nouns: Rational thought and rational behavior rarely govern either the *formation* or the *operation* of policy.—Barbara W. Tuchman, *Newsweek*
Not parallel (noun mismatched with dependent clause): Rational thought and rational behavior rarely govern either the *formation* of policy or *how it operates.*

Parallel gerunds: Sir Percy was given to *sniffing* snuff and *prattling* foolishly as a cover for the daring Pimpernel.—Thomas H. Middleton, *Saturday Review*
Not parallel (gerunds mismatched with independent clause): Sir Percy was given to *sniffing* snuff and *he also prattled foolishly as a cover for the daring Pimpernel.*

Failure to use matching grammatical structures is particularly noticeable with the correlative conjunctions *both . . . and, either . . . or, neither . . . nor, not only . . . but (also).* A simple example is given in the second rewritten version above. Here is an equally common type:

The rule is *not only* ignored by those it is directed at *but* those who are supposed to enforce it ignore it too.

It seems clear that the writer wants to emphasize how thoroughly the rule is being ignored. In revising, then, a good first step would be to place the verb before *not only:* The rule is being ignored. Who is ignoring it? Those who . . . and those who. . . . Then, with the correlative conjunctions added, the phrasing falls naturally into parallel form:

The rule is being ignored *not only by those who are supposed to* observe it *but also by those who are supposed to* enforce it.

2. Do *not* make structures parallel unless the relationship of the ideas or details they express justifies parallelism. If parallelism in structure fails to represent the logic of the material, the reader will be misled. The three grammatical elements that end the next sentence are not parallel:

My year abroad taught me a lot about the way Venezuelans earn a living, spend their leisure time, and their attitudes toward Americans.

To make the elements parallel (. . . and feel about Americans) would produce a smoother sentence, but so far as meaning goes, it would be a mistake. In the context, the way Venezuelans feel about Americans is not logically related to the way they earn their living or spend their leisure time. The best revision, then, would be to retain the first two elements in the series but turn the third into a separate sentence. How the new sentence would be phrased would depend on whether the writer was making a casual addition or introducing a significant topic:

My year abroad taught me a lot about the way Venezuelans earn a living and spend their leisure time. It also taught me a lot about their attitudes toward Americans. *Or* More important, I learned a lot. . . .

See Parallelism, Phrases 2, Shifted constructions. For further examples of the effective use of parallelism, see Periodic sentence.

Paraphrase
A paraphrase is a restatement of a writer's ideas in different words. The term *paraphrasing* is now usually applied to digesting the contents of a passage in one's own words, as in taking notes. Difficulties may arise in the next step: using the para-

phrase in a paper of one's own. First of all, the source of the materials must be acknowledged. Second, if phrases or sentences from the original are included in the paraphrase, they must be enclosed in quotation marks and either footnoted or otherwise identified as the original author's. See Plagiarism, Research papers.

Parentheses

Like commas and dashes, parentheses are used to enclose words and word groups that break away from the main structure of the sentence. Of the three types of enclosing marks, parentheses indicate the greatest degree of removal.

1. For additions. Within sentences parentheses are used to enclose words and word groups that add facts to a statement without essentially altering its meaning. They allow such additions to stand outside the frame of the principal sentence. The additions may be illustrations (as in this book), definitions, or information thrown in for good measure:

The few verb endings that English now retains (*-s, -ed, -ing*) are being still further reduced in ordinary speech.

Gresham's Law (that bad money drives out good) applies as usual in this case.

His concerts were well received in most cities (Cleveland was an exception), but he was still dissatisfied.

Like dashes, parentheses can become a bad stylistic habit. If the information they enclose is as unimportant as parentheses usually suggest, it probably should be omitted. If it is worth including, work it into the structure of the sentence in which it appears, or make it a separate sentence.

2. With other marks. When a complete sentence in parentheses comes within a sentence (notice the punctuation of this one), it needs neither a capital letter nor a period. Commas and other marks of punctuation in the main sentence always *follow* the parenthesis (as here and in the preceding sentence). (Parenthesized sentences, like this one, that do not stand within other sentences have the period before the closing parenthesis.)

3. To enclose numbers or letters in an enumeration. Parentheses are sometimes used to enclose letters or figures that mark items in an enumeration: The additions may be (1) illustrations, (2) definitions, or (3) information thrown in for good measure. Parentheses make the listed items more conspicuous.

See Brackets, Dash.

Participles

Participles are derived from verbs but do not stand as independent predicates.

1. Forms. The present participle adds *-ing* to the base form of the verb: *asking, singing*. The past participle of regular verbs adds *-ed* to the base (*asked*), and the perfect participle adds *having* to the past participle (*having asked*). In the passive, the *-ed* form is preceded by *being* (*being asked*) and *having been* (*having been asked*). Many irregular verbs have special past participle forms: *sung, having sung, being sung, having been sung*.

2. Functions.

a. In verb phrases. Participles enter into many verb phrases: I am asking, I am being asked, I have asked, I have been asked. Although participles are referred to as present and past, they do not themselves indicate definite time but time in relation to the context in which they are used. See Tenses of verbs.

b. As modifiers. When not part of verb phrases, participles are most commonly adjectivals. They are like adjectives in that they modify nouns (a *coming* era, a *frightened* cat). They are like verbs in that they may take an object (*Following these clues*, he soon found her). They are like both in that they may be modified by adverbs (*rolling crazily*). Generative-transformational grammars derive them from full underlying clauses:

The car [the car was rolling crazily] crashed into a bus.
The car, rolling crazily, crashed into a bus.

When used as an adjective, a participle should refer clearly to some particular noun or pronoun: Having opened the envelope, he began to read the letter (*Having opened* modifies *he*). A modifying participle is said to dangle when it seems to refer to a word the writer does not mean it to refer to: Kissing his wife good-bye, the door slammed behind him. Errors like this occur when the subject of the participle and the subject of the main clause differ. In "[*He* was] kissing his wife good-bye, *the door* slammed behind him," *He* and *the door* are not the same. Compare a correct modifier: [*He* was] kissing his wife good-bye, *he* let the door slam behind him. *He* in "[He was] kissing" and *he* in "he let the door slam" are the same. The first subject can be deleted. See Dangling modifiers.

c. In absolute phrases. The participle-as-adjective should not be confused with the participle in a phrase that relates to the whole sentence—to the situation—rather than to a particular word. Some such phrases have become formulas: Judging from her looks, she isn't under fifty. See Absolute phrases.

3. Stylistically objectionable participles.
Unskilled writers sometimes use a participle or a gerund where a subordinate clause would read more smoothly: The train was on time, necessitating our hurrying. *Better:* . . . so we had to hurry. Clumsy nominative absolutes should especially be avoided: The plane arriving then, we boarded it.

For *very* with participles, see *very* 2. Compare Gerunds. References: Donald W. Emery and R. W. Pence, *Grammar of Present-Day English*, 2nd ed. (New York: Macmillan, 1963), pp. 305–15; Roberts, pp. 345–55.

Particles

Of the eight traditional parts of speech, four have no inflected forms in English — adverbs, prepositions, conjunctions, interjections — and can be discussed only in terms of function and position. They are sometimes lumped under the label *particles.*

Parts of speech

Parts of speech are the categories a linguist sets up in order to describe structures in sentences and finally sentences themselves. Since it would be pointless to list all the words in English, indicating for each one whether it can serve as a subject or object or modifier, linguists group words into categories and subcategories and then describe where these categories may occur in various patterns and how they form larger structures. The "correctness" of these categories, however, depends on how the linguist wants to describe sentence structure — even on what his notion of "structure" is. Linguists working with different grammatical theories will create different sets of definitions. Thus one linguist will classify a word like *some* as an indefinite pronoun and another will classify it as a prearticle. The different names are not just terminological quibbles. They may reflect different theories that determine the definitions.

1. Three approaches. Traditional schoolroom grammarians, using a system much like that developed for describing classical languages, cite eight parts of speech: nouns, verbs, adjectives, adverbs, pronouns, prepositions, conjunctions, and interjections. Nouns and verbs are defined semantically: a noun is the name of a person, place, or thing; verbs show action. The other parts of speech are defined functionally: adjectives modify nouns; adverbs modify verbs, adjectives, and other adverbs; pronouns replace nouns; and prepositions relate a noun or pronoun to some other part of the sentence.

Because semantic definitions are imprecise (it is hard to say what the noun *lack* refers to in "There is a lack of time") and because the functional definitions are much too broad (the definition of *preposition* would, for example, cover *is* in "John is a friend"), structural linguists reject them in favor of purely formal definitions: Nouns, they say, are those words that can occur with plural and genitive endings or in positions after *the* and before a verb; verbs are those words that can occur with third-person singular -*s* endings, with past-tense inflections, with perfect inflections, and with progressive -*ing* endings; adjectives are those words that can occur with comparative or superlative endings, after *more* or *most*, and in the position "The [noun] is very _____"; adverbs are those words made up of an adjective and an -*ly* ending. The residue of words such as *and, in, can, very, the, not, all, therefore, because, please,* and *hello* are put into a large category of "indeclinable" words, or function words, which is subcategorized according to where these words occur in a sentence relative to the parts of speech already identified.

Transformational grammarians, or generativists, are much less concerned than structuralists with devising formal tests to classify parts of speech and more concerned with the most economical and general overall description. The labels for individual words are judged "correct" only if they are necessary to describe how the words behave in the context of a sentence. Generativists assume that one part of speech may derive from another, as the verb *discover* in a deep structure like "Tom *discovered* gold" becomes, in a surface structure, the noun *discovery*, "Tom's *discovery* of gold." For transformational grammarians, it is impossible to talk about parts of speech without explaining the whole grammar of a language and without distinguishing between deep and surface structures. See Deep structure.

Because structural grammars emphasize the careful and logical classification of parts of speech, we will rely chiefly on their methods here.

2. Form-class words and function words. The structuralist approach suggests that English words are of two general types: (1) form-class words, which express the primary lexical or semantic meaning of a sentence and can usually be inflected for number, tense, or comparison; and (2) function words, which perform the grammatical or structural function of connecting, relating, and qualifying the form-class words. These function words usually cannot be inflected. The form-class words are commonly called nouns, verbs, adjectives, and adverbs, with certain pronouns fitting into subgroups under the category *noun*. All other words are function (or structure) words.

a. Form-class words. In addition to expressing lexical meaning, form-class words share other characteristics. They can be inflected to indicate specific semantic meanings and grammatical relationships. Nouns (and the personal pronouns) inflect to show plural number and possession: *girl, girls, girl's, girls'; I, we, my, mine; she, her, hers; they, their, theirs*. Verbs inflect to indicate present third-person singular, past tense, present participle, and past participle: *walks, walked, walking, walked; sings, sang, singing, sung*. Adjectives and most adverbs add *-er* or *-est* (or *more, most; less, least*) to indicate comparison: *tall, taller, tallest; more fully, most fully; less difficult, least difficult*.

Form-class words are an "open" class. Borrowed words and coined words, such as *astronaut, hippie, telecast, video, stereo*, are still being added. See Origin of words 2.

b. Function words. Function words (also called structure words) have less specific lexical meanings than form-class words. (Consider the various meanings of *green* or *run* in comparison with the meaning of *by* or *the*.) Only a few groups of function words (if we choose to so classify them) can be inflected: the demonstrative, relative, and interrogative pronouns and the modal-auxiliary verbs. In contrast to form-class groups, which include hundreds of thousands of different words, most groups of function words contain a very small number; some, like *not* and *do*, contain only one. And function words are members of closed groups. The idiomatic use of certain prepositions may vary or change, but English has borrowed or developed very few new prepositions or conjunctions over the seven hundred years since it was interpenetrated by French borrowings after the Norman Conquest. In that time it has lost pronouns and has added no articles.

The most detailed description of function words from a structural point of view is that by C. C. Fries in *The Structure of English*. Fries points out that such words as *yes* and *no* (or their colloquial equivalents), *please, not,* and *let's* are used in limited contexts. He also shows that *very, extremely, considerably,* and others are quite different from such words as *quietly, thoroughly, angrily.* For example, the sentence "He collected the materials quickly" is meaningful; the sentence "He collected the materials very" is not. A structural linguist is thus forced to classify these two groups of words in two different categories—the first, qualifiers; the second, adverbs (or, in Fries' more esoteric terminology, Class 4 words).

c. Words in context. The respective grammatical roles of form-class words—to express the primary lexical meaning of communication—and of function words—to relate and give understandable structure to combinations of form-class words—can be illustrated either with regular English sentences or with nonsense sentences. Consider, for example, the sentence used by Fries: The mother of the boy will arrive tomorrow. The basic lexical information can be expressed telegraphically with the four form-class words: Boy's mother arrives tomorrow. The function words, *the* and *of,* signal the grammar of the message; *will* indicates that the arriving will occur in the future.

Or consider the nonsense sentence "The slithy toves will gyre and gimble very gluggily in the wabes." The sentence possesses only such meaning as grammatical structure (that is, word order, word forms, and function words) gives to it. The "nouns" *toves* and *wabes,* the "verbs" *gyre* and *gimble,* the "adjective" *slithy,* and the "adverb" *gluggily* can be replaced with meaningful words or with other nonsense words. But the function words *the, will, very, in* cannot be replaced if this is to be an English "sentence."

Both sentences indicate the distinctive features of the two general types of words. Form-class words can be inflected and are members of open classes: we recognize them by their forms and their position in the sentence and by the function words used to connect and relate them. Function words have almost no inflected forms (except for *will–would, this–these,* etc.); they are in closed groups; they occupy regular positions or slots in syntactic structures.

As the two illustrative sentences also indicate, we classify parts of speech according to their context in a sentence or according to their inflections. Certain words, like *walk, burn, run,* are used as either nouns or verbs. Other words, like *bomb, radio, dust,* are used not just as nouns or verbs but also, without change in form, as modifiers: bomb shelter, radio station, dust belt. The conjunction *after* (We will leave after we have eaten) may also serve as a preposition: After dinner, the group dispersed. How a word is classified in a specific instance depends upon the context in which it is used. That is why, in the chart of form-class words, we list the usual function of each part of speech.

The chart of function words lists the types that occur most frequently, along with examples and usual functions. The same words may either serve as different kinds of function words or (like some prearticles, *some, many, all*) serve as both form-class words (nouns) and function words (prearticles). See Determiners.

FORM-CLASS WORDS

PART OF SPEECH	INFLECTED FORMS	FUNCTIONS
Nouns (*boy, house, city, truth*)	Plural: *-s* (*boys*) and a few anomalous forms: *oxen, deer, teeth,* etc. Genitive (or possessive): *-'s, -s'* (*boy's, boys'*)	Serve as subject; complement; object of verbs, of verbals, of prepositions.
Personal pronouns (*I, you, he, she, it*)	Plural: *we, they* Genitive: *my, mine, his, her, its* Objective: *me, him, them*	Same function as nouns.
Indefinite nouns (*everybody, everything, everyone, no one*)		Serve in many but not all of the positions nouns do.

Other pronouns, such as *who* and *that,* are listed under function words, because they do not possess a full set of noun inflections and cannot be used in all the positions filled by nouns or personal pronouns.

PART OF SPEECH	INFLECTED FORMS	FUNCTIONS
Verbs (*walk, play, breathe*)	Present participle: *-ing* Past participle: *-ed* Third-person singular, present tense: *-s* past tense: *-ed* (For irregular verbs, see *be,* Principal parts of verbs.)	Assert an action or express a state or condition.
Adjectives (*tall, green, poor*)	Comparative: *-er* (or *more, less*) Superlative: *-est* (or *most, least*)	Modify nouns or pronouns.
Adverbs (*slow, quickly*)	Comparative: *-er* (or *more, less*) Superlative: *-est* (or *most, least*) (Some adverbs—like *here, tomorrow, everywhere*—are not compared.)	Modify verbs, adverbs, phrases, and clauses, usually indicating place, time, or manner.

FUNCTION WORDS

PART OF SPEECH	USUAL FUNCTIONS
Auxiliaries (usually called modal auxiliaries): *can, could, will, shall, may, must, get, used (to),* etc.	Precede, point to, and qualify predicating verbs or serve as substitutes for verbs.
Determiners (also called noun determiners) are subdivided into prearticles, articles, and postarticles.	
Prearticles: *some, few, several, much, many, each, both, all, neither, half, two,* etc.	Precede and enumerate nouns; they stand alone when the nouns are deleted: Several [boys] were here.
Articles: *a/an, the, some; this, that, these, those*	Specify definiteness of reference. The words traditionally defined as demonstrative pronouns—*this, that, these, those*—can be classed as a variety of article. The absence of an article indicates indefiniteness before noncount nouns and plurals: Food is expensive; Carrots are cheap.
Postarticles: *several, many, few; first, second, third,* etc.; *one, two, three,* etc.; *former, latter, next, first, last,* etc.	Follow articles and precede adjectives: the few old men, the second young woman, the three pretty girls. *Several, few*, and *many* are identical to the prearticles *some, few,* and *many*: Few of the several sick children, several of the many brave soldiers. Postarticles usually quantify or indicate an order to the head noun.
Qualifiers: *very, rather, fairly, mighty, less, least, more, most, too, quite, much,* etc.	Qualify or limit adjectives, usually by indicating degree or extent. Some qualifiers are intensifiers.
Conjunctions or connectors	
Coordinating conjunctions: *and, but, nor, yet, for, or, so,* and sometimes *not, rather,* etc.	Connect like or equal grammatical components (words, phrases, clauses, sentences).
Correlative conjunctions: *both . . . and, either . . . or, so . . . as, not only . . . but (also),* etc.	Used in pairs to connect clauses within a sentence.
Conjunctive adverbs (also called sentence connectors): *accordingly, also, consequently, hence, however, therefore,* etc.	Connect either independent clauses within a sentence or sentences within or between paragraphs.
Subordinating conjunctions: *after, as, if, since, when, until,* etc.	Join and subordinate, as a structure expressing modification or qualification, a dependent clause to another clause in the sentence. Usually the dependent clause modifies a verb, a clause, or an entire sentence.
Noun substitutes	
Interrogative pronouns: *who, which, what, whoever,* etc.	Serve as subjects, objects, or single-word modifiers in interrogative sentences or dependent noun clauses.

Relative pronouns: *who, whose, whom, which, that, when,* and also *where, wherever,* etc.	Serve as subjects, complements, objects, or single-word modifiers to link independent noun and adjective clauses to other clauses within a sentence.
Prepositions: *at, about, by, in, on, under, underneath, back of, due to, in front of, on account of,* etc.	Precede and connect object, consisting of a noun or pronoun, with or without modifiers, to other constituents of the sentence. Usually the phrase can be identified as either adjectival or adverbial.

Miscellaneous

do (did, does, done)	Used to form *yes–no* questions, to give emphasis, and as a substitute verb.
Exclamations (including interjections): *oh, ouch, no, yes, hey, never, really,* etc.	Used to show feeling or—in some instances—to indicate that the speaker is listening.
Interrogators: *when, why, where, how,* etc.	Used alone or as introductory word for a phrase or clause asking a question.
Negatives: *no, not, never*	Show negation.
Yes–no words: *yes, yeah, uh-huh; no, not at all, maybe,* etc.	Give responses or—in some instances—indicate that the speaker is listening.

See Grammar, Linguistics. References: Charles Carpenter Fries, *The Structure of English* (New York: Harcourt, 1952), Ch. 5; Francis, Ch. 5; Sledd, Ch. 2.

pass Passive voice

Change the verb or verbs to active voice.

1. Avoiding the passive. Using the passive voice without good reason will tend to make your sentences awkward and wordy, place emphasis where it doesn't belong, and at times leave your readers wondering who did what.

a. Don't use the passive to avoid using *I.*

Between Laredo and Austin the driving was done by me.
Revision: Between Laredo and Austin I drove. *Or . . .* I did the driving.

b. Don't use the passive in an attempt to sound weighty or scientific.

The proposals that were made by the administration have been received negatively by the student body.
Revision: Students disliked the administration's proposals.

c. Don't use the passive to hide or obscure the identity of the source of an action.

My roommate and I were summoned by the dean because of the waterbags that had been thrown from our windows.
Revision: The dean summoned my roommate and me for throwing waterbags from our windows. *Or (depending on the facts)* The dean summoned my roommate and me because he thought, wrongly, that we were the ones who had thrown the waterbags.

d. Don't use the passive to vary the pattern just for the sake of varying the pattern.

After finding our way through the woods, we reached the campsite. A half-dozen trips were made to bring in our supplies. By sunset we were more than ready for a hot meal.

The shifts from active to passive are unjustified and distracting. Revising the second sentence (We had to make . . .) would keep the focus clear and so make the passage easier to read.

2. Appropriate uses of the passive. The passive voice is appropriately used in at least three rhetorical contexts.

a. Passives are appropriate when the agent of the action is either unknown, unimportant, or better left unidentified:

As many as a hundred notices of teaching jobs are printed each month in a newsletter best described as a "whole education" catalogue. — Jean Collins, *Change*

The grammars could not be dismissed as inferior or crude; they were simply different. — J. J. Lamberts, *A Short Introduction to English Usage*

Postal rates are to be increased.

b. Passives can be used (as in this sentence) when the subject of the discourse would otherwise be the direct object. Because passives are the subject of this section, it's natural that the noun phrase referring to them be the subject-topic of most sentences in these paragraphs.

c. Passives allow a writer to focus on the agent of an action by shifting the agent to the end of the sentence, where it will be stressed. This is especially desirable when the agent is represented by a fairly long and complicated noun phrase:

Active: A team bigger and tougher than any you would find outside professional football defeated us.
Passive: We were defeated by a team bigger and tougher than any you would find outside professional football.

Such a shift often makes it possible for the writer to build a tighter transition from one sentence to another. The element ending one sentence leads into the subject of the sentence that follows.

See Voice.

Past tense
For past tense, regular verbs add *-ed* to the base form: *ask, asked; answer, answered.* See Principal parts of verbs, Tenses of verbs.

people, persons
People has long been used as a collective noun referring to a group, but as recently as the early part of this century, it was regarded as nonstandard when used with numerical quantifiers as the plural of *person*, as in "Five people are here." Though formal usage still tends to prefer *persons, people* is now thoroughly established in such contexts. *Person* and *persons* are frequently resorted to by writers who object to using *man* or *men* to represent both sexes. See Sexist language.

per

Per (Latin, "through, by, among," etc.) is most appropriate in phrases that are still close to their Latin originals (per capita, per diem), in commercial expressions ($125 per week, $3.00 per yard), and in some technical phrases (revolutions per minute). In less specialized contexts, *a* or *every* is preferable (a dime a dozen, a thousand words every day).

percent

In informal and general writing (but not formal) *percent* is often used instead of *percentage* or even *proportion:* Only a small percent of the class was [*or* were] present. So used, it is treated as a collective noun, sometimes taking a singular verb, sometimes a plural. With figures, *percent* (97.6 percent) is preferred to the percent sign (97.6%) except in technical and statistical material. *Percent* is also written as two words. It is not an abbreviation and should not be followed by a period.

Perfect tense

Tenses formed with *have* and a past participle are traditionally called perfect tenses: present perfect, *has laughed;* past perfect, *had laughed;* future perfect, *will have laughed.* See Tenses of verbs.

Period

1. At the end of statements. A period is used to mark the end of every completed sentence that is not a question or an exclamation. Sometimes if he is not really inquiring or exclaiming, a writer will use a period at the end of a sentence in the form of a question or an exclamation: Would you be so good as to return the book at your earliest convenience. What a day. See Rhetorical questions.

2. Miscellaneous conventional uses.
a. After abbreviations: Oct.; etc.; Mr. W. Fraser, Jr.
b. Between dollars and cents: $5.66; $0.66 (*but* 66 cents *or* 66¢)
c. Before decimals: .6, 3.14159, 44.6 percent
d. Sometimes between hours and minutes in giving precise time, though a colon is more usual: 2.36 p.m.

3. With quotation marks. When a quotation ends a sentence, most American publishers place the period inside the quotation marks whether the quotation is a complete sentence or a single word:

"The longer you put it off," he said, "the harder it's going to be."
He glared at me as he said "harder."

Periodic sentence

A periodic sentence withholds its complete meaning until its last word (as in the first sentence below) or until its last clause (as in the second and third):

Exhaustive in its scholarship, discerning in its literary judgments, sensible in its theorizing, it merits the adjective all biographies aspire to: *definitive.* – Robert F. Moss, *Saturday Review*

Not so long before he died, still receiving carloads of honors as he always had, and still receiving, as also he always had, from Right or Left in turn, fanatic attacks on his social views, Mann remarked that he was a "great, unloved name." – John Thompson, *Harper's*

The importance of disciplinary studies, the value of humanistic thinking and illumination, the urgency of facing the public with the best that the humanities can do, the clear need of bringing together the best humanists (which includes some social and natural scientists) as well as other figures such as journalists, labor leaders, businessmen, and politicians, all argue for an institution devoted to such and other ends. – Morton W. Bloomfield, *PMLA*

A great many short and simple sentences have their base structures at the end and therefore fit the definition of a periodic sentence; but rhetoricians reserve the term for sentences of some length and complexity. Because such a sentence keeps the reader in a mild or an acute state of suspense, its resolution creates a sense of satisfaction. A long periodic sentence almost always lends a passage a distinct touch of formality, for it is necessarily an artful and studied production, often using, as in the examples above, sustained parallelism. Remaining airborne through clause and phrase as it does, it can achieve unusual dramatic emphasis when it finally returns to earth – or, if poorly done, it can end with the thud of anticlimax. In appropriate contexts the periodic sentence can contribute to a variety of rhetorical purposes; but a succession of periodic sentences is tiring to read and creates a style too elaborate for everyday topics.

The prime example of the periodic sentence as cliché is the nominating speech. Here, a very long series of clauses beginning "a man who," or "a woman who," precedes the name of the nominee, which usually comes as a surprise to no one.

See Parallelism. Compare Cumulative sentence.

Person

Person as a grammatical term refers to both pronoun classification and verb inflection. Personal pronouns are in the first person, the one(s) speaking *(I, my, me, we, our, us);* second person, the one(s) spoken to *(you, your, yours);* third person, anyone or anything else *(he, his, him, she, her, hers, it, its, they, their, them).* Nouns are regarded as third person, as are most other pronouns (the relative *who* and its derivatives take their persons from their antecedents).

Except in the verb *be (I am, you are, he is . . .),* English verbs indicate person only for the third singular of the present and perfect tenses: I see, you see, he *sees;* we see, you see, they see; I have seen, you have seen, he *has* seen; etc.

Personal pronouns

The personal pronouns are *I, we, you, he, she, it,* and *they.* See Case, Person, Pronouns 1.

Personification

Personification is a figure of speech in which an object or animal or quality or ideal is given some attributes of a human being:

There has been, after all, something in the talk of American innocence. No doubt it is a false innocence, fabricated by a myth-charged education: the lady who was "once a beauty of magnificence unparalleled" nourished her complexion on genocide and slavery. Yet her beauty existed in the eyes of her children, especially her adopted, immigrant children. – Conor Cruise O'Brien, *New York Review of Books*

It is less common today than formerly, and less common in prose than in verse. Flat and unnecessary personification is likely to sound amateurish: No steam engine can brag of such efficiency. See Figurative language, Gender, Pathetic fallacy.

persons

With numerical quantifiers, *persons* is preferred to *people* in formal usage: five persons. See *people, persons*.

phenomenon, phenomena

Phenomenon is the singular and *phenomena* (sometimes *phenomenons*) the plural: phenomena of the mind. Originally, *phenomenon* meant "any observable event," but now it also means "something remarkable," and *phenomenal* is almost always used in that sense. See Hyperbole.

Phrasal verbs

A main verb preceded by one or more auxiliaries (will go, has left, was thinking, is considered, must have been punished) is called a phrasal verb or a periphrastic verb. A verb-adverb combination is also currently called a phrasal verb. See Verbs.

Phrases

A phrase is a group of words that functions as a unit in a sentence, a clause, or another phrase. In "The man in the car under the tree yelled," *the man in the car under the tree* is a noun phrase made up of an article, *the,* a noun, *man,* and a prepositional phrase, *in the car under the tree.* The prepositional phrase, in turn, is made up of the preposition *in* and another phrase, *the car under the tree.* This noun phrase is made up of the article *the* and the noun *car* and the prepositional phrase *under the tree,* which, in turn, is made up of the preposition *under* and the noun phrase *the tree.* Thus phrases can be contained in phrases ad infinitum.

Noun phrase: the *plumber*
Verb phrase: have *gone* to the store
Adjective phrase: old enough to be my father
Adverbial phrase: more *quickly* than usual
Prepositional phrase: in the house
Participial phrase: walking down the street
Infinitive phrase: to go faster

1. Function. Phrases may be further classified by their function in a sentence. *The plumber* is an adjectival noun phrase in the larger noun phrase, *my friend the plumber*. *Walking down the street* is a nominal participial phrase (traditionally called a gerund) in "Walking down the street was dangerous." *In the morning* is an adverbial prepositional phrase in "He left in the morning," an adjectival prepositional phrase in "Breakfast in the morning," a nominal prepositional phrase in "In the morning will be soon enough."

2. Phrases and style. The style of a passage depends in part on how a writer combines and coordinates phrases:

```
His ideas
        about the need
                        for intellectual renewal
                                and
                        spiritual reform
indicate the crisis
                faced not only
                                by those
                                        in places
                                                of power
                                        but
                                by those
                                        in all walks
                                                of life.
```

In this sentence, the phrases are balanced and coordinated to create a rhythm that carries the reader along smoothly to the end. In this next sentence, the phrases are merely strung out one after the other, creating a heavy, bumping kind of movement that interferes with the reader's understanding of the writer's idea:

```
Our situation
                in this century
                        of turmoil
                                in the cities
        can only be alleviated
                        by improving the living conditions
                                                in ghettoes
        in the central cities
                        which have decayed
                                beyond the endurance
                                                of most
        to live
                in them.
```

See Absolute phrases, Gerunds, Infinitives, Participles, Prepositional phrases. See also Dangling modifiers, Parallelism.

Plagiarism

Plagiarize is defined in *Webster's New Collegiate Dictionary* as "to steal and pass off (the ideas or words of another) as one's own." Plagiarism occurs in college courses for several different reasons, including panic, dishonesty, and ignorance of what plagiarism is. Sometimes it comes of an unconscious drift from paraphrasing into copying. Whatever the cause, the penalty—a failing mark on the paper and, if the cheating is chronic, a failing mark in the course—is justified. Copying someone else's work is the most complete failure possible.

The student who has not learned how to handle material obtained from reading needs guidance in the fundamentals of scholarship. Anyone using published material has a twofold responsibility: first, to make the ideas part of his own thinking and, second, to give credit to the sources he has consulted. No one is *composing* when he is merely copying. A student should read and digest the material, get it into his own words (except for the brief passages he intends to quote directly). He should be able to talk about what he has read before he writes about it, and when he does write, he should name the sources of his ideas and facts, including ideas and facts he has paraphrased or summarized. This is not only courtesy but a sign of good workmanship, part of the ethics of writing. It is also part of the legality of writing, since the plagiarist who uses copyrighted material is liable to prosecution.

In an informal essay, credit can be given informally, perhaps in a preliminary note saying "This essay is based on. . . ." Or a source may be acknowledged in the body of the essay: "Professor Martin said in a lecture . . ." or "According to an editorial in . . ." or "Here is Jackson's position as presented in last night's debate." Or credit may be given more formally in the footnotes that are a customary part of a research paper.

Plagiarizing is stealing. And besides being unethical, it is unnecessary and unproductive. By giving credit where credit is due, you gain free and legitimate access to everything in print (though if what you write is to be printed, you must secure permission to quote copyrighted material directly); and you learn to integrate the ideas of others with your own ideas. Finally, when you express what you have to say in your own words, you are not copying but composing. See Footnote form, Originality, Paraphrase, Research papers.

plenty

As a qualifier (I was plenty worried; The car is plenty fast) *plenty* is chiefly informal. It is used by some general writers, but others avoid it entirely, using instead such established adverbs as *extremely, amply,* and *quite*. In general writing, an *of* is expected between *plenty* and the following noun: We had plenty of time. Reference: Copperud, p. 213.

plurality, majority

In an election a plurality is the largest number of votes received by any one candidate but less than a majority, which is more than half of all the votes cast. See *majority, plurality*.

Plurals of nouns

The plural of the great majority of English nouns is made by adding -*s*. Some exceptions and special cases follow.

1. Special groups in -s or -es.
a. Some plurals can be pronounced only by adding a full syllable. The spelling is -*s* if the noun already ends in silent -*e*, otherwise -*es: birches, edges, misses, dishes, mazes.*
b. With a few exceptions, common nouns ending in -*y* preceded
by a consonant or *qu* change *y* to *i* and add -*es: beauties, bodies,
caddies, cherries, soliloquies.* Words ending in -*y* preceded by a
vowel add -*s: bays, boys, moneys* (but *monies* in the technical
economic sense).
c. Nouns ending in -*o* preceded by a vowel make regular plurals
with -*s: cameos, folios, radios, studios.* Some words ending in -*o*
preceded by a consonant always or nearly always take -*s: dyna-
mos, Eskimos* (or *Eskimo*), *Filipinos, pianos, solos, sopranos.*
Some always or nearly always take -*es: echoes, heroes, potatoes,
tomatoes, vetoes.* Some take either: *banjos, banjoes; cargoes,
cargos; dominoes, dominos.*
d. Some common nouns ending in -*f* or -*fe* (*calf, half, knife,
leaf, loaf, self, shelf, thief*) use -*ves* (*calves, halves, knives,* and
so on). Some have two plurals: *elf, elves–elfs; hoof, hoofs–
hooves; scarf, scarfs–scarves.* But many nouns ending in -*f*,
-*fe*, and -*ff* form regular plurals with -*s: beliefs, fifes, rebuffs.*

2. Same form for both singular and plural. Nouns with the same
form for singular and plural include names for some living
creatures (*fowl, sheep, fish*—but *fishes* for varieties of fish), all
words in -*ics* (*athletics, politics, civics*), and some common
measurements (*foot, pair, ton*).

3. Survivals of older English plural forms. Survivals include plurals in -*en* (*brother, brethren,* in church use; *child, children; ox,
oxen*) and plurals with changed vowels (*foot, feet; goose, geese;
louse, lice; man, men; mouse, mice; tooth, teeth; woman,
women*).

4. Foreign language plurals. Many nouns taken into English
from other languages keep their foreign plurals, at least for a
time. Words used chiefly in scientific or formal writing keep the
foreign form longer. *Antenna,* for instance, has the plural *an-
tennae* in biology but *antennas* in discussions of radio and TV.
When the word is in transition, both forms will be found in the
same context.
   Some common words have two plurals—the foreign (*appendices, media, nuclei*) and the English forms (*appendixes,
mediums, nucleuses*).

5. Compound and group words. Most compound words and
group words add -*s* to the end of the group, whether written as
one word or as several: *high schools, cross-examinations, book-
cases.* In a few the plural sign is added to the first element:
daughters-in-law (and other *in-law* words), *passersby, courts-
martial* (also *court-martials*).

6. Plurals of figures, words, letters. Usually the plural of a letter

of the alphabet, of a word as a word, or of a figure is written with
-'s: There are two *c*'s and two *m*'s in *accommodate;* Don't use
several *that*'s in a row; three *2*'s. But usage is divided; the plural
of figures especially is often made with -s: three 2s; no *if*s, *and*s,
or *but*s.

See Apostrophe 3; *-ful, full;* Genitive case 1a. References:
Fries, pp. 40–59; Jespersen, pp. 198–203; Long, pp. 203–27.

plus

Plus is a preposition having the sense "with the addition of." A
phrase introduced by *plus* should not therefore affect the number of the verb, but it is allowed to do so in some general writing,
particularly when the *plus* phrase is not set off by commas: The
committee report plus some newspaper headlines *were* all that
was needed. In more formal writing the *plus* would be changed
to *and* or the verb would be made singular.

Plus as a substitute for the adverb *besides* or *in addition* (The
school has a good engineering department, plus its campus is
beautiful) is informal and is objectionable to many. *Plus* is also
used as a noun (a plus for the new cafeteria is its lighting) and
an adjective (a plus factor). Some writers avoid the word entirely
except in arithmetical and commercial contexts.

p.m.

This abbreviation for *post meridiem,* "after noon," should not be
used as a noun. See *a.m. and p.m.*

Poetry

When verse is quoted, it should be lined off (as well as capitalized and punctuated) exactly as written. If possible, the quoted
lines should be approximately centered on the page, indented
according to the scheme of the original. When so spaced, lines of
verse quoted in a prose passage do not need quotation marks.
Diagonal marks, or virgules, are sometimes used to indicate line
breaks when a short passage is run into the text: It was Marlowe
who wrote, "I walk abroad 'a nights / And kill sick people groan-
ing under walls."

Point of view

**The shift in point of view in the passage marked is illogical or un-
justified.**

Your point of view in a paper is the position from which you view
your subject. The position may be physical—your location in
space and time—or psychological—your attitude toward your
subject. The correction symbol *pv* indicates that, in the context,
your change in point of view is unjustified or unmotivated or
that, in the rhetorical situation, your choice of point of view is
ineffective.

1. Don't make unjustified shifts in physical point of view. When
you write a description of an object, a place, a process, or an inci-

dent, the reader sees it through your eyes; and if he is to grasp what he is looking *at*, he must have a clear idea of where he is looking *from*. In describing a building on the campus, for example, you may begin with a head-on view and then lead the reader in full circuit, using such phrases as "looked at from the left," "the view from the rear," "the Main Street side." Or you may begin with a view from far across the campus or even a bird's-eye view—how the building would look if you approached it in a helicopter. The important thing is to keep the reader oriented. A description that jumps from facade to basement lab to clock tower to classrooms is bound to befuddle.

2. Don't make unmotivated shifts in psychological point of view. If you set out to describe your dormitory, what you show the reader, what you show in greatest detail, and what you don't show at all will differ according to your attitude toward the place. Thus psychological point of view may determine physical point of view. And psychological point of view may also lead to some role-playing. Suppose you hate your dorm and want to convince your reader that it deserves hating. Can you best accomplish your purpose by stating your attitude in the opening sentence? By being sarcastic throughout? Or by adopting an objective, analytical tone and counting on the examples and details you present to win the reader to your side? The strategy is yours to choose; but once you've made your choice, maintain your point of view consistently, or clearly justify any deviation from it. Like an erratic change in physical point of view, an unexplained switch in tone from sympathetic to contemptuous or from hostile to nostalgic will confuse and irritate the reader.

3. Don't make confusing changes in the distance between you and your reader. Point of view—physical or psychological or both—influences your choice between a *personal* mode of narration, description, or argument, in which your presence is clearly felt, and an *impersonal* mode, in which you efface yourself. The pronouns, if any, that you use to refer to yourself will signal to the reader something about the relationship you want to establish. Heavy reliance on the pronoun *I* (or *we*) may suggest casual intimacy; it may suggest restricted but personal knowledge of the subject; it may suggest real authority. Use of *you* may give the impression that you hope to engage your reader in a dialog. Use of the third person ("If one should . . .") may lend objectivity or imply remoteness. A completely impersonal approach focuses on what is being discussed without calling attention to either the writer or the audience. Once you have established yourself in one relation to your audience, it is unwise to adopt another without good reason.

Many problems in word choice and syntax stem from failure to maintain a consistent point of view. For related grammatical problems, see Passive voice, Reference of pronouns, Shifted constructions, Tense, *you*. See also Description, Details.

politics

Politics in the usual sense is treated as a singular: In almost any group, politics *is* a controversial subject. But when used in the sense of "principles," "activities," or "tactics," it may be treated as a plural: Republican politics *were* offensive to the Federalists. Avoid treating the word both ways in the same passage.

position, job

Position is the formal word for *job*. See *job, position*.

Positive degree

The positive degree of adjectives and adverbs is the base, or root, form of the adjective *(poor, high, golden)* or adverb *(slow, slowly, bitterly)*. See Comparison of adjectives and adverbs.

Possessive adjectives

See Possessive pronouns, possessive adjectives.

Possessive case

The possessive, or genitive, case is indicated by the apostrophe, with or without *-s;* by *of;* by the genitive form of the personal pronouns; and by the relative *whose*. See Genitive case.

Possessive pronouns, possessive adjectives

The personal pronouns have the following possessive forms: *my, mine; your, yours; his; her, hers; our, ours; their, theirs;* and the relative *who* has *whose*. *Its* is the only one that regularly tempts writers to use an apostrophe, through confusion with *it's*, the contraction for "it is."

My, your, her, his, our, their are used as adjectives (and sometimes called possessive adjectives) in the attributive position: my car. *Mine, yours, his, hers, its, ours, theirs* are used without a noun: Ours is better than yours.

Précis

A précis is a paraphrase of someone else's writing that condenses the original but retains its information, emphasis, and point of view. Rules for the formal précis prohibit direct quotation and call for a final version that is between one third and one fifth the length of the original. Condensation is achieved through the substitution of appositives, verbals, and series for more expansive statement and through the elimination of nonessential material. To produce a précis that accomplishes all this and is also well written calls for practice, hard work, and considerable skill.

Predicate

Almost all English sentences divide into two main elements—subject and predicate. The predicate of a clause or sentence is the verb with its modifiers and objects or complements. The predicate may be a single verb (The bell *tolled*), a transitive verb and its object (He *landed the big fish*), or a linking verb and its complement (The oldest member of the family *is usually the first to go*). Two verbs depending on one subject are known as a compound predicate: The three of them *washed* and *wiped* the dishes in fifteen minutes.

Predicate adjectives

Use an adjective here, since the verb is a linking verb.

Loudly in "The music sounds loudly" should be revised to *loud*.

The use of an adverb instead of a predicate adjective results from the habit of thinking that only adverbs follow the verb. But adjectives fill that position whenever the verb is a linking verb. In addition to *be,* about sixty verbs (*become, feel, turn, look, taste,* and so on) can perform this linking function. What follows the verb relates to or qualifies the subject, not the verb. Accordingly, an adjective — known as a predicate adjective or an adjective in the predicative position — is required, even though in its other functions the same verb is followed by an adverb. Compare: He felt *tired* (adjective, relates to subject); He felt the edge of the knife *carefully* (adverb, relates to verb).

Adjective: She acts *tired.*   *Adverb:* She acts *brilliantly.*
Adjective: She looks *cold.*   *Adverb:* She looked at him *coldly.*

The test for a linking verb is that the appropriate form of *be* can replace it: "The story rings true" is structurally the same as "The story is true." When you have identified the verb as linking, use an adjective after it.

See *bad, badly;* Linking verbs; *look.* See also Adjectives 1.

Predicate nominative

Words and word groups that follow linking verbs and function as nouns are called predicate nominatives or complements. They include nouns, pronouns, phrases, and clauses. See Linking verbs

predominant, predominate

Predominant is the adjective: a predominant sentiment, a sentiment predominant in the state. *Predominate* is the verb: The Muslims predominate there. Although increasingly common and recognized by dictionaries, the spelling *predominate* for the adjective and *predominately* for the adverb is offensive to many readers.

prefer

To is ordinarily used with *prefer:* I prefer Ireland to Spain; He preferred going by train to flying. But when an infinitive is used instead of a noun or gerund, *to* is impossible, and *than* or *rather than* is used: He preferred to take the train rather than to fly [*or* rather than a plane]. Reference: Copperud, pp. 217–18.

Prefix

A prefix is a form that can be placed before a word or root to change its meaning or function: un*tie,* im*mobilize.* See Origin of words 3a. See also Hyphen 4, Long variants.

Prepositional phrases

A prepositional phrase consists of a preposition and its object: without hope, in a hurry, toward a more abundant life. Prepositional phrases are modifiers, used in the functions of adverbs or adjectives:

Adverbial modifier: She arrived *at just the right time.*
Adjectival modifier: The man *in the black coat* has left.

See Phrases.

Prepositions

A preposition connects a noun phrase or a pronoun or a clause to some other part of the sentence. The whole phrase is usually adverbial or adjectival in its function: He showed her *to her room;* He was old *in experience;* He was surprised *at what he saw;* the click *of flying wheels.* What follows a preposition is called its object or, by some grammarians, its complement. Prepositions may be word groups (in regard to, according to) as well as single words. And many words that serve as prepositions, such as *after, but, since,* also serve as adverbs and conjunctions.

In some contexts, prepositions signal purely grammatical functions. *By* can signal the agent of an action: The window was broken by Mike. *Of* can signal either agent or object: The destruction of the city shocked everyone; The discussions of the committee were kept secret. *With* can signal instrumentality: He cut the bread with a knife. But *by, with,* and *of* can also indicate specific meaning. *By* can be paraphrased as "in a space adjacent to" in "He sat by the river"; *with* means "in the company of" in "I left with Tom"; *of* means "belonging to" in "He is a citizen of France." Even in abstract contexts (under a cloud, with ease) prepositions have meaning.

See Objects 3, Parts of speech, Prepositions and style. References: Follett, pp. 257–59; Fowler, pp. 473–75; Quirk et al., pp. 299–337.

prep Prepositions and style

Change the preposition to one that is idiomatic or less conspicuous; or supply a missing preposition.

1. Use prepositions that are exact or idiomatic. A number of words are accompanied by certain prepositions; we say "contented *with* conditions," "*in* my estimation." Some words take on different meanings with different prepositions: agree *with* (a person), agree *to* (a suggestion), agree *in* (principle).

Selecting the right preposition presents no problem with words that we use often, because we learn the words by hearing or seeing them in their typical combinations. When learning new words, learn their usage as well as their meaning: *acquiesce in* (acquiesce in a decision) rather than just *acquiesce*. Dictionaries usually give the preposition appropriate to particular words. This book treats a few idioms that are occasionally troublesome: *ability to; agree to, agree with; all of; compare, contrast; different*. See also Idiom.

When using together two words that take different prepositions, include both prepositions: The first lesson he learned was obedience *to* and respect *for* others besides his parents. *Not . . .* obedience and respect for others. When both words take the same preposition, there's no need to use it twice: The box office refused to make any allowance [ ] or refund *for* tickets purchased from an agent.

2. Keep your prepositions from bulking too large. English has a number of group prepositions that become conspicuous when they take up too much space for the work they do. A reference to "recent demonstrations on the part of dissatisfied students" is weighed down by "on the part of" where *by* would do the job. Sometimes we carry over from speech the habit of using double prepositions: *(in) back of, outside (of), off (of)*. See *as to; off of; on, onto, on to; prior to*.

3. Don't omit prepositions in general or formal writing. Sometimes prepositions are dropped:

. . . one of the best pieces written about the United States [in] this century. —Arthur Schlesinger, *New Republic*

. . . the mysterious command center beneath the Pentagon [from] where [or from which] the ultimate orders go to distant area commanders. —Mark S. Watson, *New York Times Book Review*

Although such omissions as these are increasingly common in general writing, expressions like "a couple [of] days later," "a different type [of] girl," and "outside [of] his interest in boxing" remain decidedly informal.

4. When a preposition falls naturally at the end of a sentence, leave it there. There is an old "rule" that prepositions should not stand at the end of their constructions (What did I do it for?), but postponing the preposition has long been a characteristic English idiom. Both idiom and rhythm often demand the preposition at the end, particularly with compound verbs like *dispose of* and in relative clauses with *that* or with no relative expressed. Attempts to avoid the postponed preposition are often clumsy or ungrammatical: Tell me what it is to which you object [*better:* what you object to]. Reference: Bryant, pp. 162–64.

Placing the preposition at the end is such a firmly fixed habit that in some sentences you must be careful not to repeat one that has already been expressed: He brightened the life of everyone with whom he came in contact [with].

See Phrases 2.

Present tense

The base form of a verb (*ask, answer, buy, say*) is its present tense. In most verbs -*s* is added in the third-person singular. See Tenses of verbs.

pretty

Pretty for *rather* or *fairly* gives a sentence an informal tone: "[Archibald Cox] sets pretty straight . . . the real impact of the great case of Marbury v. Madison" (Charles L. Black, Jr., *New York Times Book Review*).

Prewriting

Prewriting is the stage of thinking, worrying, and doodling that you go through before you set down even the rough form of an essay. The process is related to what is known in classical rhetoric as invention and discovery—finding out what you have to say about your subject.

People prewrite in different ways. Some scribble, apparently aimlessly, trying to find their way to a lead-in idea. Some think through the subject again and again, doing their prewriting entirely in their heads. And some look into promising sources, jot down facts, thoughts, and impressions, and try various ways of ordering their ideas to discover the points that need most emphasis.

Whether or not your exploration of your subject involves hunting up information and finding out what others have said, the end product of prewriting is not a collection of notes. It is a sure sense that you have made the subject your own. Making the subject your own means that whatever you write will be motivated by personal concern. Writing that lacks personal concern—intellectual commitment or emotional commitment or both—is very likely to be dull writing, trite and mechanical in both thought and expression. Writing that grows out of personal concern is just as likely to have some drive and freshness; it is the kind of writing that quickly engages the attention of a reader.

Though no rules can be provided that will guarantee successful prewriting, or pump priming, one practice that helps many writers is keeping a daily journal—entering sentences or paragraphs that capture thoughts and opinions, making a note of images that match half-formed ideas. Because his journal proved so rich a source for his public writing, one author called it his savings bank. Certainly keeping a journal is worth a try. You may find that, like other prewriting techniques, it will give you a running start on writing your essays.

Reference: D. Gordon Rohman, *CCC*, May 1965, pp. 106–12.

Principal parts of verbs

Change the verb form to one in standard use.

1. The principal parts of a verb. These are the base form or infinitive (*ask*), the past-tense form (*asked*), the past participle (*asked*).

Most English verbs are "regular"—that is, their past tense and past participle are formed by adding *-ed* to the base form. A number, most of them descended from Old English strong verbs, make their past-tense and past-participle forms by a change in vowel (*strike, struck, struck*). Some (*let, cost*) remain unchanged; some (*bend, make*) change the final consonant; some have less common irregularities (past forms of *teach: taught, taught*).

The trend has been toward regularity. A few verbs (*broadcast, shine, speed*) have acquired regular forms in addition to their old ones: *broadcasted, shined, speeded*. A few others (*dive, fit, prove, sew*) have reversed the general trend, acquiring irregularities that are either new or a revival of archaic forms: *dove, fit* (past tense), *proven, sewn*. For some verbs (*dream, plead, show, strive, thrive*) variant pairs have long existed side by side: *dreamed, dreamt; pleaded, pled; showed, shown; strived, strove; thrived, throve*.

The following list includes a number of verbs with irregular past-tense or past-participle forms. The forms labeled *NS* (nonstandard) and *D* (dialect) would not ordinarily be written. When doubts arise, a recent dictionary should be consulted for verbs not listed here; but usage is by no means uniform, even among speakers and writers of standard English, and neither this list nor the dictionaries record all variations.

Infinitive	*Past tense*	*Past participle*
arise	arose	arisen
bear	bore	borne
bear	bore	born (given birth to)
begin	began (D: begun)	begun
bite	bit	bitten, bit
blow	blew (D: blowed)	blown (D: blowed)
break	broke	broken (NS: broke)
bring	brought (NS: brung)	brought (NS: brung)
catch	caught (chiefly D: catched)	caught (chiefly D: catched)
choose	chose	chosen
come	came (NS: come)	come
dig	dug	dug
dive	dived, dove	dived
do	did (NS: done)	done
drag	dragged (D: drug)	dragged (D: drug)
draw	drew (NS: drawed)	drawn
dream	dreamed, dreamt	dreamed, dreamt
drink	drank (D: drunk)	drunk
eat	ate (D: pronounced et)	eaten (D: pronounced et)
fall	fell	fallen
fly	flew	flown
forget	forgot	forgotten, forgot
freeze	froze (D: friz)	frozen (chiefly D: froze)
get	got	got, gotten
give	gave (NS: give)	given (NS: give)
go	went (D: goed)	gone (NS: went)
grow	grew (D: growed)	grown (D: growed)
hang	hung	hung
hang (execute)	hung, hanged	hung, hanged
hear	heard	heard

know	knew (D: knowed)	known (D: knowed)
lay	laid	laid
lead	led	led
lend (loan)	lent	lent
lie (*see* lay)	lay	lain
lose	lost	lost
prove	proved	proved, proven
ride	rode (D: rid)	ridden (D: rid)
ring	rang, rung	rung
run	ran (NS: run)	run
see	saw (NS: seed)	seen (NS: seed, saw)
shake	shook (chiefly D: shaked)	shaken (chiefly D: shaked)
shine	shone, shined	shone, shined
show	showed	showed, shown
shrink	shrank, shrunk	shrunk
sing	sang, sung	sung
sink	sank, sunk	sunk, sunken
sit	sat (D: set)	sat (D: set)
slide	slid	slid
sneak	sneaked (chiefly D: snuck)	sneaked (chiefly D: snuck)
speak	spoke	spoken
spring	sprang, sprung	sprung
steal	stole	stolen (chiefly D: stole)
swim	swam	swum
take	took (D: taken)	taken (D: took)
tear	tore	torn
throw	threw (D: throwed)	thrown (D: throwed)
wear	wore	worn
write	wrote (D: writ)	written (D: wrote)

2. Nonstandard verbs. Linguists investigating the patterns of some Black English dialects have found a predictable and therefore grammatical structure in sentences that have traditionally been called ungrammatical:

The teacher gone right now, but she be back soon.
He always be playing records late at night.

The lack of a *be* form in the first clause—the teacher [is] gone—and the apparently incorrect form of *be* in the second— she [will] be back—result from a deletion transformation. It regularly and predictably deletes a form of *be* and other auxiliary verbs such as *will, would, have,* etc., where standard English speakers contract their form of *be*. (An exception is '*m*, as in "I'm going.") This sequence represents the process:

The teacher is   gone right now, but she will be back soon.
The teacher's   gone right now, but she'll   be back soon.
The teacher[ ] gone right now, but she[ ]   be back soon.

Where standard English speakers cannot contract a form of *be,* neither can speakers of some dialects of Black English delete it:

Standard English: I don't know who he is. *Not* I don't know who's.
Black English: I don't know who he be. *Not* I don't know who he.

The form of *be* in "He always be playing records late at night" is a different problem. It is evidently an invariant verb form that always appears as *be* to indicate a repeated action. When the action is temporary, not repeated, the first variations on *be* are found, as in "He not here right now, but he be back in a minute."

See *born, borne; do; got, gotten; hanged, hung; lay, lie; proved, proven; set, sit.* References: Atwood; Fries, pp. 59–71; Mencken, pp. 527–28; Pyles, pp. 124–30, 194–205; *Webster's Third New International Dictionary.*

principal, principle

Principal is either an adjective or a noun, *principle* a noun only. One way to remember that the adjective is spelled *principal* is to associate it with other adjectives ending in *-al: historical, political, musical.*

Principal as a noun is probably an abbreviation of a phrase in which it was originally an adjective: the principal that draws interest was once the principal sum; the principal of a school, the principal teacher; the principal in a legal action, the principal party; the principals in a play, the principal actors. These are the only common uses of *principal* as a noun.

The noun meaning "a general truth or rule of conduct" is *principle:* the principles of science, a man of high principles.

prior to

Prior to, a rather formal preposition, is most appropriate when it adds to the notion of "before" that of "in anticipation of": "He urged reform leaders to work prior to the convention so as to minimize the influence of Greeley's supporters" (Matthew T. Downey, *Journal of American History*). In most contexts, particularly in general writing, *before* is the better word.

Profanity

Using profanity — that is, referring to sacred beings carelessly or irreverently — is primarily a matter of muscular or emotional release rather than of meaning, and in writing, profanity often attracts more attention to itself than it deserves. Like other kinds of swearing, it has no place in college writing, except perhaps in dialog. See Obscenity.

professor

Write: Professor Moore; Prof. E. W. Moore; E. W. Moore, a professor of chemistry; *or* E. W. Moore, Professor of Chemistry.

The colloquial *prof* (my math prof) is a clipped word, not an abbreviation, and is written without a period.

Strictly speaking, the title *Professor* should be given only to assistant professors, associate professors, and full professors, not to those who have not reached professorial rank. When the title follows the name in an *of* phrase, exact rank is usually indicated: Professor A. B. Plant, *but* A. B. Plant, Assistant Professor of English.

Progressive verb forms

Progressive verb forms are verb phrases made with *be* and the present participle to show continuing action: I *am asking,* he *was asking,* they *have been asking.* See Tenses of verbs, Verbs.

Pronouns

A pronoun is commonly defined as a word that replaces a noun or another word or group of words used as a noun. The word or phrase or clause that it substitutes for, as *it* substitutes for *a pronoun* in the sentence you're reading, is called its antecedent: *it* is said to refer to *a pronoun*; *a pronoun* is the antecedent of *it*. Not all pronouns have antecedents. The reference of *I* and *you* depends on the identity of the writer or speaker and the audience being addressed, not on the verbal context in which *I* and *you* appear.

Like nouns, pronouns can serve as subjects and objects (though not all pronouns can serve as both). Many have a genitive form, and a few have a separate plural form. Unlike nouns, pronouns do not occur with *the* or *a*; with a few exceptions (*someone* nice, *something* useful) they are not modified by adjectives; and they are a small, closed class of words.

The traditional subclasses of pronouns are listed below. Because these subclasses don't all share the same characteristics, some grammarians assign a number of them to other parts of speech. See, for example, Parts of speech 2.

1. Personal pronouns. The personal pronouns are those words that specifically indicate person (first, second, or third), number, and, in the third-person singular, gender.

		Nominative	*Genitive*	*Accusative*
1st-person	singular	I	my, mine	me
	plural	we	our, ours	us
2nd-person	singular	you	your, yours	you
	plural	you	your, yours	you
3rd-person	singular			
	masculine	he	his, his	him
	feminine	she	her, hers	her
	neuter	it	its, its	it
	genderless	one	one's, one's	one
	plural	they	their, theirs	them

Except for the relative pronoun *who* (*whose, whom*), only the personal pronouns, and not all of them, have different forms for the three cases. Some of the most common grammatical mistakes occur because, unlike nouns, *I, we, he, she, they*, and *who* have different forms in subject and object position. See *between you and me*; Case; *it's me*; *who, whom*.

In some traditional grammars, personal pronouns in the genitive case are classified separately as possessive pronouns.

2. Reflexive pronouns. The reflexives, sometimes called the compound personal pronouns, are formed by adding *-self* or *-selves* to the genitive case of personal pronouns in the first and second persons (*myself, yourself, ourselves, yourselves*) and to the accusative case in the third person (*himself, herself, itself, themselves*). They are used when an object or a subjective complement has the same referent as a preceding noun or noun phrase in the same sentence and when no other possible antecedent intervenes:

Direct object:	He hurt *himself.*
Object of preposition:	The rope was twisted back on *itself.*
	He autographed a dozen pictures of *himself.*
Indirect object:	They made *themselves* caftans.
Subjective complement:	Ben is not *himself* today.
Object of infinitive:	Jane wanted Betty to help *herself.*

With the last example, compare "Jane wanted Betty to help her," in which the antecedent of *her* is *Jane*, not *Betty*. Since a possible antecedent, *Betty*, intervenes, the reflexive is not used.

When they serve as intensives, the reflexive forms are construed as pronouns in apposition: The owner *himself* sold the car; The owner sold the car *himself.* See Apposition, appositives.

3. Reciprocal pronouns. The reciprocals *each other* and *one another* substitute in object position for a compound or plural noun that has the same referent as a compound or plural subject when the action of the verb is directed by each member of the subject toward the other members: Tom and Bill looked at *each other;* the losers kidded *one another*. Compare: Tom and Bill looked at *themselves;* The losers kidded *themselves.*

Like the personal pronouns, the reciprocals are freely used in the genitive: They borrowed *one another's* clothes.

4. Relative pronouns. *Who, which,* and *that* are relatives. Like the personal pronouns, *who* has different forms for the genitive (*whose*) and the accusative (*whom*). *Which* and *that* are not inflected for case.

Relative pronouns introduce dependent clauses:

The student *who* submitted this paper has dropped out.
The paper *that* she submitted won an award.
Her decision to leave school, *which* caused some excitement, was never explained.

When no specific referent for the pronoun is intended, the indefinite, or expanded, form of the relative is used: *whoever, whomever, whichever, whatever.* Unexpanded *what* is also an indefinite relative pronoun:

Whoever receives this will be pleased.
I will support *whomever* you nominate.
They will believe *whatever* he says.
They will believe *what* he says.

See Relative clauses.

5. Interrogative pronouns. The interrogatives *who, whose, whom, which,* and *what* are used to introduce direct and indirect questions: *What* happened? He asked me *what* happened.

6. Demonstrative pronouns. *This, that, these,* and *those* are considered adjectives when they modify nouns (*this* hat, *these* books), pronouns when they function as nouns: *This* will fix it; *Those* are too large; I prefer *these.* The demonstratives discriminate between referents close at hand (*this, these*) and referents that are more remote (*that, those*).

7. Indefinite pronouns. *Some, any, every,* and *no* compounded with *one* (*someone*), *thing* (*everything*), and *body* (*nobody*), and other words like *all, any, some, each,* and *either,* have traditionally been called indefinite pronouns. When used as subjects, the compounds take singular verbs, and pronouns referring to them are usually in the singular: Everyone *is* expected to do *his* part. Since the indefinite pronouns do not replace noun phrases and generally have no specific referent, some grammarians find it more logical to classify them as indefinite nouns.

Informally, *they* is also used for indefinite reference: They ought to do something about these roads. See *they*.

See Antecedent, Determiners, Parts of speech, Reference of pronouns. References: Archibald A. Hill, *Introduction to Linguistic Structures* (New York: Harcourt, 1958), pp. 145–52; Jespersen, Chs. 14–18; Quirk et al., pp. 203–25; Roberts, pp. 53–89; John Ross in *Modern Studies in English,* ed. David A. Reibel and Sanford A. Schane (Englewood Cliffs, N.J.: Prentice-Hall, 1969), pp. 187–200.

Proofreading
Checking the final copy of an essay for mechanical mistakes that may have slipped into the last draft is an essential part of preparing a manuscript. See Careless mistakes, Caret, Manuscript form, Typewritten copy.

Proper adjectives
Proper nouns that are used like adjectives are capitalized, and so are adjectives that are directly derived from proper names if they still refer to the place or person. After proper adjectives lose the reference to their origins, they become simple adjectives and are no longer capitalized: the Indian service, india ink; the Roman forum, roman type. See Capital letters.

proved, proven
Prove is a regular verb, forming a past tense and past participle with -*ed: proved. Proven* has been used for centuries as an alternative past participle of *prove* and is now established in all varieties of usage. References: Bryant, pp. 165–66; Pooley, pp. 157–58.

provided, providing
Both are in standard use as connectives. Formal writing strongly prefers *provided;* in general writing usage is divided.

You can't even argue, much, with the picture, providing you look at it only as a clever Western. — David R. Slavitt, *Yale Review*

Anyone who can get into M.S.U. can get into Justin Morrill, provided he is willing to work. — Duncan Norton, *Fortune*

Reference: Copperud, p. 223.

Psychologese

Psychologese, a jargon made up of words from the technical vocabulary of psychology, is used enthusiastically if inexactly by many outsiders: *instinctual* for *instinctive*, *operant* for *operating*, *motorical* for *motor*. A great many other terms from psychology (*empathy*, *motivational*, *neurotic*, *paranoid*, *relate*, *traumatic*) have entered the general language, become vogue words, and lost much of their technical meaning.

public

Meaning "the people as a whole," *public* is a collective noun and can be treated either as a singular or as a plural. A plural construction is more common: The public depend on TV newscasts for most of their information. But in the sense "a group of people with a common interest," *public* is more often singular: "There is a foreign policy public that is considerably smaller than the general public" (Carl N. Degler, *American Historical Review*).

pn Punctuation

Insert necessary punctuation, or change your punctuation to conform to standard usage.

no pn No punctuation

Delete the unnecessary punctuation.

The basic purpose of punctuation is to mark off sentences and to link, separate, and set off elements within sentences in ways that will make the meaning clear to readers. A good rule to follow is to use all punctuation required by current convention and as much optional punctuation as you consider necessary to help your reader. Don't use unnecessary punctuation, which may make reading more difficult. And don't rely on punctuation to bail out awkwardly constructed sentences. Instead, rewrite.

1. To end sentences. Use periods to end statements. Use question marks to end sentences that ask direct questions. Use exclamation marks to end sentences (or to follow words or phrases) that express strong emotion and demand special emphasis. See Exclamation mark, Period, Question mark.

2. To separate.
a. Use a comma before the conjunction to separate independent clauses joined by *but*, *for*, or *so*. You may also use a comma before the other coordinating conjunctions in compound sentences. To indicate a stronger separation, use a semicolon. See Comma 1, Semicolon 1c.
b. Use a comma after a long introductory phrase or dependent clause to separate it from the main clause. You may use a comma after all introductory phrases and clauses. Do not use a comma after introductory *but*, *and*, or other conjunction. See Comma 2a.
c. Use a comma before a nonrestrictive dependent clause or

phrase that follows the main clause. Do not use a comma before a restrictive modifier that follows the main clause. See Comma 2b.

d. Use commas to separate the units in a series and to separate adjectives modifying the same noun. To separate the units in a series that already includes commas, use semicolons. See Comma 5, Semicolon 2.

e. Do not use a comma between subject and verb, between verb and object or complement, or, in most cases, between the verbs in a compound predicate. See Comma 8.

3. To set off.

a. Use paired commas to set off nonrestrictive modifiers.

b. Use paired commas, paired dashes, or parentheses to set off interrupting elements. Commas mark the least separation, parentheses the most. Setting off short interrupters is optional. See Comma 4a.

4. To link.

a. Use a semicolon between main clauses when you want to link them rather than to separate them with a period. See Semicolon 1.

b. Use a colon (*not* a semicolon) to link a series, a quotation, or other material to the sentence element that introduces it. See Colon 1.

c. Use a dash to link to the end of a sentence a word, phrase, or clause you want to emphasize. See Dash 1.

d. Use a hyphen to link syllables and words. See Hyphen.

5. Other uses.

a. Use quotation marks to identify direct quotations. See Quotation marks 2.

b. Use ellipses to indicate omission of words. See Ellipsis.

c. Use apostrophes to indicate possession and to indicate the omission of letters in contractions. See Apostrophe 1, 2.

References: Summey; Whitehall, Ch. 10.

Puns

A pun is a figure of speech in which a word is simultaneously used in two senses or substituted for another word of similar sound but different meaning (effluent society, the whine of sour grapes). Deliberate punning may serve serious purposes as well as humorous ones, but unintentional puns should be weeded out in revision.

Qualifiers

Qualifiers are words used not to convey meaning in themselves but to qualify—usually by intensifying—the meaning of adjectives. They include the first words in the phrases "much older," "very quiet," "too old," "somewhat sick," "rather careless," "quite intelligent" and degree adverbs like *slightly*. Though sometimes effective in speech, qualifiers are more likely to weaken writing than to strengthen it. See Parts of speech.

Question mark

The chief conventions governing the use of the question mark are these:

1. As an end stop. The principal use of the question mark is as the end stop of a direct question: What was the real reason?

A question mark is not used after an indirect question: He wanted to know what the real reason was.

A request that is phrased as a question may or may not be followed by a question mark, depending on the formality of the style:

Formal: Will you please return the book at your earliest convenience?
General: Will you please get the book back as soon as you can.

2. With quotation marks. When a question mark and a closing quotation mark fall together, the question mark belongs outside the quotation mark if the sentence that encloses the quotation is the question (Did you really say, "I thought you were older than that"?), inside if the quotation is the question (He asked, "Did you really say that?"). If both are questions, only the inside question mark is used: Did she ask, "How many are coming?"

3. Within sentences. Usage is divided over a question built into a sentence: Should I quit school now [ ] I ask myself. A question mark after *now* would emphasize the question; a comma would make it less emphatic. If quotation marks were used around the question, a question mark would be appropriate.

4. Miscellaneous uses. A question mark is used to show that dates are approximate or uncertain: Geoffrey Chaucer 1340?– 1400 *or* Geoffrey Chaucer 1340(?)–1400.

A question mark in parentheses to indicate humor or sarcasm is out of date and out of favor: her fashionable (?) outfit.

Questions

1. Signals of questions. A question may be introduced by a pronoun (*Who* was that? *What* can be done?), an adjective (*Which* way did he go?), or an adverb (*Where* shall we eat?). A question may also be indicated by inverted word order, with the verb or part of the verb coming before the subject (Was he there?). Ordinarily a verb phrase is used, with part of it coming before the subject as a sort of compromise inversion: *Do you think* he can do it? (Here the auxiliary *do* is meaningless but allows us to begin the question with one verb while keeping the main verb, *think*, in its normal position after the subject.) A statement may also be turned into a question by adding an inverted clause at the end: He didn't try, *did he*?

2. Direct and indirect questions. A direct question is a question as actually asked, not just reported. It begins with a capital (unless it is introduced parenthetically into another sentence) and ends with a question mark: Who killed Cock Robin?

An indirect question is not a question as actually asked but a question reported as a subordinate element of another sentence. An indirect question does not begin with a capital or end with a question mark, and it is not set off by quotation marks. When a direct question is turned into an indirect one, the tense of the verb in the question is made to match the tense of the verb in the independent clause, and a subordinating conjunction is often introduced:

Direct: "What are our plans for tomorrow?"
Indirect: He asked *what our plans for tomorrow were.*

Direct: He asked, "Do you really understand what you have read?"
Indirect: He asked us *if we really understood what we had read.* He always asks us *whether we understand what we have read.*

3. Leading questions. A leading question is one phrased to suggest the answer desired, like "You wouldn't do that, would you?" (*Compare:* "Would you do that?") See Rhetorical questions.

4. Questions as transitions. Occasionally, but only occasionally, asking a question is a good way to introduce a new topic: What do we mean by *immoral?*

Quotation marks

Make the quotation marks conform to conventional usage.

1. Methods of indicating quotations.
a. Double quotes, not single, are the usual marks in the United States.
b. For quotations within quotations, double and single quotes are alternated; single quotes are used inside double quotes and so on: " 'Perry's instinct,' he says, 'soundly chose the point at which to halt the extension of the term "formula" ' " (Joseph Russo, *Yale Classical Studies*).
c. When a quotation is longer than one paragraph, quotation marks are used at the beginning of each paragraph but at the end of the last paragraph only.
d. When long quotations or a series of quotations are indented or are set in smaller type, as in this book, no quotation marks are used. In double-spaced typewritten copy, such block quotations are usually indented and single spaced.

2. Principal uses of quotation marks.
a. Quotation marks are used to indicate all passages taken from another writer, whether a phrase or a page or more (except when the quotation is indented). Any change of language within the quotation should be indicated—omissions by ellipses, additions by brackets. The quoted matter may stand by itself or may be worked into the writer's own sentence. Both methods are shown in this passage, the more formal first:

The most that could be said for Haig was said by Churchill: he "was unequal to the prodigious scale of events, but no one else was discerned as his equal or better." (Lloyd George, more succinctly, said he was "brilliant to the top of his army boots.") – Geoffrey Barraclough, *New York Review of Books*

When brief passages of conversation are introduced not for their own sake but to illustrate a point, they are usually incorporated in the paragraph:

I am having a drink with the manager, Yves Blais. "You don't speak French," he starts off by saying, "but that is all right because you are from Ontario, which is another country. I will speak English with you. But I have no British accent. I have a pea-soup accent." Blais volunteers the obvious – that he is a separatist. "I'm glad to be. I don't care. I refused to accept a Canada Council grant of $8,000. But it has nothing to do with my shows." – Jon Ruddy, *Maclean's*

b. There are no half quotes. A sentence is either an exact quotation and therefore in quotation marks, or else it is not an exact quotation and so is not quoted. By paying scrupulous attention to the exact language of the material to be quoted, you can avoid using quotation marks with pronouns and verb tenses appropriate only to indirect statements: He boasted that he "could do twice as much work as me." The boast must have been, "I can do twice as much work as you." The choice is between – but not halfway between – direct and indirect quotation: He boasted, "I can do twice as much work as you"; *or* He boasted that he could do twice as much work as me.

3. Miscellaneous uses of quotation marks.
a. Quotation marks enclose titles of poems, articles, stories, chapters of books, and, in most newspapers and many magazines, the titles of books themselves. See Titles 2a.

b. Words that are used as words rather than for their meaning usually appear in italics in formal writing, in quotes in general writing. But usage is divided:

There is the ugly and almost universal use of "like" for "as." – Douglas Bush, *American Scholar*

The word *bluff* is old in the English language. – Webb Garrison, *American Legion Magazine*

c. A word from a conspicuously different variety of speech is sometimes put in quotation marks, but this only calls attention to it. If you decide that such a word suits your needs, use it without apology:

He spurns aspirants not of his clique, thereby creating a tyranny of taste that soon will have every center of imaginative expression . . . under its cheesy [not "cheesy"] thrall. – Benjamin DeMott, *New American Review*

d. A word may be put in quotation marks to show that the writer refuses to accept its conventional sense in the context:

In numerous cases it is impossible to maintain on any solid ground that one pronunciation given is "better" than another, as, for example, that one pronunciation of *swamp* is better than the others given. – John S. Kenyon and Thomas A. Knott, *A Pronouncing Dictionary of American English*

But putting a word in quotation marks to signal sarcasm or derision (The "cute" Great Dane had eaten my sweater) is on a par with putting a question mark in parentheses to get a laugh.

e. Directly quoted *yes* and *no* (sometimes capitalized, sometimes not) frequently appear without quotation marks when they are built into the sentence in which they appear: Steve said Yes, so we went to work at once. When they are not actually spoken, they should not be quoted: If he had said no, I was prepared to resign.

4. Quotation marks with other marks.

a. When a question mark or an exclamation mark ends a quotation, it is placed inside the quotes:

"Don't go near that wire!" he shouted.
Later he said, "Aren't you wondering what would have happened?"

When a question mark or exclamation mark belongs to the construction that includes the quotation, it is placed after the quotes: What is an ordinary citizen to do when he hears the words, "This is a stick-up"? See Question mark 2.

b. American practice is to place periods and commas within the quotation marks, colons and semicolons after the closing marks.

c. "He said" and all its variations are normally set off by commas from the quotations they introduce:

"History," it is said, "does not repeat itself. The historians repeat one another." — Max Beerbohm, *Works*

But the quoted phrase may be so closely built into the sentence that no comma is wanted:

Any moron can say "I don't know who done it." — Francis Christensen, *Notes Toward a New Rhetoric*

raise, rear

Raise in the sense of bringing up a child has become suitable in all varieties of usage. *Rear* is now somewhat formal. See *bring up*. Reference: Copperud, pp. 227–28.

reaction

Reaction has drifted from the scientific vocabulary into general usage and become a counter word for nearly any response, whether emotional or mental, general or specific. Reference: Copperud, p. 229.

real, really

Ordinarily *real* is the adjective (a real difficulty, in real life), and *really* is the adverb (a really significant improvement; I really thought so). Both are overused as qualifiers; television commercials could barely exist without them. Adverbial *real,* as in sentences like "Write real soon" and "It's real pretty," is informal.

rear, raise
As applied to bringing up children, *rear* is the formal choice. See *raise, rear.*

reason is because
In formal writing there is a strong preference for *reason is that,* on the grounds that *reason is because* is redundant. Even in general writing, *that* is much more common when there are no intervening words (My only reason is that I have to work tonight) or when the intervening words don't constitute a clause with a subject of its own (The reason usually given for such failures in sports is that there was inadequate concentration). But when many words or a clause with a separate subject intervenes, *reason . . . is because* often occurs in both formal and general prose:

One reason why music can stand repetition so much more sturdily than correspondingly good prose is because music, of all the arts, is by its nature least suited to the psychology of information, and has remained closer to the psychology of form. — Kenneth Burke, *Psychology and Form*

And the reason the press isn't a menace, Reston says, is because it has divested itself of so much of its power. — *Newsweek*

Even though *reason is because* has a long history in literature and is regularly used by educated speakers, writers should remind themselves that to some readers *reason is because* is a hobgoblin. References: Bryant, pp. 170–71; Copperud, p. 230; Pooley, pp. 128–29.

Reciprocal pronouns
Each other and *one another* are called reciprocal pronouns. See *each other,* Pronouns 3.

reckon
Used to mean "suppose" or "think," *reckon* is a localism. See Localisms.

Reduced clauses
Constructions that function like clauses but lack a full verb or a subject or both are sometimes called reduced clauses: I'm happy *if you are* [happy]; John will go to the barbecue *if Jan will* [go to the barbecue]; *Although* [he was] *tired,* he agreed to attend. See Clauses 2.

Redundancy
In writing, words and phrases that are repetitive or simply unnecessary are redundant. See Repetition, Wordiness.

Reference of pronouns

Change the pronoun marked (or revise the sentence) so that the reference will be clear and the pronoun appropriate to the context.

In the sentence "Because my brother loves to ski, he spent Christmas vacation in Colorado," the pronoun *he* replaces the nominal *my brother. My brother* is called the antecedent of *he; he* has the same referent as *my brother.* In "He got so frostbitten I scarcely recognized him," the pronoun *I* has a referent (the speaker), but it does not have an antecedent. Both categories of pronouns — those that have antecedents and those that don't — create some problems for writers.

1. Clear reference. If the meaning of a pronoun is completed by reference to an antecedent, the reference must be unmistakable. Clear reference is a matter of meaning, not just the presence or position of certain words. Confusion may arise
a. When the pronoun seems to refer to a nearby noun that it can't sensibly refer to:

The next year he had an attack of appendicitis. *It* burst before the doctor had a chance to operate.
Revision: . . . His appendix burst. . . . (*It* can't sensibly refer to *appendicitis.* Such slips in reference are common when a sentence boundary separates a pronoun and its antecedent.)

b. When there is no noun nearby:

He isn't married yet and doesn't plan on *it.*
Revision: . . . and doesn't plan to marry.

c. When the pronoun refers to a noun used as a possessive or as an adjective:

Bill was skipping stones across the swimming hole. One cut open a young girl's head *who* was swimming under water.
Revision: . . . One cut open the head of a young girl who. . . .

Nancy longed for a chinchilla coat, though she wouldn't have dreamed of killing one.
Revision: . . . of killing a chinchilla to get one.

d. When two or more pronouns are crossed so that the exact reference can't be readily determined:

Businessmen without regard for anyone else have exploited the mass of workers at every point, not caring whether *they* were earning a decent living but only whether *they* were making big profits.
Revision: . . . not caring whether they paid a decent wage but only whether they were making big profits. (The sentence needs a complete rewriting, but this revision at least makes both *they*'s refer to the same antecedent.)

2. Broad reference. General English uses *which, that, this,* and sometimes *it* to refer not to a specific word or phrase but to the idea of a preceding clause. Formal avoids broad reference.

General: Her friend was jealous of her clothes and money and had taken this way of showing *it.*
Formal: . . . and had taken this way of showing her feeling.

General: They have also avoided titling the categories, so that the arrangement gently and effectively forces itself on the reader's consciousness, *which* adds a good deal to the effect of the whole.
Formal: . . . on the reader's consciousness—a fine choice, which adds a good deal to the effect of the whole.—Deborah Austin, *Journal of General Education*

3. Indefinite reference. Often pronouns are used to refer to the readers or to people in general instead of to specifically mentioned individuals. *One* has a severe, formal, sometimes pompous connotation. *We* and *you,* which seem slightly more personal and more expressive, are often preferred. Whether to choose *you, they, we, one,* or *people* or some other noun is a question of style, not grammar.

Keep indefinite pronouns consistent: When you have worked a day here, you have earned your money. With *one,* a shift to *he* is common: When one has worked a day here, he has earned his money. But *not* When one has worked a day here, you have. . . . See *one.*

Don't substitute an indefinite pronoun for a definite personal pronoun: For me there is no fun in reading unless you can put yourself in the position of the characters and feel that you are really in the scene. *Revision:* . . . unless I can put myself in the position of the characters and feel that I am. . . .

As a common-gender pronoun meaning "he or she," *he* is used in formal English, *they* in informal. General usage is divided between these forms, *he* being more conventional, *they* often more practical. See Agreement 2, Sexist language.

4. Avoiding and misusing pronouns. Writers who are uncertain about the reference or agreement of pronouns sometimes try to avoid them by repeating nouns. The result is usually unidiomatic or clumsy: Arrest of the woman yesterday followed several days of observation of the woman's [her] activities by the agents. On the other hand, overuse of *this* and *that* deprives writing of clarity and force: *This* is the first thing the agency has accomplished; *That* is something to be thankful for.

Referent
The referent of a word is the thing it refers to: in a specific context, "Ann Jackson" and "the love of my life," referring to the same person, would have the same referent. Words without referents are called noise by some semanticists.

Reflexive pronouns
Myself, yourself, himself, herself, itself, ourselves, yourselves, and *themselves* are reflexive pronouns. See *myself,* Pronouns 2.

relate
In the shoptalk of psychology the verb *relate* is a convenient term meaning to "have a realistic social or intimate relationship," as in "the patient's inability to relate." This sense of *relate* has passed into everyday usage, but the relationship is usually—

and preferably—specified by a *to* phrase: They find it almost impossible to relate to adults. *Relate* is a vogue word.

Relative clauses

Relative clauses, often referred to as adjective clauses, are introduced by relative pronouns (*that, which,* or *who*) or by relative adverbs (*where, when, why*). A relative clause stands after the noun it modifies:

The rain *that began in the morning* kept on all night.
The coach was abused by alumni *who two years before had cheered him.*
The road to the left, *which looked almost impassable,* was ours.
The first place *where they camped* turned out to be a swamp.

In general usage, when the clause is restrictive, the adverb, or the pronoun if it is not the subject, is often omitted:

He will never forget the time *you tried to cheat him. Formal:* . . . the time *when you tried to cheat him.*

The man *I met that afternoon* became my closest friend. *Formal:* The man *whom I met.* . . .

When relative clauses are introduced by indefinite relatives (*who, what,* and the compounds with *-ever*), they function as nouns:

The stranger at the door wasn't *who we thought he was.*
What actually happened was very different from *what the newspapers reported.*

Several relative clauses in succession make for an awkward house-that-Jack-built sentence: People who buy houses *that* have been built in times *which* had conspicuous traits of architecture *which* have since been abandoned often have to remodel their purchases completely. See Subordination 1.

See Pronouns 4; Restrictive and nonrestrictive; *that; which; who, whom.* Compare Noun clauses. Reference: Randolph Quirk, *Essays on the English Language Medieval and Modern* (Bloomington: Indiana Univ. Press, 1968), Chs. 9–10.

Relative pronouns

The relative pronouns are *who (whose, whom), which (of which, whose), that, what, whatever,* and *whoever (whomever):*

Somebody *who* was sitting on the other side shouted, "Put 'em out."
The Senator, *whose* term expires next year, is already worrying.
I haven't read the same book *that* you have.

That refers to persons and things, *who* to persons. *Which* in standard English now refers to animals or objects or situations and also to collective nouns, even if they refer to persons:

The army *which* mobilizes first has the advantage.
The Board of Directors, *which* met on Saturday. . . .
The Board of Directors, *who* are all bankers. . . .

In older English—and still in nonstandard—*which* applies also to persons: "Our Father which art in heaven. . . ."

The use of *as* in place of *that* in sentences like "I can't say as I do" is informal and dialectal.

See Pronouns 4: Restrictive and nonrestrictive; *that; which; who, whom.*

 ## Repetition

Get rid of the ineffective repetition of word, meaning, sound, or sentence pattern.

Repeating words, meanings, sounds, or sentence patterns is often effective in writing, giving prose both clarity and emphasis. This article reviews some kinds of repetition that ordinarily call for revision.

1. Of words and phrases. You are bound to repeat nouns unnecessarily if you don't use pronouns:

Ann accepted the boy's challenge and proceeded to teach the boy [him] a lesson. When the boy [he] stayed at the base line, Ann [she] ran the boy [him] from one side of the court to the other. When the boy [he] charged the net, Ann [she] beat the boy [him] with passing shots.

If you write hurriedly and don't take the time to read over what you've written, you are likely to end up with some careless repetition:

I'm having financial difficulties and need to *get* out of housing. So the hassle I *got* when I tried to *get* released from my dorm contract upset me.

When you use the same word in two different senses, the result may be worse: After falling only a few *feet* my left *foot* found *footing;* I would like to find a job with a *concern* that shows some *concern* for the environment. In cases like these, the repetition is obvious enough to be caught and corrected with little trouble – either by omitting the unnecessary repetition or by substituting synonyms. But it does call for that little trouble.

Harder for writers to spot but equally conspicuous to readers is the pet word or phrase that pops up three or four times in the course of an essay. If it's a cliché or a vogue expression, as it's likely to be, it may bother some readers on its first appearance and become increasingly irritating thereafter. In going over a first draft, then, keep a cold eye out for expressions that recur. Some of the repeated words and phrases will be unavoidable, some desirable. But you may also spot some pets that you have repeated simply because they are pets. Sacrifice them.

2. Of meaning. In reviewing what you've written, watch for words and phrases that unnecessarily repeat what you've already said. For example, a gift is free and a fact true by definition, so drop the adjective from "free gift" and from "true fact." If the setting of many TV plays is San Francisco, then San Francisco must frequently be the setting of TV plays. Writing "In many TV plays the setting very often is San Francisco" adds words but subtracts sense. So does "at 8 a.m. in the morning."

3. Of sounds. Jingles and rhyming words (hesitate to take the bait, a glance askance at the dance) are distracting in prose because they draw attention from sense to sound. So are noticeable repetitions of unstressed syllables, especially the *-ly* of adverbs and the endings of some abstract nouns, like *-tion*. Reading first drafts aloud is the best way to catch unintentional repetition of sound. See Adverbs and style, Alliteration, Assonance.

4. Of sentence patterns. If you unintentionally use the same pattern in one sentence after another—beginning three sentences in a row with a dependent clause, for example, or writing three successive compound sentences, or using the same coordinating conjunction in a series of sentences for no rhetorical purpose—your reader is likely to begin nodding. Sometimes this sort of repetition sets up a rhythm even more distracting than the repetition of sound within sentences. Sometimes it simply begins to bore the reader; he feels that he is being led over the same path again and again. Deliberate varying of sentence patterns is not often called for, but if you find yourself recycling the same pattern, make an effort to get untracked. See Parallelism.

Requests
Requests are often expressed in the form of questions: Will you please cooperate? Sometimes the question mark is omitted. See Commands and requests.

Research papers
The research paper—sometimes called the reference paper, library paper, investigative paper, or source paper—is the culminating assignment in many college courses, including Freshman English. Done well, it serves as a valuable introduction to scholarship, for preparing a good paper requires resourcefulness in using the library, ingenuity in following up leads, judgment in analyzing data, and skill in organizing and writing an essay of some length and complexity. Because a research project is an ambitious undertaking, often extending over several weeks, it should be planned carefully and worked at methodically. The main steps are these:

1. Choosing a topic. The best topic is one that you know something about but not nearly enough to satisfy you. The motivation to learn more gives point and direction to your research. And the motivation to learn more about something *in particular* will protect you from taking on an impossibly large topic. "Robert E. Lee and the Civil War" is too big; "Lee at Gettysburg" is manageable. But neither title tells enough about what kind of reading, thinking, and writing you will need to do. Decide early whether your essay is to be primarily a report or a thesis paper. A report assembles the material available on the subject, recovering or reclaiming information and perhaps presenting it from a fresh perspective. A thesis paper shapes the evidence into support for a hypothesis; it argues a point. The decision to make the paper primarily expository or primarily argumentative has some bearing on the sources you investigate and more on the use you make of the material.

2. Preparing a working bibliography. In your initial canvassing of sources, move systematically from the card catalog to indexes or periodicals to appropriate reference books and special encyclopedias. For information about reference books in your field of interest, consult Constance M. Winchell's *Guide to Reference Books* (8th ed.; Supplements, 1966–68). For each source that looks promising, make out a bibliography card: copy accurately on a 3″ × 5″ or 4″ × 6″ filing card the facts of publication as well as author and title (see Bibliographical form), and note where the source is located in the library. Keep your working bibliography flexible. As you begin your reading, you will discard items that looked promising but turn out to be dead ends, and you will add items from the new sources that keep coming to your attention.

3. Taking notes on sources. In addition to making out bibliography cards that identify your sources, you will need to take notes on what the sources have to say. Record these notes on the same kind of filing cards you use for bibliography notes or, if you prefer, on the pages of a loose-leaf notebook. In either case, restrict yourself to one note – fact, opinion, quotation, or summary – per card or page, with the source and the page number in the upper right corner and, in the upper left corner, an identifying word or phrase to indicate the specific phase of your topic the note bears on.

As you make notes, be sure they distinguish clearly between an author's facts and his opinions, between direct quotation and summary, between what you are taking *from* the source and observations you are making *on* the source (see Paraphrase). You will find it helpful to keep on a separate pad a running log of notes to yourself – comments, questions, hunches that will remind you, when you begin to sift through and arrange your notes, of leads to be followed up, conflicting sources to be weighed, puzzles to be solved, and hypotheses to be tested.

4. Developing an outline. Early in the note-taking stage, sketch a tentative outline for your paper. Keep it fluid. Let it give direction to your thinking, but don't let it channel your ideas too early. Try to divide your material into logical blocks – from five to eight, perhaps – and then keep shifting these units around until you have them in the right order. Once you can discern the shape of the whole, you can write (and rewrite) one section at a time.

5. Writing drafts. Much of a research paper consists of a digest of sources that lead to, support, or elaborate on the researcher's findings or generalizations. In summarizing, interpreting, and analyzing your sources, it is important to represent them accurately and to do so in your own words. But you will not be able to free yourself of the original phrasing unless you first achieve full comprehension of the ideas. Then you can express them in your own words. If you merely tie together a succession of direct quotations from a source, you display no mastery of the material. If you use phrases and clauses from a source without putting them in quotation marks, you leave yourself open to the charge of plagiarism (see Plagiarism).

As you write, keep a close check on the sources you are consulting and summarizing, so that you can give accurate and adequate credit (see Footnote form). Be meticulous in reproducing direct quotations (see Quotation marks 2b). And when you quote, make sure that the passage bears directly on the point you are discussing, that you present it so that its relevance is immediately clear, and that you fit it smoothly into your text.

The style of a research paper should be comparatively formal and impersonal. This does not mean that it should be stilted or dull. Nor does it mean that you need avoid *I;* in some published research, *I* appears regularly. It does mean that you should keep the focus on the subject and what you have managed to find out about it—not on your feelings about it. But since all good research papers reveal the writers' interest in their topics, communicating your own interest will be a natural consequence of engaging yourself fully in your subject.

6. Documenting the paper. Your readers' chief interest will be in the substance of your paper—what you have found out about your subject—and the clarity and force with which you present it. They will also examine the documentation, the footnotes and the bibliography that record your journey of exploration. Check and recheck details of bibliographical form and footnote form for accuracy and consistency.

References: James D. Lester, *Writing Research Papers*, 2nd ed. (Glenview, Ill.: Scott, 1976); Kate L. Turabian, *Student's Guide for Writing College Papers*, 2nd ed., rev. (Chicago: Univ. of Chicago Press, 1970).

rest Restrictive and nonrestrictive

If the modifier marked is restrictive, don't separate it from the word it modifies by a comma. If it is nonrestrictive, set it off by a comma or by two commas.

"Lemmon, who isn't Jewish, plays Jews who aren't Jewish either" (Pauline Kael, *New Yorker*). The first *who* clause in the quoted sentence tells us something about Jack Lemmon, but it doesn't set him apart; it can be dropped from the sentence without destroying the meaning: Lemmon plays Jews who aren't Jewish. But the *who* clause modifying *Jews* is essential to Kael's point: the Jewishness of the characters Lemmon plays is superficial and trivial. Dropping this clause would leave us with "Lemmon plays Jews," which isn't what Kael is saying. Separating the second *who* clause from the main clause with a comma would give us "Lemmon plays Jews, who aren't Jewish," which is nonsense. The first *who* clause is nonrestrictive. The second *who* clause is restrictive.

1. Restrictive modifiers. An adjective (or relative) clause or an adjective phrase is a restrictive (or bound, or limiting) modifier when the information it provides about something in the main clause is essential to the meaning the writer intends.

If you speak a sentence before you write it, or read it aloud after you have written it, you can usually tell whether a clause or phrase is restrictive:

The girl *whose book I borrowed* has dropped the course.
The books *stolen from the library* were found in that locker.

When the modifier is restrictive, there is no pause between the word modified and the clause or phrase that modifies it.

You can be quite sure a clause is restrictive if you begin it with *that:* The year *that I dropped out* is one I'd be glad to forget. And a clause is restrictive if you can omit the relative pronoun: The year [*that*] *I dropped out;* The people [*whom*] *we met;* The plan [*which*] *they came up with.*

2. Nonrestrictive modifiers. An adjective (or relative) clause or adjective phrase that can be dropped from a sentence without changing or blurring the meaning is nonrestrictive and should be set off by a comma or commas. The importance of the information the modifier provides is not the deciding factor. If you write, "The bullet *which came within an inch of my head* smashed my mother's favorite teacup," the content of your adjective clause is certainly dramatic and significant. But unless you are using the clause to specify *this* bullet among a number of bullets, you must set it off with commas.

If *which* were used to launch only nonrestrictive clauses, as *that* is used to launch restrictive clauses, *which* and *that* clauses would cause few problems. But there are times when *which* seems a better choice for starting a restrictive clause: That was the bad news *which we had been given every reason to expect.* (*Which* avoids the repetition of *that.*) And some clauses are restrictive in one context, nonrestrictive in another. In a different context, the clause *whose book I borrowed,* used as an example of a restrictive clause in the preceding section, can be nonrestrictive: The girl, whose book I borrowed, left soon afterward with an older woman. So can the example of a restrictive phrase: The books, stolen from the library, later turned up in a second-hand store.

Your job, then, is to know what you mean. In the modifying clause or phrase, do you mean to say something that the sentence requires for its basic meaning, or do you mean to offer information which—no matter how important—could be omitted from that sentence without detracting from its central message? If the former, the modifier is restrictive—no commas. If the latter, the modifier is nonrestrictive—commas. Say the sentence out loud. Do you make a definite pause before the modifier? Then it's nonrestrictive—commas.

You may find the same advice useful in punctuating other modifiers. Traditionally, the restrictive/nonrestrictive distinction has applied to a dependent clause introduced by a relative pronoun and functioning as an adjective. Some grammarians extend the principle to all adjectival modifiers, to appositives (see Apposition, appositives), and to some adverbial modifiers, including final adverbial clauses (see Comma 2b). References: Christensen, pp. 95–110; Quirk et al., pp. 261–62, 622–25, 638–48, 858–76.

rhetoric

In its classical, neutral sense of "the art of persuasion," *rhetoric* is now used mainly in formal contexts. In textbooks like this one, it is broadened to mean "the study of the making, the qualities, and the effects of verbal discourse." But *rhetoric* has a wide range of other interpretations, some of which stress its baser uses, some its more dignified, as in these quotations from the same issue of the *Shakespeare Quarterly:*

. . . the great Swiss writer, Ferdinand Ramuz, whom no one has ever accused of rhetoric. – Robert Speaight

A lucid, chaste Virgilian rhetoric. . . . – Howard Felperin

In general usage, where derogatory senses of the word prevail, *rhetoric* frequently suggests flamboyant insincerity, unprincipled manipulation of emotion, or empty verbiage. Currently a writer can assume that most audiences will regard *rhetoric* as a term of abuse.

The suggestion of empty verbiage is equally strong in current uses of *rhetorical:* "It will be interesting to see how many men are prepared to give more than rhetorical support today to the sex from which they have, for centuries, demanded and accepted so much" (Adrienne Rich, *Chronicle of Higher Education*).

Rhetoric

Whenever a writer asks anything of his reader – agreement, understanding, belief, action, even just a laugh – he is within the province of rhetoric. As he composes an essay, every decision he makes, from the selection of the material to the choice of a particular word, should be guided by his sense of the rhetorical situation. Some of these decisions he makes intuitively, some out of habit, some after carefully weighing alternatives.

The chief elements in a rhetorical situation are the writer, his subject, his purpose, and his audience. Each of these elements is influenced by the other three; each offers opportunities and imposes limits. As you plan an essay, and especially as you revise it, questions like the following will sharpen your sense of the rhetorical situation:

What do I want to say about this subject?

Do I have enough information and evidence now, or do I need to dig for more?

Who are my readers? How much do they know about the subject, and what is their attitude toward it? What are their tastes, habits, values, fears, hopes, prejudices?

What common ground is there between us, what shared assumptions? What can I take for granted, and what do I have to explain or argue for?

How can I make my readers see what I want them to see, think the way I want them to think, do what I want them to do? Should I start by declaring what my purpose is, or would my readers be more responsive if I invited them to take part in an inquiry with me, if I raised problems that we would try to solve together?

How can I make my readers identify with me, share my feeling about the situation? How can I make them understand and adopt my point of view?

Will this detail, this bit of evidence, have more weight than that one? If so, should it come first or last? How can I phrase this idea so that it will be both clear and compelling? How can I make this sentence say precisely what I mean?

Will *this* word, *this* image, *this* mark of punctuation work with *this* audience? Do I need to make my style simpler, more relaxed, or does my relationship with my readers require increased distance, greater objectivity, a style that is altogether more formal?

What side of my personality do I want to come through in this essay? How do I want my readers to see me?

As these questions suggest, you can assess the appropriateness of what you are saying and how you are saying it only in a specific rhetorical situation. The arguments you advance, the evidence you offer, the organization you adopt, the language you select—all these should be tested, as you revise your essay, for their fitness in communicating to the particular audience your thoughts and feelings about your subject.

See Introduction, pp. 1–7. References: Douglas Ehninger, *Contemporary Rhetoric* (Glenview, Ill.: Scott, 1972); Porter G. Perrin in *Perspectives in English,* ed. Robert C. Pooley (New York: Appleton, 1960), pp. 121–32; Joseph Schwartz and John A. Rycenga, eds., *The Province of Rhetoric* (New York: Ronald, 1965); W. Ross Winterowd, *Rhetoric: A Synthesis* (New York: Holt, 1968).

Rhetorical questions

Rhetorical questions are really statements in the form of questions, since no direct answer is expected: "Did not Henry James, in using the family letters, perversely alter William's Old Abe into President Lincoln?" (Lewis Mumford, *New York Review of Books*). As a stylistic device, the rhetorical question will be a flop if the reader rejects the answer the writer intends.

right

In the sense of "very," *right* is a localism, in good standing in the South: We'll be right glad to see you. The use of *right* before phrases of place and time (right across the street, right after the show) is avoided in most formal writing but is established in general usage.

Phrases like *right here, right there, right now,* and *right then* are similarly avoided in formal contexts though commonplace in general. Idioms like *right away* and *right off* ("at once" or "now") and *right along* ("continuously" or "all the time") are slightly more informal.

rise, arise, get up

In referring to standing up or getting out of bed, *arise* is formal and poetic; *rise* is somewhat less formal; the general idiom is *get up.*

rob

A person or place is robbed. What is taken in the robbery is stolen. *Rob* for *steal* (They're the ones who robbed the money) is an old usage considered nonstandard today.

Roman numerals

Roman numerals may be either lowercase (iii, v, x) or capitals (III, V, X). See Numbers 3.

round, around

Round is a preposition and adverb in its own right, often interchangeable with *around:* "an easy irony, good for a laugh the first two or three times round" (Stanley Kaufmann, *New Republic*). It should not be written with an initial apostrophe ('round).

Around for "approximately" (around 1920, a cast of around forty) is now found in all varieties of usage.

The general adjectives *all-round* and *all-around* are overused, particularly with *athlete.*

Run-on sentence

The label *run-on sentence* is applied variously to a sentence in which two independent clauses are run together with no punctuation between, to a sentence in which two independent clauses are joined with only a comma between, and to a sentence in which a series of independent clauses are joined with coordinating conjunctions. As a result, *run-on* is more confusing than useful. See Comma fault, Fused sentence.

said

As a modifier (the said person, the said idea) *said* is legal language. In general writing, *that* or *this* or simple *the* is the right choice.

saint

The abbreviation *St.* is commonly used in names of places (St. Albans, St. Louis) and often before the names of saints (St. Francis, St. Anthony of Padua), though some stylebooks call for spell-

ing out *Saint* in both cases. The plural of the abbreviation is *SS*.
(SS. Peter and Paul). Occasionally the French feminine form,
Sainte, is used (Sault Sainte Marie); the abbreviation is *Ste*.
Spanish forms are common in the West; San Diego, Santa Bar-
bara. In writing a personal name beginning with *Saint* (Camille
Saint-Saëns) or *St*. (Louis St. Laurent), the spelling established
by the bearer should be followed.

same

Because *same* without *the* suggests legal or commercial jargon
(We enclose payment for same), it is obtrusive and inappropriate
in normal prose.

say

Say is the usual word for "speaking" and can also be used for
what is written: In his journal, Gide says. . . . In dialog the repetition of "he said," "she said" is almost always preferable to the
use of strained alternatives like *expostulated, muttered, bab-
bled*. *State*, which implies a formal "saying," is a poor substitute
for *say*, whether in dialog or in ordinary text: "To be able to state
this of the new work of an American poet of 50 is, to state the
least, unusual" (Aram Saroyan, *New York Times Book Review*).
Assert and similar substitutes are also unsatisfactory in most
contexts. See *claim*. Reference: Copperud, p. 240.

　　Say in the sense of "approximately," "for instance," "let us
say," is used in all varieties of writing: "the specialist in the literature of, say, the English eighteenth century" (Howard Mumford Jones, *Journal of the History of Ideas*).

scarcely

Since *scarcely* means "probably not," adding a *not* as in "can't
scarcely" is redundant. See Double negative 2.

scenario

A vogue word of the 1970s, *scenario* has taken on meanings having little connection with "script" or "synopsis." Often it should
be replaced with *plan, prediction*, or *possibility*. The difficulty
for the reader is in deciding which: "The scenario isn't as far-
fetched as it may sound" (Joann S. Lublin, *Wall Street Journal*).

seem

Seem is often used needlessly to qualify a statement: They [seem
to] run with a gang that can't [seem to] keep out of trouble. So
used, it loses its power to distinguish between appearance and
reality. Limit your use of *seem* to situations in which you must
be tentative; don't say something *seems to be* when you mean
something *is*. See *can't help but, can't seem to*.

self

Self as a suffix forms the reflexive and intensive pronouns: *myself, yourself, himself, herself, itself, oneself, ourselves, your-*

selves, themselves. These are used chiefly for emphasis (I can do that myself) or as objects identical to the subjects of their verbs (I couldn't help myself). See *himself, herself; myself;* Pronouns 2.

As a prefix, *self* is joined to the root word by a hyphen: *self-control, self-explanatory, self-made, self-respect.* When *self* is the root word, there is no hyphen: *selfhood, selfish, selfless.*

semi-

Semi- is a prefix meaning "half or approximately half" (*semicylindrical*), "twice within a certain period" (*semiweekly, semiannual*), or "partially, imperfectly" (*semicivilized, semiprofessional*). It is a live element in forming new words.

✎ *semi* Semicolon

Use a semicolon as the link between these sentence elements.

1. To link coordinate clauses.

a. Between clauses without connectives. Use a semicolon, especially in a rather formal context, to link two independent clauses whose relatedness you want to emphasize:

The auto industry has become a state within a state; its activities cannot and should not escape continuing public scrutiny. — *Consumer Reports*

Some years ago, a learned colleague who was old and ill complained to me that he could no longer read German; it made his legs feel queer. I know that feeling well; I have had it while trying to read Henry James. — P. B. Ballard, *Thought and Language*

b. With conjunctive adverbs. Use a semicolon to link clauses connected by a conjunctive adverb such as *however, moreover, therefore:*

His popularity was undiminished; however, he no longer enjoyed the work.

Finally, despite the hopes and prophecies described before, we do not really agree on philosophical and political values; therefore the conference, moved by the same desire for survival and development as the world at large, carefully avoided exposing the ideological differences that remain. — Stanley Hoffman, *Daedalus*

A comma before *however* or *therefore* in these sentences would produce a comma fault. See Conjunctive adverbs.

c. With coordinating conjunctions. Consider using a semicolon between clauses connected by a coordinating conjunction (*and, but, for, or . . .*) if the clauses are long, if they contain commas, or if for some reason — perhaps for contrast — you want to indicate a more definite break than you could show with a comma:

Words that are beautifully written by a scribe seemed to address his eye and mind in a personal way that was obliterated by mechanical type; and a manuscript illuminated by hand-painted miniatures gave him a pleasure that no woodcut could equal. — Edgar Wind, *Harper's*

I do not suggest that as English teachers we stop talking about planning and organization; nor am I saying that logical thought has nothing to do with the organizational process. — Robert Zoellner, *College English*

2. To separate units with internal commas. The units may be figures, scores, verbal items in series, or internally punctuated clauses:

Three things which a social system can provide or withhold are helpful to mental creation: first, technical training; second, liberty to follow the creative impulse; third, at least the possibility of ultimate appreciation of some public, whether large or small. — Bertrand Russell, *Proposed Roads to Freedom*

3. Semicolon and colon. Don't use a semicolon to introduce a quotation or a listing or to perform conventional functions of the colon (see Colon 3). In linking clauses, however, you sometimes have a choice. The colon is more formal and carries a suggestion that the second clause will explain or illustrate the first; but often the choice is chiefly if not solely stylistic.

4. Semicolons and style. Semicolons are more suitable in the longer, more complicated sentences of formal styles than in general and informal writing. Since they slow the pace, they are more common in exposition than in narrative. In general styles commas are often used where semicolons might appear in formal writing, or clauses that could be linked by semicolons are written as separate sentences. The use of a semicolon, then, is often as much a matter of style as of correct punctuation.

Compare Colon, Comma. References: Follett, pp. 418–23; Summey, pp. 97–101; Whitehall, pp. 121–22.

sensual, sensuous

Both *sensual* and *sensuous* refer to the senses, but the connotations of *sensual* are more physical, of *sensuous* more aesthetic. Sensual music and sensuous music are two different things.

Sentence fragment

A sentence fragment is a part of a sentence that is punctuated as if it were a complete sentence. See Fragment.

Sentences

1. Classifying sentences grammatically. On the basis of their clause structure, sentences are classified grammatically as simple, complex, compound, and compound-complex. Each of these types of sentences can be expanded by making subjects, verbs, and objects compound and by using appositives and modifiers. According to transformational theory, all such expansions, as well as all dependent clauses, represent sentences in the deep structure that have been embedded in the surface-structure sentence. Even a grammatically simple sentence is usually the product of some embedding — the normal process of packing meaning into sentences. See Absolute phrases, Clauses, Deep structure.

2. Analyzing sentences rhetorically. A sentence is not only a grammatical unit but also a rhetorical unit. A rhetorical analysis of a sentence takes into account the order of elements, the repetition of grammatical structures, and the appropriateness of such ordering and repeating to the idea expressed. See Balanced sentence, Cumulative sentence, Parallelism, Periodic sentence, Phrases 2.

3. Building sensible sentences. A writer should build his clauses and arrange their parts so as to bring out the natural and logical relationships in his material. Subordination and parallelism, for example, clarify such relationships when they are properly used. Misused, they blur or distort them. If embedding is a way of packing more meaning into a sentence, reversing the process – converting some elements into separate sentences – can unburden an overloaded sentence and improve its unity and clarity. See Coordination, Shifted constructions, Subordination.

Although some structures that lack an independent subject-verb combination are rhetorically effective, most sentences have at least one independent subject-verb combination. Generally, faults in sentence construction result from failure to recognize the difference between a dependent clause and an independent clause or from failure to show the relation between a modifier and what it modifies. See Comma fault, Dangling modifiers, Fragment, Fused sentence.

Sequence of tenses
In some sentences the tense of a verb in one clause is determined by the tense of a verb in another: When he drives, I brace [*not* braced] myself. See Tense 3.

Series
A succession of words, phrases, or clauses that are grammatically coordinate makes a series. Sometimes the units are simply separated by commas – "the people who cared for Eliot – Cross, Lewes, Edith Simcox, Maria Lewis, Sara Hennell" (Michael Wood, *New York Review of Books*) – but usually the last unit is joined to the rest by a coordinating conjunction. Usage is divided over putting a comma before the conjunction:

It was a novel, confusing, and unnecessary argument. – Richard Harris, *New Yorker*

Another patron . . . came to see the go-go boys with her mother, her sister [ ] and her Kodak movie camera. – Jeannette Smyth, *Washington Post*

Though many writers, especially in general and informal styles, omit the comma, its presence helps to indicate that the units are equivalent, and in some instances it prevents misunderstanding (see Comma 5). If the units are long or have commas within them, they are often separated by semicolons (see Semicolons 2).

For the rhetorical effects of a series, see Parallelism, Parallelism and style, Phrases 2.

set, sit

In standard English, people and things *sit* (past: *sat*) or they are *set* (past: *set*)—that is, are "placed":

I like to sit in a hotel lobby.
I have sat in this same seat for three semesters.
She set the soup down with a flourish.
The post was set three feet in the ground.

A hen, however, sets (on her eggs), cement sets, and the sun sets. A large dining room table sits eight, and few city people know how to sit a horse. Reference: Pooley, pp. 160–63.

Sexist language

Since the revival of the movement for equality of the sexes, there has been much criticism of sexism both in current usage and in the grammar of formal English. Examples of usage that patronizes or denigrates women include labels like *working girls, coed, the little woman, the weaker sex, boss lady, woman driver,* and *lady doctor* and the suffixes *-ess* and *-ette: poetess, Jewess, suffragette, usherette.* Similarly offensive to many is the use of first names for women where men's full names or last names are used: Before Robert Browning came to know her, Elizabeth was already considered a rival of Tennyson.

Add to these the words for certain occupations and offices that seem to imply that women are excluded: *policeman, businessman, chairman, Congressman.* And to many most galling of all is the use of *man* and *men* to stand for *men-and-women* (*manpower, the common man, man-made, free men*) and for the whole human race (*prehistoric man, mankind,* "all men are equal," "the brotherhood of man") and the use of *he* (*him, his*) as the pronoun referring to a noun that doesn't specify gender or to an indefinite pronoun (*student, citizen, spectator, person, anyone, no one*).

Although some feminists attach relatively little importance to sexist language, others see it as a subtle but powerful conditioner of attitudes toward the sexes from very early childhood. For those who are seriously concerned, the substitution of *-woman* for *-man* in the words for occupations and offices (*policewoman, businesswoman, Congresswoman*) is no solution to the problem. Like *lady doctor* and *woman driver,* it calls attention to gender where gender is not, or should not be, of any significance. (*Male nurse* belongs in the same category. Opponents of sexist language deplore terms that stereotype either men or women.)

Person(s), people, and *humans* are common substitutes for *man, men, mankind* when both sexes are intended. An increasing number of writers now avoid the traditional use of *he* to stand for *he or she* by using the latter in its various forms: Everyone must turn in his or her theme. . . . But because the wordiness is easily compounded and awkwardness is almost inevitable (. . . if he or she wants a passing grade), there is now a growing tendency to write in the plural (All students must turn in their themes . . .) or to treat *they* as an indefinite common-gender singular (Everyone must turn in their themes . . .). See Agreement 2, *he or she, they.*

If you consider sexism in language an issue of overriding importance, then as a writer you will avoid all the usages described as sexist, including the use of *man* for an individual of either sex and any age and the use of *he* for *he or she*. If you don't believe that sexism exists in the language, or don't care if it does, or applaud the masculine bias, you will ignore the whole matter. But if you belong to neither of these extremes, there are choices to be made. Even if you are mainly satisfied with the language as it is used, you should be aware that your readers may not be. You can easily avoid the more obtrusive sexist usages, such as descriptive terms that classify women physically when their looks have no relevance (the senator's red-headed wife) or that imply a general lack of intelligence and competence (a cute pre-med student). You may also decide to seek substitutes for the *-man* words and to cut down on your use of generic *he* in sentences like "When a young person says he is interested in helping people, his counselor tells him to become a psychiatrist."

How far you go will depend in part on your own sensitivities as writers. If your sense of style causes you to wince at *he or she* (or *he/she*), if the connotations of *artificial* make it impossible for you to accept it as a substitute for *man-made*, if *persons* and *humans* bother you at least as much as generic *man*, then you face much more difficult choices than those who can settle the problem to their own satisfaction with the rhetorical question, "What's more important – syntax or souls?" For those truly torn between the demands of feminist ideology and the demands of stylistic grace and flow, the only solution is a long grind of writing and revising and rewriting until at last the conflicts are resolved and both ideological and aesthetic demands are satisfied.

In this book *he* is used to refer to *student* and *writer* not because of bias or obtuseness but in the interest of economy and style.

shall, will

Since the eighteenth century some grammarians have insisted that in expressing determination, obligation, or prohibition in statements about the future, *will* should be used with first-person subjects and *shall* with second- and third-; but practice has never been uniform. In current American usage either auxiliary occurs with all three persons. *Will* is more common. The same grammarians have sought to keep the single function of indicating the future distinct by urging that *shall* be used with first-person subjects and *will* with second- and third-; but again, in standard usage *will* is much more common than *shall* with all persons. In questions, *shall* is common only in the first person: Shall I go first? Will you come later? See *should, would.* References: Bryant, pp. 182–83; Copperud, pp. 243–44; Fries, pp. 150–67; Pooley, pp. 47–52.

Shifted constructions

Avoid the unnecessary shift in construction.

Shifted constructions are needless changes in grammatical form or point of view within a sentence. In speech and in much informal writing, shifted constructions are common, but in general and formal prose they are avoided because they trouble a careful reader. The many types of needless shift include the following:

1. Between adjective and noun: This book is interesting and an informative piece of work. *Revised:* . . . interesting and informative.

2. Between noun and clause: The most important factors are time and temperature, careful control at every point, and the mechanical equipment must be efficient. *Revised:* . . . and efficient mechanical equipment.

3. Between adverb phrase and adjective phrase: Along these walks are the cottages, some of which have stood since the founding but others quite recent. *Revised:* . . . but others for only a short time.

4. Between gerund and infinitive: Carrying four courses and to hold down a job at the same time will either develop my character or kill me. *Revised:* Carrying four courses and holding down a job . . . .

5. Between gerund and finite verb: I have heard complaints about the plot being weak and that the setting is played up too much. *Revised:* . . . and the setting being played up. . . .

6. Between participle and finite verb: You often see a fisherman trying to get quietly to his favorite spot but instead he broadcasts warnings with his rhythmical squeak-splash, squeak-splash. *Revised:* . . . but instead broadcasting warnings. . . .

7. Between transitive verb and copula: Anyone who has persistence or is desperate enough can get a job on a ship. *Revised:* . . . who is persistent or who is desperate enough. . . .

8. Between past and present: The tanks bulled their way through the makeshift barricades and fan out across the enormous plaza. *Revised:* . . . and fanned out. . . .

9. Between active and passive: The committee members disliked each other heartily, and their time was wasted in wrangling. *Revised:* . . . heartily and wasted their time in wrangling.

10. Between personal and impersonal: When one is sick, you make few plans. *Revised:* When one is sick, one [or he] makes. . . .

No enumeration of shifted constructions could be complete: there are too many constructions to shift.

See Parallelism and style; Point of view; Reference of pronouns; Tense 2, 3; *when, where.*

Shoptalk

Shoptalk is the words that people in the same occupation use among themselves to refer to the things they regularly concern themselves with in their work: the noun *mud* among bricklayers to mean "mortar," the verb *docket* among lawyers to mean "make an abstract."

No occupation gets along without shoptalk; all have everyday terms that may be unintelligible to outsiders but are indispensable to those who practice the trade or profession. Especially convenient are short, informal substitutes for long technical terms. So a *mike* may be a microphone in a broadcasting studio, a microscope in a laboratory, a micrometer in a shop; a *hypo* is a fixing bath to a photographer, a hypodermic injection to a nurse. Many such words are metaphoric (the television *ghost*) or imitative (the radar *blip*). Much shoptalk is so specialized or colorless that it has never spread to the general vocabulary—printshop words, for example, like *chase, em, pi, quoins.*

Many words and meanings from shoptalk are given in general dictionaries with the names of the occupations they belong to, but most are listed and adequately defined only in more specialized books. So long as they remain narrowly specialized, they are inappropriate in writing for general audiences.

See Jargon. See also Gobbledygook, Psychologese, Slang. References: Mencken, pp. 709–61, and many articles in *American Speech.*

should, would

In indirect discourse, *should* and *would* can function as the past tenses of *shall* and *will.* "We will go" can be reported as "He announced that we would go," and "We shall go" as "He announced that we should go." Since *should* has a connotation of obligation or propriety that may not be intended, *would* is preferred. See *shall, will;* Tense 3. Reference: Pooley, pp. 52–53.

sic

Sic, the Latin word meaning "thus," is properly used to indicate that what precedes it has been quoted correctly. See Brackets.

sick, ill

Ill is the more formal, less common word. In the United States they mean the same thing. In British usage *sick* is usually restricted to mean "nauseated": "The mere touch of the thing would make me sick or ill, or both" (Richard Jones, *The Three Suitors*). In American usage *sick* in that sense is made clear by adding a phrase: It made me sick to [at/in] my stomach.

Simile

A simile compares with *like* or *as:* He swims like a winded walrus; straight as a lodgepole pine. See Figurative language.

Simple sentence

A simple sentence consists of one independent subject-predicate combination. See Clauses 1.

since

As a subordinating conjunction, *since* has the meaning "because": Since we were already late, we didn't rush. See *because.*

sit, set

People and things *sit* or *are set.* See *set, sit.*

-size

Size is typical of a class of nouns (*age, color, height, shape, width, weight* . . .) that also function as apparent modifiers: *medium-size, standard-size, life-size, outsize, oversize.* The *-size* words are redundant in compound modifiers with adjectives that might modify the head nouns directly: not "small-size box" but "small box," and similarly with "round-shape table," "younger-age students," "dark-color hair," and so on. See Wordiness 1.

Slang

Drawing a line between slang and other sorts of informal English is difficult. Many people use the term *slang* too broadly, applying it to almost any informal word, and dictionaries have been too generous with the label, marking as slang many words that simply suggest spoken rather than written style. In fact, there is no fully accepted criterion for marking off the segment of the vocabulary that constitutes slang, as disagreement among and between dictionaries and handbooks makes clear.

Though some of the words labeled slang in current dictionaries—*lulu, corker, deadbeat*—have been around for generations, the central characteristic of slang comes from the motive in using it: a desire for novelty, for vivid emphasis, for being up with the times or a little ahead; for belonging—either to a particular social group or, more broadly, to an age group or, more broadly still, to the in-group that uses the current slang. These are essentially qualities of style, and the tone and connotation are as important as the meaning of the words. Other varieties of language have ways of expressing the ideas of slang words, but their tone is more conventional. Young people like novelty, as do grown-ups with youthful ideas, and entertainers need it in their trade. In-groups, both legal and illegal, have their slang vocabularies, which often spill over into general English: some of the slang of the drug culture has wide circulation among nonusers.

Slang is made by natural linguistic processes. It abounds in clipped words (*marvy, natch, hood*) and in compounds and derivatives of ordinary words (*screwball, sourpuss, cockeyed, put-on, rip-off*). Many are borrowed from the shoptalk of sports and the popular arts, especially jazz and rock. And a great many are figurative extensions of general words: *nut, dope, egg* (applied to people); *heavy, hung up, spaced out.* Sound often contributes a good deal, as in *barf, booboo, goof, zap, zip, zonk.*

Since many slang words have short lives, any discussion of slang in print is bound to be out of date. *Twenty-three skidoo, vamoose, beat it, scram, hit the trail, take a powder, drag out, shag out, cut out, split* succeeded each other almost within a generation. Words for being drunk (*soused, plastered, bombed*), for girls (*baby, doll, chick, bird, sister*), and words of approval (*tops, neat, the most, cool, groovy, out of sight, baddest*) and disapproval (*all wet, cruddy, gross, a hype*) change from year to year—though some survive and some recur. Many slang words prove permanently useful and become a part of the informal vocabulary (*blind date, boy friend, go steady*) or the general (*highbrow, lowbrow*).

The chief objection to slang in writing, aside from its conspicuousness, is that it elbows out more exact expressions. A slang cliché is at least as boring as a cliché in standard English, and slang that names general impressions instead of specific ones is in no way preferable to comparable words in the general vocabulary, like *nice* and *good.* If slang expressions are appropriate to the subject matter and the audience and if they come naturally to the writer, they should be used without apology (that is, without quotation marks). If they are not appropriate, they should not be used, with or without quotation marks.

References: Mencken, Ch. 11; Harold Wentworth and Stuart Berg Flexner, eds. and comps., *Dictionary of American Slang,* 2nd ed. (New York: Crowell, 1975).

slow, slowly

Both *slow* and *slowly* are used as adverbs. *Slow* is more vigorous and is widely used in speech and in informal writing in place of *slowly,* but in general usage it is restricted to only a few contexts: He drove *slow; but* He drove away *slowly.* See Adverbs and style 1, Divided usage. Compare *bad, badly.* Reference: Copperud, p. 246.

so

1. *So* and *so that.* To introduce clauses of purpose, *so that* is ordinarily expected in formal contexts, but *so* by itself is respectable in general use:

[The ghost of] Patroclus comes to ask Achilles to bury him quickly so that he may pass into the realm of Hades.—Anne Amory, *Yale Classical Studies*

I might have tried . . . to give a clearer idea of the rest of the contents, so readers could gather some notion of whether or not this kind of material might interest them. — John Thompson, *New York Review of Books*

To express consequence or result, both *so* alone and *so that* are found in all varieties of usage. *Speculum: A Journal of Mediaeval Studies* had these two passages in the same issue:

The old bishop was better known as a fighter than as a churchman, so we may reasonably assume that it was prudence and not cowardice which prompted him. — Herbert L. Oerter

He quotes frequently from the Old French, so that the reader gains a very good appreciation of the style. — Alfred Foulet

2. So as substitute. *So* can substitute for a whole clause: I think *I will win;* at least I hope *so.*

3. So as an intensive. As an intensive, *so* is informal: He's so handsome!
   References: Bryant, pp. 190–93; Copperud, pp. 246–47.

so . . . as

So . . . as is sometimes used in negative comparisons of degree: not so wide as a barn door. See *as . . . as* 3.

so-called

If you have to use *so-called*, don't duplicate the idea by putting the name of the so-called object in quotes: the so-called champion, *not* the so-called "champion."

some

1. As a subject. *Some* as a subject takes either a singular verb (Some of the material is difficult) or a plural verb (Some of the tests are easy), depending on the context.

2. As an adverb. *Some* as a qualifier is informal: He is some older than she is. More formal usage would have *somewhat.* Informally, *some* is also used to modify verbs (The springs were squeaking some).
   In formal writing the adverb *someplace* is still avoided in favor of *somewhere*, but in the last generation or so *someplace* has moved from informal to general usage: "I began to get some idea of what I came to call the Civilization of the Dialogue, a phrase I am sure I stole someplace" (Robert M. Hutchins, *Saturday Review*). *Somewheres* is nonstandard. Compare *any.*

3. As one word or two. The compounds *somebody, someway, somewhat, somewhere* are written as one word. *Someone* is one word (Someone is coming) unless *one* is stressed (some one of them). *Someday* is written as either one word or two. *Sometime* in "Drop in sometime" means "at some time [two words] in the future."

sort

Sort takes a singular verb even when it is followed by *of* and a plural noun: That sort of men deserves shooting. See *kind, sort.*

Sound

In good writing, sound reinforces sense. In bad writing, sound distracts attention from sense. See Alliteration, Assonance, Repetition 3.

Spelling

Correct the spelling of the word marked, referring to a dictionary if necessary.

Use your dictionary, and when alternative spellings are listed, choose the first. The following *Index* articles deal with spelling:

Apostrophe	Foreign words in English	Plurals of nouns
Capital letters	Hyphen	Principal parts of verbs

See also Analogy in language, British English, Divided usage.

Split infinitive

An infinitive is said to be split when an adverb or an adverbial element separates the *to* from its following verb: The receptionist asked them to kindly sit down.

The split infinitive gets more attention than it deserves. Many people have been taught to avoid it scrupulously; and sometimes there is good reason to do so. Certainly, long intervening elements are awkward and should be moved, often to the end of the sentence: After a while he was able to, although not very accurately, distinguish good customers from disloyal ones.

On principle, moreover, formal writing does rather consistently avoid the split infinitive, even when the adverb cannot be placed at the end of the clause:

We must have sufficient foresight and vision patiently to guide the peoples of the world along the road they have chosen to follow. — Bernard Kiernan, *American Scholar*

The Chinese model . . . never eclipsed the local differences that made Japan always and Korea sometimes so distinct from China as properly to constitute a separate civilization. — William H. McNeill, *The Rise of the West*

But if long intervening elements are awkward, short adverbs that modify the infinitive may fit most smoothly and clearly between the *to* and the verb; and for such reasons split infinitives often occur in unquestionably reputable general writing. The first of the following citations, for example, would be ambiguous if "really" were placed before "to" and unidiomatic if it were placed after "hate." In the second, "precisely to locate" might be ambiguous, and "to locate precisely enough" would invite misreading:

To really hate the old ruling class we would have to live under it in its days of decay. — John K. Fairbank, *New Republic*

The major mission of Apollo 10 was to precisely locate enough lunar landmarks to prevent the crewmen of Apollo 11 from dropping onto terrain for which they would be unprepared. — John Lear, *Saturday Review*

When the prejudice against the split infinitive makes a writer bend over backwards to avoid it, his meaning is often unclear:

She had demonstrated her inability to rear properly numerous other children.

Myrdal replies that it should be the proper function of planning constantly to strengthen nongovernmental structures.

In the first sentence the adverb "properly" can be read as if it modifies "numerous"; in the second, "constantly" might modify "planning." Both sentences can be improved by splitting the infinitives.

References: Bryant, pp. 194–97; Follett, p. 313; Fowler, pp. 579–82; Fries, pp. 132, 144–45; Pooley, pp. 96–101; Quirk et al., p. 725; Roberts, pp. 204–206.

Spoken and written English

Though talking and writing are related, overlapping skills, they differ in several respects. Speech is peppered with expressions that seldom appear in writing other than recorded dialog: "OK," "y'know," "y'see," "Right?" and all the grunts and murmurs that ask for and provide feedback in conversation. When we talk, we pay less attention to the shape of our sentences than when we write. We are more casual about pronoun reference and agreement; we let *and* do most of the work of joining statements; we rarely make the effort to build phrases and clauses in parallel series; and we scarcely ever use the nonrestrictive clause. (We might write, "Picasso, who was born in Spain, never lost his fondness for Barcelona"; but we would probably say, "Picasso was born in Spain, and he always loved Barcelona.")

The number of significant differentiations in sound that all of us use is much larger than the number of symbols in our writing system. In talk, words are always part of a pattern involving pitch and stress, for which the marks of punctuation provide only the barest hints. Writing therefore blurs or overlooks a great many speech signals—including the stance, the gesture, even the slight rise of an eyebrow that may reinforce or modify the messages sent by speech. Whether "more" modifies "competent" or "competent men" in "more competent men" would be shown in speech by stress (heavier stress on the "more" that modifies "competent men"). To make the distinction in writing, rewording might be necessary: more men who are competent, more truly competent men.

But if we can communicate some things more directly in talk than in writing, the reverse is also true. Punctuation indicates quotations efficiently, including quotations within quotations. Spelling distinguishes some homophones that would be ambiguous in speech: We'll halve it; We'll have it. Because writing can be reread, it's a surer means of communicating difficult material—detailed, complicated instructions, for instance. And because writing can be repeatedly revised, it can be more precise, better organized, more economical than talk.

Though language originated as speech and though writing came very late in its history (only some six thousand years ago), it is legitimate to speak of the written language (or at least of the writing styles of a language) as an entity in itself. Most prose literature was written to be communicated through the eye, not the ear; and though reading aloud often increases its effectiveness, the survival of literature depends mainly on its capacity for communicating without the direct use of sound.

Yet in spite of their differences, written English and spoken English have a close relationship. When we say someone "talks like a book," we mean that his talk is uncomfortably elaborate or stiff; it is more often a compliment to say that he "writes the way he talks." For most purposes we value writing that has the colloquial flavor of good talk. But having the flavor of talk and being just like talk—even good talk—are by no means the same. Even informal written English, the written English that comes closest to casual speech, has to be far more coherent, far more selective, far less casual than casual speech if it is to be read with ease and comprehension.

See Colloquial English.

spoonful, spoonfuls

Spoonfuls is the plural of *spoonful.* See *-ful, full.*

Squinting modifier

A squinting modifier looks in two directions: it may refer to the word or phrase that precedes it or to the word or phrase that follows it. See Ambiguity 2a, Split infinitive.

Standard English

Standard English is the social dialect used by the American middle class. Because the educated members of that class use it, they approve it; and because they are the dominant class in the United States, what they approve is standard. Both spoken standard English and written standard English can be divided into formal, general, and informal, as in this book, or into different and more numerous categories. But when used appropriately, all the locutions called standard are supposed to be acceptable to all educated users of the language. In fact, there is disagreement, in dictionaries, English texts, and books on language etiquette, about a good many usages. Nevertheless, there is agreement about the great majority of them, and it is the chief purpose of this book to call attention to the areas of agreement and to encourage the intelligent use of standard English. See Introduction, pp. 3–7; Nonstandard English; Usage.

state

When you mean no more than *said*, don't use *stated.* See *say.*

strata

In formal usage *stratum* is singular and *strata* plural. In general English *strata* is sometimes construed as a singular, but readers who know Latin condemn that usage. Reference: Copperud, p. 251.

Style

Style is choice. Style consists of the choices a writer makes—choice of words, choice of sentence patterns, even choice among optional ways of punctuating. If there were not many different ways of expressing ideas, there would be no such thing as style.

Style is character. Or, as the famous aphorism has it, "Style is the man." How a writer attacks a problem, how he arranges his material, the manner in which he makes his assertions, the "voice" he speaks in—all these reveal something about that writer's personality, his values, his *life* style.

There need be no contradiction between these two views of style if we think of style as the sum of choices, *conscious or unconscious*, that a writer makes among the options offered by the language. Such matters as basic word order in sentences and the ways of forming plurals and indicating verb tenses are part of the structure of English and therefore not stylistic. But other matters—the ways sentences are linked, their relative length and complexity, the placing of those elements that are movable, the connotations and figurative values of the words used—give a passage the distinctive features that we call style. Some of these features are the result of unconscious choice, reflecting linguistic habits and ways of thought that the writer is not aware of; some of them are the product of deliberate calculation. To the extent that style is the result of such conscious choice, it can be improved.

A style is good or bad, effective or ineffective, insofar as it achieves or fails to achieve the writer's purpose, wins or fails to win the response he wants from his readers. One of the best ways of improving your style is to analyze the prose of writers you admire, trying to determine how, in their choosing of words and shaping of sentences, they have won your response. The more you know about the choices the language affords, the more likely you are to write with clarity, force, and grace, qualities that are the foundation of all good styles. And through constant experimenting and rewriting, you will, if you have something you want to say, find your own style, your own voice.

Because syntax, usage, rhetoric, and style are all interrelated, the great majority of the articles in this *Index* have a bearing on style.

Subjective case

A noun or pronoun that is the subject of a verb or the complement of a linking verb is in the subjective, or nominative, case.

Subjects

1. Definition. The subject of a sentence can be defined in at least four ways:

a. The subject performs an action or is in a particular state of being. But this does not explain such sentences as "These socks wear out too quickly" or "He received the condemnation of millions." Neither *socks* nor *he* is the performer of any action. On the contrary, both are the objects of an action.

b. The subject is the person, place, or thing that a sentence is about. But this does not explain "I just heard that a car hit the mayor." The sentence is, quite clearly, not "about" the speaker or a car. It is about the mayor.

Both these definitions could be correct for some sentences: The mayor defeated his opponents in three elections. This is "about" the mayor, the performer of the action—*defeated*.

c. The subject is the word, phrase, or clause that usually stands before the verb and determines whether the verb will be singular or plural. Where the first two definitions are based on meaning, this one is based on formal criteria—on position in the sentence or on the relationship between inflections for number in the subject and the verb: The woman is here; The women are here. When a sentence is transformed into an expletive *there* sentence, the subject is the noun following the *be* verb that the number of the verb agrees with: There *is a woman* outside; There *are women* outside.

d. In one form of a transformational grammar, the subject in the deep structure is the first noun phrase before the verb. This deep-structure subject does not always occur as the surface-structure subject:

Deep-structure pattern	Surface-structure pattern
Someone witnessed the accident	*The accident* was witnessed.
Bees swarm in the garden	*The garden* swarms with bees.
Someone wears out socks fast	*Socks* wear out fast.
Someone opened the door with a key	*The key* opened the door.

In each case the deep-structure subject has been replaced by another noun phrase that becomes the surface-structure subject. See Deep structure.

The difference between definitions *c* and *d* is now clear: *c* is a surface-structure definition; *d* is a deep-structure definition. And the similarity between *a* and *d* should also be clear. The semantic definition of a subject in *a* seems to correspond to the semantic function of the first noun phrase in the deep structure. It is usually an agent of some kind, an actor, a performer of an action. But in the examples a transformation has changed a deep structure into a surface structure in which the subject is not the actor. Very often, of course, the deep-structure subject and the surface-structure subject are the same: The boy saw the man.

Thus in defining elements in a sentence, it is important to know what grammatical theory we are working with. Different theories will define elements in different ways.

2. Subjects and style. Despite the qualification in definition *b*, the surface-structure subject is very important because the subject is often the *topic* of a paragraph. Continuing the same grammatical subject from sentence to sentence, with variation provided by synonyms and pronouns, helps keep the focus of a paragraph clear. Further, in direct, vigorous writing, the subject and verb usually express the central action in a sentence. See Nominalization, Passive voice.

See Agreement 1, Comma 8, Compound subject. For subjects of gerunds and infinitives, see Gerunds 2, Infinitives 3.

Subjunctive mood

Traditionally, English grammar recognizes three verbal moods: indicative, imperative, and subjunctive. Subjunctive forms were common in the past in nonfactual and indirect expressions, such as wishes, beliefs, contrary-to-fact conditions, and hypothetical statements, in order to contrast them with statements of known fact: Long *live* the queen (vs. the queen *lives* long); *Were* I you (vs. I *am* you); They insisted he *be* there (vs. He *is* there). Such examples are the remnants of a system of verb inflection that has been mostly replaced by special words, such as *would* or *if* followed by an ordinary verb, and by special uses of certain verbs, such as *were* with *I, he, she, it,* or a noun (*Were* John here, he *would* be pleased).

In modern English very few forms can be surely identified as subjunctives, and the use of those few is so inconsistent that definite syntactical criteria are hard to state. Generally, the subjunctive is optional, a means of setting one's language, consciously or unconsciously, a little apart from everyday usage. It is not always a trait of formal style, though there are formal contexts, such as resolutions, that use the subjunctive regularly.

1. Form of subjunctives.
a. Simple subjunctive. The identifiable forms of the subjunctive are *be* throughout the present tense of that verb, *were* in its past-tense singular, and *s*-less forms of the third-person singular of the present tense of other verbs that normally have an -*s*. Some past-tense forms with present or future reference are also subjunctives.
b. Auxiliaries as subjunctives. Some grammarians include as subjunctives all the locutions that can be used in expressing ideas that may also be expressed by the subjunctive and the forms that could be used in translating into English the subjunctives found in other languages. Under this system several auxiliaries—*may, might, should, would, let, have to,* and others—become subjunctives (or subjunctive markers). Because this broad interpretation makes consideration of the subjunctive unduly complicated, only the simple subjunctive is considered here.

2. Uses of the subjunctive.
a. Formulas. The subjunctive is found in numerous formulas, survivals from a time when the subjunctive was used freely.

Today we do not make other sentences on the pattern of "Far be it from me."

Suffice it to say	Heaven forbid	As it were
Long live the king	God bless you	Be that as it may

Some of these formulas are used in all levels of the language; some, like "Come what may," are rather formal.

b. *That* clauses. The subjunctive is relatively frequent in demands, resolutions, recommendations, and the like, usually in formal contexts. Ordinarily, alternative expressions without the subjunctive are available.

Formal: I ask that the interested citizen *watch* closely the movement of these troops.
General: I ask the interested citizen to watch the movement of these troops closely.

Formal: Who gave the order that he *be dropped?*
General: . . . the order to drop him?

Formal: It is necessary that every member *inform* himself of these rules.
General: . . . that every member should inform himself. . . . *Or* . . . for every member to inform himself. . . . *Or* Every member must [should] inform himself. . . .

c. Conditions. The subjunctive may be used in *if* clauses when the fulfillment of the condition is doubtful or impossible: "If one good were really as good as another, no good would be any good" (Irwin Edman, *Four Ways of Philosophy*). The subjunctive *were* is not necessary to convey the meaning, which the past indicative *was* would convey just as well by its contrast between past form and present or future sense.

A large proportion of the conditions with the subjunctive are real or open conditions, not contrary to fact:

We set up standards and then proceed to measure each judge against these standards whether he be a sixteenth or nineteenth or twentieth century judge. — Louis L. Jaffe, *Harvard Law Review*

Stunkard recorded each subject's stomach contractions for four hours, and at 15-minute intervals asked him if he were hungry. — Stanley Schachter, *Psychology Today*

In such conditions a choice is open between the subjunctive and another verb form. There is no special virtue in using the subjunctive, and it should be rejected when it gets in the way of natural, idiomatic expression. See Conditional clauses.

References: Copperud, pp. 252–53; Fowler, pp. 595–98; Fries, pp. 103–107; Jespersen, Ch. 27; Pooley, pp. 53–56; William M. Ryan, *AS*, Feb. 1961, pp. 48–53, and May 1962, pp. 114–22; Richard L. Tobin, *Saturday Review*, Aug. 8, 1970, pp. 45–46.

Subordinate clauses

A dependent, or subordinate, clause (when day is done) has a subject and verb but cannot stand as a sentence. See Clauses, Comma 2.

Subordinating conjunctions

The most common subordinating conjunctions – words that relate dependent clauses to independent clauses – are these:

after	before	since	until
although	how	so that	when (whenever)
as	if	that	where (wherever)
as . . . as	in order that	though	whether
as if, as though	once	till	while
because	provided	unless	why

The relative pronouns (*who, which, that, what*) also function
as subordinating conjunctions. See also *for*.

Subordination

Correct the faulty subordination.

Faulty subordination relates to the handling of dependent
clauses – clauses introduced by subordinating conjunctions or
by relatives and used in the grammatical functions of nouns,
adjectives, and adverbs. Three types of faulty subordination are
commonly distinguished:

1. Tandem or excessive subordination occurs when you write a
succession of dependent clauses, each modifying an element in
the clause before it. The weakness is in style, not grammar:

Tandem: For his teachers, he had carefully selected those who taught
classes that had a slant that was specifically directed toward students
who intended to go into business.

Revised: . . . those who slanted their courses toward students intending
to go into business [*or* toward future businessmen].

2. Thwarted subordination occurs when you add *and* or *but* to a
dependent clause that is already connected to the independent
clause by its subordinating conjunction or relative pronoun. It is
a grammatical lapse, most commonly found in the form of *and
which* and *but which* (see *which* 4).

Thwarted: In the first semester of the course we used three textbooks,
and which were continued for the second semester.

Revised: . . . three textbooks, which were continued for the second semester.

Compare the appropriate use of a coordinating conjunction to
join two dependent clauses that are parallel: Tolerance is a virtue [which] all of us praise but [which] few of us practice.

3. Upside-down or inverted subordination occurs when you fail to
use subordination in such a way as to make the relationship
between statements sensible and logical. Since it is not a blunder in grammar or in style, it is harder to discuss in isolated sentences, for often only the context determines whether subordination is upside-down. In one writing situation, "Pearl Harbor was
attacked when Roosevelt was President" would be satisfactory;
in another, "When Pearl Harbor was attacked, Roosevelt was

President" might be much better. Without a context, we can't be sure which statement should be put in the independent clause and which in the dependent clause. But the nature of the statements may make the choice relatively easy. In most contexts this sentence would sound odd: When I was recovering from the accident, fighting broke out in the Middle East. Some such statement as this would be more likely to make sense: I was recovering from the accident during the week when reports of fighting in the Middle East filled the news. Ordinarily, upside-down subordination is corrected by turning the dependent clause into an independent clause and vice versa. Often, as in the example just given, some rewriting is advisable.

See Coordination.

Substantive

Substantive refers to nominals—nouns and pronouns and other words or groups of words used in the functions of nouns.

such

As an intensifier, *such* is somewhat informal (it was such a hot day; I have never seen such energetic people). In formal and most general writing, the construction would usually be completed by a *that* or an *as* clause (It was such a hot day that the tar melted; I have never seen such energetic people as I saw in Ballydavid), or the basis of the comparison would be indicated elsewhere in the passage:

In spite of high winds and raging seas, they were out in their boats before dawn. I have never seen such energetic people.

As a pronoun, *such* is used to refer to the idea of the preceding sentence or clause, particularly in formal styles.

When the Illyrians did achieve victory on the frontier, an invasion followed. Such was the situation in 359 B.C.—Harry J. Dell, *Classical Philology*

This or *that* commonly serves the purpose in general writing.

Formal usage often has *such as* to introduce examples, where general would have *like*. *Such as* is preferable when the example is only loosely or nonrestrictively connected to the preceding noun: "A number of big processors, such as Campbell and Heinz, still make their own cans" (*Fortune*).

When *such* is used to modify a singular, countable noun, an indefinite article precedes the noun: Such a man is needed. But in the negative the article should be omitted: No such man is needed.

Such is used with *that* to introduce result clauses: There was such a crowd that [*not* so that] we couldn't even get to the door. When *such* comes immediately before the *that*, the form is distinctly formal: . . . a crowd such that we couldn't. . . .

Reference: Bryant, pp. 199–201; Copperud, p. 253; Pooley, pp. 92–94.

Suffix

An element that can be placed after a word or root to make a new word of different meaning or function is called a suffix: *-ize* (*criticize*), *-ish* (*foolish*), *-ful* (*playful*), *-th* (*warmth*). See Origin of words 3a.

Superlative degree

Hottest, *most pleasant*, *quickest*, and *most surely* are examples of adjectives and adverbs in the superlative degree. See Comparison of adjectives and adverbs 3.

sure

Sure in standard written English is primarily an adjective (sure footing; as sure as fate; Are you sure?). As an adverb meaning "certainly," *sure* is informal to general, while *surely* is general to formal:

It's a novel interpretation, but it sure saves oranges. — Horace Sutton, *Saturday Review*

The Art Commission said it surely did want to honor this splendid son of Italy. — Donovan Bess, *Harper's*

The idiom *sure* (never *surely*) *enough* is in general use: "And sure enough, in all the fearful discussions about computers, the question that inevitably comes up . . ." (Robert Langbaum, *Yale Review*).

Surface structure

According to transformational theory, the surface structure of a sentence — the sentence as it is spoken or written — is arrived at through a series of transformations from the deep structure. See Deep structure.

Syllabication

When you're not sure where to break a word at the end of a line, consult a dictionary. For general rules, see Division of words.

Syllogisms

A syllogism represents deductive reasoning reduced to a pattern consisting of a major premise, a minor premise, and a conclusion. If the rules of inference are observed, the reasoning will be valid. Good arguments must satisfy another condition as well: the premises must be true. The rules of inference are concerned only with validity.

1. Common patterns for syllogisms.

a. Hypothetical syllogisms:

Major premise:	If P, then Q	*or*	If P, then Q
Minor premise:	P		Not Q
Conclusion:	Therefore Q		Therefore not P

Arguments that follow this pattern will not be valid if the minor premise is "Not P" and the conclusion is "Therefore not Q," or if the minor premise is "Q" and the conclusion is "Therefore not P." The major premise gives no grounds for either of these inferences.

b. *Either-or* syllogisms:

	Disjunctive	Alternative
Major premise:	Either A or B but not both	Either A or B
Minor premise:	A	Not A
Conclusion:	Therefore not B	Therefore B

Arguments that follow the pattern of the alternative syllogism will not be valid if the minor premise is positive – that is, "A" or "B." The major premise does not exclude the possibility of both A and B; it simply requires one of the two.

c. Categorical syllogisms:

Major premise:	All M are P
Minor premise:	S is an M
Conclusion:	Therefore S is a P

Arguments that follow this pattern will be invalid if they introduce a fourth term (in addition to M, P, and S); if they shift the meaning of a term; if the middle term (M) is not distributed (that is, if one or more of the premises in which it appears fails to affirm or deny something about the whole class the term stands for); or if a term that has not been distributed in a premise is distributed in a conclusion.

2. Testing arguments. Although a syllogism or, more likely, a series of interlocking syllogisms is the underpinning of most solid arguments, writers normally don't construct arguments by first formulating a syllogism and then searching for evidence to support the premises. Nor does a writer set forth his ideas in statements that fall naturally into the pattern of syllogisms. Nevertheless, an elementary acquaintance with the rules of inference can help a writer in two ways.

First, it can make him aware of the premises that underlie his argument. "It's not a poem; it doesn't rhyme." The first clause is the conclusion and the second clause the minor premise of an incomplete syllogism that has as its major premise a proposition something like "If the lines of the passage do not rhyme, the passage is not a poem" or, to put it another way, "All poems rhyme." That unspoken assertion is too controversial to be allowed to go unsupported. If the writer intends to base an argument on it, he had better argue for it.

Acquaintance with the rules of inference can also help a writer check the validity of his line of reasoning.

Why do colleges waste time teaching students material they can understand or skills they can learn on their own? Instead of giving courses in science fiction, they should teach double-entry bookkeeping. *That's* a skill students can't pick up on their own.

This bit of reasoning might be spelled out as three syllogisms, each of which invites the reader to raise questions about the va-

lidity of the reasoning as well as about the truth of the premises.
To take just one of the syllogisms:

> If students can learn a skill on their own, a college shouldn't teach it.
> (If P, then Q)
>> Students cannot learn double-entry bookkeeping on their own. (Not P)
>> Therefore, colleges should teach double-entry bookkeeping. (Not Q)

Quite aside from questions of truth, the reasoning is invalid. The
major premise has not asserted that a college should teach *all*
the skills a student can't learn on his own.

See Deduction, Fallacies, Logical thinking.

Synecdoche

Synecdoche is a figure of speech in which the whole stands for
the part (a nation adopts a policy) or a part stands for the whole
(a baseball player's bat wins a game). See Figurative language.

Synonyms

Broadly, synonyms are words that mean the same thing. More
strictly, they are words that share at least one cognitive meaning. Very few words are completely interchangeable, since no
two are likely to share all their meanings and to have the same
connotations. At the very least, they will differ in sound and
therefore in stylistic value.

Choosing among synonyms requires consideration of both
sense and sound. The chosen word must be exact in meaning
and in suggestions, and it must fit the sound pattern. Relying on
books of synonyms to improve vocabulary often results in a stilted, pretentious style.

See Connotation. Reference: Bolinger, pp. 211–15.

Syntax

Though the meaning of the term varies from one theory of grammar to another, *syntax* refers in general to the order and relations of the elements of sentences. That the subject of a sentence, for example, ordinarily comes before the predicate is a
feature of English syntax.

T

Tandem subordination

Tying a succession of dependent clauses together is called tandem subordination. See Subordination 1.

teach, learn

A teaches *B*, who is taught by *A*. *B* learns from *A*. See *learn,
teach.*

Technical writing

Good expository writing conveys information accurately, clearly, and concisely. When such writing is about specialized subject matter – in engineering, for example, or physics or chemistry – it is called technical writing. More particularly, technical writing appears in the reports, articles, and manuals produced by professionals in science and technology.

Whatever the subject matter or the nature of the communication, the first obligation of the technical writer is to present his information so clearly that it can't be misunderstood by his audience. In addition to presenting information, he must often analyze data, weigh alternative solutions to problems, make predictions, argue for a course of action. Always he needs to take into account what his readers already know and what they want to find out.

1. The technical writer and his audience. The technical writer is the expert on his subject. Nobody knows as much about his project as he does. When addressing his peers (professional associates at a convention, for instance), he will naturally use the specialized terms of his profession. When writing reports for his superiors or giving directions to subordinates, however, he has to gauge their probable familiarity with a vocabulary that is second nature to him. (The president of a potash firm may well have been chosen for his managerial ability rather than his knowledge of potash. In reporting to him, the technical writer may have to work as hard at translating shoptalk as he would if he were addressing a general reader.) Even graduate students in Aerospace Engineering might have trouble understanding this announcement of a lecture by an expert in the field:

He will talk about flow visualization experiments of a turbulent water jet in a confined tank modeled to simulate certain flow conditions expected in the Anechoic Chamber/Jet Noise Facility.

Although the gap between general English and technical vocabularies is often large, what blights technical writing for both layman and professional may not be so much vocabulary as the tangled syntax that results when a writer relies heavily on nominalization, passive verbs, and strings of prepositional phrases (four in the sentence quoted above). Some industrial firms and professional societies have recognized the problem. The American Chemical Society, for one, gives short courses in communication skills for chemists and chemical engineers. Notes on a recent course stressed the need for directness, simplicity, and brevity and recommended the use of the active voice and, on occasion, the first-person pronoun.

2. Technical reports. The merit of any technical report lies in its efficiency in communicating its content to its intended audience. Its format should therefore be carefully planned.

Technical reports differ visually from other expository writing. They are divided into sections, which are often numbered. They

have no long stretches of consecutive writing. They use subheads, tables, charts, diagrams. Many, though not all, present
at the beginning a summary (or abstract) of the findings, results, or recommendations. In this format, everything vital is
in the summary. No crucial new information is introduced as
the report proceeds through its next three or four or dozen sections. Subsequent headings depend on the nature of the report;
the order in which they appear depends on the nature of the
audience. One general, adaptable format follows:

   I. Summary—important results, conclusions, recommendations

  II. Introduction—background, purpose, problem being addressed,
scope

 III. Review of previous work—if short, a part of the Introduction

 IV. Description of present study—details of apparatus used, if the investigation is experimental; derivation of equations; procedures
followed

  V. Presentation (in table or graph form) and discussion of results—
comment on salient features of the data

 VI. Conclusions and recommendations—interpretation of results; inferences; recommendation of a solution, action, or future investigation

VII. Appendices—supporting data, usually highly specialized

The technical writer who is preparing his report for several
different audiences will choose a format that permits him to
move from the simple to the complex in content and in vocabulary. He will begin with a summary phrased in nontechnical
language and will keep his introduction as uncomplicated as
possible. He will then proceed directly to conclusions and recommendations, again presenting them so that the least informed of
his readers can follow them. The experimental section, the discussion of results, and subsequent sections will be increasingly
technical, and the final sections will supply data likely to be understood only by specialists. The advantage of this format, with
its progression from simple to complex, is that each reader can
continue until he has satisfied his interest or reached the limit of
his understanding. Even the reader who is ignorant of the tech-
nicalities of procedures, operations, or calculations will have a
grasp of the general purpose, scope, and results of the study.

See Abstract language, Nominalization, Passive voice, Phrases 2, Shoptalk.

tense Tense

**Make the tense of the verb conventional in form, or make it consis-
tent with, or in logical sequence with, other verbs in the passage.**

1. Use the standard form. In general English, avoid nonstandard
forms like *drawed* and *had went* (which signals past time twice)
and dialectal forms like *drug* (for *dragged*), *throwed*, and such

double auxiliaries as *might could* and *used to could*. See Principal parts of verbs.

2. Make the tense consistent with others that refer to the same time. Consistency does not mean that you must use the same tense for verbs throughout a sentence or a paragraph or an essay. Choose the verb form or verbal phrase that expresses the distinction of time that you intend. In a single sentence you may have occasion to refer to past, present, and future time: When I *was* ten, I *planned to be* a veterinary surgeon; but now I *know* that I *will spend* my working life as an accountant. Through skillful use of verbs you can interweave particular events with habitual action:

Summers we generally *follow* a simple routine. Every day we *travel* the fifteen miles to our lakeside cabin. We *start off* at dawn, Mother driving and the kids rubbing sleep from their eyes, and we seldom *get* home before dark. Once there, we *fall* into bed, tired from a day outdoors. One night last July our simple routine *was wrecked*. Just before we *turned* into the driveway, we *saw* that the lights *were* on all over the house. Since we *knew* we *had left* the lights off and the doors locked, we *were* puzzled and a little frightened. My brother *offered* to reconnoiter. When he *came* back to the car, he *said* he *had seen* . . .

But though it's natural and easy to shift tense, don't make a shift unless it serves a purpose—normally, to mark a change in time. Careless shifts like the following are distracting:

The observers unobtrusively *slipped* in the back door while the children *were* still getting settled at their desks. The class *begins* with the teacher reading a short passage from *Christopher Columbus, Mariner,* at the end of which she *asked* for comments.

To keep the tenses consistent, *begins* should be *began*. Or, if there were a reason for doing so, all the verbs might be put in the historical present: *slips, are, begins, asks*. See Tenses of verbs 3a.

3. Observe the conventional sequence of tenses. In certain contexts, considerations of actual time are subordinated to the conventions of tense sequence, a pattern of adjustment between verbals and verbal phrases.
a. Between independent and dependent clauses. A dependent clause that is the object of a verb in the past tense is usually put in the past tense even though it refers to an existing state of affairs:

What did you say your name *was*?
They didn't tell me you *were looking* for an apartment.

But when the dependent clause describes a timeless state of affairs, the present tense is often used: He told me that I always *remind* him of my father. And when the point of the sentence is the current existence of the state of affairs reported in the dependent clause, the present tense is common:

Simply observing the people and comparing them with those I had seen three decades ago, I was convinced that they are a lot better off materially than their predecessors. — Robert Shaplen, *New Yorker*

b. From direct discourse to indirect discourse. When a dependent clause reports something said, its verb is ordinarily shifted from present to past (He said, "I *am* leaving" *becomes* He said he *was* leaving) or from past to past perfect (He said, "I *did* it" *becomes* He said he *had done* it). But this formal sequence can sometimes be misleading. To report the statement "I am optimistic about the outcome of the election" as "He said that he was optimistic . . ." invites doubt as to whether the optimism persists. "He said that he is optimistic about the outcome of the election" removes that doubt.

c. With infinitives and participles. Infinitives and participles express time in relation to the time of the main verb. Use the present infinitive to indicate time that is the same as that of the main verb or later than that of the main verb:

I plan *to go* to Washington, and I expect *to see* him there.
I planned *to go* last week and expected *to see* him today.
I would have liked *to see* him on his last trip.

Use the perfect infinitive for action prior to that of the main verb:

I would like *to have seen* him on his last trip.

Use the perfect form of the participle to express time that is prior to that of the main verb, the present form to express time that is the same as that of the main verb:

Having driven safely through the worst blizzard in local history, he slid off the edge of his own driveway and, *jamming on* the brakes too fast, overturned the car.

See Tenses of verbs.

Tenses of verbs

1. Time and tense. Time has three divisions: present, past, future. One of the ways we indicate which of these divisions we are referring to is by changing the form of the verb or by adding a modal auxiliary: He runs (present time); he ran (past time); he will run (future time).

It is a mistake to assume that the time indicated is the name of the tense. When we say, "He leaves for New York tomorrow," we are talking about future time, but the inflection -s on *leaves* shows we are using present *tense*. When we say "He has left," we are talking about the past, but the inflection -s on *has* shows we are again using present *tense*.

It is also a mistake to assume that the only function of tense is to show time. Sometimes *could* is the past tense of *can* (He could swim better last year than he can now), but in other uses the difference between *can* and *could* has nothing to do with time (Can you please come right away; Could you please come right away).

In English, then, there is no simple correspondence between tense and time. The term *tense* refers to inflection, or change in form. English verbs have only two tenses: present (he leaves) and past (he left). There is no single-word verb, no inflection, that applies solely to the future. Nevertheless, we find various ways of referring to future time. We use the present tense accompanied by an adverb (He leaves tomorrow) or an auxiliary before the uninflected verb (He will leave tomorrow). Or we say, "He will be leaving" or "He is going to leave" or "By this time tomorrow he will have left." Some grammarians call *will leave, will be leaving*, and so on, the future tense; others do not.

2. Tense and auxiliaries. If we use no auxiliaries, the only tenses we can form are present and past (or past and nonpast, as some linguists prefer to call them). But because through using auxiliaries we can refer to times in the future as well as the past extending into the present, the past not extending into the present, the past of a certain time already past, some grammarians speak of six tenses, which roughly translate the six of Latin:

Present:	He eats	*Present perfect:*	He has eaten
Past:	He ate	*Past perfect:*	He had eaten
Future:	He will eat	*Future perfect:*	He will have eaten

Still more tenses emerge if we consider the uses of *do* (emphatic: *does eat, did eat*) and *be* (progressive: *is eating, was eating*). If the past of *shall* and *will* is also taken into account, we can speak of a past future *(would eat)* and even a past future perfect *(would have eaten)*.

The emphatic tenses—those with the auxiliary *do*—may be analyzed as transformations. *Do* is added to a verb to produce the emphatic transformation, as well as negatives and questions, only when no other auxiliary is present. "He has eaten" can be made emphatic by putting primary stress on the auxiliary: He *has* eaten. To make "He ate" emphatic requires the addition of *do* to carry the stress: He *did* eat. (The past-tense marker has been shifted from *eat* to the first element in the verb phrase.) Likewise, "He ate" can be transformed into a question or the negative only with the addition of *do* (Did he eat? He did not eat.) See Auxiliaries.

3. Special uses of simple present and past.
a. In addition to its basic function of referring to something going on now, the present tense is used to refer to a state of affairs that is generally true, without reference to time (Oil *floats* on water); to habitual action that continues into the present (He *writes* in his journal every day); and, when accompanied by an adverbial, to a time in the future (She *goes* to college in the fall). Other special uses of the present tense are illustrated in

I *hear* you are going to Europe.
He'll come if you *ask* him.
Thoreau *urges* us to do without luxuries.
Skirts *go* up and down with the economy: in the prosperous Twenties *they're* short; in the Depression Thirties *they're* long.

The third example is sometimes known as the *literary present* (Thoreau died in 1862), the fourth as the *historical present*.

b. The simple past tense is normally used to refer to something
that took place in the past, either a single occurrence (He *broke*
his leg) or a repeated occurrence (He *skied* at Vail every Christmas). But in certain contexts the past tense does not refer to past
time. It is regularly used in a dependent clause that is object of
the verb in the independent clause when the main verb is in the
past (I *heard* that you *were* in town). It is used in the *if* clause
that refers to a hypothetical situation (If you *knew* him, you
wouldn't be surprised). It is the polite alternative in questions or
requests (*Would* you send me the catalog).

See Auxiliaries, Tense, Verbs. References: Jespersen, Chs.
23–26; Joos, Ch. 5; Geoffrey N. Leech, *Meaning and the English Verb* (London: Longman, 1971); Long, Ch. 7; Quirk et al.,
pp. 84–97.

than

At its simplest level, the choice of case after *than* can be illustrated by the sentences "He is taller than I" and "He is taller
than me." Both are used in general writing. Conservatives favor
the nominative after an intransitive or linking verb, but many
writers use the objective.

When the verb before *than* takes an object, however, the nominative and objective cases after *than* may have different meanings: She likes him more than I [do]; She likes him more than
[she likes] me. Hence in standard English the case of the pronoun used with *than* after a transitive verb is what would be used
if the dependent clause were written out. Use of the nominative
case where the objective case is called for, as in the following
example, is considered hypercorrect: Though the jury said we
were both guilty, the judge gave my partner a lighter sentence
than [he gave] I.

For *different than*, see *different*. References: Copperud, pp.
256–57; Jespersen, pp. 132–33; Pooley, pp. 163–67.

that

1. *That* or *which*. Writers are often urged to use *that* to introduce
restrictive clauses and *which* to introduce nonrestrictive clauses; and the advice has value for those who use *which* everywhere, in the belief that it is more elegant than *that*. In general
practice, however, the choice between *which* and *that* in restrictive clauses is more likely to depend on rhythm, sound, emphasis, and personal taste than on any rule. If *that* has already been
used in the sentence, writers may shift to *which* to avoid repetition. On the other hand, when the restrictive clause is compound, *which* may be chosen as a clearer signal to the reader
that the construction is being repeated: "He had an exploratory
operation for cancer which the doctors were reluctant to under-
take but which he was convinced he needed" (David Halber-
stam, *Atlantic*). *Which* normally introduces nonrestrictive
clauses in all varieties of usage.

2. Redundant *that*. When *that* introduces a noun clause in which a modifying phrase precedes the subject, *that* should not be repeated after the modifier: "It must seem to many outsiders that if there was room for honest argument [that] a reasonable doubt had to exist, but the America's Cup Committee hasn't given house room to a reasonable doubt in 119 years" (Red Smith, syndicated columnist).

3. Clauses without *that*. A complex sentence like "The work [that] he does shows [that] he has talent" is perfectly correct without either *that.* The dependent clauses "he does" and "he has talent" are related to the rest of the sentence clearly enough to need no explicit signs of subordination, like *that.* No writer should handicap himself by thinking a *that* should be inserted wherever it will fit. *That*-less clauses are common:

He thinks that the Italians neither approved of Fascist terror nor were really terrorized by it. He thinks [   ] they became numb, resigned, apathetic, and cynical. — Naomi Bliven, *New Yorker*

The convention [   ] we accept unthinkingly had not as yet established itself. — William Nelson, *Journal of English Literary History*

To use *that* to stress the subordination of short clauses is often to rob them of their force: He knows [that] I'm sorry; I'm glad [that] you're here; Take anything [that] you want.

But *that* is necessary in writing when the clause comes first (That he might be hurt never occurred to us) and when a clause has no other subject (There is a moral standard that has long been accepted). When a modifier stands between two clauses, *that* is sometimes needed to show which clause is being modified: Mr. Wrenn said [   ] after the guests were gone [   ] Mrs. Wrenn should pack her bags. Depending on the intended meaning, *that* is needed either after *said* or after *gone.*

See *this.* References: Copperud, pp. 257–59; Jespersen, pp. 350–51, 360–65.

that is

That is introduces the equivalent of, or the explanation of, what it precedes. It is a rather formal connective and is best kept to introduce series or complete statements. Usually it is preceded by a semicolon and followed by a comma: The men worked continuously for three whole weeks to complete the dam on time; that is, they worked twenty-four hours a day in three shifts, seven days a week. In briefer constructions a comma or a dash would be adequate: They used the safest explosive for the purpose — that is, dynamite. Better yet, *that is* could be omitted: . . . explosive for the purpose — dynamite.

their

Their is the genitive of *they. Theirs* is the absolute form: This table is exactly like theirs. Except in formal usage, *their* is often used as a common-gender singular to refer to words like *somebody, anybody, everyone:*

Almost nobody has the words to really talk about their lives. — *Time*

It is necessary to make anyone on the streets think twice before attempting to vent their despair on you. — James Baldwin, *Show*

See Agreement 2.

then

Then is an adverb of time that is frequently used as a connective (conjunctive adverb): The next three hours we spent in sightseeing; then we settled down to the business of being delegates to a convention. Often *and* is used before *then*, with a consequent change in punctuation: He ate a good meal, and then he took a nap before starting home.

Adjectival *then* (the then President) is common in general writing, rare in formal. Some readers dislike the usage.

then, than

Then, the adverb of time, and *than*, the conjunction in clauses of comparison, should not be confused: *Then* the whole crowd went to Louie's; It was better as a movie *than* as a novel.

there is, there are

When *there* is used as an anticipatory subject, the verb ordinarily agrees in number with the "real" subject, which follows the verb: "There is still occasional sniping at the 'supersquad' and there are still lazy, indifferent homicide detectives" (Barbara Gelb, *New York Times Magazine*). When the subject is compound and the first element is singular, usage is divided. Some writers follow the rules of formal agreement and use a plural verb; others find a plural verb awkward before a singular noun:

There are much good history, intelligent analysis of social problems, and good writing. — David Fellman, *American Historical Review*

There is no jargon, few footnotes, some repetition, few insights and little analysis. — Lewis A. Froman, *American Political Science Review*

Like repeated use of *it is* . . . , repeated use of *there is* . . . , *there are* . . . constructions has a deadening effect on style, mainly because it robs a sentence of a strong subject-verb combination. See Subjects 2. References: Bryant, pp. 13–14; Copperud, p. 260; Fries, pp. 56–57.

Thesis statement

A thesis statement is the most explicit statement the writer can make of his purpose — what he wants to assert or prove. Whether or not it appears in the essay itself, the thesis statement must be firmly fixed in the writer's mind, guiding him as he selects and organizes his material. See Outline form 2, Topic sentence 3.

they

They occurs in all varieties of usage with no explicit antecedent: "One thinks of Tolstoy, and the story that all day long they had to be beating omelets for him in the kitchen" (Louis Kronenberger,

New York Times Book Review). The indefinite reference is troublesome, however, when the pronoun clashes with the suggestion of particular individuals (Around campus they were saying that they had a plan to boycott classes); and often impersonal *there* is preferable: There have been [*instead of* They have had] no serious accidents at that crossing in years.

They, and especially *their,* is frequently used to refer to *everyone* and similar words that are treated as singular in formal English. See Agreement 2, *he or she*. Reference: Bryant, pp. 211–12.

thing

Thing often encourages the accumulation of deadwood in writing: [The] first [thing] you [do is to] get a few twigs burning.

this

Though often criticized as a sign of lazy writing, *this,* like *that,* is regularly used to refer to the idea of a preceding clause or sentence: He had always had his own way at home, and this made him a poor roommate. Confusion is caused not when *this* clearly refers to the idea of a clause or sentence but when it refers to only some part of the idea or to an antecedent that is not actually expressed. See Reference of pronouns 2. References: Bryant, pp. 172–74; Copperud, p. 261; Long, pp. 290–93.

though

After a period of literary disuse, during which it was considered colloquial, *though* in the sense "however, nevertheless, for all that" now appears in all varieties of writing: Two things are clear, though.

thus

Thus at the beginning of participial phrases has a tendency to encourage loose modifiers. In sentences like this one there is no noun or pronoun for the participle to modify: "D. Eldred Rinehart's term on the racing commission also is expiring, thus opening up the chairmanship" (*Washington Post*). See Dangling modifiers.

Thwarted subordination

Subordination is said to be thwarted when a coordinating conjunction precedes the subordinating connective: By the end of the summer he had completed three reports, [and] which were accepted for publication. See Subordination 2.

till, until

In all varieties of writing, *till* and *until* are interchangeable both as prepositions (Wait till/until tomorrow) and as conjunctions (Wait till/until they get here). As a clipped form of *until,* '*til* is sometimes found in informal contexts, but it is not recognized by most dictionaries.

Titles

1. Composing titles. Since it can help stir the reader's interest, a striking and easily remembered title is an advantage for an essay. But titles that strain for originality or impact often fail. If no good title comes to mind, simply name the subject of the essay as precisely as possible in a few words. Because the title is considered a separate part of the essay, it should not be referred to by a pronoun in the opening sentence: not "This is an important issue today" but "The parking problem is an important issue today."

2. Referring to titles.
a. Italics vs. quotation marks. For most purposes there is a simple rule of thumb: Italicize titles of long works (by underlining them) and quote titles of short works. Italics are traditional for titles of books, magazines, pamphlets, long poems, plays, movies, symphonies, and operas. Quotation marks are usual for essays, short stories, short poems, songs, television shows, chapters of books, lectures, paintings, and pieces of sculpture.
b. Capitalizing. General practice is to capitalize the first and last words of titles and all intervening nouns, pronouns, verbs, adjectives, and adverbs; some styles also capitalize prepositions and conjunctions that contain more than five letters: *Wit and Its Relation to the Unconscious; Peace through* [or *Through*] *Meditation;* "Hills like White Elephants"; "Nobody Knows You When You're Down and Out." Capitals are similarly used, without italics or quotation marks, in titles of unpublished works, book series, and books of the Bible and in the words *preface, introduction, table of contents,* and *index* when they are used for parts of a manuscript or published work.

The (or *a*) is capitalized and italicized or set within quotation marks only if it is part of the recognized title: *The Yale Law Review* but the *Harvard Law Review; The American Historical Review* but the *American Sociological Review; The New York Times* but the *Los Angeles Times.* In some styles initial *the* is never treated as part of the title of a newspaper or periodical. Within the pamphlet entitled *The MLA Style Sheet,* that publication is referred to as "the *MLA Style Sheet.*"
c. Consistency. A writer should choose an accepted style for handling titles and stick to it. For example, the name of the city in a newspaper title may be either italicized or not italicized: the *Los Angeles Times,* the Los Angeles *Times.* Similarly, while strict formality may demand that a title be given in full each time it appears, current styles permit the use of short forms and the omission of initial articles when they would cause awkwardness: Hemingway's [*A*] *Moveable Feast* provides background for his [*The*] *Sun Also Rises.*

Many newspapers and magazines have their own rules for handling titles. Some use quotation marks around book titles and merely capitalize the names of periodicals. For the more rigid and elaborate rules governing very formal writing, as in dissertations and scholarly articles, consult such detailed treatments as Kate L. Turabian, *Manual for Writers of Term Papers, Theses, and Dissertations*, 4th ed. (Chicago: Univ. of Chicago Press, 1973), and the *MLA Style Sheet*.

too, not too

In the sense "also," *too* is sometimes set off by commas, sometimes not. At times commas are necessary for clarity. Without them, the sentence "Bob, too, frequently interrupted rehearsals to give advice" could be taken to mean that Bob interrupted excessively often.

Though *too* is used to modify past participles after linking verbs in all varieties of usage (She was too excited; He was too concerned), conservative stylists prefer another adverb of degree between *too* and the participle (too greatly excited, too much concerned). Objection is strongest when the participle could not be placed before the noun or pronoun as a modifier: He is not too identified with the opposition; Priests are too removed from real life. In such cases, many writers would insist on intervening adverbs — "too closely identified," "too far removed" — particularly in formal contexts.

Some formal stylists would continue to criticize both examples on the grounds that the constructions are incomplete — "not too closely identified" for what? "too far removed" for what? And many would reject the "not too" phrase, a popular informal substitute for "not very" that is always rather vague and sometimes ambiguous.

Topic sentence

Normally, the topic sentence is the broadest, most general statement in a paragraph, the one that expresses most directly the idea that the paragraph as a whole conveys. The other sentences of the paragraph develop the idea, particularize it, illustrate it, or qualify it.

1. Position. The topic sentence has no fixed position in a paragraph. Most often it is the first sentence, as it is in this paragraph, or the second sentence, coming immediately after a transitional sentence. But it sometimes stands at the end of a paragraph, pulling details and observations together into an inclusive statement. And occasionally it occurs midway through a paragraph, introduced by particulars that lead up to it and followed by further particulars that support or qualify it. In textbooks and in other types of explanation and instruction where it is vital that the reader have a firm grasp of each stage of the discussion, the writer sometimes sets forth the central idea at the start of a paragraph and restates it in a somewhat different way at the end.

2. Rhetorical use. Topic sentences keep a reader fully informed of the chief points being made. Phrasing topic sentences keeps the writer on track, too, encouraging him to stick to his subject and so maintain the unity of his essay. But in some situations —

certainly in describing and narrating and also at times in arguing—he may deliberately shun the explicitness of topic sentences, feeling that his purpose is better served if he simply supplies details and impressions and leaves it to the reader to infer a conclusion or generalization. If the writer has done his work well, the reader will come to the right conclusion.

3. Topic sentence, pointer sentence, and thesis statement. If a reader asks what a paragraph adds up to, it probably needs a topic sentence. If he asks why he is suddenly in the middle of a new subject, it probably needs a pointer sentence. If he asks what the upshot of the whole paper is—what it all adds up to—the writer needs to formulate a thesis statement for himself.

A topic sentence sums up what a paragraph or sequence of paragraphs *says*. A pointer sentence tells what the paragraph or sequence of paragraphs will *do* (or, sometimes, what it has done). "There are three kinds of joggers" is a pointer, an organizational signpost indicating that each kind of jogger will now be described. "But what do we mean by *détente*?" is an implied promise to explain the term.

An expository or argumentative essay usually has several topic sentences and perhaps a pointer or two. By contrast, it has just one thesis statement, and that statement may or may not appear in the essay. Whether or not it does, it is the writer's expression of the controlling idea of his entire essay. It is his reason for writing the essay.

See Outline form 2, Paragraph indention, Thesis statement, Unity 2.

toward, towards

These words are identical in meaning, and the choice of one or the other is a matter of taste. *Toward* is more common, but both appear in all varieties of usage. References: Bryant, p. 220; Copperud, pp. 8, 264.

Transformation

In transformational grammar a transformation is a rule that changes the surface structure of a sentence while retaining the meaning of the basic deep structure (see Deep structure). Each of the following groups of sentences has the same deep structure, although the surface structures are different:

Tom gave the money to Bill.
Tom gave Bill the money.

I held the man up.
I held up the man.

I can read German and Bill can read German, too.
I can read German and Bill can, too.
Both Bill and I can read German.

The above sentences illustrate optional transformations. Many others are obligatory. In embedding a relative clause, for example, the substitution of a pronoun for a noun is required:

The man [The man lives next door] is very noisy.
The man   who   lives next door is very noisy.

In elliptical clauses of comparison, deletions are obligatory:

John is older than I am old.
John is older than I (am).

trans Transition

Make the transition between these sentences (or paragraphs) clear and smooth.

Transitions are words or phrases or sentences that show the relation between one statement and another, one paragraph and another, one part of an essay and another. When you write a sentence or paragraph as an isolated unit — as if nothing had preceded it and nothing was to follow it — your reader is bound to be puzzled. A lack of transition between one paragraph and another is sometimes a sign of faulty organization and sometimes simply evidence that you've neglected to provide a signpost that will show the reader where he's been or where he's going. A lack of transition between sentences usually indicates that you haven't thought through the relationship between consecutive statements.

1. Transitions as signals. The most familiar of the markers that indicate relationships and knit a piece of prose together are conjunctions and adverbs — *and, but, still, yet, for, because, then, though, while, in order that, first, second, however, moreover, therefore,* and so on.

Some of the choices available to indicate the common logical relationships are these:

a. Addition. When you want to call attention to the fact that you're adding something, *and* is the usual connector. Others that indicate equivalent, coordinate, or similar ideas are *also, again, once again, too, likewise, moreover, furthermore, then, in addition, by the same token, similarly, analogously.* You can indicate restatements with such phrases as *that is, to clarify, more simply* or by clauses like *what this means is.*

b. Contrast. When the relation is one of contrast, ranging from direct contradiction through various degrees of opposition, qualification, restriction, and concession, some of your choices are *but, yet, however, nevertheless, nonetheless, by contrast, at the same time, instead, in place of, conversely, actually, in fact, to be sure, at any rate, anyway, still, of course, on the other hand, provided that, in case.*

c. Alternatives. You can call attention to an alternative or option by using *or, nor, either, neither, alternatively, on the other hand* (often following *on the one hand*).

d. Causal relations. You can indicate a causal relation with *for, because, since, then, as.* You can point to result or consequence with various words and phrases, among them *so, then, therefore, thus, hence, accordingly, as a result, in consequence.*

e. Illustration. When the relation is inclusive — when what follows illustrates what has come before or particularizes it in some way — some of your choices are *for example, for instance, thus, to illustrate, in particular, namely.*

f. Sequence. When the relation is sequential, your transitions may indicate temporal or spatial relations in the subject itself, or they may point up the organization of the essay. Sample time indicators are *then, soon, after, now, earlier, later, ten years ago.* Sample space indicators are *here, there, on top, in the middle, below, on the left, on the right, beyond.* You can indicate sequence by transitions like *for one thing, for another; first, second, third; to begin with; in short, in brief; finally, to summarize, in conclusion, as we have seen.* Other transitions bring out the relative importance of points — *more important, less important, above and beyond.*

2. Transitions and style. A transition should give an accurate indication of the relationship you intend. Beyond that, the transition should be in keeping with the style and tone of your essay.

a. Accurate markers. *Actually* and *incidentally* are overworked as transitions. Since *actually* often introduces a correction and *incidentally* a digression, both may be signs that revision is needed. (But when a digression is justified, it should be clearly identified as a digression.) An unwarranted transition — for example, a *therefore* when the case has not been made — can be seriously misleading.

b. Apt markers. Though *first, second, third* are preferable to old-fashioned *firstly, secondly, thirdly,* they should be supplied only when the material demands such emphatic division. Overuse of any of the heavier connectives (*however, nevertheless, consequently*) can clog your style. Often you can make a transition that is just as clear, less obtrusive, and stylistically more pleasing by repeating a key word from sentence to sentence, by using a synonym or a pronoun to echo or pick up the key word, and by binding sentences or parts of sentences through parallel structures. Whether overt or subtle, transitions are your chief means for giving a piece of writing coherence.

References: Stanley Greenbaum, *Studies in English Adverbial Usage* (Coral Gables: Univ. of Miami Press, 1970), Ch. 3; W. Ross Winterowd, *College English,* May 1970, pp. 828–35.

Transitive and intransitive verbs

A transitive verb is one that is used with a direct object; an intransitive verb is not so used: The janitor put [transitive] the books on the shelf, but they soon vanished [intransitive]. Some verbs may be transitive in one sense and intransitive in another (He grows corn; The corn grows well), and in the course of time intransitives may become transitives (as *answer* has done) or transitives may become intransitive (some senses of *withdraw*); but at any one time in the history of English, a given verb in a given sense can be classified according to its use with an object or without. We can disappear, but not disappear something, put something somewhere, but not just put. See *lay, lie; set, sit.*

transpire

Long objected to in the sense of "happen" or "occur" because of its literal meaning in botany and its related figurative meaning "to emerge or come to light," *transpire* is regularly used to mean "happen" in general and formal writing and is understood by many people in no other sense. But this usage still has its critics. For that matter, so does the "correct" usage, to mean "become known." Reference: Copperud, p. 265.

 Triteness

Replace the trite expression with one that is simpler and fresher.

The most troublesome trite expressions, or clichés, are worn-out figures of speech or phrases: the picture of health, the break of day, reign supreme, from the face of the earth, crack of dawn, acid test. What was once fresh and striking has become stale and hackneyed from being used again and again with no sense of its figurativeness. This passage compresses a great number of trite expressions into small space:

The Blushing Bride

I suppose it is natural that I should have been asked to step into the breach on this happy day, if only because I have had the privilege of knowing Geraldine since she was so high. . . . Onlookers see most of the game, you know, and it is easy to be wise after the event, but I thought I could see which way the wind was blowing last August.

They say marriages are made in Heaven, well, be that as it may, these two look as happy as the day is long. It was a great pleasure to me to see Hubert give away his one ewe lamb to such a regular chip off the old block as our friend here. Like father like son, they say, and I think his father deserves a pat on the back. As for Geraldine, bless her, she is a real Trojan, and has been a tower of strength to her dear mother, who doesn't look a day older than when I first set eyes on her, far longer ago than either of us cares to remember.

At moments like this, when family ties are stronger than ever, these young things should remember how much they owe to their parents.

One last word, I must not fail to remind Geraldine that the way to a man's heart is his stomach, and to warn Bertrand that the hand that rocks the cradle rules the world.

Now, I mustn't take up any more of your valuable time, I feel sure you will all join me in drinking the health of the happy couple, and wishing that all their troubles may be little ones. — Georgina Coleridge, *I Know What I Like*

One way to guard against triteness is to recognize figurative language for what it is and to avoid using it unless you mean it — that is, unless the figure conveys an intended extension or nuance of meaning. Remember, too, that triteness is not a matter of age. Yesterday's vogue expression can be as worn a cliché as one handed down for generations. So if you find yourself writing down a phrase without even stopping to think about it, stop and think about it — think twice. Trite expression is the natural vehicle for trite ideas.

But the rhetorical situation should be decisive. Depending on your purpose and your audience, the same words can be either a cliché that you should avoid or a well-established phrase that, with its connotations, expresses your meaning accurately and succinctly. Going out of your way to avoid an expression only because it has been used many times before may force you into awkwardness, incoherence, or absurdly "fine" writing.

See Figures of speech, Vogue words. References: Theodore M. Bernstein, *Miss Thistlebottom's Hobgoblins* (New York: Farrar, 1971), pp. 156–58; Copperud, pp. 48–49.

try and

Though the idiom *try and* – "Neither Congress nor the Court itself seemed prepared to try and force him to resign" *(Newsweek)* – appears regularly in general and informal contexts, formal style usually demands *try to*. References: Copperud, p. 267; Pooley, pp. 124–25.

-type

The use of *-type* in compound modifiers (Polaris-type missile, new-type car, family-type programs) has spread in all varieties of usage, but outside of technical and commercial contexts it arouses strong distaste in conservative stylists. Most writers prefer *type of* (Polaris type of missile) or, where possible, simply omit *type* (new car, family programs). The practice of shortening *type of* and *make of* to *type* (this type letter) and *make* (this make car) is informal. Reference: Copperud, p. 268.

Typewritten copy

Use only one side of the sheet, leave wide margins at both left and right, keep type clean, and change the ribbon regularly. In first drafts, using triple space and leaving extra space between paragraphs will provide room for revision. Double space the final draft.

Indent the first lines of paragraphs five spaces. Long quotations may be indicated in double-spaced copy by indenting each line as in a paragraph indention and single-spacing the quoted matter. No quotation marks are used with block quotations.

For the figure 1, use the small *l*, not capital *I*. For a dash use two hyphens. Leave a space after all other punctuation marks except at the end of sentences, where two spaces should be used.

Transposed letters should be erased and retyped or corrected with a curved line.

Strikeovers [*not* Strikeovers] are often hard to read.

A few mistakes can be corrected in ink, but any page that contains several should be retyped. See Caret.

Underlining

Underlining in manuscripts is used to mark titles that are not quoted, words used as words, foreign expressions that have not been anglicized, and – sparingly – words or word groups that, for one reason or another, you want to emphasize. See Italics.

Understatement

Understating is one means of emphasizing: Income taxes are not universally popular. See Figurative language, Figures of speech.

uninterested

To be uninterested is to lack interest; to be disinterested is to be neutral, which is not the same thing. But see *disinterested, uninterested.*

unique

In strict formal usage *unique* means "single, sole, unequaled" and consequently is not compared. In general usage, *unique*, like so many other words that formerly had an absolute meaning, has become an adjective of degree. As an emphatic *rare* or *remarkable*, it is often found compared with *more* or *most:* "The more unique his nature, the more peculiarly his own will be the colouring of his language" (Otto Jespersen, *Mankind, Nation and Individual from a Linguistic Point of View*). Because of this varied usage, a reader may find the unqualified word ambiguous. The writer of the following sentence may have been guarding against that possibility: "It is a unique festival, and there is nothing like it in the world" (Harold C. Schonberg, *New York Times*). While redundant by formal standards, the second clause is probably practical. See Comparison of adjectives and adverbs 4. References: Copperud, p. 55; Evans and Evans, pp. 528–29.

United States

Like many proper nouns, *United States* is often used as an attributive: "There are some who think that the United States attempt to overthrow the Castro government was an act of international immorality" (Richard H. Rovere, *New Yorker*). No apostrophe is needed. Since *United States* has no adjectival form, the construction often sounds awkward; and in most contexts *American* – or, where confusion is possible, *of the United States* – is preferable. See *American.*

un Unity

Unify this passage.

A sentence, a paragraph, or an essay is unified when its parts fit together to make a consistent whole. The major threat to unity is material that, however interesting, stands outside—or seems to stand outside—the core of thought or feeling that the writer intends to communicate.

Your first obligation as a writer is to have a purpose in writing and a controlling idea against which you can test your sentences, your paragraphs, and your complete essay. Your second obligation is to build your sentences and paragraphs in such a way that your train of thought, and ultimately your purpose, will be clear to your audience.

Failures in unity can be real, as when a writer introduces irrelevant material, or apparent, as when a writer doesn't make plain to his audience a relationship that is perfectly plain to him. The first is a failure in thinking (see Logical thinking); the second is a failure in composition, especially in continuity (see Coherence, Transition). A sentence, a paragraph, or an essay may be coherent but not unified; it may also be unified but not coherent. Good prose is both coherent and unified.

Out of context—and here context means both the writer's thinking about his subject and his expression of his thought—it is difficult to decide whether a passage is lacking in unity or in coherence. But some hints can be given about ways of strengthening passages that have been criticized for lacking unity.

1. Unity in sentences. For a sentence that lacks unity, there are three possible remedies:
a. Delete any phrase or clause that is unrelated to the central thought. In the sentence "Parking space on the campus, which is one of the most beautiful in the state, has become completely inadequate, and recently the city council voted to increase bus fares again," delete the *which* clause.
b. Subordinate one statement to another to show the logical relationship. Even if readers of the quoted sentence can figure out a connection between the shortage of parking space and the cost of public transportation, the coordinating *and* obscures the writer's point. A possible revision: At a time when the shortage of parking space makes commuting to campus by car almost impossible, the city council has discouraged the use of public transportation by increasing bus fares once more.
c. Separate seemingly disconnected statements, making two sentences, and bring in material that will provide a logical link between them. Between a sentence about inadequate parking space and a sentence about increased bus fares, this sentence might be introduced: But the commuting student is hardly being encouraged to switch to public transportation. See Coordination, Sentences, Subordination.

2. Unity in paragraphs. As a general rule, a paragraph lacks unity when one or more of its sentences fail to contribute to the central idea of the paragraph. When that idea is expressed in a topic sentence, it is fairly easy for both writer and reader to see exactly where the discussion slides away from the main point. You would be wise to provide topic sentences when dealing with a subject so complex that a reader might need help in following your treatment of it. On the other hand, you can do without topic sentences if the logic of your thought, or the pressure of your emotion, creates a unified topic *idea* that the paragraph transmits to your audience.

Sticking to a subject does not in itself guarantee unity. In a paragraph on Robert Frost, all the sentences may be about the poet, but the paragraph is not likely to be unified if two sentences deal with his current reputation, one with his last public appearance, one with his marriage, and three with his poem "After Apple-Picking." Bringing together several loosely related ideas usually means that no one of them will be adequately developed and that the paragraph will badly lack unity. See Paragraph indention, Topic sentence.

3. Unity in essays. Even when each paragraph in an essay is satisfactorily unified, the essay as a whole may not be. Each paragraph should bear on the writer's intent in writing the essay (whether or not that purpose is expressed in a thesis statement); and the paragraphs should be in such an order and should be so linked that the reader understands the relation of each to the controlling idea.

A useful way of testing an essay for unity is to outline it. Questions of relevance and relatedness can be more easily answered when you have seen through the surface of what you have written to the underlying structure of thought.

Reduce each paragraph to a heading. If your essay is brief — four or five paragraphs, say — each heading may represent a main point; but in a longer paper the paragraphs should fall into logical groups, with each sequence developing a theme. Be on the lookout for a heading that doesn't logically follow another heading or lead into another heading. If you find one, consider dropping the paragraph it stands for. If you find a sequence of paragraphs that strays from your central thesis, rethinking and rewriting are in order. See Organization, Outline form, Thesis statement.

until, till

Until and *till* (not *'til*) are interchangeable. See *till, until*.

up

Up is a member of many typical verb-adverb combinations in general use (*give up, grow up, sit up, use up*). Because they have developed meanings that are not the sum of the meanings of their parts, they are usually entered separately in dictionaries, and they behave like independent verbs. *Up* also appears in a number of other combinations to which it contributes no new element of meaning (*divide up, fill up, raise up, join up*). These idioms are usually avoided in formal.

Upside-down subordination

Subordination is said to be upside-down when logically the dependent clause of a sentence should be independent and the independent clause dependent. See Subordination 3.

Usage

The study of usage is based on an accumulation of specific instances and depends on wide observation of what people say and write in various situations as a basis for judging the standing of particular words, forms, and constructions. Works on usage include scholarly studies of the ways the language is used, and has been used, in speech, in print, in letters, and so on; polls to determine attitudes toward particular usages; and guides to usage based in large part on the authors' taste. Both the polls and the guides focus on disputed usages, and it is this area of usage study that has most interested the general public. J. Lesslie Hall dealt with disputed usages in his pioneering *English Usage* of 1917. Sterling A. Leonard used the polling technique to investigate cultivated usage for his *Current English Usage* of 1932. In 1938, in *Facts About Current English Usage*, Albert H. Marckwardt and Fred G. Walcott reported on the actual practice of writers in using the locutions evaluated in Leonard's poll.

As methods for systematic study of usage became established, some scholars spoke out against the classroom approach to "good English." Robert C. Pooley criticized it in *Grammar and Usage in Textbooks in English* (1933) and *Teaching English Usage* (1946). C. C. Fries' *American English Grammar* (1940) provided evidence that educated writers of standard English showed more variation in usage than had been assumed. Information on actual usage from a wide variety of scholarly sources was brought together and summarized in Margaret M. Bryant's *Current American Usage* in 1962. More evidence was provided in *Computational Analysis of Present-Day American English* (1967) by Henry Kučera and W. Nelson Francis.

These works and others built up a picture of what educated users of American English say and, more especially, write. But for many people who are interested in usage, what *is* is not nearly so important as what *should be*. Most of the popular guides to usage are conservative—that is, they prescribe usages and constructions that this *Index* associates with formal English. Roy H. Copperud's *American Usage: The Consensus* (New York: Van Nostrand, 1970) brings together recommendations (often conflicting) from six guides—Theodore M. Bernstein, *The Careful Writer* (New York: Atheneum, 1965); Roy H. Copperud, *A Dictionary of Usage and Style* (New York: Hawthorne, 1964); Bergen Evans and Cornelia Evans, *A Dictionary of Contemporary*

American Usage (New York: Random, 1957); Rudolf Flesch, *The ABC of Style* (New York: Harper, 1964); Wilson Follett, *Modern American Usage: A Guide,* ed. and completed by Jacques Barzun (New York: Hill, 1966); and H. W. Fowler, *A Dictionary of Modern English Usage,* 2nd ed., rev. by Sir Ernest Gowers (New York: Oxford Univ. Press, 1965) — as well as from Bryant's *Current American Usage* (New York: Funk, 1962), *Webster's Third New International Dictionary of the English Language* (Springfield, Mass.: Merriam, 1961), the unabridged edition of the *Random House Dictionary of the English Language* (New York: Random, 1966), and *The American Heritage Dictionary of the English Language* (Boston: American Heritage and Houghton, 1969).

The appearance of *Webster's Third,* as the edition is popularly known, offered clear proof that, for an articulate minority, concern about usage is intense. The publishers of the dictionary had decided to apply usage labels much more sparingly than in the past, on the grounds that the primary role of a dictionary was to record usage, not evaluate it, and that it was often impossible to label with any precision words taken out of context. Praised by many scholars, the decision was attacked in newspaper editorials and magazine articles as an abandonment of standards. More recently the polling technique introduced into usage study in the 1930s has been borrowed by publishers. Panels made up of journalists, novelists, columnists, commentators, and others concerned with verbal communication have registered mixed opinions on individual items for *The American Heritage Dictionary* and *Harper's Dictionary of Contemporary Usage* by William and Mary Morris (New York: Harper, 1975).

What this concern with the etiquette of usage indicates is that the writer should be aware of the attitudes of his audience — which are not always consistent with the audience's own usage. Most disputes involve matters of divided usage within standard English. Judgments vary, and as letters to the editors of newspapers and periodicals frequently reveal, conservative attitudes are often passionately held. Such letters also reveal that while word watching can make anyone's reading more interesting and his writing both richer and more precise, it can also be an unfortunate obsession. It is bad when the watcher (and listener) insists on "correcting" the usage of others. It is much worse when he makes usage the criterion for judging not only their educational and social level but their character and intelligence.

Like every writer, you must make your own choices. But they should be intelligent choices, based on sound information. The best safeguard against avoidable bias is awareness of some principles of selection; the principle proposed in this *Index* is appropriateness. And there is the intangible called taste. If, like most of us, you find some locutions too stuffy or too crude, you can simply not use them. Although no one can control the usage of others, everyone can control his own.

See Introduction, pp. 1–7.

utilize

Utilize means "put to use." The verb *use* is almost always preferable.

Verb-adverb combinations

In "I looked up at the top of the tree," the verb *look* is used in its ordinary sense and is modified by the adverb *up.* In "I looked up the word in the dictionary," *looked up* is a verb meaning "investigated," a meaning not explained by a literal use of the two words. A person may *break out* (literally) of jail or *break out* with measles; he can *look after* a departing car or *look after* the children. In each of these pairs of expressions, the first has a verb modified by an adverb in its ordinary meaning, and the second is really a different verb, with a meaning of its own, composed of two elements. The second word in these two-word verbs, commonly referred to as a particle, can sometimes have more than one position in a sentence: I *looked up* the word in a dictionary; I *looked* the word *up* in a dictionary.

Hundreds of such verb-adverb combinations are in use, most of them one-syllable verbs with adverbs like *about, around, at, by, down, for, in, out, through, to, up, with.* They are widely used in general English and often give an emphatic rhythm differing from the more formal *investigate (look into), sacrifice (give up), surrender (give up).* This pattern is now the most active way of forming new verbs. When the combinations develop meanings beyond what their elements imply, they are separately entered in dictionaries.

Reference: Dwight Bolinger, *The Phrasal Verb in English* (Cambridge, Mass.: Harvard Univ. Press, 1971).

verbal, oral

Although *verbal* is widely used to mean "spoken," many word watchers insist on *oral* for that meaning. See *oral, verbal.*

Verbals

The parts of a verb that function as nouns or adjectives are called verbals. For their various uses see Gerunds, Infinitives, Participles.

Verbs

1. Forms. If we exclude *be* and the modal auxiliaries, all verbs can be identified by their capacity to add to the base form (*ask, sing, tear*) the suffix -*ing* (*asking*), the suffix -*s* (*asks*), and the suffix -*ed* (*asked*) or use some other change in form as the equivalent of the -*ed*—*sing, sings, singing, sang, sung; tear, tears,* *tearing, tore, torn. Be* has eight forms (*be, am, is, are, was, were, being, been*); *can, may, must,* and other modal auxiliaries have only one or two forms. We recognize verbs by their form and sentence position even when we don't know their meaning. In "I am sure that his words will coruscate," we know that *am, will,* and *coruscate* are verbs—*am* and *will* because we have already learned their forms, functions, and meanings, and *coruscate* because it depends on *will,* even if we have no notion of its meaning.

Verbs fall into two classes, a closed one (no new ones are added) whose function is primarily grammatical, and an open one (new ones are constantly added) whose lexical meaning is important. In "He got hurt," *got* performs the grammatical function of showing past tense and passive voice, and *hurt* carries the lexical meaning. See Auxiliaries, Gerunds, Infinitives, Participles, Parts of Speech, Principal parts of verbs, Tenses of verbs, Voice.

2. Function. The syntactic function of verbs is typically to form the predicate of a clause or sentence—that is, to join with a subject, and perhaps an object, to form a single construction. For convenience we are using *verb* instead of some more specific word like *predicator* to indicate this function as well as to indicate the part of speech. See Agreement, Linking verbs, Objects, Subjects, Transitive and intransitive verbs.

3. Verbs and style. The rhetorical function of a verb is usually to comment on the topic of a sentence. Generally speaking, the important action in a sentence should be in the main verb after the topic-subject has been stated. In the sentence "The possibility of a decision in regard to an investigation of reasons for student transfers exists," the one verb is *exists;* it states only that the very long and complicated topic-subject is there for the reader to consider. But the important action is not that a possibility exists; it is that someone may decide to investigate why students transfer: [The president?] may decide to investigate why students transfer. This sentence has three verbs: *decide, investigate,* and *transfer.* Those are the crucial actions in the sentence and should be represented in verbs, not in the abstract nouns related to the verbs.

Too often the main verb of a sentence is a lexically empty verb like *make, have, give,* and *get,* and abstract nouns related to lexically full verbs are subjects or objects. Unless there is good reason to keep a sentence abstract and impersonal, it usually should be rewritten with the abstract nouns changed into lexically vivid verbs:

The *intention* of the teacher is to make a selection of the best papers.
Better: The teacher *intends* to select the best papers.

See Absolute phrases, Conditional clauses, Nominalization, Passive voice, Subjunctive mood, Tense, Verb-adverb combinations. References: Robert L. Allen, *The Verb System of Present-*

Day English (New York: Humanities Press, 1966); Joos; Long and Long, Chs. 23–30; F. R. Palmer, *A Linguistic Study of the English Verb* (Coral Gables: Univ. of Miami Press, 1968); Quirk et al., Chs. 3, 12.

Vernacular

Vernacular once meant "the local language as opposed to Latin." In England the word was used to refer to natural spoken English as opposed to formal literary English, and this usage gained social and political overtones in the United States. Vernacular humor—that is, comic writing in the English of the farm and the frontier—often celebrated Jacksonian democracy, rural interests, and naturalness and ridiculed the East, city ways, and "fancy" language. Since Twain and Whitman, it has been impossible to flatly oppose the literary language to the vernacular language, for the vernacular has been more important to American literature than the formal or academic. Thus while *vernacular* is still encountered as a term for nonstandard English, it is also the term for a literary style derived from the speech of particular classes or regions. See Colloquial English.

very

1. As a qualifier. *Very* is so much used as a qualifier that it may weaken the expression it is meant to intensify. The *Emporia Gazette* once described its war upon *very* this way:

"If you feel you must write 'very,' write 'damn.'" So when the urge for emphasis is on him, the reporter writes "It was a damn fine victory. I am damn tired but damn well—and damn excited." Then, because it is the Emporia (Kan.) Gazette, the copy desk deletes the profanity and the quotation reads: "It was a fine victory. I am tired but well—and excited." That's how the Gazette attains its restrained, simple, and forceful style. Very simple.

2. With past participles. The argument against using *very* before a participle is that a participle is not an adjective but a verbal, conveying not a quality but an action, and therefore cannot be modified by *very* ("extremely"), which is indicative of a degree of quality. By this argument, an adverb of degree, such as *much* or *greatly*, must stand between *very* and the participle (not "very distressed" but "very much distressed"). But in general usage many participles, both present and past, have for a long time been compared like adjectives and freely modified by *very* and *too: disturbing, more disturbing, very disturbing, too disturbing.* With past participles a scale can be set up: some take *very* (very tired), some *much* (much improved), some either (very pleased, much pleased), some neither (brightly [*not* very *or* much] lighted). References: Bryant, pp. 222–23; Copperud, p. 276; Long, pp. 58–59.

viable

Viable was originally used for newborn infants in the sense "capable of living" and then extended to ideas, institutions, and plans with the metaphysical senses "capable of growth," "capable of sustaining itself in existence," and "capable of being put into practice." As a vogue word, *viable* developed more new senses than the dictionaries could keep up with; but in many contexts it means no more than "workable": a viable program, a viable organization.

Vogue words

Particular words and expressions are constantly enjoying great popularity in one social or professional group or another, but a true vogue word is one that has moved into general usage and there become a fad. Some begin in the slang of the black ghetto or the campus and find their way into the copy of advertising writers; others start in the academy or the bureaucracy and become clichés through the efforts of journalists and commentators. As P. A. Duhamel has said, "The jargon of the day can so fascinate some speakers that they will repeat it mindlessly, substituting incantation for communication" *(Boston Herald-Advertiser)*. Writers are not immune to this weakness.

Some vogue words and expressions have little specific meaning to begin with in the contexts in which they appear. At various times "like," "you know?" "see?" and "right?" have been used in place of grunts as conversation fillers. Worse, in that the speaker or writer often believes he is saying something, are expressions like "That's the name of the game," "That's the bottom line," "It's a whole new ballgame," and "That's what it's all about." Other vogue words lose what force and meaning they had *(actually, basically, meaningful, relevant)* and become counter words. Still others take on so many meanings in so many different contexts as to become almost meaningless *(scenario, concept, massive, one-on-one)*. The thing that all vogue words and expressions have in common is that they have become a bore. Writers should make every effort to avoid using them.

See Cliché, Counter words, Triteness.

Voice

1. Forms. *Voice* is a term borrowed from the grammars of the classical languages, where it usually differentiates distinctive endings on verbs. In English, *passive voice* refers to constructions made with the past participle and some form of the verb *be* (was killed); all other verb forms are *active.*

	Active	*Passive*
Present:	he asks (is asking)	he is asked (is being asked)
Future:	he will ask	he will be asked
Perfect:	he has asked	he has been asked
Infinitives:	to ask, to have asked	to be asked, to have been asked
Participles:	asking, having asked	being asked, asked, having been asked.

Get is also used for the passive, especially in informal English:

If he should get elected, we'd be lost.
Our house is getting painted.

2. Definition. The traditional semantic definition is often a useful guide in identifying active and passive verbs, but there are many exceptions. When the subject of a verb is the doer of the action or is in the condition named by its verb (and predicate), the verb is traditionally said to be in the active voice: The congregation sang "Abide with Me"; They will go swimming; His father gave him a car. When the subject of a verb receives the action, the verb is said to be in the passive voice: "Abide with Me" was sung by the congregation; He was given a car by his father; They had been caught.

There are, however, patterns in English that are formally active but semantically passive to the degree that the subject actually "receives" the action: Your car drives easily; This wood doesn't burn as well as that wood; I received one rebuff after another. According to generative-transformational theory, these patterns and the formal passive with a form of *be* and the past participle of the verb result from transformations of a deep structure in which the noun phrase that moves into the subject position is in some sense originally an object. This is clearest in the passive, where the change involves just three simple steps. The direct object becomes the subject, a form of *be* and the past participle are added to the verb, and the original subject becomes the object of the preposition *by:*

The truck   pulls   the car.
The car   is pulled   by the truck.

Other transformations are responsible for the other illustrative sentences. In each case, somewhere in the deep structure the apparent subject has been an object, a "receiver" of an action. See Deep structure.

3. Active vs. passive. Some verbs have no passive version (She resembles her mother), and some are seldom used in the active (She bore four children); but most verbs can be put in either voice. In much written English, as in spoken English, the active voice is more common and more natural because we are accustomed to the actor-action-goal pattern of expression. Active verbs that are not just fillers in a sentence are usually more direct and lively than the corresponding passive:

Passive: The idea that we should leave was suggested by Kevin.
Active: Kevin suggested that we should leave.

Though the passive occurs less frequently than the active, it is legitimately used when the action is more important than the agent of the action, when the agent is unknown or unimportant, or when continuity of idea or emphasis requires shifting the agent to the end of the sentence. See Passive voice 3.

References: Copperud, pp. 207–208; Jespersen, Ch. 12; Joos; Long and Long, pp. 273–77, 285–90.

W

wake

English is oversupplied with verbs for waking from sleep (intransitive) and waking someone else from sleep (transitive). Most common is *wake (woke* or *waked; woke, waked,* or *woken),* to which *up* is frequently added in general writing. *Awaken (awakened, awakened)* is almost as common but somewhat more formal. *Awake (awoke* or *awaked; awoke, awaked,* or *awoken)* is rather formal. *Waken (wakened, wakened)* is least used.

want

Except in the rather rare sense "have need" (They want for the bare necessities of life), *want* should not be followed by *for:* I want [for] you to go. Nor should it be followed by a *that* clause: I want that you should go.

Want for "ought, had better" – You want to review all the notes if you're going to pass the exam – is informal.

Want in, want out, without a complementary verb, is seen in general and informal writing but not in formal. References: Bryant, pp. 224 – 25; Copperud, p. 279.

way, ways

Way in the sense "far" is established in general writing, though not in formal:

A stock can be selling at two cents and be way overpriced. – Thomas W. May, *Atlantic*

It goes way back to his red-baiting days. – T.R.B., *New Republic*

There is some prejudice against the use of *ways* to mean "distance" (a little way[s] down the road).

we

We is frequently used as an indefinite pronoun in expressions like "we find" and "we feel," to avoid passive and impersonal constructions. It is also used to mean "I and others," as in writing for a group or institution. And there is the *we* of the newspaper editorial page, the royal *we* of kings and popes, the corporate *we* of business letters, and, particularly since the spread of radio-television interview and "talk" shows, the *we* that can only mean "I," as in a singer's "We always draw well in Las Vegas."

We for *I* has been taken up by ordinary individuals, with no hint of publicity agents, teammates, or bureaucratic associates, on the peculiar grounds that it is more modest than *I.* But the ambiguity of *we* for *I* is even worse than the condescension of *we* for *you* as in the kindergarten *we* (We won't lose our mittens, will we?) and the hospital *we* (How are we feeling this morning?).

well, good

Well is either an adjective (He looks well) or an adverb (She swam well); *good* is an adjective (a good feeling). See *good, well.*

what

When a predicate nominative connected to a *what* clause by a linking verb is singular, the verb is singular: What I wish to discuss is the responsibility of students. When the predicate nominative is plural, usage is divided:

What we are getting is old answers to old questions.—Daniel Boorstin, *Look*

What he wanted were people who could stimulate. . . .—Anthony Starr, *Esquire*

When *what* is the subject of its clause and the *what* clause is the subject of the sentence, usage is consistent if the *what* clause, linking verb, and predicate nominative agree in number: What is needed is a change; What are needed are changes. But when the *what* clause is singular and the predicate nominative is plural, the linking verb may be either singular or plural:

What is required is neither military bases, pacts, nor conspiracies. —Anatole Shub, *Foreign Affairs*

Still, what holds all his work together are stylistic qualities.—Richard Kostelanetz, *New York Times Magazine*

See *but that, but what.*

when, where

Although the *when* or *where* clause is probably the standard form for defining in informal usage and occurs often in general contexts, there is strong prejudice against it: Welding is when [*or* where] two pieces of metal are heated and made into one. The grammatical argument is that an adverbial clause may not serve as the predicate complement of a noun, which requires as its complement another noun or a noun phrase or clause.

whether

Or is required after *whether* when *whether* introduces a complete or elliptical adverbial clause: Whether [he is] right or not, we owe him respect. In noun clauses, *or not* may be used for emphasis, but it is not strictly necessary:

Whether readers find him successful will depend on their patience. —Charles F. Mullet, *American Historical Review*

If the child at home wonders whether he is loved, the pupil in school wonders whether he is a worthwhile person. — Robert Dreeben, *Harvard Educational Review*

When the alternatives are fully expressed, *or not* is redundant: Whether or not the move is good or bad is debatable.

Repeating *whether* after *or* can be usefully explicit when the alternatives are long and complex, as in some formal contexts.

See Conditional clauses; *if, whether.* References: Copperud, pp. 284–85; Fries, p. 217.

which

1. For broad reference. The use of *which* to refer to the whole idea of a preceding clause (They plan to tear it down, which is a pity) is well established; but objections are properly raised when the reference is so loose that the *which*, at first reading, seems to refer only to the preceding word: She liked the book, *which* was puzzling. Similarly, a reader should not have to grapple with two *which*'s, one of specific and one of broad reference, in a single short sentence: I worked Saturdays to earn money *which* was owed on the car, *which* pleased my parents.

2. In the genitive. *Whose* as the genitive of *which* is older and less cumbersome than *of which* and is preferred by most writers: "a pattern whose outlines are clearly visible" rather than "a pattern the outlines of which are. . . ." Reference: Pooley, pp. 167–69.

3. In parallel clauses. The coordinating conjunctions *and* and *but* connect equivalent *which* clauses having the same antecedent. Sometimes a writer omits the relative pronoun before the first clause only to find that he needs it before the second: "It seems to hold as much promise for American politics as the second-hand legislative reforms [   ] Sinclair propounded in his novels, and which successive Democratic administrations enacted" (Andrew Kopkind, *New York Times Book Review*). In such cases, insertion of *which* will provide balance.

Sometimes an adjective *which* clause, which is subordinate, is mistakenly attached to a main clause by *and* or *but*: "I took to my heart the memorable statement in Joseph Pulitzer's will, now reprinted every day on the editorial pages of the *St. Louis Post-Dispatch*, and which I subsequently tacked to the wall of my office" (Willie Morris, *North Toward Home*). This sentence could be construed as another case of equivalent clauses, to be revised by inserting *which is* before *now;* but it seems more likely that the writer intended to have the single *which* clause ("the memorable statement in Joseph Pulitzer's will . . . which I . . . tacked to the wall") and inserted the *and* to provide some separation from "the editorial pages of the *St. Louis Post-Dispatch*." In careful writing, a conjunction before a single adjective clause should be avoided, even at the cost of considerable revision. See Subordination 2.

4. *Which* or *that*. For the choice between *which* and *that* as relative pronouns, see *that*.

Reference: Copperud, pp. 15–16.

while

As a temporal conjunction, *while* means "during the time that": While the rest were playing cards, he was studying. In general English it is also used to mean "although" or "whereas" (While the cast is talented, the play is a bore) and to introduce the second of two clauses where *though* or *but* might stand (The beagle was a thoroughbred, while the rest of the pack were mongrels). There is some prejudice against *while* when no sense of time is involved. References: Bryant, pp. 231–32; Copperud, p. 284; Fries, pp. 236–37.

who, whom

Ideally, function determines form: *who* is used for subjects and *whom* for objects. In all varieties of English, subjects are consistently rendered as *who* except when they are immediately followed by the subjects of interspersed clauses. Then what *The New Yorker* used to refer to as The Omnipotent Whom is common, as if the pronoun rather than its clause were the object of the interspersed clause: "a solemn old man whom American officials thought might just possibly make a decent guide" (Theodore H. White, *Saturday Review*). As subject, *who* is the right form in such constructions.

Where *whom* is called for, formal usage observes the proprieties, but informal and general often break the traditional rule. General usage permits *who* in questions like these:

And who was the hard sell aimed at? – Mary McCarthy, *New York Review of Books*

Who are they trying to impress? – Bruce Price, *Washington Post*

And though general usage much prefers *whom* in the object function at the beginning of dependent clauses, it sometimes accepts informal *who:* "How [elections] come out depends on who the voters have to choose between" (James Q. Wilson, *Commentary*).

The reason educated writers accept *who* as object when they would recoil from objective *I, we, he, she,* and *they* is that *who* is so often in subject territory, preceding the verb. When the pronoun functions as subject, function and position are in harmony, and *who* is the natural choice. When the pronoun functions as object, function and position are at odds. In formal contexts most writers take the trouble to ignore position and let function determine form. In casual conversation, position is allowed to determine form. General usage usually favors the demands of function except when the pronoun introduces the whole sentence (Who can we turn to?). In college writing, subject *who* and object *whom* are normally the appropriate choices, even though *whom* may sound pedantic in some contexts.

See *one of those who.* References: Bryant, pp. 232–34; Copperud, pp. 285–86; Long and Long, pp. 343–46; Pooley, pp. 68–72; Edward Sapir in Hungerford, Robinson, and Sledd, pp. 327–36.

whose

Whose is interchangeable with *of which* and often the better choice. See *which* 2.

will, shall

Whether pointing to the future and expressing determination, prohibition, or obligation or simply indicating the future, *will* is more common than *shall* with all three persons. See *shall, will.*

-wise

This suffix has long had a limited currency in forming adverbs from nouns (*edgewise, lengthwise, slantwise*). Some years ago it increased in faddish use, especially in an abstract rather than a special sense (*average-wise, budget-wise, legislation-wise, tax-wise*) until new *-wise* words became a joke. Now both the overuse and the ridicule have died down. When a noun has no established adjectival form, a *-wise* coinage may serve a need and have the virtue of concision. But often the *-wise* word lacks precision (*production-wise*); sometimes it represents no saving (*economy-wise* versus *in economy*); and it may simply duplicate an existing word (*drama-wise* for *dramatically*). The connotation of jargon is a further liability. Reference: Copperud, p. 287.

with

According to formal rules, a singular subject followed by a *with* phrase (or *along with, together with*) takes a singular verb: The sheriff along with his three deputies was [*not* were] the first to reach the scene. In general and informal English *with* is often treated as if it created a compound subject. Reference: Copperud, pp. 287–88.

woman, lady

An adult human female is a woman. She may or may not be a lady—"Miss Hepburn is always a lady, a person of integrity" (Edwin Wilson, *Wall Street Journal*)—just as a man may or may not be a gentleman.

Wordiness

Replace the wordy expressions with more compact and exact ones.

There are two cures for wordiness—surgery and treatment. Surgery means excision, simply cutting out words. Treatment means repair, rewriting.

1. Cut out deadwood. Deadwood is the type of wordiness that contributes nothing but clutter:

At [the age of] forty he was a handsome [looking] man.

He was aware [of the fact] that he had failed.

The architecture [of the buildings] and the landscaping [of the grounds] speak of town pride.

[It also happened that] we were the same age.

He kept things moving in [the field of] basset breeding throughout [the entirety of] his career.

The most common deadwood consists of unnecessary phrases like "green *in color*," "seven *in number*," "rectangular *in shape*" and clichés like "in the business world" and "in the field of economics," which we often use without thinking. But good writing requires thought, and when a first draft is revised, every phrase should be looked at closely. Does "green in color" mean anything more than "green"? Doesn't "in business" say everything that "in the world of business" says?

Sometimes a phrase that contributes nothing to the meaning of a sentence nevertheless fits its rhythm or has some other stylistic justification. Perhaps adding "in my life" to "for the first time" provides a desired emphasis even though it's tautologous. But, in general, simply eliminating deadwood is a step toward a compact, direct, honest prose style.

2. Compress inflated passages. When deadwood is involved, no replacement is necessary, but loose, unfocused expression often demands rewriting:

The reason that I'm telling all this is because I want to demonstrate in the clearest way possible that the cultural background of my family was of such a nature as to encourage my interest in the reading of books, magazines, etc.
Rewritten: All this shows that my family background encouraged me to read.

Using unnecessary words produces flabby writing. You can often improve a first draft greatly by reducing long-winded phrases and other circumlocutions to single words that are more direct, more emphatic, and just as clear:

Instead of		
	in this day and age	today
	at this point in time	now
	during the time that	while
	in the event that	if
	at the conclusion of	after

See Nominalization, Passive voice.

wo Word order

Change the order of words or other elements so that the meaning is clearer or the phrasing is more natural or more effective.

The placing of words and word groups in a sentence is the most important means of showing their grammatical relationships. Word order plays a major role in style, particularly in achieving emphasis.

1. Interrupted constructions. Keep your subjects close to your verbs. When a word or words interrupt a construction, the effect is usually clumsy unless the interrupter deserves special emphasis:

Between subject and verb: Newspaper headlines *in these trying and confused times* are continually intensifying our fears.
More natural: In these trying and confused times, newspaper headlines are. . . .

2. Wandering modifiers. Keep your modifiers close to the words they modify. When modifiers are separated from their head-words, the result is frequently awkward, sometimes misleading:

Bob recovered from exhaustion plus what apparently was a bug making the rounds following two days' bedrest. —Grace Lichtenstein, *New York Times*
Better: Following two days' bedrest, Bob. . . .

Her uncle, King Leopold, was even unable to influence her.
Better: Even her uncle. . . .

I decided that if I moved in the direction of the apple tree growing beside the fence calmly, I might make it before the bull charged.
Better: . . . moved calmly in the direction. . . .

3. Word order and emphasis. Don't change normal word order unless you have a reason for doing so. As a rule an element shifted from its usual position receives increased emphasis, as when the object is put before subject and verb:

Object first: I was surprised to find Salinger's novel on the list. *That book* I read when I was fourteen.
Predicate adjective first: Lucky are the ones who need no longer worry.

See Ambiguity, Dangling modifiers. Reference: Fries, Ch. 10.

Words
Index articles containing general discussions of words and their uses include Abstract language, Diction, Figurative language, Origin of words, Slang, Synonyms, and Vogue words.

world
Inflated phrases with *world* —"the business world," "the fashion world," "the publishing world," "the world of science (economics, finance, politics . . .)" —can usually be collapsed: After graduation he went into [the world of] advertising. "Today's modern world" means "today." In other cases, more specific language is preferable: This is especially true in the world of jazz [*better:* among jazz musicians]. *Area, field,* and *realm* are misused in the same way.

would, should
In indirect discourse, *shall* as well as *will* is likely to be reported as *would:* She said, "We shall see"; She said that we would see. See *should, would.*

would have, would of
Writing *would of* for *would have* is nonstandard. See *have* 3.

ww # Wrong word

Replace the word marked with one that says what you mean.

No word is right or wrong in itself. As a correction symbol, *ww* means that the word does not convey a meaning that makes sense in context. In the sentence "What he said showed real comprehensibility of the problems of Asia," *comprehensibility* does not make sense; it's the wrong word. *Comprehension* would be the right word. In "Some people remain stagnant to the lessons of life," *stagnant* needs replacing; *oblivious* is one possibility. In "I remember explicitly my first puff of a cigarette," *clearly* would be a good choice to replace *explicitly.* Errors like this occur when the writer is attempting to use words whose meaning he is not sure of, when he confuses words of similar sound, or when he simply writes too hurriedly and fails to proofread his work. See Careless mistakes.

 Correct the obvious error.

See Careless mistakes.

Xmas

X is the first letter of the Greek word for Christ. It has been used for centuries as an abbreviation in the word *Xmas*, pronounced exactly like *Christmas.* Today, however, *Xmas* is most likely to be pronounced *eks'mus*, and for many its popularity with advertisers has given it unpleasant commercial connotations. Except for purposes of irony, *Xmas* is inappropriate in serious writing.

yet

Yet is both an adverb (The books haven't come yet) and a coordinating conjunction roughly equivalent to *but:* His speech was almost unintelligible, yet I found that I enjoyed it.

you

In giving instructions, as in a how-to essay, *you* is often a good stylistic choice (Then you glue the bottom strip . . .), certainly preferable to repeated use of the passive. As an impersonal pronoun, *you* is more common than *one* in general usage and not at all rare in formal:

In a sense, Richard III, as Shakespeare sees him, is the little boy who has found out that God does not strike you dead when you tell a lie.—Arnold Edinborough, *Shakespeare Quarterly*

There are at least three ways to treat any philosophical work: (1) You may inquire into its background, its history. . . .—Frederick Sontag, *Journal of Religion*

Writers should avoid switching back and forth between *you* and *one* and take care that their *you, your* is clearly indefinite, not personal. "Your parents depend on alcohol and pills to get them through the day" might better be "Our parents. . . ."

See *one, they*. Reference: Bryant, pp. 238–39.

youth

As a collective noun, *youth* meaning "young people in general" can be followed by either singular or plural verbs and pronouns. In American usage the singular construction is much the more common: "Russian youth wants to avoid military confrontation as sincerely as American youth does" (George Feifer, *New York Times Magazine*). But when *the* precedes *youth,* a plural verb is often desirable to show clearly that more than a single person is meant: The increase in tuition made education too expensive for the youth who were most in need of it.

Though the collective use includes both sexes, *youth* meaning "a young person" ordinarily refers to a young man, and the ordinary plural is *youths.*

Youth has been so overused by journalists and commentators that sometimes almost any alternative—*young man* (or *men*), *boy(s), adolescent(s), young people, girls and boys*—would be welcome. See *kid*.

 A correction symbol indicating approval: "good idea," "well ex-pressed," and so on.

Additional Correction Symbols

Correction Chart

To the student: When one of these correction symbols calls attention to a weakness in your essay, look up the *Index* article that discusses the problem, and make the revision. The symbols in the chart are arranged alphabetically; page numbers for the articles follow the instructions.

ab Write out this word. Or use the standard abbreviation. 11

abst Make this word or passage more concrete or more specific. 14

adj Reconsider your choice of adjective. 19

adv Correct the form or change the position of the adverb. Or reconsider your choice of adverb. 22

agr Make the verb agree with its subject or the pronoun with its antecedent. 24

amb Make your meaning unmistakable. 30

apos, ˅ Insert or remove an apostrophe as required. 36

awk, k Rewrite this passage to make the phrasing smoother and more effective. 42

beg Revise the beginning of your essay to make it lead more directly and smoothly into your subject or to arouse your reader's interest. 44

cap Capitalize the word marked. 56

case Correct the mistake in case. 59

cf Revise this sentence to correct the comma fault. 75

coh Make clear the relation between the parts of this sentence or between these sentences or paragraphs. 65

colon, ⁀ Use a colon here. Or reconsider the use of this colon. 67

comma, ˄ Insert or remove a comma here: C_1 between independent clauses, 69; C_2 with preceding or following elements, 72; C_3 with nonrestrictive modifiers, 72; C_4 with interrupting and parenthetical words and phrases, 73; C_5 in lists and series, 73; C_6 for clarity, 74; C_7 for emphasis, 74; C_8 with main sentence elements, 74; C_9 in conventional uses, 75; C_{10} with other marks of punctuation, 75.

comp Correct the fault in comparing the adjective or adverb marked. 78

concl Revise the ending of your paper to round out the discussion. 82

conj Make this conjunction more accurate or more appropriate to the style of the passage. 84

coord Correct the faulty coordination. 89

d Replace this word with one that is more exact, more appropriate, or more effective. 102

det Develop this passage more fully by giving pertinent details. 101

div Break the word at the end of this line between syllables. 106

dm Revise the sentence so that the expression marked is clearly related to the word it is intended to modify. 92

emp Strengthen the emphasis of this passage. 112

fig Replace this trite, inconsistent, or inappropriate figure of speech. 128

form Make this word or passage less formal, more appropriate to your style, subject, and audience. 136

frag Make this construction a grammatically complete sentence, or join it to a neighboring sentence. 137

glos See this *Index* for an article on the word marked.

id Replace this expression with standard idiom. 155

inf Make this word or passage less informal, more appropriate to your style, subject, and audience. 160

ital Underline to indicate italics. 163